Strategic Military Surprise

Strategic Military Surprise
Incentives and Opportunities

Edited by
Klaus Knorr and Patrick Morgan

With Contributions by
MICHAEL DOYLE
MICHAEL HANDEL
RICHARD BETTS

Transaction Books
New Brunswick (U.S.A.) and London (U.K.)

Library of Congress Catalog Number: 82-2784
ISBN: 0-87855-912-4 (paper)
Printed in the United States of America

Library of Congress Cataloging in Publication Data
Knorr, Klaus Eugen, 1911-
     Strategic military surprise.

     1. Strategy—Addresses, essays, lectures.
2. Surprise—Addresses, essays, lectures.   I. Morgan,
Patrick M., 1940-   . II. Title.
U163.K63   355.4′3   82-2784
ISBN 0-87855-912-4   AACR2

Contents

Acknowledgments

The project has been shaped throughout by the intellectual, organizational, editorial, and financial support supplied by Professor Frank Trager and his assistant Hila Rosen of the National Security Program at New York University. Every chapter bears the imprint of their suggestions and comments, and indeed the project would never have been completed without their participation. We wish to express our appreciation to them, and our gratitude to the other contributors who have met deadlines with dispatch and provided work of such high caliber as to require a minimum of editorial attention.

CHAPTER ONE
Strategic Surprise: An Introduction

Klaus Knorr and Patrick Morgan

Surprise is a familiar phenomenon in the history of statecraft, and the constant companion of the statesman. In the fluid and dangerous realm of contemporary world affairs, governments are more concerned than ever about their vulnerability to surprise. They invest heavily in resources for predicting the future course of events and for coping with unexpected developments. Their rate of return on these outlays is less than ideal; statesmen periodically find themselves caught in situations they did not adequately anticipate, where the consequences of having failed to do so are quite nasty.

It seems appropriate, then, that surprise would be a prominent target of analysis and research, for we need to hone our understanding of when, why, and how it occurs. In this book the focus is on the most significant kind of surprise arising from the deliberate actions of states, which is the unanticipated and devastating military attack. We are not interested in tactical military surprise, if by "tactics" one means concepts and practices for winning battles as opposed to winning wars. Thus this book leaves aside those efforts to spring limited surprises in ongoing conflicts which military leaders develop as a matter of routine. It concentrates instead on grand strategy in the use of force, in the adoption of which governments (not just military leaders) play a major or decisive part.

The purpose of a strategic attack is to inflict a striking defeat that sharply alters the military situation and possibly determines the outcome of the conflict. It must be conceded that it is not always clear where tactics end and strategy begins; in fact, the application of wholly new tactics that had a decisive effect on the larger outcome falls within our area of interest. In the main, however, our objective is to explore the major attack designed by a government to be a critical step in achieving its strategic objectives vis-à-vis the opponent. The term *strategic* here does not refer solely to certain types of nuclear weapons or to the involvement of great powers—we define it in

1

terms of the purposes of the attack and its context, not the nature of the actors or weapons.

An attack of this sort need not have surprise as a key ingredient. When it does, then we have a strategic surprise. There are three types of actions that, in the framework of a strategic attack, can deliver a most unpleasant shock to the victim: the unexpected initiation of hostilities, the unexpected extension of a war to a new theater, or the use of an unexpected mode of warfare. The Japanese attack on Port Arthur in 1904 is a good example of the first, the German invasion of Norway in 1940 illustrates the second, and the atomic bombing of Japanese cities in 1945 exemplifies the third.

We are intrigued that a surprise of strategic dimensions has occurred in one of these three ways on numerous occasions. Normally this is by design; the attack has been elaborately planned as a surprise, under conditions of strict secrecy and perhaps the use of deception. However, we are interested as well in those occasional instances in which a state is caught by surprise even though the opponent had not planned this. Thus a state may experience a strategic surprise whenever its opponent develops and implements a strategy or mode of warfare for which it was unprepared, regardless of the opponent's intent.

We have chosen to review cases of strategic surprise drawn from the last 120 years. This decision reflects the fact that by roughly the middle of the nineteenth century a combination of factors had begun to alter the nature of war in such a way as to increase the opportunities for strategic surprise and the incentives for exploiting those opportunities. Throughout history, of course, actors had been able to surprise opponents on the battlefield by introducing new tactics, adopting bold strategies, employing deception, and developing exceptional troop discipline. But it was hard to achieve a truly strategic surprise by such methods. Strategic surprise did not figure prominently in the wars of the eighteenth century and the Napoleonic era, and Clausewitz—that discerning student of all aspects of warfare—paid little attention to the subject, presumably because armies moved ponderously and weapons did not change dramatically in a short period of time.

In many ways, however, the Napoleonic wars marked a turning point, for they demonstrated that it was becoming possible, due to political and organizational changes, to manage huge armies that could inflict smashing defeats and bring about the occupation of major states. As the century progressed, improvements in communication, transportation, and weapons made it increasingly plausible to conduct war via swift yet very large attacks that could settle the conflict in short order. New bureaucratic structures (such as general staffs) and novel procedures for systematic problem solving (another part of the industrial revolution and the advance of the scientific spirit) added to the capabilities of states to mount strategic surprises. Prussia was the first state to realize and exploit these developments, in its wars with Austria and France in 1866 and 1870 respectively.

At the same time, these developments were enlarging the potential scale and destructiveness of wars if they were not kept short and settled quickly. This escalated the incentives to consider seeking decisive victories via strategic surprise, as well as by other methods, lest even the victor have to pay far too great a price. This was widely appreciated prior to World War I, but the carnage and exhaustion of that struggle drove the point home and it has helped to shape approaches to warfare ever since.

Thus it is not just that technological change over the past 120 years has sometimes provided a state with new weapons that could be used to surprise and overwhelm an opponent, the facet of strategic surprise which preoccupies many analysts today. There have been occasions when this occurred, when new weapons were the crucial ingredient or an important contributing factor. More significant, however, is that a cluster of political, social, and technological changes many years earlier combined to put a premium on modes of warfare and strategies in which strategic surprise plays a central role. This context has guided many states' planning for war in this century, with the result that there are far more examples of attempts at strategic surprise since 1900.

It could be argued that another turning point has arrived: technological change has made surveillance so sophisticated and omnipresent in international affairs as to virtually rule out equivalent surprises today. For numerous reasons which are reviewed in the final chapter, this does not appear to be the case, either where nuclear weapons in a constant state of readiness are involved or where such weapons are not present and it is conventional forces that constitute a potential threat. The prospect of a strategic surprise will remain a worrisome feature of the statesman's craft.

Despite the emergence of the phenomenon over more than a century and the accumulation of examples, the historical and theoretical literature on strategic surprise was rather thin until the last two decades. Most monographic case studies and nearly all theoretical analyses in the public domain are of recent origin.[1] Much of the latest work was provoked by the Israeli experience in the 1973 war in the Middle East, and interest has also been stimulated by growing Soviet military strength amid fears in the West that Moscow might be tempted to strike at American nuclear forces or to attack in Europe. Analysis has been facilitated by the emergence in recent years of a better understanding of perception and misperception—individual, organizational, and governmental—as it affects state behavior, which has permitted a better appreciation of the position of the victim in cases of strategic surprise.

As a result of previous work, substantial components of a theoretical grasp of the subject are now in place. In view of the growing interest, this seems an opportune time to add to and refine these components, while seeking to extract lessons for the improvement of statecraft in this regard. Hence this volume.

The emphasis in most previous studies has been on exploring the informational and the cognitive/psychological elements that combine to make governments vulnerable to being surprised. In addition to this important aspect of the subject, we have attempted to examine others: the nature of the incentives that give rise to efforts at strategic surprise, the kinds of capabilities that a state needs to achieve a strategic surprise, and the other factors—particularly political considerations—that contribute to a state's vulnerability.

Much of the prior theoretical work has been based on intensive study of relatively few examples of strategic surprise. In this volume, twenty cases are examined, involving a wide variety of states—large and small, highly industrialized and economically less developed, Western and non-Western, militarily superior and inferior. The method employed is comparative and moderately inductive. The contributors have posed a set of questions as guides for the investigation and reporting of each case, in the hope that this would yield further insights and new theoretical propositions while facilitating an evaluation of existing ones in the literature. (The questions are listed in the appendix.)

The contributors initiated the project by meeting to establish a common frame of reference, to form the questions and the working definition of strategic surprise, to select the examples to be studied, and to allocate the preparation of the case studies. One member of the original group, Bruce Kuniholm, was forced by the pressure of events in Iran to withdraw from the project to give full attention to his duties at the State Department. As a replacement, Michael Handel generously agreed to add the project to his busy schedule.

After initial drafts of the case study chapters had been prepared, the group met again to critique the work and plan revisions. On the basis of the new versions of the case studies, the editors drafted the comparative analysis chapters, which were then submitted for comment and criticism to the other participants. After suitable alterations, the final versions emerged as they appear here. A deliberate effort was made to hold footnoting to a minimum and to list only some of the works consulted in the development of the case studies, with an eye to enhancing the accessibility of the volume for the reader.

NOTE

1. For a sample and description of available studies see Klaus Knorr, ''Strategic Intelligence: Problems and Remedies,'' in Laurence Martin (ed.) *Strategic Thought in the Nuclear Age* (London: Heinemann, 1979) pp. 90–91.

APPENDIX

The Framework for the Case Studies

I. A's Incentive Structure
   A. Why did A seek a strategic surprise? Was it:
   For defensive purposes, perceiving a future attack by B?
   For offensive/aggressive purposes:
       To win quickly?
       To win cheaply?
       To win at all?
   B. What was the salience of surprise in A's planning?
   Was surprise the basis for the action contemplated, or primarily designed to facilitate it?
   C. What were the origins of A's incentives to seek a strategic surprise?
   Possibilities:
   Perception of an opportunity given some deficiency in B.
   A predisposition to use surprise due to historical experiences.
   A predisposition due to cultural factors.
   A predisposition due to elite values.
   A predisposition due to the personalities of key leaders.
   A predisposition due to implicit or explicit models of international politics used in A.
   Perception of an opportunity given the international and domestic contexts.
   D. Were there disincentives for seeking a strategic surprise, was there opposition within A to doing so? What were the disincentives and where was the opposition located? (See the categories listed under C. for analysis of the roots of the opposition.)
   E. To what extent was A united concerning the use of strategic surprise? How broadly was it known that this was being contemplated?
   Political, bureaucratic limits on consensus.
   Effect of the nature of the government.
   Cohesiveness of the elite.
   To what extent could A behave as a unitary actor on this score?
   F. How strong was A's net incentive to seek a strategic surprise? Under what circumstances is it likely that A would not have carried out the planned surprise?
   G. To what extent were A's expectations and estimates grounded on reasonable assessments, as opposed to misperceptions, irrational judgments, etc.
   H. Were there indicators of A's incentives a watchful B could have observed?
   I. Were there interesting combinations of these factors?

II. A's Opportunity Structure

   A. Did the opportunity arise primarily because of A's capabilities in one or more of the following:

   Military strategy, doctrine, plans;

   Superior forces in quantitative terms, or in qualitative terms—weapons, leadership, training, morale;

   Superior ability to mobilize forces;

   Deployment and mobility of forces;

   Use of new military and related technologies;

   The ability to reduce the strategic risks of seeking a surprise;

   The ability to maintain secrecy;

   The ability to practice deception?

   Were there relevant trends in such capabilities?

   B. Did the opportunity arise from A's perception of B's being vulnerable due to some deficiency in B's capabilities, preparations, perceptions, or behavior?

   C. Did the opportunity arise because of domestic conditions in A—nature of the leadership, degree of cohesion, bureaucratic factors, etc.?

   D. Were A's assessments of the opportunity—in terms of anticipated immediate and long-term results, reactions by B and other parties—reasonably realistic? Were the assessments based on hard evidence carefully analyzed or were they largely fortuitous? Where the assessments were incorrect, what were the contributing factors?

   E. Was the strategic surprise planned at length for a particular time, planned at length for a suitable opportunity, or mounted quickly because some need or opportunity had arisen?

   F. Were there indicators of A's perception of an opportunity for strategic surprise and its probable response to it that B could have observed? Were there indicators in the behavior of third parties that B could have observed?

   G. What steps by B might have led A to decide an opportunity did not exist or existed no longer?

   H. Did A perceive B as having had various opportunities to learn of the impending attack? If so, what led A to proceed anyway?

   I. Were there notable patterns to the perceived opportunities for strategic surprise?

III. B's Vulnerability to Strategic Surprise

   A. Was B vulnerable because of weaknesses in its military capabilities, in such areas as:

   Relative size of forces;

   Relative speed of force mobilization;

   Relative quality of forces;

   Structure and deployment of forces;

   Military strategy, tactics, and plans?

B. Were there weaknesses in B's threat perception? If so, what were the contributing factors: deception by A, "noise," or other elements?
C. Were there weaknesses in B's assessment of its vulnerabilities? Did B overestimate its security, its intelligence capabilities, its military capabilities? If so, what were the contributing factors: deception by A, "noise," or other elements?
D. Was B readily penetrated by foreign intelligence in ways enhancing vulnerability to strategic surprise?
E. Did internal disunity—due to domestic politics, bureaucratic politics, domestic sympathizers with A—or difficulties with allies lead to vulnerability to strategic surprise?
F. Were there any special vulnerabilities (e.g., Israel on Yom Kippur)?
G. Which indicators of these weaknesses were observed by A?
H. To what extent did some people in B perceive a surprise attack as very likely? Why weren't their perceptions acted upon? Possibilities:
   Psychological resistance to such information.
   Financial disincentives to preparing for a possible attack.
   Political liabilities of preparing for a surprise attack, including the desire to avoid a provocation.
   Reliance on alternative indicators to determine that a surprise attack was near.
I. Were there interesting patterns to these factors?

IV. *The Relationship of A and B to Third Parties*
A. The strategic surprise is initiated by one small power against another, when both have ties to great powers. How does this affect A's incentives and opportunities and B's vulnerability (e.g., the Arab-Israeli Wars in 1967, 1973)?
B. The surprise initiated by A against a small power B is also of considerable consequence and a major surprise to a great power associated with B. How does this affect A's incentives and opportunities, and B's vulnerability (e.g., the outbreak of the Korean War)?
C. The surprise is initiated by a great power A against a small power B associated with another great power. How does this affect A's incentives and opportunities, and B's vulnerability (e.g., the Bay of Pigs)?

CHAPTER TWO
Strategic Surprise in Four European Wars

Klaus Knorr

THE WAR OF 1866[1]

On the eve of the war of 1866, Austria was generally regarded as militarily much superior to Prussia—a belief fully shared in Vienna—and expert observers were stupefied by the decisiveness of Prussia's victory at the battle of Sadowa. There is no doubt that Austria's leaders were surprised by their defeat and by the Prussian strategy that led to it. A war between the two states to settle the question of supremacy in the Germanies was widely expected. Its outbreak did not cause surprise. Rather, strategic surprise resulted from the Prussian design of a new mode of warfare.

Following the war of liberation against Napoleon, the Prussian army fell into a state of considerable decay in numbers and quality. It fought no major war for fifty years and was rated as far from first-rate. A French visitor observing its autumn maneuvers as late as 1861 remarked that it was "compromising the whole profession."[2] It was not until 1858, when Prince William became regent of the kingdom, that concern over the evident weaknesses of the country's military system began to crystallize and, in the face of parliamentary opposition, the early 1860s saw a considerable expansion and vast improvement of its capabilities.[3] Indeed, the feat of achieving so much in a few years in itself contributed to the subsequent surprise.

A number of other factors helped to bring about the Prussian victory in 1866. The Prussian infantry was by then superior to the Austrian. It was better trained, better led by literate noncommissioned officers, and better equipped. In fact, the first analyses of the unexpected Prussian success attributed it mainly to the new breech-loading rifle—which permitted more rapid fire and greater accuracy at larger ranges than the Austrian muzzle-loader—and to the introduction of tactics that made the most of this technical superiority. Subsequent studies cast doubts on this interpretation and concluded that this advantage, although a contributory factor, was not decisive,

9

in part because the Austrian army possessed superior artillery and cavalry, and fought with superb bravery.

The critical factor, it is now accepted, was the Prussian development of a new military system for preparing for war. This system was developed and applied by General von Moltke, Prussia's chief of general staff. By the mid-century, the industrial revolution was profoundly transforming west and central European economies and societies. In essence, Moltke was the first to adapt concurrent advances in science, technology, and management to the military art. There were three distinct, although interrelated, modes of adaptation.

First, Moltke developed the Prussian general staff as a superb organization capable of designing grand strategy and its implementation far in advance of war, and of doing so in meticulous detail. Fostering modern means of gathering information and analytical tools for formulating and solving strategic problems, Moltke created an elite corps of officers whose professionalism included advance planning and new administrative skills. The result was a resource that other contemporary armed services lacked or possessed only in rudimentary form. As Michael Howard observed, development of the general staff was perhaps the greatest military innovation of the nineteenth century.[4]

Second, Moltke and his staff recognized the full military utility of the expanding railroads and telegraphic communication for purposes of waging war. Properly employed, these new logistical assets facilitated the quick mobilization and deployment of massive military forces. Without them, in fact, it would have been difficult to bring to bear the new larger armies which the industrial revolution and the vast increase in labor productivity permitted to be released from civilian labor. With approximately 450,000 combatants, the battle of Sadowa was larger than any preceding ones. To move and supply armies on this scale required means of mass transportation. It was also clear to Moltke that speed of mobilization and deployment could yield great advantage in seizing the strategic initiative at the beginning of hostilities. He planned to seize this advantage, but political circumstances caused the carefully prepared plans of the general staff to be put to use only with appreciable delay. War against another German people was not popular in Prussia, and the Prussian king was extremely reluctant to accept the necessity of war with Austria. While the Austrians began their call-up on April 21 and accelerated it on April 27, it was not until May 12 that Prussia's mobilization was authorized. But the extraordinary efficiency of the Prussian system permitted lost time to be made good.

The third and related component in Moltke's new mode of warfare was his strategy of moving troops into battle not in one move and direction, but in having three separate armies, approaching from different directions, join on the battlefield. He thus dismissed traditional wisdom about the advantages of concentrating troops at once and operating on interior lines. His novel concept permitted the sweeping use of large spaces for strategic maneuver.

The adoption of Moltke's strategy had to overcome considerable obstacles. The mere presence of an innovating mind was far from a sufficient condition for the achievement of strategic surprise. Until 1864, the position of the Prussian chief of the general staff was ambiguous. He and his organization were subordinate to the minister of war and enjoyed no direct access to the king or contact with the commanding generals. The king had been impressed by Moltke's staff work in the brief campaign against Denmark in 1864 and became increasingly interested in his advice. But it was only in June 1866, shortly before the outbreak of war against Austria, that the king authorized orders from the general staff to be communicated directly to the operational commands. There was plenty of distrust of this arrangement and of Moltke and his plans in the Prussian command structure. The critics either did not understand or did not approve of Moltke's strategy, especially his daring plan that the concentration of forces should be consummated only on the battlefield, not before. They disliked preconceived plans to begin with, and were very sensitive to the risks involved in the separation of armies prior to battle. It is doubtful that Moltke's strategy would have been implemented without strong backing by the king.

While the Prussians intended to win and elaborated a new strategy for doing so, it was the Austrians themselves who did much to produce their experience of surprise. As mentioned, deficiencies in Austrian weaponry, strategy, and tactical doctrine contributed to their defeat. Thus, the Austrian military believed in the simple offensive strategy of frontal assault and in infantry shock tactics that were misplaced in the face of superior Prussian rifle fire. Their mobilization process was extremely slow because of an inefficient call-up system and a poor railroad net. They had only a single line for advancing into Moravia while the Prussians had five lines at their disposal for moving toward Bohemia.

Yet the major Austrian contribution to their shocking defeat was their failure to inform themselves properly about Prussia's military developments even though they had a fairly good espionage service (in fact, a better one than the Prussians). Two reasons essentially accounted for this failure of threat perception and assessment. First, the Austrians were overconfident. They thought that they had the better army and were not much worried about the approaching war. Overconfidence tends to stultify threat perception.

Second, and probably more important, was an Austrian conception of military strategy that had no room and hence no appreciation for the strategic analysis and preparation that characterized the Prussian general staff. Austrian anticipation was virtually the antithesis of Prussian planning. Benedek, the Austrian commander-in-chief, was an experienced general who looked on the conduct of war in traditional terms. He placed great emphasis on the use of the traditional virtues of dash and courage, and regarded strategy as something fairly routine. His style was utterly different from Moltke's and, in this respect, he was representative of the entire Austrian officer corps, which had an aristocratic liking for the business of fighting but was hardly given to intellectual application in these matters. There was the beginning of a general staff, but it was small, deficient in competence, not highly regarded by the commanders, and hence it played an insignificant role before and during the war. It is not surprising, under the circumstances, that the Austrian military had little interest in what the Prussian general staff might be up to either in the design of strategy or in the painstaking preparation for mobilizing troops and moving them quickly into battle. As it was, Benedek had no idea of how to maneuver an army of 230,000 men into position for decisive battle.

In conclusion, a leadership that is both overconfident and uninnovating lacks proper alertness to what an opponent might do who attempts to design a bold and new strategy and carefully prepares for its implementation. The Austrians were blind to this, and this blindness was of their own making. The strategic surprise they suffered in 1866 was largely self-inflicted.

THE WAR OF 1870[5]

The factors that made France suffer strategic surprise in 1870 are basically very similar to the factors that operated in 1866. This is all the more remarkable because the French had the opportunity to study the causes of the Austrian debacle and to derive appropriate lessons from it. As it was, the military destruction of imperial France by Prussia and its German allies astounded the world, for France had been regarded as the leading European military power since the French Revolution. The world as well as the French were surprised. Henceforth it was Germany that held preeminent rank. As in 1866, it was not the outbreak of war that caused surprise in 1870—it was the Prussian mode of warfare that surprised, this time the French.

A number of factors impinged on the outcome of the war, but most had no decisive effect. In contrast to 1866, this time the Prussians had the superior artillery, but also the inferior infantry rifle. The French may have had the edge in the overall incompetence of commanders but, except for Moltke, the difference was not great. Nor was the imprint of Moltke's strategic genius very effective after the initial phases of the war. As on the French side, poor intelligence, disobedient commanders, and chance left little scope for continuous strategic planning. But Moltke was quick to realize and exploit any advantages that unexpected circumstances offered. The great victories at Metz and Sedan were achieved by "brilliant opportunism."[6] Moltke was also more resolute than his opponents. On the other hand, the French armies generally benefited from the fact that the weapons technology in use favored the defense over the offense. Hence, the bloodiness of individual battles.

The outcome was determined overwhelmingly by the same sort of differences in the preparation for war that had led to the Prussian victory over Austria. Crucial among these were superior organization and superior manpower in the initial stages of war. As in 1866, the Prussians benefited from their superb general staff, which had prepared elaborate plans for rapid mobilization and —with a superior railroad system at its disposal—deployed huge military forces with great speed, thus lending Prussia and its allies the strategic initiative and the superiority of numbers. Moltke and his officers had studied a number of plans for war against France, selected Lorraine as the area of decisive encounter, and calculated that they could put into the field more troops than the French at the very start of hostilities. Before these began, Moltke stated in a memorandum: "Our mobilization is prepared to the last detail. Six railroad lines are available for troop transport to the area between Mosel and Rhine. The schedule for each troop unit is fixed for departure and arrival."[7]

Napolean III and his top military leaders operated within a frame of mind that made them disinclined to assess and prepare for the German military threat. It was not that they were not forewarned.

Records of the war of 1866 were there to be studied, but the then-favorite conclusion that the Prussians had won because of the new needle gun gave no cause for alarm since the newer French chassepot was superior to the Prussian infantry rifle. Colonel Stoffel, the French military attaché in Berlin, reported on Prussian military preparations with considerable insight and reported in detail about the important role which the Prussian general staff had played in Austria's defeat. Napoleon and a few other Frenchmen had formed some understanding that Prussia's victory in 1866 resulted in considerable part from the efficient training of a large, short-term conscript army and a capacity to mobilize and deploy at great speed. Yet most of the French military were too conservative to be alert to such new developments. Napoleon, increasingly ill and feeble, discovered that proper countermeasures—such as switching from a professional army and a modest corps of trained recruits to a mass army based on universal conscription—were politically unpopular in Paris. So he fell in with carefree attitudes and opinions prevalent among the French military.

In command of what was widely regarded as Europe's best army, French generals adopted a strategy of immediate attack even though they expected their troop strength to be on paper inferior to that of the Germans. They felt that they could depend on French qualitative superiority and they grossly overestimated their capacity for quick mobilization relative to their opponent's.

War having been declared on July 14, 1870, both sides began to mobilize on July 15. While German mobilization and deployment in three armies was completed by August 2, the French machinery for mobilization and deployment proved extremely inefficient and quickly broke down. Unlike the Prussians, the French had done little to prepare the logistical effort. Transportation facilities were soon overtaxed and inoperative; chaos spread, and the French found themselves under widespread and heavy attack before they could get ready for offensive warfare. The French assumption that they could move faster than the "lumbering" Prussians proved to be sheer wishfulness. It made little difference, under the circumstances, that with the French general staff being underdeveloped, no particular concepts for attack had been prepared. It was more serious that, faithfully dedicated to the "irresistible French élan," the French had done little to train their troops in tactical defense.

None of the deficiencies were obvious prior to hostilities. In fact, the French had done a great deal to improve their army during the last years before the war erupted and, when it did, French soldiers fought with exemplary bravery before their situation became catastrophic. The French army was in excellent condition to fight any force constituted, trained, and led like itself. What the French, unlike the Prussians, had failed to realize is that the technological revolution had also ushered in a new military age. They had not understood the key problem of producing much larger forces than were previously possible, and of moving them quickly into decisive battle.

As Michael Howard put it, the fundamental weakness that set the French up for a shocking experience of strategic surprise was a faulty—that is, obsolete—military system.[8] While Prussian planners understood and exploited the effects of the ongoing scientific and technological revolution on the conduct of war, the French had not. The Prussians developed an elaborate staff system, espousing new analytical tools, that recruited itself from the best brains in the officer corps and gained increasing respect among the Prussian military. The French staff organization was far inferior in working methods and influence. Educational standards at the French military schools were very low and their graduates nursed a deep distrust of military theorizing. There was thus little ability and inclination to study the growing systems of railroads and the electric telegraph for solving logistical problems. Not having conceptualized these problems, the French were naturally surprised by the new mode of warfare introduced by Moltke and his staff.

The French obviously made a vital contribution to the strategic surprise they experienced at the hands of the German states. This contribution is all the more astonishing because the Prussian mode of warfare was in its essence no longer new. It had been demonstrated in 1866, and some of the novel features (i.e., the effective use of modern means of communication) had also emerged during the American War of Independence from 1861 to 1865. Plenty of warning was available. French insensitivity to it can perhaps be explained partly by the fact that France as a society was slower than the German states in accepting and absorbing the industrial revolution and its ramified repercussions. As Michael Howard points out, the military system of a country tends to reflect its underlying social systems.[9]

In any case, although French planners were prepared to adopt technical improvements in particular weapons, they saw nothing wrong with their basic organization for warfare. They remained rigidly fixed on a past mode of war in which their nation had excelled for a long time, and in which they had great confidence. It was no doubt this attitude of overconfidence that made them ignore the danger signals. Even given this fixation, which completely distorted French threat perception, it is hard to explain how the French military could have so grossly overestimated their capacity for quick mobilization and deployment, and so grossly underestimated that of their opponents, except that this faulty estimate permitted comforting assumptions to be preserved. Napoleon III had more than an inkling of the troubles a war with the Germans might produce. But, in addition to being in poor health, he was surrounded by military leaders who thought otherwise and he was confronted by powerful political elites over which he had little influence and which resisted any profound reforms of their country's military organization.

THE GERMAN SURPRISE ATTACK IN 1914[10]

In the opening phase of World War I, powerful German forces swept quickly through Belgium, violating that country's neutrality and crushing its resistance, in order to envelop their French and British opponents in the north and, then turning southward, to annihilate the bulk of the French army from the rear. Favored by strategic surprise, they came close to winning the war in the west in a matter of weeks. Although the French command had intended to seize the strategic initiative, it was the Germans who did so to the surprise of their enemies.

The ingredients of this case of surprise are fairly clear. The Germans had a strong incentive to seek a quick decision in the west. In view of the France-Russian alliance, they anticipated a war on two fronts if hostilities broke out. Knowing Russia's capacity for mobilization and deployment was very low, they decided to concentrate most of their forces for achieving a quick victory over France and then to cope with the Russian threat. Their famed general staff was also aware of the technical superiority of defensive over offensive operations (although not to the same extent after the introduction of the efficient machine gun). In order to win quickly they needed a superior strategy and the initiative to put it into effect. The Germans knew they could amass armies in the west substantially superior in numbers to the opposing forces in the west; by means of their formidable machine for mobilization and deployment, already demonstrated in 1866 and 1870, they hoped to do so with such dispatch that the strategic initiative would be theirs. Because the narrowness of the Franco-German frontier permitted little room for strategic maneuver, and because the French armies would be concentrated there, German ideas focused on outflanking the French by rapidly piercing through neutral Belgium. This strategy was gradually formulated between 1895 and 1907 by General Schlieffen, the chief of the general staff. The plan consisted of leaving only a thin screen of defensive forces in the east in order to stem Russian attacks as best they could; of placing only weak forces also in the southwest, luring the French into the western fringes of Germany; and of striking with overwhelming mass through Belgium like a vast scythe, enveloping the opponent where he was relatively weak and, wheeling south, crushing the main French armies from behind.

The Germans had at their disposal vital assets—mass, mobility, and a bold mode of attack—for achieving strategic surprise and, they hoped, a quick victory.

Unfortunately for them, Schlieffen's successors in the general staff gradually diluted his plan. Reluctant to permit a temporary French advance into Germany, General Moltke (nephew of the famous chief of staff some decades earlier) strengthened the German forces in the south at the expense of the crucial right wing in the north.[11] Yet Schlieffen's strategy, or what was left of it, still produced much of the surprise experienced by the French. Three other factors contributed to it: an unexpected display of mobility (much of it achieved by hard marching troops), the overall deployment of twice as many troops as the French had anticipated, and the German ability to conceal their precise movements in the early stages of the offensive.

But it was the plans and decisions of the French themselves that made their experience of strategic surprise so complete. Before 1900, the French had likewise realized the technological advantage of defense over offense, and accepted the dogma that any frontal attack was doomed to failure. Following 1900, however, leading French strategists began to ignore this conventional wisdom and, under the leadership of General Langlois, fervently embraced the "mysticism of the offensive." Cool technical analysis was replaced by a psychological construct. The plodding course of the Russo-Japanese war, shaped by the relative power of defensive warfare, did not disturb them. The new doctrine, focusing on attack conducted with utmost élan, inspired the notorious Plan XVI of 1908. When Joffre became chief of the general staff in 1911, he accepted this doctrine and set out to shape French forces and their training accordingly. Yet Plan XVI did not really contain a strategy. Beyond setting forth the twin objectives of assembling all available forces at the outbreak of war and immediately seizing the initiative, there was no war plan of strategic implementation, no strategy of exactly where and how to attack. This lack reflected a type of military thinking—completely different from that of the German staff—which was pithily expressed by Marshall Foch when he said that strategy was "merely a matter of character and common sense."[12]

Moreover, French military intelligence grossly underestimated German strength. It expected the Germans to operate with 45 active divisions in the west. This intelligence failure was based on the assumption that the Germans would not use their reserves—whose quality the French underrated—for anything but defensive purposes. Actually, Germany deployed 83 divisions, including reserves that fought very well. Because France was inferior to Germany in population and numbers of trained soldiers, the French assumption had been comforting, and one wonders whether it was not inspired by wishfulness.

Finally, the French knew about the Schlieffen plan, which had received considerable public discussion. A big war game, based on this plan and carried out by the German general staff in 1906, had also come to their attention. Joffre and his aides could not be certain that the Germans would actually apply the Schlieffen plan, but they were aware of it as a possible choice and marginal changes were made in Plan XVI to provide for the contingency of a German violation of Belgian neutrality. Modest French forces were positioned toward the northwest. Yet, aside from the fact that the French expected to seize the initiative by their own attack and thereby foil German plans in the northwest, French planners complacently assumed that any German thrust would not penetrate the heart of Belgium but proceed through the difficult wooded mountains of the Ardennes. The French thus misjudged the wideness of the German sweep, which constituted a much vaster enveloping movement than the French command regarded as a contingency. Once the war had begun, General Lanrezac, commanding the 5th Army that was covering it, guessed the true dimensions of German intentions, but was permitted to move further in the critical direction only belatedly, after repeated urging.

That French planners did not take the Schlieffen plan and a German penetration of most of Belgium more seriously is all the more astounding because, once they learned about the Schlieffen plan, Joffre and his staff became interested in the possibility of preventive action by a quick French march into Belgium as soon as war broke out. However, the French government firmly ruled out this possibility, in large part because a French violation of Belgian neutrality would have offended Britain and might have jeopardized her entry into the war on the French side. Although this cannot be documented, one has the feeling that the French military leaders thought of foiling German plans by an *offensive* of their own through Belgium. This would have been in keeping with their faith in the virtue of the offensive spirit. But to foil

German strategy by sufficient *defensive* deployment in the north would have required offensive action in the east to be abandoned.

To conclude, French military behavior played into the hands of the Germans. The preconceived French attachment to their "offensive á outrance" conflicted with proper defensive deployment, and was doomed in any case because the Germans enjoyed the strategic initiative and because the French armies were numerically too inferior. Rigid preconception conflicted with proper and feasible threat perception. The gross underestimate of opposing German force levels and the comfortable assumption that any German violation of Belgian territory would proceed through the Ardennes and remain shallow suggests a considerable element of wishfulness.

As it turned out, decisive success escaped the Germans despite stunning victories. The ultimate failure of strategic surprise to work according to Schlieffen's plan does not reflect on a weakness in Germany's capability to inflict strategic surprise. There was nothing wrong with Schlieffen's plan, and the Germans had at their disposal virtually all the assets to implement it with success (i.e., quick mobilization, massive superiority, and impressive mobility in the field). The main trouble was that strict adherence to this daring plan allowed only a thin defensive cover along the Franco-German boundary. The younger Moltke preferred to be safe everywhere and thus compromised the boldness of the plan. This insistence on playing it safe ran counter to the essence of Schlieffen's boldness. The crucial right wing was weakened and, in large part for this reason, its commander wheeled prematurely before the Paris region was reached. The French were able to hold. Gradually the tide turned and the war of attrition began, which Germany could not win against a coalition superior in manpower and material resources.

1940: GERMAN OCCUPATION OF NORWAY AND DENMARK[13]

On April 9, 1940, Germany launched a lightning strike to occupy neutral Denmark and Norway. The quick occupation of Denmark posed no military problem. Norway did. Small German assault forces (fewer than 9,000), landing from ships and airplanes, seized Oslo and five other Norwegian port cities all the way to Narvik in the extreme north, to be strengthened by more troops shipped in during the following days.

Success depended on two factors. First, it required unfailing execution of a bold and carefully prepared plan designed to affect simultaneous landings over a coast stretching about 1,000 miles to the north. Any breach of simultaneity would have given warning and reaction time to opposing forces. To make this possible, unescorted German merchant ships, carrying mostly military equipment, left German ports on April 3. German warships, carrying the bulk of the invading troops, went to sea on April 7. About 500 transport aircraft flew in the airborne forces on April 9. Strategic surprise was the second condition to success. The operation went almost exactly as planned. Small opposing British forces were landed in central Norway but faced a hopeless task and were quickly withdrawn. A larger Anglo-French force put ashore subsequently to capture Narvik was evacuated when Germany launched its blitzkrieg in the west in May.

Despite warnings from several sources, the German invasion of Denmark and Norway surprised Britain. The "British were taken wholly by surprise."[14] General Ismay, chief of staff to the minister of defense, admitted: "I realized, for the first time in my life, the devastating and demoralizing effect of surprise."[15] Of course, the Danes and Norwegians were surprised as well.

The Germans decided on the invasion of Norway in order to prevent her invasion by the British. It was to be a preventative action. The Germans had been well content with Scandinavian neutrality. They depended on Swedish iron ore which—during the winter months when the Baltic is frozen—was received through the Norwegian port of Narvik; and, hugging Norwegian coastal waters, German ships were able to sail into the North Atlantic. The British, on the other hand, had good reason for wanting to cut these lanes of transportation. Anglo-French plans for occupying Narvik were duly prepared, in particular at Churchill's instigation, but Prime Minister Chamberlain and other officials balked at the proposal to violate Norwegian neutrality.[16] In the end, the British Cabinet agreed on April 5 to start the mining of Norwegian waters despite strong Norwegian protests. At the same time, British troops were embarked in ships to sail for Narvik and other Norwegian ports in the event the British action provoked military countermeasures by Germany. While both British and German forces were set to converge on Norway, the Germans got there first.

All along the Germans had received information on British plans. In order to cover this contingency, Hitler ordered the supreme command of the armed forces to study the problem on December 13, 1939, and on January 27, 1940 he demanded the development of an operational plan under the codeword "Weserübung." German leaders became convinced that British action in Norway was imminent when the British boarded the German ship *Altmark* in Norwegian waters on February 16 in order to liberate British prisoners on board. If they were to act, the Germans felt it necessary to do so by early April, which was the end of the time period during which they could count on cloud cover and dark nights.[17]

The German planners calculated that the achievement of strategic surprise was indispensable to the occupation of Norway. First, Britain enjoyed vast naval superiority in the area. Only surprise could negate this obstacle. Also, the Norwegians might offer considerable resistance unless they were caught unawares. Second, Norway would not be a decisive theater of war, and the

Germans were shortly to start their big offensive in the west. Therefore, only very modest land forces could be spared for the Norwegian operation. As the plan stated: "Numerical weakness must be offset by bold action and surprise."[18]

The Germans carefully chose the means essential to the achievement of surprise. One was the design of a plan so audacious and original that opponents were most unlikely to consider it as a contingency. Another was the requirement that all invasion targets were to be hit at precisely the same time. A third was to insure quick success by reckless commitment. It was recognized that, in view of the risks, only unhesitating action could succeed. The loss of half of the naval forces involved was accepted in German calculations. As already mentioned, German planners timed the attack so that it would benefit from protective weather conditions. Finally, great pains were taken to insure secrecy of preparations. Hitler ordered General Falkenhorst, the designated commanding officer, to impose strict rules of secrecy in the planning phase, including the choice of a very small staff. Maps and interpreters were procurred discreetly, and deployment of troops at the ports of exit was concealed as long as possible. Divisional commanders were briefed on their tasks only at the beginning of March, and personnel below battalion commander not until after embarkation. The German Foreign Office was not informed until the day before the invasion was scheduled.

Implicit in these capabilities were top decision-makers, or a top decision-maker, capable of authorizing an audacious and riskful strategy. At least at this phase of World War II, Hitler had the capacity to make such decisions. He displayed remarkable gifts as a strategist. Distrustful of the military professionals—who seemed to him, among other things, given to excessive caution—he did not hesitate to make the final decisions himself. In this he was helped by a deep familiarity with weapons systems, by an ability to take political and psychological factors into consideration, and by an intuitive understanding of the strategic issues involved. His decisions were also marked by a strong penchant to do daring things.[19]

Most strategies aiming at surprise carry considerable risks, and leaders are apt to be divided on weighing these in relation to promised advantages. Therefore, such strategies can be adopted only if internal doubts and opposition are overcome. The German attack on Norway and Denmark is an interesting case from this point of view. The German military understood the risks involved in the strategy. Especially the plan to enter the defended Oslo Fjord and to occupy Narvik in the extreme north was regarded as extremely hazardous. Still more riskful seemed the diversion of forces to a peripheral enterprise from the impending offensive in the west. The naval staff was for the most part unenthusiastic but went along. The top generals of the army, however, lodged protests on January 1, 1940 and, again, on March 1. Annoyed by this opposition, Hitler started to bypass the Oberkommando Heer (OKH), which sat at the top of the army command structure, and to entrust leadership to the Oberkommando Wehrmacht (OKW), a small headquarters directly under Hitler as commander-in-chief (since February 1938) of all three services.[20] This meant the establishment of a unitary actor for the conduct of war. Hitler was thus able to make his gamble stick.

It is fair to say that the British made a considerable contribution to the surprise that was inflicted on them . They were aware that their own designs on Norway—intent on disrupting vital German iron ore supplies and a maritime egress to the North Atlantic—might provoke German countermeasures. They even considered the possibility of German preemptive action. On March 12, Chamberlain ordered that the military force assembled for a British landing in Narvik stand down on the grounds that if the Germans heard of it, they would be given an excuse to invade Norway. Indeed, when it was decided to lay mines in Norwegian waters, the British thought that any military reaction by Germany would induce Norway to call for military assistance by the allies which, in turn, would permit the British to move into Narvik.[21] But these calculations only contemplated a form of German riposte which the British felt confident could be put down easily. They ruled out precisely the all-out attack which the Germans were about to launch. They did so on the assumption—perfectly sound as far as it went—that such an enterprise (which would give the British time to react in force) was precluded by the vast extent of British naval superiority in the region. With their long historical experience with landing operations from the sea, they understood the problem and would themselves never have laid on such an action under the circumstances. They simply did not expect the Germans to do anything so foolhardy. In holding this view, the British did not recognize, or take properly into account, that Norway's airspace was closer to German than to British bases and that, although inferior at sea, the Germans might count on local air superiority. More importantly, the British did not ask themselves—and herein lies their mistake—: under what conditions could the Germans hope to take Norway despite British seapower? The obvious answer would have been: only under conditions of complete surprise. It was not perhaps much of a mistake because it is difficult to conceive of a boldly original plan unless one feels compelled to do so. Yet it does take imagination and the will to put it to work if one desires not to be taken by surprise.

The British government did receive warnings of possible German military moves, especially shortly before the invasion date when German ship and troop concentrations could no longer be concealed. European capitals were seething with rumors. The trouble was that rumors and warnings, even when not contradictory, were compatible with quite different assumptions about what the Germans might be up to. On several occasions up to February 1940, the British chiefs of staff résumés included items drafted by MI 3 (Military Intelligence) that summarized secret service reports about German plans but were hedged with qualifications. The résumé of February 3 dismissed the idea of preparations for a German expeditionary force on the grounds that the Germans would need from 25 to 30 divisions for an invasion of Norway and Denmark and that only six divisions could be traced in the deployment area to which reports had drawn attention.[22] (In the end, it was six divisions that did it.) On March 26, the head of the Northern Department in the Foreign Office minuted on a warning telegram from the air attaché in Stockholm. "I wish I could believe this story. German intervention in Scandinavia is just what we want."[23]

By April 3, British military intelligence became more cautious and advised the chiefs of staff that the latest reports might portend the invasion of Scandinavia. But it concluded on April 4 that the evidence did not at the moment support the probability of a German invasion. As before, there were lots of signals but no unambiguous confirmation. Also, all the warnings that were received by the British reached different branches of intelligence and were never collated, so significant connections between clues were overlooked. As long as ambiguity prevailed, information was easily seen to fit preconceived assumptions. In the admiralty, for instance, intelligence did not challenge the belief of Winston Churchill, the first lord, that a landing in Scandinavia was beyond German means, or the conclusion of Churchill and the naval staff that Germany intended instead another naval break-out into the Atlantic. Many bits of information could be seen as pointing in this direction.

On April 7 a few officers in the admiralty were beginning to credit a message from the British ministry in Copenhagen that the Germans planned to invade Jutland and Narvik, but they did not marshal other evidence in such a way as to present a convincing case to themselves or their superiors. On the same day, the director of Naval Intelligence remarked that "all these reports are of doubtful value and may well be only a further move in the war of nerves."[24] While other British officials believed by April 7 that a German attempt at invading Norway was underway, they thought of much more limited actions than what the Germans had in train.[25] The admiralty, continuing to interpret warning signals as indicating a break-out of the German fleet into the North Atlantic, dispatched British ships to bring the German fleet to action. As a result of ambiguous intelligence, rough weather, and poor visibility, the British force failed to make contact. On April 8, a Polish submarine near Skagerrak sank a German transport, and German soldiers rescued by Norwegian fishermen disclosed that they were part of a force bound for Bergen. But when the British received this information, their fleet units were already at sea on a different mission, and no capacity for quick British action was available.

Great Britain was not, of course, the only country surprised by Germany.

Among others, Norway and Denmark are especially interesting cases.[26] The posture of neutrality had kept the Scandinavian countries out of World War I and, when World War II broke out, the maintenance of neutrality was their cardinal principle in foreign policy. Militarily weak as Denmark and Norway were, this was obviously an attractive stance. Yet the governments of both states should have nursed less confidence in it than they felt. To begin with, they should have been warned by the very nature of the Hitler regime—amply displayed in previous action against Austria, Czechoslovakia, and Poland— that the new Germany was far more aggressive, daring, and ruthless than had been imperial Germany. Moreover, they had undertaken no defensive military preparations to make a violation of their neutrality more costly. To do so was perhaps hopeless for the Danes, but it was not for the Norwegians who could have counted on timely British intervention if they would hold out for a time against a German attack. Although the Norwegian government had been reassured by Germany on September 1, 1939, that it intended to respect Norwegian neutrality, this declaration was made conditional on Norway's status not being breached by a third party.

The Norwegian government staunchly resisted all Allied pressures that would have compromised their neutrality. But this was evidently not enough to calm German apprehensions about a possible British move into Norway. As German preparations for Weserübung became observable, the Norwegians received plenty of warnings of German plans for an overseas expedition. On April 4, Colonel Oster of the German counterintelligence service, who was anti-Nazi like his Chief Admiral Canaris, informed the Dutch military attaché in Berlin about the German plans. The Dutch official promptly passed the news to the representatives of other neutral governments. Norwegian officials in Berlin filed several memoranda reporting on ominous German troop and ship concentrations and suggested that the Germans were preparing a strike toward the north. As already mentioned, German soldiers picked up by Norwegian fishermen when their troop ship was sunk by a Polish submarine on April 8 admitted that they had been on the way to Bergen. When reports of this incident reached Berlin, the German planners assumed that the element of surprise had been lost and that the German invaders would now meet stiff resistance throughout Norway. They need not have worried. The Norwegian government and military had received all these warnings with considerable disbelief. And at the end, when they were taken more seriously, the Norwegians decided against immediate mobilization in the hope of avoiding any step that the Germans might have construed as a provocative act.

On the day before the invasion, the chief communications officer of the Norwegian admiralty spent the evening at the home of the German air attaché in Oslo. Despite the bad news that kept coming in, he was not called away from his social engagement before 11:30 p.m., and it was not until 1:00 a.m.

of April 9 that the Norwegian admiralty issued orders for the activation of mines in Oslo Fjord. That move came too late as German ships had already entered the fjord. The Norwegian army was also caught unawares. On the night of April 8-9, the chief of the operations section of the Norwegian general staff was asleep at his home. Shortly after 1:00 a.m. of the 9th, a telephone call from the Army chief of staff informed him that the fortresses at the mouth of Oslo Fjord were under attack.

The Danish government was likewise informed of the danger of a German invasion. It ignored these reports and took no action. Although counsels were divided at repeated Cabinet meetings, optimism invariably prevailed. During a session on the afternoon of April 8, the Cabinet rejected a proposal by the military to order general mobilization. The majority and the king still believed that a German attack was improbable. Early the following day, the German ambassador informed the Danish government that German troops had invaded the country. Unlike the Norwegians who, however belatedly, fought as long as they could, the Danes decided that resistance was hopeless. Both the Norwegians and the Danish government were caught in the comfortable disposition not to believe that the worst was happening.

Why did the Norwegian government fall victim to surprise? First, preconceptions played a crucial role. The key actor on the Norwegian side was Halvdan Koht, the foreign minister who was a highly regarded dominating personality and whose views easily prevailed. Based on the success of Norway's neutrality in World War I, and perhaps swayed also by wishful thinking, Koht believed that a neutrality policy was as workable in 1940 as it had been before. He thought that the Germans preferred this status—which was indeed true before they began to doubt Norway's ability to maintain it in the face of Anglo-French pressure and schemes. Koht did not perceive that this neutrality status had been losing credibility. Second, his strategic assessment accepted the British assumption that German occupation of Norway was impractical against Britain's superiority at sea. The Norwegian's faith in the Royal Navy's power of deterrence and denial was supported by current misconceptions of recent changes in military technology that enabled the German air force— capable of operating in much of Norway's airspace from bases closer than those of British aircraft—to offset British naval superiority in good part by achieving local superiority in the air.

Third, Koht was preoccupied with possible British moves that might endanger Norway's neutrality by provoking his country into entering the war on the side of the Allies. He regarded any threat from Germany as a reaction to Anglo-French initiatives. Fourth, as did the British, the Norwegians failed to recognize Germany's incentive to act by surprise, if at all, and also underrated her willingness to accept high strategic risks. Fifth, Koht did not expect—as Stalin was not to expect subsequently—that Germany would strike without first precipitating a crisis and issuing demands as Hitler had done prior to marching into Austria, Czechoslovakia, and Poland. Sixth, Koht overestimated the strength and readiness of Norway's defenses. Finally, Norway's vulnerability to surprise was facilitated by Koht's position of preeminent actor. He preferred to consider and make decisions alone and was allowed to do so. While his views were shared or accepted by most of the government and military, his domination precluded the opportunity for different opinions to emerge and be heard. His assumptions and conclusions—which proved to be wrong—carried the day without challenge.

In view of this mindset prevailing on the Norwegian side, it is not difficult to understand why strategic warnings of a possible German attack were given insufficient attention. Because, as is usually the case, the signals of what was to come were ambiguous, and because twice before (in December 1939 and in January/March 1940) warnings of possible German naval preparations against Norway had proved unfounded, there was a strong tendency to regard the later warnings as unsubstantiated.

1940: BLITZKRIEG IN THE WEST[27]

After the outbreak of hostilities in 1939, France and Britain—not expecting to develop their full strength for two years—decided against any serious offensive action against Germany until then. Aside from occupying Norway and Denmark, the Germans used the period of the "phoney war" for rapidly increasing their military capabilities and planning an all-out attack on the Allies in the west.

The Allies could hope only to win a prolonged war. This was also Hitler's estimate. Already in November 1939 he had said that "time was on the side of the Western powers."[28] He feared that a protracted struggle would lead to the entry of other powers on his opponents' side. Therefore, Hitler wanted a quick decisive victory in the west, knocking out France and inducing the United Kingdom to negotiate a peace treaty. Because Hitler intended to strike without delay, he opposed any total economic mobilization for war. November 12, 1939 and January 17, 1940 were the first dates fixed for the attack. Both had to be cancelled on account of bad weather, and the offensive finally began on May 10.

The German planners had learned the chief lesson of World War I. The loser tends to be more eager than the victor to study past mistakes. It was so in this case. Wanting to avoid prolonged positional warfare, the Germans were intent on designing a strategy that would combine three elements—concentration of force at the decisive point, utmost mobility, and surprise—in order to cut deeply through the armies of the Allies and roll them up from the rear in a great battle of encirclement. To do so would have been impossible where the famous Maginot Line of fortifications protected the French frontier in the east. As the Germans had already concluded before World War I, the only promising area for an outflanking maneuver was in the neutral Low Countries. Geography presented no other option. The German plan that was finally executed was brilliantly original in two ways. First, the German army, unlike the French and British, had understood the military revolution made possible by the use of massed tank formations, in combination with assault gun units and dive bombers for ground support, in thrusting speedily through enemy lines of defense. Since quickness of movement was of the essence, the Panzer divisions did not wait for slow foot infantry to catch up, but raced ahead, their confident commanders being unworried about exposing flanks to counterattacks and leaving gaps in their forward movement. It was not that the Germans had more tanks than the French, but rather that, instead of dispersing them over the entire front, they were concentrated for massive shock effect. The Germans thus created a new doctrine that, temporarily at least, overcame the basic technological superiority of defense over offensive operations, and completely outclassed their adversaries. Second, the shock of surprise was produced not only by this novel form of fighting but also by the choice of the Ardennes for the critical breakthrough even though this mountainous and densely wooded area was far from ideally suited for rapid movement en masse. In this respect, deception contributed to surprise. Once the Germans had selected the Ardennes as the area for their decisive thrust, they hoped that another army rapidly invading the Netherlands and Belgium further north would give the enemy the impression that it represented the major threat.[29] Furthermore, the Germans managed the preliminary moves into position for attack in the Ardennes by gradual stages so that their troops were ready to move in strength on May 10 without having given the Allies the opportunity to observe last-minute preparations.[30]

The Allies were surprised on both counts. They had not expected the attempt of a breakthrough in the Ardennes, and they were unprepared for the speed and force of the German offensive which was, indeed, something new in warfare. The German columns moved with the speed of an avalanche, leaving no time for defensive countermoves to get underway.

There were additional factors that contributed to Germany's victory. In terms of static numerical comparisons of men and arms, the Germans were not superior to the Allies. But such comparisons are often misleading. The Germans enjoyed some important qualitative advantages. The Peace Treaty of Versailles had limited the German army to 100,000 men and to strictly defensive arms, e.g., no tanks and no aircraft. Hitler had swept these restrictions aside only a few years before the war. The recency of German rearmament meant that, unlike in France, none of its military equipment was outmoded; the small German professional army had been used as an outstanding school for developing excellent officers and noncommissioned officers. When war broke out, German troops were better led and trained, and enjoyed better morale than the French and British troops. These advantages no doubt helped in the execution of blitzkrieg. But the stunning success in the west was primarily the result of a new strategic concept and of the surprise inflicted on Germany's enemies.

It is interesting to analyze in some detail the tortuous way in which the winning German strategy was chosen. To do so will throw light on the problems of selecting a strategy of surprise; it will also show the difficulties confronting the target state in avoiding the experience of surprise.

As already indicated, German planning turned on two major questions: how to strike a decisive blow (mode of attack) and where to strike (choice of area for a concentrated breakthrough). The chief merit for forging the instrument for the mode of attack was in General Guderian's plan. As an idea, the concept of armoured breakthroughs at high speed had surfaced in other countries, including France (General de Gaulle) and Britain (Liddell Hart), but failed to attract acceptance by the military leadership. These leaders either did not understand or distrusted the massive use of tanks in a war of movement, and preferred their dispersed deployment in support of infantry.

Guderian was the innovator who translated the idea into an operational concept and a trained operational force. In Germany as well, however, the more conservative military—many of them at the top levels of planning and command—were very critical of this innovation. They regarded the infantry as the preeminent service and the proposed use of Panzer divisions as adventurist, inviting too many risks, and depending excessively on the achievement of complete surprise, which they thought was often a matter of luck. The German general staff was also unimaginative in choosing the area for concentrated attack. In response to Hitler's directive of October 9 to work out an offensive plan, the OKH proposed that the major advance by Army Group B proceed through the Netherlands and north Belgium, and that a subsidiary feinting attack by Army Group A take place in southern Belgium and Luxembourg. This represented only a slight revision of the Schlieffen plan as applied in 1914, and Hitler was not all enthusiastic. But its sponsors argued that the events of 1914 had proved the essential soundness of the strategy and that it had then failed in the end only as a result of faulty leadership. The proposed plan was essentially what the French expected to be the most likely German choice. Its execution would not have surprised them.

It was at this point that General Manstein—the chief brain behind the blitzkrieg that was eventually launched—intervened. He objected that the Allies would be prepared for the proposed attack and that it would therefore lack the benefit of surprise—which had been an essential part of the old

Schlieffen plan. At best, he pointed out, the planned offensive would produce only a partial victory, not a crushing and decisive one. Manstein's alternative was to strengthen Army Group A, especially its armored components, pierce the enemy lines by advancing through the difficult terrain of the Ardennes, and then cut off the retreat of the Allied forces that would have moved into Belgium. His aim was a grand battle of annihilation. By selecting the Ardennes as the principal area of breakthrough, Manstein expected to achieve strategic surprise. He acknowledged that his plan was risky, but he deemed it also to offer the best chance of success.

Guderian fully agreed with Manstein that a quick and powerful advance through the Ardennes was feasible. However, when the plan was submitted to OKH, it met stiff opposition. That might have been the end of it and the blitzkrieg actually launched later would not have happened. Yet Hitler had not liked OKH's plan—he as well did not think it would give the advantage of surprise—and, on November 12, he directed that Army Group A be somewhat strengthened. It is unclear whether he did so on his own intuition or because some version of the Manstein plan had reached him through unknown channels. By the end of November 1939, Hitler veered further away from OKH's plan. He decided that the decision on whether the main breakthrough should be entrusted to Army Group B or A should be delayed until the outcome of the initial fighting was known. Manstein regarded this compromise as strategically wrong because it would militate against greatly strengthening one army group at the expense of the other and because it would leave too much to chance. In his view, the place of breakthrough should be determined in advance.

At this point an accident intervened. On January 17, a German aircraft carrying a courier with the somewhat amended plan of OKH made an emergency landing in the Netherlands. The Germans had to suppose that knowledge of the plan would leak to the Allies. (Incidentally, it was conveyed to the Allies who, however, suspected that the document was planted by the Germans for purposes of deception.)[31] This fortuitous event made Hitler and his generals more disposed to undertake a radical revision of the offensive design. Manstein was now given the opportunity to submit his ideas to Hitler, and his plan was studied in two war games in February. The OKH again objected to Manstein's strategy as being too risky. General Halder, the chief to the general staff, called it "senseless" and advocated a slower advance in order to permit infantry to move up in support of armored thrusts. Guderian, however, strongly emphasized the importance of using all available Panzer divisions together and with surprise at the decisive point, of breaking through quickly and not worrying about exposed flanks. But nothing was decided at this point.[32]

On February 17, Hitler ordered another briefing by Manstein and then, on March 15, by Guderian. It was at this latter meeting that Hitler made the decision. When Guderian asserted that he expected to cross the Meuse River on the fourth day, Hitler asked: "And what will you do then?" Guderian replied that he would continue the thrust unless stopped by contrary orders, that the high command would have to decide whether he should slash through toward Paris or Amiens on the coast, and that the latter direction would be most effective strategically. Hitler nodded. Subsequently, when the blitzkrieg was launched, Guderian received no further directional orders once he had crossed the Meuse and before he had reached the Channel.[33] But in various ways his superiors at OKH were still fighting the strategy by repeatedly ordering him to slow down and by attempting to divert troops from his command. At one point (May 17), Guderian asked to be relieved of his command.[34] But in the end he succeeded in what he had set out to do.

It is clear from this account that the adoption to the blitzkrieg strategy, including the seizure of surprise, was helped by fortuitous circumstances and would have been impossible without Hitler's personal fiat, his authority to impose his will on the German army leaders, his own flair for understanding military problems, and his proclivity for accepting daring and risky courses of action.[35] In view of the cautiously conservative cast of mind prevailing at the top of army planning, it is no wonder that, in a sense, the Germans as well as the Allies were surprised by the capabilities the German army demonstrated in the blitzkrieg in the west.[36] Finally, it would have demanded extraordinary perceptiveness for the French to have anticipated what was to befall them.

The French did unwittingly everything to be surprised by the German blitzkrieg. As junior partners in land warfare, the British went generally along with French dispositions. Until a few years before May 1940, when lightning struck, the French nation, more interested in material welfare and its domestic distribution, had neglected its defenses, especially during the crucial years from 1934 to 1936 when Hitler was already in power and the German armament effort was in training. Although not fully understanding the nature of the looming German threat, the French became nervous about their unruly neighbor and sharp increases in defense expenditures occurred from 1938 to 1939. But this tardy effort was inadequate relative to Germany's and left France with a great deal of obsolete and obsolescent military equipment in 1940. These deficiencies reflected a deeply divided society in which one half distrusted and hated the other. Under these circumstances, the nation was incapable of generating the vitality of defensive effort that might have stopped the Germans.[37]

It was against this unpropitious background that military leaders had fashioned French strategy. The army was not a popular institution in the state. Its top echelon, mindful of their eventual victory in World War I (although achieved only with the help of powerful allies) was opinionated and uninspired. French doctrine was based squarely on the lesson of World War I, which had proved the defense to be technologically superior to the offense. Concentrated modern fire power was seen as giving scant scope to any war of movement. This conviction prompted the French to build the magnificent Maginot Line of fortifications all along the Franco-German frontier. Exploiting favorable topographic features, the Maginot Line was generally thought to be impregnable. And in fact it was. The Germans did not attack the line, and it had not been breached at the time the French surrendered. The trouble was that the Maginot Line was not extended along the Franco-Belgian boundary to the Channel. Unlike eastern France, the region adjoining Belgium was densely industrialized and populated, and lacked conditions of terrain suitable for fortifications. The French had also worried that a prepared line of defenses in this location would weaken the defensive spirit of the Belgians.

The French military suspected that the Germans were likely to attack through Belgium. The problems presented by such an offensive had been the subject of Anglo-French staff studies. With their eastern frontier secure, the French planned to advance with their best troops into Belgium as soon as the Germans were on the move and meet them there head-on. This would have been facilitated if joint plans could have been formulated with Belgium and the Netherlands. However, the Dutch were flatly opposed and, although tempted, the Belgians refused in the hope that strict maintenance of neutrality would induce Hitler to spare them. (Belgium had declared its permanent neutrality in 1936.) The French and British nevertheless stuck to their plans of moving into Belgium as soon as the Germans did.

The French planners were not wrong in perceiving that weapons technology basically favored defense. What they failed to recognize is that some recent developments permitted a new form of offensive warfare—a concentration of tanks, self-propelled guns and dive-bombers that could punch through the defense line of an opponent unprepared for blitzkrieg. French strategists should have been forewarned. They had witnessed the rapidity with which German forces has sliced through Poland in 1939. These operations hinted at what was likely to come.[38] The French were aware of the development of German tank divisions and their exercises. General Gauché of the Deuxième Bureau (military intelligence) made a detailed study of the Polish campaign. But the French high command paid no attention to it.[39] It was not really curious about recent German military thinking. It had itself studied the use of tanks and dive-bombers but concluded that such use involved unacceptable risks and was unlikely to achieve decisive results.[40] This judgment was not exactly stupid. It was in fact not unlike that of the conservative school of thought prevalent at the top of the German planning structure, which also held that the ideas of Guderian and Manstein were unsound. And there is no question that the German plan of blitzkrieg involved the substantial risk that the spearheads of the German advance—mobile units lacking infantry support—might be cut off. But this risk would have been serious only against an enemy who was unsurprised, had comprehended the essence of blitzkrieg *and was fully prepared* to exploit its inherent weaknesses.[41] To be able to do this, they would have had to perceive fully Germany's revolutionary doctrine and plan against it—which they did not.

The British likewise failed to perceive the threat of blitzkrieg. Prior to the war, they were aware of the German development of Panzer divisions but did not take them seriously because they deferred to French judgment. British intelligence also studied the German use of tank columns in Poland, but the army remained unimpressed.[42]

Too sure of themselves, and their minds closed to new ideas, the leading French strategists were unable to envisage alternative strategies that were open to the Germans, and they stuck therefore to a defensive concept that was outmoded by German plans and capabilities. Moreover, the German decision-makers knew this and could plan on it. In the end, the much-touted Maginot Line had served no useful purpose. It had, however, stimulated German planners to design a strategy that would bypass it; and, making the French overconfident, may have helped to blind them to unaccustomed dangers. Right up to the day disaster struck, the French army maintained the same fixity of posture that it had developed by the time the war with Germany had begun. One French historian remarked: "the impression left is . . . that of an army of victims patiently waiting for the day the enemy had decided to carry out the death sentence."[43]

In the west, the Germans could not hope to achieve the complete surprise they had enjoyed in Norway. Intelligence branches in Paris and London expected a German offensive and had agreed, on April 29, that a German invasion was imminent and that possibly all of the German armored divisions would be committed to it. But intelligence was unable to say where and precisely when the blow would fall.

Regarding the "where," four main possibilities were kept under review: an attack limited to the Low Countries, and perhaps Holland alone; an offensive through the Low Countries aimed at turning the Maginot Line in the north; a frontal attack on the Maginot Line; and an attack through Switzerland.[44] Eventually, attention concentrated on the first two possibilities. The British seriously considered that Germany might limit its offensive to seizing Belgium and the Netherlands in order to acquire better bases for air attacks on England. French intelligence concluded by the end of April that the Germans had opted for the second possibility. But the French high command firmly discounted the possibility that the major German thrust would come through the Ardennes. This view was professionally not unsound. Most of the German senior planners agreed with it. But, again, the French lacked the imagination to ask themselves: what unlikely thing might the Germans do if they want to surprise us?

Two factors contributed to this failure. First, as already mentioned, the Germans took great care to keep their change of plan secret. Their northern Army Group B was meant, by rapidly advancing into Belgium, to give the Allies the impression that it—and not Army Group A—represented the main thrust, thus inducing their opponents to swing into Belgium as they had planned to do, and set themselves up to be trapped. Second, the French and British staffs took no serious interest in military intelligence. The Germans did not make it easy for the Allied intelligence services. Prior to the day of the offensive, they kept wireless traffic as near normal as possible in order not to give anything away on volume count. Aerial reconnaissance, although handicapped by bad weather, supplied some disturbing information. Yet these signals were not fully appreciated by the French high command. General Gamelin, the French commander-in-chief, had staked his reputation on the assessment that the Germans could and would not attack through the Ardennes.[45] The French estimate of the German order of battle (with correct figures in parentheses) was:[46]

Opposite Dutch-Belgian frontier (Army Group B)	37 divisions (29)
Eifel-Moselle (Army Group A)	26 divisions (45)
Opposite Maginot Line	41 divisions (20)

Furthermore, while the Allied staffs had not been unmindful of the risks their armies assumed by marching into Belgium,[47] the dominant assumption about German strategy made it impossible to appreciate fully the extent of the risk.

When the thunderbolt fell on May 10, the Allies and the Germans had about the same number of divisions in the field. The French army manned the Maginot Line in the east with as many as 30 divisions, maintained a feeble cover force of 12 mediocre divisions in the center, and in the north advanced with its British allies slowly into Belgium. The Germans overran the Netherlands, quickly broke Belgian resistance, and broke through in the center. By the time the Allied command began to grasp the situation on May 16, Guderian had smashed through the French lines at Sedan and pushed 50 miles beyond. On May 20, he reached the Channel at Abbéville. The Allies were "breathless, confused, and eventually dazed."[48] Utterly surprised, they had been too slow to react and too rigid to improvise. All that was left for the victors to do was to mop up.

The collapse was military. It was not caused by defeatism in the rear. But the military business had been distasteful to most of the French nation and its governments. Provision for deterrence and defense had come grudgingly and tardily, and the hidebound military doctrine to which its military leadership clung, suited—as Charles de Gaulle put it—"the spirit of the regime."[49] The Nazi regime in Germany, by contrast, was strongly militarist, open to innovation, and willing to gamble in order to overthrow the consequences of World War I.

THE GERMAN INVASION OF RUSSIA: 1941[50]

Stalin experienced the shock of strategic surprise when Germany invaded the Soviet Union in 1941. He had not expected Hitler to order the attack and, despite the German performance in the blitzkrieg in the west a year earlier, the Soviet high command was ill-prepared for the mode of fighting practiced by the German army. Unlike the previous German offensives in Norway, the Low Countries, and France, this one, although seemingly very successful in its initial stages, did not produce a knock-out victory. But this ultimate failure came about even though strategic surprise had been achieved.

Hitler felt subjectively compelled to conquer the USSR. The conclusion of the Soviet-German nonaggressive pact on August 23, 1939 between deadly ideological antagonists, which had surprised the rest of the world, had simply been a convenient tactic that secured Germany in the east while it was fighting in the west. Hitler knew already in 1939 that his country lacked sufficient economic potential for winning a prolonged war of attrition against a materially superior coalition of enemies. Successful short wars, for which Germany was superbly ready, were to create a much enlarged and self-sufficient state or empire.[51]

The dazzling victory in the west had knocked out France, but the United Kingdom did not negotiate peace, as Hitler had hoped; it quickly became clear to him that Germany lacked the naval forces or the crushing superiority in the air that would have permitted a successful invasion of the British Isles. In consequence, Hitler feared the eventual development of a hostile alliance that would include the Soviet Union and especially the United States. He said in 1940 that "England's hope rests with Russia and the USA."[52] Peripheral campaigns in the Mediterranean would fail to be decisive even if they brought brilliant victories. Nor was he convinced that the German alliance with Japan would keep the United States tied down in the Pacific and Far East. Increasingly his worries about the probable enmity of that country—which Hitler knew could vastly outproduce Germany in military materiél—moved to the center of his strategic thinking.[53] There were additional considerations that pushed Hitler toward war with Russia, especially his deep ideological hatred of bolshevism. But it was anxiety about the United States that made the conquest of the Soviet Union imperative. Germany was vitally dependent on Soviet oil and raw materials, and Stalin, Hitler suspected, would exploit this dependence for blackmailing Germany once the United States became belligerent, and might well join his enemies in the end. The only way, Hitler thought, of making Germany strategically secure was by directly controlling the resources of the Soviet Union.[54]

Hitler also believed that his country possessed the present military means for beating the Red Army. The German forces had performed stunningly every task he had set for them—in Poland, Norway, and the west. Moreover, as is clear from the ultimate failure to win in the east, the Germans underestimated Soviet military resources. This fatal underestimate of the armed forces and military potential of the USSR resulted from various considerations. Although, as a closed society, the Soviet Union was insusceptible to normal operations of military intelligence, the Germans had good information on the numerical strength of the Red Army.[55] They understood that their adversary had more troops deployed then they themselves would put into the field, and that it possessed several times as many tanks and aircraft as the Germans did. However, German planners were not impressed. They also knew that most of these tanks and planes were obsolete and that Soviet strategists, although early on keenly interested in employing armor in mass formations, had—like the French—decided on dispersing them for close infantry support. The Germans assumed that the Soviets had studied the German technique of blitzkrieg applied against Poland and France, but they also thought the Soviet leaders were unable to change their doctrine for the use of tanks, or for defense against tank armies, quickly and effectively. Actually, the Soviet military had been so alarmed by the rapid fall of France that they started to form armored corps. But the decision did not come quickly enough and the Soviets were caught in the midst of reorganization. Furthermore, the Germans calculated that Stalin's massive purge of the Soviet officer corps in 1938 had greatly impaired Soviet military efficiency in the higher echelons. Finally, the German image of Russian military weakness, demonstrated in World War I, seemed corroborated by the poor showing of the Red Army in the winter war against Finland (1939-1940)—overlooking the fact that the Soviet government had been unprepared for this war and that, after the initial reverses, its armed forces did rather well under trying climatic conditions.

Many components of this estimate proved correct. But the German perception of some of the qualitative factors in Soviet military capacity was grossly flawed and led to a falsely optimistic net assessment. Underlying German estimates was an assumption of Soviet military inferiority that was ultimately inspired by racial and ideological biases and, to some extent, by unconscious wishfulness.[56] Soviet soldiers were regarded as incapable of resisting a modern army operating with élan, and Soviet leaders as incapable of organizing an effective defense effort. Also, the factors of vast Soviet territory and harsh climatic conditions were not taken properly into account.

At bottom, the German strategists were blind to some critical military realities that confronted them and fell victim to a "collective illusion" that generated gross self-deception.[57]

There were some doubters among the high German military. By now, however, Hitler had proved them wrong several times and they were no longer sure of themselves or willing to challenge their master. The decision was wholly Hitler's. Even he had some somber thoughts on the very eve of the invasion, but he quelled them and went ahead.[58] For the most part, the strength of Soviet resistance after the first few months of fighting came as a surprise to the German military.

Hitler had decided as early as September 1940 to attack the Soviet Union. In December he ordered his planners to be ready by May 15, 1941. Delayed by the war in the Balkans, the date for the attack was finally set for June 22. On the basis of their faulty estimates, Hitler and his advisors had concluded that another blitzkrieg taking about twenty weeks would demolish the Red Army—an expectation that was shared by military analysts in Britain and the United States.[59] The initial German victories were indeed spectacular but adverse weather conditions and overextended supply lines stopped the German advance before Moscow could be taken. Gradually the Soviet government brought up reinforcements and mobilized for a prolonged war, which it finally won—although not without the substantial support, in particular material, of the Western powers.

Intent on smashing the Soviet armies in a campaign of a few weeks, the German planners depended on speed of operations and on inflicting strategic surprise. They took every precaution to cultivate the chance of surprising their opponent. Hitler ordered all operational planning to be shrouded in utmost secrecy. "Need to know" channels were defined very narrowly. The ranks of middle level officers, the Foreign Office, and allies were informed only when delay had become clearly dysfunctional. Nonetheless rumors began to flourish as more and more people had to be informed. Above all, the additional mobilization and gradual eastward deployment of troops could not be concealed for long from Soviet or other intelligence services.

Hitler understood that only deception could permit this observable deployment to proceed without sacrificing surprise. Disinformation would be issued in order to mislead the victim's analysis of the information that could not be kept from reaching him. The German general staff had instituted a special disinformation service in World War I. In World War II, this activity was resumed and directed by Hitler through his personal military staff (OKW). The deception campaign[60] played on four major themes: First, that the eastward deployment of troops was part of preparations for the invasion of England (in the east training could take place out of range of British bombers and reconnaissance plans); second, that it put up a contingency shield against a possible Russian attack; third, that it was a build-up for operations in the Balkans and beyond; and fourth, that it would serve to threaten Moscow for extracting concessions, especially economic. Lots of rumors were started to propagate these themes.

In retrospect, it is not easy to see how the Soviets let themselves be subjected to strategic surprise either by the mode or the fact of attack. When German forces struck across the Soviet frontier on June 22, 1941, the Red Army groups standing in their way were remarkably unready and disintegrated rapidly; approximately 1,400 Soviet aircraft were destroyed on the ground. The mode of attack could be anticipated after its preceding exhibitions. Stalin himself had been alarmed by the Germans' lightning campaigns in Poland, the Low Countries, and France. Yet even though Soviet leaders were aware of blitzkrieg as the kind of attack for which Germany was organized, they were not prepared for meeting it effectively, in part because they assumed the Red Army to be tougher than the forces previously overrun by the Germans.

It took, of course, a failure of intelligence for the USSR to be surprised by the German decision to invade. But this failure was not rooted in ineptitude. Plenty of warnings reached the Soviet Union from its own and other intelligence services, from foreign governments, and even from German anti-Nazis.[61] The difficulty of arriving at a realistic estimate of German intentions did not result from the fact that Soviet intelligence at the time was highly fragmented and not very efficient in collating and interpreting information. In fact, most of the information is known to have reached Stalin who acted as his own central intelligence analyst. Nor was it a decisive factor that he distrusted British and American warnings, which he suspected of being designed to bring Russia into the war against Germany. The crucial difficulty (common to virtually all situations of strategic surprise the author has studied) was that the total stream of information—signals (true as seen in retrospect), noise, and German disinformation—was as a whole ambiguous about Hitler's plans.

This supply of information fit at least three plausible hypotheses:[62] First, that Hitler indeed intended to attack regardless of Soviet behavior; second, that he meant to attack if the Soviet Union failed to meet the conditions of an ultimatum he was about to announce; and third, that Hitler only intended a bluff in order to obtain Soviet concessions. Stalin rejected the first (true) hypothesis on the basis of two assumptions. Aware of the traditional German aversion to fighting major powers on two fronts, he did not believe that Hitler would be foolhardy enough to start a war with the USSR before he had defeated Britain or made peace with her. Stalin had also noticed that Hitler's past military aggressions had been preceded invariably by the provocation of an intense crisis and the issuance of strident demands on his opponents. Stalin assumed, therefore, that the Germans would not attack before confronting him with an ultimatum, in which case he would have the choice of responding to it by a conciliatory offer.

While both assumptions turned out to be erroneous, they were certainly not unreasonable; it is interesting to note that the very same assumptions also led most foreign governments to misjudge German intentions until a few days before the German offensive was launched.[63] For example, the British—with Churchill and Sir Stafford Cripps (ambassador to Moscow) among them— had been more inclined right after the fall of France to believe that Germany might attack the Soviet Union without provocation. At that time, in fact, Hitler had not yet made his decision to do so, and one supposes that, after the evacuation from Dunkirk, the British were given to wishfulness in this matter.[64] As Germany deployed increasing forces eastward, British intelligence received a great deal of information to this effect. However, British officials understood that this deployment expressed no unambiguous signals about Hitler's intentions. At first, they likewise came to believe that he would not take on the Red Army as long as he remained at war with the United Kingdom, and they also concluded that Germany's military threat would be used to present Stalin with new demands in the form of an ultimatum. From June 14 on, intelligence was obtained (through the previous breaking of the German military code) that left no doubt about the imminence of attack. Yet even then, intelligence found it hard to discard the belief that Hitler's plan went beyond intimidating the Soviet Union.[65]

The Soviet authorities also struggled with the problem that the total volume of information received continued to remain ambiguous about Hitler's true intentions. Stalin's choice of interpretation agreed with the majority view in London. By mid-spring 1941, the Soviets had become apprehensive enough to alert some selected officials and military leaders to the *possibility* of war.[66] On May 5, when Stalin addressed the graduating class of academy officers, he intimated that a German attack was *possible* but *unlikely*, that Soviet diplomacy would seek to forestall an attack until at least the fall when weather conditions would rule it out for some time, and that war would break out almost inevitably in 1942.[67]

Stalin was apparently too sure of himself in sticking to the ultimatum hypothesis. There is considerable evidence for supposing that his tenacity in the matter was reinforced by wishfulness. He knew that the Red Army was not in good shape for a war with Germany and that it needed time to improve itself. He was therefore prepared to buy time by making concessions to Hitler when the expected ultimatum would come. This remained his position to the very end. A Tass communique of June 13 stated that, despite tensions between the two states, rumors of Germany's intention to attack were devoid of all foundation and that the USSR intended to honor the terms of the nonaggression pact of 1939. It hinted that the Soviet Union stood ready to negotiate about any issue of concern to Germany. When the German ambassador informed Molotov (commissar for foreign affairs) on June 22 of the German declaration of war, Molotov exclaimed: "Surely we have not deserved that."[68] When Churchill, at a meeting in August 1942, reminded Stalin of his early warning of a German attack, the latter replied: "I remember it. I did not need any warnings. I knew war would come, but I thought I might gain another six months or so."[69]

Since Stalin and other Soviet officials, although believing in the ultimatum hypothesis as the most plausible prediction of Hitler's behavior, evidently regarded a German attack without preceding ultimatum and crisis as "possible," they cannot be said to have been completely surprised by the outbreak of war on June 22. They were surprised only in terms of having put their bet, hopefully and wishfully, on an alternative estimate of Hitler's intention. But if they did not regard a German attack without preliminaries as impossible, one might ask why—in a matter of such enormous consequence—they did not take some precautionary action to cover the worst-case assumption. They could certainly have placed the Red Army on a high state of alert. Yet Stalin and his associates were unwilling to consider this because they feared that any such precautionary measures might be regarded by Hitler as provocative and thus as likely to increase the probability of a war they were trying to avoid.[70] This was another preconception which, although not unreasonable, proved to be wrong. Hitler's plans to invade did not in fact depend on Soviet behavior at all. In order to buy time, the Soviet posture was one of sheer temporary appeasement, and it was a posture that, under the circumstances, was doomed to fail.

Like any failure of intelligence, Soviet inability to avert the strategic surprise the Germans were intent on inflicting was caused mainly by the usual ambiguity of information, even though this was plentiful. Among the difficulties were those of sorting out the signals from the noise and of identifying the clever disinformation disseminated by the Germans. In interpreting the many warnings received, Stalin operated on assumptions and preconceptions that, although reasonable, proved incorrect. The assumption that, as several times before, Hitler would not start a war without the prior fomentation of a grand crisis accompanied by demands for extraordinary concessions rested on the belief that an actor would be sure or very likely to continue with a pattern of conduct exhibited regularly in the past. Actors, however, are capable of altering their behavior if doing so helps them to surprise an opponent. The assumption that Hitler would not start hostilities in the east as long as he was at war with a major power in the west, was informed by recorded longstanding German anxieties, and Hitler's decision to the contrary indeed ushered in a war on two fronts which he ultimately lost. But, as we have seen, Hitler hoped to overwhelm the Soviet Union quickly in order then, in control of its resources, to be able to face a war in the west, which he expected the United States would join inevitably. Stalin's preoccupation with the fear that Soviet behavior, if provocative, could induce Hitler to attack and, if conciliatory, would postpone conflict, was also off the mark. Finally, the rigidity of Stalin's threat perception to the very end was rooted in wishfulness.

On the German side, the incentive to attack the USSR was extremely strong, powerful enough to dare a war with major powers on two fronts. The Germans were very resourceful in concealing the nature of their military threat to the Soviet Union. They masked their true intentions. The taut system of central control established by Hitler helped in this respect. The Germans as well, however, suffered strategic surprise in the end. They lost a war they felt sure to win because they underestimated basic Soviet resilience and—like Napoleon before—the obstacles presented by inclement climate and huge distances. This faulty estimate resulted from inaccurate assumptions about the low fighting quality of the Soviet soldier and the low competence for government attributed to Stalin's regime. The intervention of subconscious predispositions in German perceptions contributed to these misperceptions. A degree of wishfulness was present also on the German side. But even more potent in leading perception astray was the Germans' euphoric overconfidence in their military prowess. After the blitzkrieg in the west, they felt that nobody could stop them in a war on land.

NOTES

1. This case study is based on Gordon A. Craig, *The Battle of Königgrätz* (Philadelphia: Lippincott, 1964); Hans Delbrück, *Geschichte der Kriegskunst*, V (Berlin: George Stilke, 1928); Michael Howard, *War in European History* (London: Oxford University Press, 1976); Eberhard Kessel, *Moltke* (Stuttgart: Koehler, 1957).
2. Craig, *The Battle of Königgrätz*, p. 16.
3. Michael Howard, *The Franco-Prussian War* (New York: Macmillan, 1961), pp.12-20.
4. Howard, *War in European History*, p. 100.
5. This case study is based mainly on the definitive work of Michael Howard, *The Franco-Prussian War*. Also consulted were: Hans Delbrück, *Geschichte der Kriegskunst*, VI (Berlin: Georg Stilke, 1932) and Kessel, *Moltke*.
6. *Howard, War in European History*, p. 140.
7. Quoted in Kessel, *Moltke*, p. 541.
8. Howard, *The Franco-Prussian War*, pp.1-4.
9. Ibid., p.1.
10. This part of the study is based on George H. Allen, Henry C. Whitehead, and F. E. Chadwick, *The Great War*, III (Philadelphia: George Barrie's Sons, 1916); B. H. Liddell Hart, *History of the First World War* (London: Cassell, 1970); *The Personal Memories of Joffre* (New York: Harper, 1932); Girard L. McEntee, *Military History of the World War* (New York: Scribner's, 1937).

11. After the outbreak of war, when this wing was on its mission, it was weakened further by a high command apprehensive over developments in the east. Two divisions were detached to reinforce the defense against Russia. Ironically, the German forces in the east brilliantly defeated the·Russians while these troops were still in transit to East Prussia.

12. Sir George Aston, *The Biography of the Late Marshal Foch* (New York: MacMillan, 1929), p. 137.

13. This case study is based mainly on T. K. Derry, *The Campaign in Norway* (London: HMSO, 1952); F. W. Hinsley, *British Intelligence in the Second World War* (London: HMSO, 1979); Walter Hubatsch, *"Weserübung"* (Göttingen: Messerschmidt, 2nd ed., 1960); J. L. Moulton, *The Norwegian Campaign of 1940* (London: Eyre and Spottiswoode, 1966).

14. Stephen Roskill, *Hankey, Man of Secrets*, III (London: Collins, 1974), p. 458.

15. *The Memoirs of General Lord Ismay* (New York: Viking, 1960), p. 119.

16. On these plans see Derry, *The Campaign of Norway;* Moulton, *The Norwegian Campaign of 1940.*

17. See Hubatsch, *"Weserübung."*

18. Ibid., p. 63.

19. See Felix Gilbert, ed., *Hitler Directs His War* (New York: Oxford University Press, 1950), Introduction; and Percy Ernst Schramm, *Hitler: The Man and Military Leader* (Chicago: Quadrangle Books, 1971), especially pp. 20, 104-09.

20. See Walter Görlitz, ed., *The Memoirs of Field Marshal Keitel* (London: William Kimber, 1965), pp. 104-05; Walter Warlimont, *Inside Hitler's Headquarters 1939-45* (London: Weidenfeld and Nicholson, 1964), pp. 67-79.

21. Moulton, *The Norwegian Campaign of 1940*, pp. 57-58.

22. On British intelligence on this matter see Hinsley, *British Intelligence*, pp. 116-24.

23. Ibid., p. 118.

24. Ibid., p. 123.

25. Derry, *The Campaign in Norway*, p. 22.

26. The following works were consulted on Norwegian and Danish perceptions: T. K. Derry, *A History of Modern Norway, 1814-1972* (Oxford: Clarendon Press, 1973); Johan J. Holst, "Surprise, Signals, and Reaction," *Cooperation and Conflict*, vol. I (1966), pp. 32-45; Hubatsch, *"Weserübung";* Richard Petrov, *The Bitter Years, The Invasion and Occupation of Denmark and Norway April 1940-May 1945* (New York: William Morrow, 1974).

27. The literature mainly used in this case study: Anthony Adamthwaite, *France and the Coming of the Second World War, 1936-1939* (London: Frank Cass, 1977); General André Beaufre, *1940, The Fall of France* (London: Cassell, 1965); J. R. M. Butler, *Grand Strategy*, II (London: HMSO, 1957); Guy Chapman, *Why France Fell: The Defeat of the French Army in 1940* (New York: Holt, Rinehart and Winston, 1968); Basil Collier, *The Second World War: A Military History* (New York: William Morrow, 1967); Gerhard Foerster, *Totaler Krieg und Blitzkrieg* ((East) Berlin: Deutscher Militaerverlag, 1967); Paul Marie De La Gorce, *The French Army* (New York: Braziller, 1963); Col. A. Goutard, *The Battle of France* (London: Frederick Muller, 1958); B. H. Liddle Hart, *The Other Side of the Hill* (London: Cassell, 1948); Andreas Hillgruber, *Hitler's Strategy, Politik und Kriegsfuehrung, 1939-1945* (Frankfurt: Bernard & Graefe, 1965); F. W. Hinsley, *British Intelligence in the Second World War* (London: HMSO, 1979); Alistair Horne, *To Lose a Battle: France 1940* (London: Penguin, 1969); Eich von Manstein, *Verlorene Siege* (Bonn: Athenaeum, 1955); Vivian Rowe,

The Great Wall of France, The Triumph of the Maginot Line (New York: Putnam's, 1961); Kurt von Tippelskirch, *Geschichte des Zweiten Weltkriegs* (Bonn: Athenaeum, 1951); John Williams, *The Ides of May: The Defeat of France May-June 1940* (New York: Knopf, 1968); Gordon Wright, *The Ordeal of Total War, 1939-1945* (New York: Harper & Row, 1968).

28. Hillgruber, *Hitler's Strategy*, p. 46.
29. Tippelskirch, *Geschichte*, pp. 85-87.
30. Hinsley, *British Intelligence*, p. 135.
31. Ibid., p. 114.
32. Heinz Guderian, *Erinnerungen eines Soldaten* (Heidelberg: Kurt Vohwinckel, 1951), p. 80.
33. Ibid., pp. 81-82.
34. Ibid., pp. 82-100.
35. Hillgruber, *Hitler's Strategy*, pp. 48-62.
36. Tippelskirch, *Geschichte*, p. 9.
37. Beaufre, *1940, The Fall of France*, pp. 59-60; Adamthwaite, *France and the Coming*, pp. 162-66, 356-57.
38. Air Vice-Marshal E. J. Kingston-McCloughry, *The Direction of War* (New York: Praeger, 1954), p. 98.
39. Hinsley, *British Intelligence*, p. 113.
40. Collier, *The Second World War*, p. 107.
41. Beaufre, *1940, The Fall of France*, p. 64; Michael Howard, *War in European History*, p. 132.
42. Hinsley, *British Intelligence*, pp. 76-77, 113.
43. De la Gorce, *The French Army*, p. 289.
44. Hinsley, *British Intelligence*, pp. 127-28.
45. F. W. Winterbotham, *The Utra Secret* (New York: Harper & Row, 1974), pp. 31-32.
46. Hinsley, *British Intelligence*, p. 130.
47. Butler, *Grand Strategy*, p. 163.
48. Beaufre, *1940, The Fall of France*, p. 185.
49. Charles de Gaulle, *The Call to Honour, 1940-1942* (New York: Viking, 1955), p. 8.
50. This case study is based mainly on: Alan Clark, *Barbarossa: The Russian-German Conflict, 1941-45* (New York: Morrow, 1965); Collier, *The Second World War;* John Erickson, *The Road to Stalingrad* (New York, Harper & Row, 1975), and *The Soviet High Command, A Military-Political History, 1918-1940* (London: St. Martin's, 1962); Hillgruber, *Hitler's Strategy, Politik und Kriegsfuehrung; The Memoirs of Marchal Zhukov* (New York: Delacorte Press, 1969); Albert Seaton, *The Russo-German War 1941-1945* (London: Arthur Barker, 1971); Boris Semjonovitch Telpuchovsky, *Die sowjetische Geschichte des Grossen Vaterlaendischen Krieges, 1941-1942*, ed. Andreas Hillgruber and Hans-Adolf Jacobsen (Frankfurt: Bernard and Graefe, 1961); Tippelskirch, *Geschichte des Zweiten Weltkrieges;* Barton Whaley, *Codeword Barbarossa* (Cambridge, Mass.: MIT Press, 1973); Wright, *The Ordeal of Total War.*
51. Hillgruber, *Hitler's Strategy*, pp. 33-34, 255-58.
52. Ibid., p. 199.
53. Ibid., pp. 199-200.
54. Ibid., p. 534.
55. Tippelskirch, *Geschichte*, pp. 206-08.
56. Hillgruber, *Hitler's Strategy*, p. 214.

57. Ibid., pp. 230, 390-97.
58. Wright, *The Ordeal*, p. 38.
59. Hillgruber, *Hitler's Strategy*, p. 444; Collier, *The Second World War*, pp. 202-03.
60. Whaley, *Codeword Barbarossa*, ch. 7.
61. Ibid., ch. 3-5.
62. Ibid., p. 223.
63. Ibid., p. 227.
64. Hinsley, *British Intelligence*, pp. 430-31.
65. Ibid., pp. 479-81.
66. Whaley, *Codeword Barbarossa*, p. 201.
67. Ibid., p. 209.
68. Ibid., p. 129.
69. Ibid., p. 63.
70. Ibid., pp. 32, 193-94, 216.

CHAPTER THREE
Examples of Strategic Surprise in the Far East

Patrick Morgan

The cases reviewed in this chapter range from the use of a surprise attack in initiating a conflict to its application in seeking to terminate one. Japan is prominent in all of these cases, either as the party seeking surprise or the one on the receiving end. All but one of the cases had a profound effect on world affairs in this century, particularly in the Far East. They collectively demonstrate the creative daring of which military leaders and civilian statesmen are sometimes capable.

PORT ARTHUR[1]

In its day, the Russo-Japanese War was a major event and attracted considerable attention, but two world wars have almost pushed it out of the history books. The genesis of the war can be traced to the initiation of the Trans-Siberian Railway construction in 1891. As the railroad grew, so did Russian ambitions in the Far East, which naturally produced apprehension in Tokyo. A significant step along the road to war was the Triple Intervention of 1895. In 1894–95 Japan had overwhelmed Chinese forces in a short war and secured the Liaotung Peninsula, which juts down from Manchuria into the Yellow Sea and terminates at what was then Port Arthur. This seemed to guarantee Japanese predominance in Korea and influence in Manchuria, thwarting St. Petersburg's ambitions in those areas. So the Russians arranged to be joined by Germany and France in insisting the Japanese give back the peninsula. Tokyo had no choice but to agree, but resentment at the Russian action was profound, spurring nationalist feelings. The Russians then rubbed salt in the wound in 1898 by pressuring the hapless Chinese government into granting them a long-term lease on Port Arthur and the surrounding province, while permitting it to be linked by rail with the Chinese Eastern Railway. From its strengthened position in Manchuria, Russia was also increasing its interests and activity in Korea, about which Japan was particularly sensitive.

Perhaps the Japanese were simply biding their time, for one of their reactions to these events was a ten-year effort to strengthen their military forces.

However, the standard view of observers then and historians since is that the initial Japanese response was conciliatory. The preeminent concern was Korea; its control by another power was seen by Japan as a direct threat to national security. In the years prior to 1900 Japan negotiated protocols with Russia to ease friction over Korea, and it suggested to St. Petersburg the outlines of a deal—Russian recognition of its preeminent influence in Korea in exchange for Japanese recognition of Russia's dominant position in Manchuria. This was as far as Japan was prepared to go, but the Russians were not interested. They already had much of what they wanted in Manchuria, so they were being asked to give up something for nothing. Then there was the fact that Japanese domination of Korea would provide a base for meddling in Manchuria. Finally, Russian officials were imbued with the notion that, as a great power, their state hardly needed to defer to the wishes of a secondary country such as Japan.

The Russians seized on the opportunity provided by the Boxer Rebellion in 1900 to move more troops into Manchuria and occupy it completely, brushing Japanese protests aside. This apparently convinced Tokyo it should take a harder line. Another inducement was the fact that the upgrading of its armed forces was nearing completion. The first move was to join in an alliance, in January 1902, with Great Britain to ensure British support and bring more pressure to bear on St. Petersburg. Initially this seemed to work; the Russians soon signed a convention with Peking promising to remove their troops from Manchuria. But then elements in favor of bolstering Russian interests in the Far East gained the ear of the tsar and prominence in court politics. The withdrawal was never carried out and negotiations to resolve the issues made no progress—the Russians refused to bend despite Japanese concessions, were insultingly slow in their responses to Japanese proposals, and generally behaved so as to forfeit popular and diplomatic support around the world.[2] Nearly everyone's sympathies, it seems, were with the Japanese. As a result, the surprise attack with which the war began was widely regarded in the West as a clever and intelligent move, against a country that had asked for a war and now was getting one. The Japanese minister in St. Petersburg announced on February 5, 1904 that negotiations were being broken off and diplomatic relations suspended. The attack on Port Arthur was mounted at night February 8, and formal declaration of war was made two days later.

The Japanese were able to attack at once because they completed their preparations for war alongside their last diplomatic efforts to settle the dispute, efforts the government had anticipated would be unlikely to succeed. An imperial conference in June 1903 concluded Japan must control Korea either by agreement with Russia or war, so in a sense the decision for war was taken then. Those who opposed war were forced out of the government at that point.

Japanese military men had long anticipated a war with Russia and believed that the strategic advantage temporarily lay with Japan because the Russians were unprepared. But if Russia was allowed to strengthen its forces in the Far East and complete the Trans-Siberian Railway, that advantage would shift. Since the summer of 1902 the Russians had been moving precisely in that direction; more troops had been sent to Manchuria, work on the fortification at Port Arthur and elsewhere had been hurried along, and numerous naval vessels had been shifted to the Far East. In other words, time was not on Japan's side. The same applied to the war itself. The chief Russian asset was immensely superior resources; if the war dragged on and these resources could be brought to bear, Russia would win. Japan had to win relatively quickly—it needed a short, sharp victory.

Within this overall strategy, the move against Port Arthur had several tactical objectives. Japan had to seize the initiative—psychologically and militarily—and the Russian positions most readily attacked were those along the Yellow Sea. Japan also needed to land troops in Korea and march quickly into Manchuria to cut Russian communications, and to do this it was vital to seize command of the sea. Otherwise, the Russians could bring up the resources to invest Korea and eventually threaten Japan itself. Yet Russian naval forces in the Far East, at least numerically, were about on a par with the entire Japanese navy. Accordingly, there was a very strong incentive for a surprise attack to nullify those forces at the start.

To carry out the attack at Port Arthur, surprise was crucial. In addition to the fleet stationed there, the Russians had constructed big guns to guard the harbor. Japanese naval leaders knew the Russians were not alert; they also knew that the harbor channel was too narrow and too shallow to pass through quickly and that the Russian fleet was therefore often at anchor in the roadstead outside the harbor and thus more accessible to an attacker. Aside from detection of the opportunity and the obvious incentives to conduct a surprise attack, it is difficult to trace the decision to any other factors. It is not clear that Japan was predisposed to such an attack by its culture, history, or elite values. Admiral Togo, in charge of the Japanese fleet, was a conscientious and aggressive commander, but not one given to highly risky operations.

A point of interest is that there was little internal opposition to the attack or to the war itself. By the time it arrived the war was widely regarded as inevitable in Japan, and there had been strong public clamor for getting tough with the Russians for months. The commitment to the war, and to doing what was necessary to win it, had already been made. Only Russian concessions or the elimination of the possibility of surprise at the last minute could have led Japan to cancel the attack. It should be noted that Japanese leaders were not confident the war could be won; it was in a subdued mood that they concluded the conflict was unavoidable. This led them to send a high official, a former friend of Theodore Roosevelt, to Washington to lay the groundwork for American mediation as soon as hostilities commenced.

The Russians might have readily noted the strength of Japan's incentives to strike, if they had been aware of the depth of her concerns and her corresponding willingness to go to war. Once her intentions were understood, Japan's strategy flowed fairly logically. But the Russians were quite insensitive to Japanese perspectives and many were convinced Japan would not fight. Thus they ignored an obvious possibility.

The actual opportunity to conduct a surprise attack was almost entirely of the Russians' making. Tokyo enjoyed a qualitative edge in capital ships, and the Japanese fleet was in better shape in terms of training, discipline, and morale, plus being more ably led. Yet these were not decisive factors in the initial engagement. Nor did the Japanese make use of any new tactics or military technology. The Russians knew relations with Japan were very strained and that war was a distinct possibility—deception on this point was not the key to Togo's success.

Actually, Admiral Togo failed to make the most of the glorious opportunity the Russians handed him, because the true dimensions of that opportunity were not clear at the time. Japanese intelligence information was substantial, much of it gathered in Port Arthur itself. Even so, it was incomplete. Togo knew main fleet was in port and had a map of its disposition. But he thought part of the fleet was at Dalny and sent eight of his own ships there, uselessly as it turned out. More importantly, he did not know the Russian shore batteries were not ready for action. Thus he prudently withheld his large ships from the initial engagement, relying instead on having destroyers sneak in late in the evening and fire torpedos at the Russian ships. He could have sailed in with his entire fleet and smashed the Russian forces and the harbor; instead, of the 18 torpedos fired only 3 exploded, seriously damaging two battleships and a cruiser. The attack had been planned for some months, with the crews given suitable practice, and one of its attractions was that Togo did not have to risk his fleet—which was essentially the heart of his country's navy—in the initial engagement of the war.[3]

The sources of Russian vulnerability were numerous and profound. Underestimation of the Japanese has already been mentioned; "The Russians in Port Arthur scarcely considered the Japanese to be people."[4] Few Russian leaders thought the Japanese would fight, and they expected tsarist forces to outclass them badly if they did. In fact, no one in the Russian government had ever advocated war with Japan and the war ministry and general staff were quite unenthusiastic about the idea. With nobody seeking war and many not expecting one, there was little attention to preparing for it. Reports by military attachés on Japanese military strength were pigeonholed, the most accurate ones being treated by higher level officers as unreliable. Only one officer on the general staff was assigned to assess Japan's armed forces and he was apparently a poor choice in terms of his diligence and competence.

Port Arthur itself was almost totally unready. The viceroy, Eugene Alexiev, had earlier been informed by some anxious subordinates about Japanese military preparations, including the massing of troops and transports. In January 1904 he wired St. Petersburg asking permission to mobilize the troops in Manchuria. Back came a response from the tsar himself—Alexiev was to do nothing to provoke a war, and was to permit Japanese landings in southern or eastern Korea. Japan was to be left to fire the first shot.

On the evening of February 8, the great ships were anchored in the roadstead with their lights blazing; crew members on board were asleep. Many crew members and their officers were enjoying the rather crude delights available on shore at this frontier outpost. The fleet commander had earlier in the evening hosted a party. Sometime before, he too had been worried about a possible attack in view of the deteriorating situation and had tried to ready his fleet but with little effect. For instance, he had ordered that his ships prepare to repel torpedos but since he gave no further instructions some of his captains did nothing. The ships in the harbor had torpedo nets out amidships but not protecting bows or sterns. Several times the commander had asked permission to further prepare the fleet for action, but Alexiev had repeated the tsar's instructions not to aggravate the situation and provoke a war.

On shore, things were no better. The big guns were still in their coating of grease for protection against winter weather. The recoil cylinders of the largest ones had been drained, immobilizing them. Preparation for an emergency was such that chaos reigned in the wake of the attack, with men dashing about aimlessly and guns firing wildly. The fleet did have two destroyers patrolling out to sea and they actually encountered the approaching Japanese ships. They turned back in order to report this news but did nothing else, and the Japanese destroyers simply followed them in and delivered the news in their own way. The first ships in port to spot the Japanese destroyers assumed they were the Russian destroyers returning from patrol.

Some of the deplorable conditions in the fleet could be traced to the incompetent commanders that court politics and the pretensions of aristocrats produced. Jealousies and rivalries among these commanders played a part, as did the fact that Russian naval officers in the Far East had little knowledge of modern naval affairs and combat. There were the inevitable effects of low pay, inexperience, and sagging morale in the ranks. But back of much of this was the preoccupation of the military leaders in St. Petersburg with the Baltic and affairs in Europe. The most significant factor was that no one had taken the possibility of an attack seriously. Thus the Far Eastern fleet was split between Port Arthur and Vladivostok, and two ships from Port Arthur were at Chemulpo, now better known as Inchon. Divided, the fleet was vulnerable to being bottled up.

The results of the attack merit a careful assessment. On February 8, as

already indicated, the Russians had three capital ships disabled (none per-
manently) and they lost two more at Chemulpo the next day. On that second
day Togo's entire fleet also cruised past Port Arthur and shelled the harbor,
doing modest damage and suffering some in return from Russian shore batteries. But the harbor entrance was not closed and in the next few weeks
Togo made several attempts to sink old steamers in the harbor channel entrance
but failed.

Thus the achievements of the attack were these. First, the Japanese closed
Port Arthur, allowing unhampered troop landings in Korea because the Russian naval units at Vladivostok were also contained. Second, the Japanese
gained a strong psychological advantage; they had the initiative, and their
morale was enhanced while the Russians were depressed by the defeat. At
one stroke Togo had established Japan as a significant sea power in the Far
East.

Yet the Russian fleet was not severely damaged and could have eventually
sallied forth to menace Japanese sea lanes. Admiral Stephen Makaroff arrived
to take command in March and he quickly began to drive the fleet into shape
to do just that. A forceful and aggressive commander, by April he was
beginning to take the fleet out for periodic encounters with Togo's forces.
But on one of these forays his flagship struck a Japanese mine and was instantly
obliterated. With his death, these promising Russian efforts came to an end.

Thus the attack did not determine the ultimate outcome of the war. That
required major land battles, which pushed Japan's resources to the limit. The
Port Arthur surprise was not a massive stroke delivered at great risk. It was
a cautious, limited exploration of an enemy's self-imposed vulnerabilities that
produced significant but restricted initial advantages. It took later Russian
mistakes and misadventures to convert those advantages into a Japanese victory.

PEARL HARBOR[5]

In considering the Pearl Harbor attack as a strategic surprise it is important
to keep certain facts about the Japanese government in mind. The supreme
command authority flowed directly from the emperor to the chiefs of staff of
the army and navy, not through the prime minister or the army and navy
ministers in the cabinet. The army and navy ministers had to be military men
on active duty and thus subject to the authority of their respective chiefs of
staff. As a result, no cabinet could be formed unless the armed forces agreed
on the men to fill these two posts and a cabinet would fall if the military
withdrew its support. This gave the two services an extraordinary degree of
autonomy which they jealously guarded, particularly on operations matters.
The various factions which composed the government moved in concert to
decide on war with the United States, but the navy enjoyed great latitude in

the matter of how that war was initiated at sea and was responsible for the decision to attack Pearl Harbor. Therefore the attack was not the result of a decision by the government so much as it was the navy's solution to the onerous problems inherent in the government's determination to make war on the United States.

For a number of years the government had been a collection of units only loosely coordinating their activities. Meetings of four or five key ministers and liaison conferences among key civilian and military leaders were required to produce a sufficient consensus to make policy. On the eve of Pearl Harbor these officials had come to share a broad view of the world, which helped generate sufficient agreement and cooperation, but they frequently failed or refused to share important information about the activities of their agencies. The attack at Pearl Harbor is a good case in point. Hideki Tojo, a leading army officer and then prime minister, only learned about the plan a week before it occurred and was given no details. His personal aide of twelve years never heard about it until it was implemented. Few civilian cabinet members or high court officials were told about the plan.[6]

Over the course of the preceding decade the domestic political power of the army had steadily grown, particularly after the onset of the war with China in 1937. That war brought a direct conflict with the United States, which insisted on a Japanese withdrawal from China. This the army steadfastly refused to do, and its power within the ruling circles made it impossible to pursue such a policy. In the end, that power was formally confirmed by having Tojo named the prime minister. Thus we can lay much of the responsibility for the approaching war on the army, which took a relatively optimistic view of Japan's chances for victory. Various civilian leaders, risking assassination, attempted to find some way to meet Japan's national interests short of war. For its part the navy was hesitant, with high officers frequently expressing doubts over how a long war would turn out. However, navy leaders used army support and the rising tensions in the Pacific to win more appropriations for navy ships, and thus they were unwilling to openly oppose the army on expansion in Southeast Asia, leaving that to civilian leaders.

However, by late 1941 all major elements in the ruling elite saw war with the United States and the European colonial powers in Asia as probably unavoidable. This view had its roots deep in modern Japanese history and had been steadily emerging as the dominant one during the previous decade. The key to Japan's development and survival as a great nation appeared to be an empire with appropriate human, economic, and natural resources. This perception of the national interest lay behind the seizure of Manchuria in 1931, and the Sino-Japanese War initiated in 1937. The only alternative, it was widely believed, was the humiliation of second class status as a nation of little power or significance.

This expansion was increasingly resisted by the United States and the European colonial powers. Japanese resentment was widespread and profound. The Western powers were blamed for Japan's inability to liquidate the war in China and accused of encircling Japan in an effort to squelch her legitimate aspirations. Even officials determined to try diplomatic solutions held that if those governments would not acquiesce in a degree of Japanese expansion then war would be unavoidable.

And so it was. By July 1941 Japan had occupied the northern half of Vietnam, and it now moved to take over the remainder of this French colony. The American response was to freeze Japanese assets and thus end the sale of scrap iron and oil. Similar British and Dutch moves cut Japanese access to the raw materials of Malaya and the East Indies. This action more than any other forced a decision for war. Japan had oil reserves for two years at the most, perhaps only eighteen months. Unless something was done, Japan would soon lose all capacity for independent action. The decision was to pursue a two-track policy: strong efforts would be mounted to obtain a diplomatic settlement with the United States and at the same time, in the event that those efforts failed (as many anticipated), Japan would prepare for war.

The trouble with the latter option was that it was hard to be optimistic about war with the United States, Britain, and Holland given the great disparity in the two sides' resources. Numerous officials realized that war would be a grave risk. Yet they were induced to take that risk by a series of developments and perspectives. One was the enormous German military success in Europe, culminating in the attack on the Soviet Union. The British, French, and Dutch had been gravely weakened and their Asian possessions lay open to attack. Russia, the traditional foe to the north, would be too preoccupied to strike from behind if Japan sought further expansion in the south.

Another was the embargo, which seemed to leave Japan little choice between humiliating concessions or war. The natural inclination was to seize on anything that suggested a war might be won. Hence a contributing factor was the fact that Japan had begun military buildup in 1936, enhanced by the war with China from 1937 on, while the United States had only recently begun to enlarge its forces. Japan was just reaching the point at which its forces could most favorably compare with those of its opponents. If it was to make war at all, the best time for doing so was fast approaching. The navy, in particular, saw late 1941 and the first half of 1942 as the peak period of its relative strength and preparedness. By fall 1941 a comparison of Western naval forces in the Pacific with Japan's looked like this:[7]

	Battleships	Carriers	Cruisers	Destroyers	Submarines
Allies	11	3	36	100	69
Japan	10	10	36	113	63

However, the Japanese entered the war with no clear conception of how it was to be won. As early as 1923 the armed forces had discussed a possible conflict with the United States. In 1941 the overall strategy called for slashing attacks to seize the areas with the raw materials Japan needed plus other places necessary to create a strong defensive perimeter around the empire. A fierce defensive struggle would then be waged until the enemy tired of the war and negotiated a settlement. China would finally be cut off from outside help and forced to surrender, and attacks on British possessions in Asia would enable Germany to knock Britain out of the war. That would leave only the U.S., which would be preoccupied by the war in Europe and the Atlantic and, it was believed, would therefore not wish to prolong its conflict with Japan. In other words, the strategy encompassed no plan for defeating the United States; it rested instead on frustrating American efforts to defeat Japan.

The navy's task would be to clear and hold the southern and western Pacific while assisting the army to seize the Philippines, Malaya, the East Indies, and the islands that would constitute the empire's defensive perimeter. Herein lay the specific incentive for the surprise attack at Pearl Harbor. Admiral Isoroku Yamamoto had grave misgivings about making war on the United States. Forthright expressions of his views made him a target for assassination by fanatical zealots at middle levels in the armed forces, one reason he was made commander-in-chief of the combined fleet in August 1939 (and thus moved out of Tokyo). This put him in a crucial position for planning a future war. Within the overall strategy, the bulk of his naval forces would have to participate in the drive to the south. But the navy's plans, of many years standing, for war with the United States called for luring the American fleet across the Pacific, harassing and weakening it as it moved toward Japan, and then destroying it in a mighty battle near home waters (as in Admiral Togo's climatic battle of the Tsushima straits in the Russo-Japanese War). Yamamoto became obsessed with the fear that once the war began the American fleet would sail across the Pacific as anticipated but his forces would be caught far to the south. How was this to be avoided?

Yamamoto's solution was to destroy much of the American fleet at the outset, clearing the flank of the naval sweep to the south. For such an attack surprise was an absolute necessity, for it would entail risking the bulk of the fleet's carriers. This made the plan extremely controversial in naval circles; nevertheless, Yamamoto was strongly predisposed to make the attack. As a commander he was inclined to bold and risky moves, as he would later demonstrate in the battle of Midway. He believed strongly in fate and gambled accordingly. He shared the bias in his military subculture toward recklessness, total commitment, and élan as the dominant elements in war. He and his colleagues also shared the cherished heritage of the victory over Russia in 1904–05 in which a surprise attack had opened the war. Finally, he was the preeminent champion in the navy of the potential of air power and he had now uncovered a unique opportunity for his carrier forces.

Yamamoto's stature and command responsibility were such that his ideas could not be ignored, but resistance to them in the naval general staff was such that they could not readily be adopted either. Yamamoto initiated the planning in January-February 1941 and soon began the necessary training for the attack, but without the attack having been authorized. As preparations mounted and opposition persisted, Yamamoto threatened to resign if the general staff cancelled the project. Early in September war games were held at the Naval War College near Tokyo to test and refine plans for the outbreak of war in the Pacific. Yamamoto's plan did not fare well—his force was discovered and two of his carriers were "sunk," reflecting the general staff's apprehensions.

Where Yamamoto detected a glorious opportunity, the staff officers saw grave risks. Yamamoto's plan would hide the fleet by crossing the North Pacific, always stormy and hence deserted in winter, but the staff officers anticipated American air patrols would detect the fleet before it reached its launch site. And that same nasty weather would make the necessary refueling of the ships at sea highly dangerous, perhaps impossible. In such weather the carriers might not even be able to launch their planes. And what if the U.S. fleet had been moved by that point? The general staff preferred the older plan of bringing the American fleet nearer Japan for the climactic battle, concentrating naval forces to the south in the meantime. Yamamoto finally received approval on November 3, after still more arguments.

After the war other officials claimed that had they known of Operation Z, as the attack was called, they would have objected on various grounds (moral, political, or psychological) but at the time the only real resistance possible was from within the navy—so tightly held was information about it. It is intriguing to speculate that such a daring plan might never have achieved the necessary support throughout the government, that it was possible solely because so few people in the end had to agree to it. In this sense, the highly fragmented Japanese government was close to being a unitary actor for purposes of this decision. The attack was ultimately the product of an intriguing mix of contrary assessments. In the services and among some civilians there were unrealistic estimates of Japan's relative military capacities that bolstered the decision for war. Yamamoto shared none of these misperceptions, but that was why he sought to inflict the maximum possible damage on the foe in the initial engagement. The traditional navy strategy for a short war, a Tsushima-style decisive battle in home waters, was simply adapted by Yamamoto into a smashing strike in enemy waters.

It must be pointed out that there were other important misperceptions of factors that made the attack unnecessary in the short run and disasterous over the long run. For years American planning for war with Japan called for just what Yamamoto feared, a navel offensive thrust across the Pacific. But the war in Europe, once the United States entered, was bound to siphon off much of the American naval strength in the Pacific and the prospect of this was already having an effect. American military planners had shifted to Rainbow 5, a plan adopted in June 1941; priority was to go to Europe and the naval posture in the Pacific was to be initally defensive, conceding the loss of many of the areas Japan expected to incorporate into its defensive perimeter. Thus Yamamoto sought to forestall an American response that the Americans had already decided not to attempt early in the war.[8]

As for the long run, the attack did nothing to solve the gravest Japanese weakness at sea, the vulnerability of the empire's lines of communication to submarines. Japanese estimates of their maximum annual merchant marine losses were exceeded in the first months of the war, and eventually these losses reached catastrophic proportions. The attack also instantly unified the United States for a maximum war effort, invalidating the expectation that the United States would be willing to negotiate a settlement out of war weariness. In this respect the attack shared the flaw in all Japanese planning for the war—no clear conception as to how it was to be won and no realistic analysis of what a long, total war would mean. There were excessively optimistic estimates of probable German military successes, of Japanese oil production and shipbuilding capabilities, and of American unwillingness and inability to fight.

What made the attack feasible were certain important Japanese military capabilities. Yamamoto had given priority to developing naval air power and to bombing stationary ships. He took note of the successful British air attack on the Italian fleet in the harbor at Taranto in November 1940 and reports that the British had modified aerial torpedos so they would work in Taranto's shallow waters. Eventually wooden fins were attached to the torpedos dropped at Pearl Harbor, thereby circumventing one of the geographical features that led Americn naval officers to believe the fleet was safe from attack.

Planning for the attack began in January-February 1941 and at the same time Yamamoto asked naval intelligence to gather data about Hawaii and the U.S. Pacific Fleet. As the plans matured specific training of the pilots was carried on with great intensity. Like the government, the navy was planning on two tracks: one involved the Pearl Harbor attack, the other did not. Thus the attack was planned at length even though the decision to attempt it came barely a month before the event. At that point only an American withdrawal of the fleet from Pearl, a last-minute diplomatic settlement or discovery of the Japanese fleet headed for Hawaii would have cancelled the plan.

The American vulnerability can be traced to a combination of factors. The Pacific Fleet was not traditionally based at Pearl Harbor, but at San Diego;

it had been moved to Hawaii in April-May 1940 by the president as a visible symbol of deterrence to Japanese expansion. The fleet commander, Admiral Richardson, had objected on grounds that the fleet could be kept much better prepared at San Diego. Apparently he objected too strenuously, a factor in his replacement by Admiral Husband Kimmel in February 1941. As the tension in the Pacific rose, it became diplomatically and politically more difficult to return the fleet to San Diego. The Japanese might see such a move as evidence of a desire to be conciliatory. Domestic groups agitating for a tough posture toward Japanese expansionism would also be roused.[9] So the fleet stayed at Pearl.

There was nothing secret about the fact that war was at hand. Japanese preparations had been noted, including the fact that radio communications with a number of Japanese carriers had ceased. Japanese convoys heading south had been spotted. Messages in broken Japanese codes clearly indicated to the Americans that a deadline for some serious event was fast approaching. Chief of naval operations, Admiral Stark, on November 24 told Admiral Hart in Manila and Kimmel on Hawaii that Japanese offensive operations could come soon, and followed this on November 27 with a "war warning" which stated that "an aggressive move by Japan is expected within the next few days."[10] On November 25, the president met with his major security advisers and suggested Japan might well attack in the next few days, and without warning in view of its past history of surprise attacks.

The theoretical possibility of an attack on Pearl Harbor had not been overlooked. In 1932, a Navy war games aerial attack on Pearl Harbor early on a Sunday morning found the defenses nil and "sank" all the major vessels in port. In late spring 1941 a joint army-navy study of Pearl Harbor's defenses forecast a possible Japanese attack that was, in the end, correct as to the direction, size of the force used, and strategy—it even anticipated that it could come early on a Sunday morning. The report predicted submarines might also be used, as they were, and pointed to a Japanese history of initial attacks without warning. The British attack at Taranto did not go unnoticed in Washington; Navy Secretary Knox sent Army Secretary Stimson a memo suggesting that immediate steps be taken to protect Pearl Harbor, sentiments with which Stimson agreed, and which led both to issue various orders to better guard against an attack. As soon as Yamamoto began planning Operation Z, Ambassador Grew in Tokyo reported rumors of a massive attack on Pearl Harbor if war broke out.

Thus the essence of the American fleet's vulnerability lay elsewhere, in the following factors: a general underestimation of Japanese determination to fight and overall military capabilities, a mental framework that led to misinterpretations of the evidence available, the ready accessibility of Pearl Harbor to Japanese intelligence, and the local command's unwillingness to adopt the most appropriate precautionary measures.

On the first of these, American leaders generally regarded Japan as not a particularly significant military power. Japanese ships and naval gunnery were frequently disparaged. Their aircraft were considered second rate, when in fact many were of superb quality. American estimates of Japanese aircraft production were too low by about half. Japanese pilots were supposedly poor in quality, but were to turn out to be exceedingly well trained. All such errors lent support to the widespread belief that Japan would not fight, or if it did it would just attack British possessions to try to avoid war with the United States.

As to the effect of preconceptions on the interpretation of available evidence, everyone anticipated Japanese attacks to the south and, perhaps, on the Philippines and the evidence was assessed accordingly. For instance, naval intelligence had lost track of the Japanese fleet carriers, but this had often happened before and in any case when Tokyo planned a major move the carriers were usually kept on home waters in case of a hostile reaction. Since the Japanese were obviously up to something in the south, the carriers were presumed to be in port. The general view that they would never be so foolish as to risk all their fleet carriers in one operation eliminated one possible alternative conclusion.

As Roberta Wohlstetter has effectively pointed out, the "noise" of confusing, contradictory, and irrelevant signals made an accurate assessment difficult, so these misinterpretations went undisturbed. Preoccupied with the Atlantic and Europe, Washington thought a direct attack by Japan on the United States was unlikely. This made it all too easy to not react to Tokyo's request for detailed information from its consulate about ship movements at Pearl, when similar requests were sent concerning the Panama Canal and other major U.S. ports. Intercepted and decoded diplomatic cables indicated something serious was about to happen, but just what that would be was never specified.

The most sensitive intercepts went to a few top officials in bits and pieces, who had to do their own analysis. No experienced central intelligence unit existed to pull all available information together. The report from Ambassador Grew on rumors that Pearl Harbor would be attacked was sent to Admiral Kimmel with the comment that naval intelligence discounted the possibility. The November 27 "war warning" (like other messages from Washington) anticipated attacks on "either the Philippines, Thai, or Kra Peninsula, or possibly Borneo."[11] From their different perspective in Washington, officials assumed the war warning had meant the fleet was now at sea. But on Hawaii the chief threat was believed to be sabotage; the main response to the war warning was to bunch planes together for easier protection, making them lovely targets on the morning of December 7.

While sabotage was not a problem, Tokyo did have agents reporting regularly on fleet movements and the state of Pearl's defenses right up to the day of the attack. The carrier pilots had excellent information as to what they would find when they arrived. In a broader sense, however, the available intelligence was faulty. Certain carrier units had been sent to the Atlantic without Tokyo's knowledge. The Japanese fleet did not know until just before the attack that the remaining carriers—the primary targets—were not in port. Up to the last moment it was not known if the fleet was protected by torpedo nets.

The local commanders compounded the effects of all the factors making for surprise by failing to adopt the best precautions, for what seemed like good reasons at the time. The previous periods of tension and earlier warnings had deadened everyone's sensitivity to the indications that this time war was coming. In addition, military leaders at Pearl were not fully informed of the extent of the diplomatic impasse and all the signals that something big was brewing, and thus they lacked the context in which to best react to warnings from Washington. Responsibility for the defenses of the islands was split among three commanders and as they were short on resources it would have taken almost perfect coordination to mount the best possible defenses. It is not surprising that less than everything possible was done.

Torpedo nets were not strung because they hampered movements in the harbor, and for the same reason the harbor barriers (to submarines) were left open. Kimmel ordered a mild alert but not a complete one for that would have interfered with the intensive training that newly arriving units were going to need if war was just about to break out. Aerial surveillance was limited in part to contain the incidence of breakdowns. Also important was the fact that the United States was playing a delicate game of getting the Japanese to strike the first blow. Kimmel and others were ordered to avoid taking such aggressive precautions that they might provoke a Japanese military response. Washington's goal was to absorb a modest first blow, with the attendant political and psychological advantages, while being sufficiently alert to keep the costs down. No one anticipated the first blow would be at Pearl.

In sum, the attack was a striking success in terms of the surprise achieved and the damage done to the specific targets. Eight battleships were damaged (two lost for good), four smaller ships were destroyed, five other ships (including three cruisers) were damaged, and 150 aircraft were smashed. But it was not altogether necessary and it failed to hit some of the premium targets including the oil supplies and permanent facilities at Pearl, the loss of which would have been far more crippling to the fleet in the coming months. It damaged battleships, but the war was to belong not to battleships but to the fast carriers. It took an unusual leader in a political system that accorded him an exceptional degree of autonomy to make the decision for the attack possible. And it required an intriguing set of circumstances to catch a government fully anticipating war at any moment so completely by surprise.

OTHER SURPRISES ON DECEMBER 7, 1941[12]

December 7, 1941 (December 8 in the Far East) is best remembered for Pearl Harbor, but it is important to keep in mind that Japan launched other surprise attacks; Pearl Harbor was only the most spectacular. In fact, the ultimate strategic surprise on that fateful day was the scale and audacity of the Japanese operations.

After July 1941 the military supreme commands in Tokyo considered three alternative plans for the Japanese thrust to the south, with different timetables for seizing major objectives *in sequence.* In each case one service or the other objected that the plan left one or both flanks uncovered and gave the enemy more time to prepare to defend some targets. So they compromised by adopting the most ambitious and daring plan of all—hitting many of their objectives *simultaneously!*

The goal was to sweep Western power out of Asia. The initial step was to carry out strikes on 29 separate targets in the first few days. Pearl Harbor, the Philippines, Malaya, Thailand, Guam, Wake, and Hong Kong were hit from the air, and eventually occupied. This entailed the use of 10 divisions, over 500 transport vessels, more than 2,000 aircraft, 169 surface warships, and 64 submarines. Close coordination was necessary to keep one attack from compromising the surprise necessary for another to be successful. Then the armed forces pushed into the Bismarks, Borneo, and Burma as well as converging in a great pincer movement on Sumatra and Java. The plan called for driving China, Australia, and New Zealand out of the war, while establishing a defense perimeter that was to enclose an empire of something like half the world's population.

There were two broad aspects to the surprise this imposed. One was a pervasive sense of superiority, ultimately racist in nature, that inhibited a realistic Western appraisal of Japan's ambitions and capabilities. The British, Dutch, and Americans shared the view that Japan was not a great military threat, that its forces were inferior in fighting ability, equipment, and imagination. The other aspect was an underestimation of the ultimate potential of forces such as Japan possessed, of what such forces could do if employed in a clever and daring fashion. Piling one gamble on another and stretching her forces to the limit, Japan mounted simultaneous operations on a scale far beyond anything the Western powers anticipated. The fleet carriers were risked in attacking Pearl Harbor. In the Philippines, much depended on success in the initial air strikes, yet the Americans would have several hours warning time once they heard about Pearl Harbor. Japanese naval and air forces had to control the China Sea or face the possibility of grave losses in attacks on their convoys to Malaya. In each case the gamble paid off.

The effects were devastating. Reviewing all of the attacks here is unnecessary, but two—the attacks on the Philippines and Malaya—are worth some attention as they display many features commonly associated with cases of strategic surprise. They can even be discussed together, for there were eerie parallels between the two situations.

For years the Philippines and Singapore were to be defended if trouble arose (from Japan, it was assumed) by the home country sending out a fleet. As threats mounted in Europe, London and Washington had to abandon such plans. The British had not been overly concerned about physically defending Malaya, as long as Singapore was impregnable. Now the Americans began to write off the Philippines in a similar fashion.

Then there emerged, rather late in the day, a renewed desire to hold onto these territories. The British discovered in the late 1930s that Singapore was vulnerable to an attack moving down the Malay Peninsula—to defend Singapore, Malaya had to be held. For the Americans, this occurred in 1940–41. Douglas MacArthur returned to active duty as commander in the Philippines and began insisting they could be defended, while others saw the islands as a good place from which to forestall or beat back Japanese expansion to the south.

Alas, a desire to defend did not guarantee the wherewithal to do so. As already mentioned, neither government had the appropriate naval units available any longer. The same applied to ground forces; British units were desperately needed in Europe and the Middle East, and the United States was just beginning to rearm. Malaya and the Philippines were hardly at the top of anyone's list of priorities, and thus the military forces stationed there were undermanned, undertrained, and underarmed.

It is not surprising, then, that big things were expected from air power. The British built a series of airfields in northern and eastern Malaya so they could maul any expeditionary force landing on the coast. In the Philippines great numbers of B-17s were to offset any threat to the islands. But the available planes were just as badly needed elsewhere as men and ships. British planning called for 336 modern planes in Malaya, but local commanders had to settle for less than half as many antiquated aircraft. The United States envisioned moving 165 heavy bombers to the Philippines, with more to come later, but only 35 were at hand when Japan attacked. This weakness led directly to disaster when Japanese plans stressed surprise attacks on the airfields and the early seizure of fields for their own use. As a result, Allied air power simply evaporated; over 60 percent of their local air strength was lost on the first day, eliminating the main prop of the defenses.

Malaya and the Philippines were also hit with multiple amphibious assaults. The local commanders had anticipated a number of the landing sites and prepared suitable defense plans, which were not carried out effectively. Due to deficiencies in their forces, plus confusion and disorder, the defenders wasted many of the assets they had, while the enemy exploited the chaos.

There had been plenty of evidence, correctly appraised, that Japanese attacks were likely. War games and special studies, some dating back a decade, had made clear to the British how, where, and even when a Japanese invasion of Malaya would most likely occur. American fears of a Japanese attack were focused on the Philippines, and the fleet there was at a higher state of readiness than the one at Oahu. There was also last minute evidence sufficient to cancel the attacker's advantage of surprise if acted upon. In each case this information was not exploited. The Japanese landings were mostly unopposed, their initial bombing of Allied airfields was a great success, and their plans went smoothly while those of their opponents had to be discarded almost at once.

In part this could be traced to the desire in Washington and London that Japan fire the first shot. The British had a plan to seize harbors in southeast Thailand before the Japanese landed, taking the initiative once Japanese convoys were spotted. But the British commander did not give the order until too late, fearing that Britain was being lured into invading Thailand so that the Thais would invite Japanese assistance. In the Philippines close to ten hours elapsed between first word of Pearl Harbor and the initial Japanese air attack. American planes did go out looking for attackers and, as luck would have it, most had landed for refueling just when the Japanese arrived. But the time could have been used to bomb Japanese airstrips on Formosa; it was not, because the necessary reconnaissance had not been done, and that was the case in part because of a desire to avoid doing anything provocative in the preceding days.

The attacker had not been so circumspect. The Japanese had excellent intelligence information about Malaya and the Philippines, based on the work of agent networks, on-site visits by infiltrated military officers, and frequent overflights. This activity had been carefully monitored by the Americans and the British, who accurately guessed what it was for. Thus, gathering the information necessary for an effective attack risked compromising the secrecy necessary for complete success.

Finally, Allied commanders and political officials on the scene shared with their countrymen elsewhere remarkably similar misestimates of the relative strength of their forces and those Japan would employ. Often this extended to the belief that Japan would not fight; if it did as a nation it would be drained by the long fighting in China, with poor soldiers and weapons. In short, the Allies were psychologically unprepared for being militarily outclassed. The most glaring example was the parade of the British battleship *Prince of Wales* and the battlecruiser *Repulse* on December 9 up the east coast of Malaya, hoping to harass the Japanese landing sites, with no real grasp of the capabilities of Japanese pilots and aircraft. The two largest Allied warships in the Far East were sunk in an engagement lasting about two hours. The Japanese lost three planes.

THE USE OF THE ATOMIC BOMB[13]

This case differs significantly from other instances of strategic surprise. Such a surprise has often been sought at the outset of a war or as an attempt to sharply alter its course; here we have a radical military step near the end of a war, when the final outcome was not seriously in doubt. Also unusual is the fact that its purpose was not only to affect the war but, to the degree revisionist views are accepted, to influence a third government on issues to which the target state was not a party. Finally, this is a case where, to an unusual degree, key facts are still in dispute and likely to remain so.

For purposes of analysis, the complexities of this case intrude first on the matter of incentives. Why did the United States seek this strategic surprise? The weight of the evidence and of historians' judgments allows no conclusive answer. Those who made the decision to drop the atomic bomb on Hiroshima and Nagasaki insisted that the preeminent objective was to shock the Japanese government into surrender, thereby shortening the war and saving American (and Japanese) lives. Many historians have accepted this as reasonably correct. Since the war ended, however, critics have insisted that the United States was interested in more than a surrender; it wanted a demonstration of its military power so as to make the Soviet Union more tractable on postwar issues. The bomb was not used to end World War II so much as to initiate the Cold War. The incentives are so different depending on which view is adopted, that we shall consider each perspective before suggesting a suitable synthesis.

According to the first view, the bomb was attractive because it would come as a great shock, a crushing demonstration of prospective devastation should the war continue. This was needed because the Japanese government had been dominated for years by the armed forces, with their well-known fanaticism. Thus the primary objective in using the weapon was psychological, which affected the choice of targets. This concern also shaped consideration of the alternatives. One option was to seek a negotiated settlement by adjusting the unconditional surrender formula. The Japanese had been putting out peace feelers since at least December 1944, mainly by seeking Soviet mediation, and the United States intercepted the messages from Tokyo to its embassy in Moscow. But there were fears that Japan was simply maneuvering to keep Moscow out of the war and ease American military pressures. Also, the Japanese continued to resist unconditional surrender even in the intercepted messages, as in the foreign minister's cable on July 12:

> . . . it is His Majesty's heart's desire to see the swift termination of the war. In the Greater East Asia War, however, as long as America and England insist on unconditional surrender our country has no alternative but to see it through in an all-out effort for the sake of survival and the honor of the homeland.[14]

A departure from unconditional surrender, to the extent of allowing the emperor to remain, had been considered by various American officials but such a decision was not made until the Japanese proposed surrender on that basis. That is, the Japanese took the initiative here, the American government did not. Why not? Prior to the atomic bomb, Japanese statements were vague because the government was bitterly divided over suing for peace and the minimum conditions for surrender. This conveyed to Washington the message that Japan was still not disposed to quit. Also, there were those in the administration and the Pentagon who wished to see the emperor deposed and this lack of consensus helps explain why Truman and others did not act sooner.

Another alternative was victory by conventional means. Japan was under naval blockade, suffering enormously from bombing raids, short of food and raw materials. The Soviet Union was about to enter the war. The United States was prepared to invade. Any one, and surely all, of these things could do the trick. The trouble was that the Japanese armed forces might not quit and then the costs could be very high. Estimates of potential American casualties in an invasion ran as high as 1,000,000. How could such costs be justified if a weapon was at hand that could prevent them?

Was there a less costly way to use that weapon? Various options were discussed and rejected. If the United States simply announced the bomb existed and demanded a surrender, how could the Japanese government be convinced this was not a trick? If a demonstration was arranged over some remote spot, using a prior public announcement to the Japanese, they might shoot down the plane or move the American prisoners to the site. What if the bomb proved to be a dud—the diehards in Tokyo would be strengthened. And if it worked, the Japanese still might not appreciate what they were seeing, might not be sufficiently shocked.

These matters preyed on Secretary of War Stimson's mind. They were discussed by the Interim Committee set up to advise Stimson, and through him the president. They were considered by an advisory panel of top scientists attached to the Interim Committee. These officials were well aware that if the bomb was used, the postwar world would be much more complicated and dangerous. Yet they concluded, virtually unanimously, that no suitable warning or technical demonstration could be devised and that the bomb should be dropped on an urban target at the earliest moment. As the United States had only two bombs at the time, the risks of failure in a demonstration were magnified. Everyone knew the bomb would work on a test platform, but that did not guarantee the results in a combat situation.

Surprise was essential for the intended effect and that is why the bomb was delivered on Hiroshima with no advance warning. Nagasaki was also hit without warning, primarily to make the point that the United States had more than one bomb. The use of a second bomb has often been particularly criticized as unnecessary. The best explanation of it is that the administration's decision was to drop bombs, not a bomb, and there was no consideration given to dropping one and then waiting to see its effect.

Thus American incentives to use the bomb arose from the desire to stop the war, the hardening of officials' sensibilities in matters of death and destruction, and their image of the opponent as treacherous and fanatical. The disposition to take this step cannot be traced to personalities, elite values, or cultural factors, nor to any special opportunities presented by the international situation.[15] It was essentially a wartime decision to use a new weapon to hurt the enemy badly. The consensus as to what should be done converted the small number of officials and scientists who helped decide on its use into something like a unitary actor.

There were disincentives certainly, although their extent is hard to measure. Secretary Stimson gradually came to see that the bomb would usher in a new era because other states would insist on developing it. If effective international controls were not established, a nuclear arms race would occur and in a future war civilization could be destroyed. Exploding the bomb would set off the race. Perhaps the only road to salvation was to approach the Soviet Union before it was used, to allay Soviet suspicions, and initiate the international cooperation that would be necessary. The secretary raised these considerations with Roosevelt and Truman, and some scientists associated with the Manhattan Project found them compelling. The Franck Report, written by several of these men and submitted to Stimson in June 1945, envisioned a nuclear surprise attack. It correctly predicted that Russia could imitate the U.S. accomplishment in a few years, a decade at most. The United States should therefore seek to arrange international controls within an atmosphere of trust and cooperation. The bomb should be used against Japan only as a last resort, and then only after suitable warning.

Thus there was opposition to seeking a complete surprise, opposition top officials and scientists rejected. Preparations for using the bomb had been made for some time, and the actual orders were approved by President Truman at Potsdam on July 24 or 25. Shortly thereafter, the Potsdam Declaration demanded that Japan surrender or face "prompt" and "utter destruction." Only acceptance of that declaration would have brought suspension of those orders, but the Japanese government was unable to agree on the terms for surrender. Through an unfortunate choice of words in a speech the premier seemed to reject the declaration outright. Thus the orders for the attack were never retracted.

From a revisionist perspective, the American incentives look rather different. Even if there was some interest in ending the war, a more compelling goal was to strengthen the United States in its dealings with the Soviet Union. Disputes were emerging and the Soviets seemed to have too many bargaining advantages—including the American desire that they enter the war against Japan. The atomic bomb would remove the need for Russian participation and bolster the American negotiating position.

For this reason, the United States hurried to use the bomb before the war ended, and downplayed evidence that Japan might be induced to surrender in some other way. Truman timed the Potsdam Conference to coincide with the first test of the bomb, but a public display of its awesome power was still needed. Therefore, the administration avoided doing the one thing that it knew might produce a surrender, telling the Japanese they might retain their emperor. The Potsdam Declaration merely repeated the demand for unconditional surrender and gave no hint of the bomb.

Thus American incentives to use the bomb lay at least partly in the emerging political/diplomatic problems of the postwar world. Of particular importance was the growing feeling that the United States had to be firm in dealing with the Russians. A conciliatory posture meant telling the Russians about the bomb and seeking international controls. A firm posture meant insistence on American positions backed up by economic and military pressure. This means the decision reflected the growing power of those who were to become the cold warriors within the government. Also assigned responsibility is the personality and background of the president himself. To his natural anticommunism was added an inclination to be assertive and a lack of experience in foreign affairs; a subtle appreciation of the difficulties of dealing with the Russians was lacking. He did not need to reach beyond his advisors for more information about this momentous decision, and he did not fully grasp the objections some had raised.

This preoccupation with the Kremlin can be used to explain the heavy emphasis in the wartime security arrangements on hiding the Manhattan Project from the Russians. It is why the Russians were told only when the initial test was completed and the U.S. capacity had been demonstrated. This also might explain the fact that since there was no real military pressure to use the bomb (the invasion was not scheduled to take place until October), the United States might have waited several months after the Potsdam Declaration but instead chose to use it almost at once. It is why the bomb ceased to be a military necessity for winning the war by the summer of 1945 but was rushed to completion and used anyway. The scientists who opposed use without warning were entirely correct in their analysis, but the dominant diplomatic considerations precluded accepting it.

It is difficult to accept one view and flatly reject the other. It must be said that in the summer of 1945 the American government behaved very much as if it considered the final defeat of Japan a formidable task. Elaborate plans to invade were drawn up and thousands of troops were shifted to the Far East for that purpose. Most of the military leaders who knew of the bomb remained skeptical that it would really work. An invasion remained most likely, and plans for the initial landings were approved by the Joint Chiefs of Staff on June 29. The estimated casualties were very high in view of the fanatical resistance on Iwo Jima and Okinawa and the heavy losses incurred from kamikaze attacks. (Kamikaze planes had sunk over 30 vessels and damaged more than 100.) American officials were impressed with the political power of the armed forces in Japan and their fanaticism. Thus it was not unreasonable to expect Japan to continue to fight hard. The arguments raised against a warning or a demonstration before using the bomb were not specious or irrelevant. It would have been hard to justify accepting more American casualties with the atomic bomb in hand.

Also important is the fact that the bomb project had acquired enormous momentum. Billions had been spent and many talented people had devoted themselves to it. A congressional investigation was inevitable and all connected with the project would have to justify their actions, a political fact of life which was not overlooked. With all that had been invested it is not surprising that, in Stimson's words,

> At no time, from 1941 to 1945, did I ever hear it suggested by the President, or by any other responsible member of the government, that atomic energy should not be used in the war.[16]

It would have taken a rather radical departure from all that had gone before to not use the bomb. The decision was not treated as an extraordinary one requiring unusual procedures, and become relatively routine instead. This is how Truman described it in his memoirs.

However, the revisionists have a point. FDR, Truman, Stimson, Byrnes, and others did not hesitate to include the bomb in their thinking about how to deal with the Soviet Union. In their discussions there were frequent references to the assistance they expected the bomb to provide, a view Churchill also vigorously espoused. It seems clear that this was an additional incentive for using the bomb.

What seems most likely is this. The momentum of the project made it *very probable* the bomb would be used if developed in time. The desire to save lives and end the war made it *certain* the bomb would be used, unless the concern that this would poison postwar cooperation with the Soviet Union became paramount. This concern bothered Stimson and might have influenced Roosevelt. But Truman and his advisors were soon persuaded that the Soviet Union would have to be pressured more than pleasured. The bomb they intended for other purposes was now seen to offer this additional advantage. The intent to use the bomb that had been there from the start was simply reinforced, and the military necessity for its use, which had declined, was not carefully reconsidered.

As with the decision to employ the bomb, there is disagreement about its results and thus about whether the American assessment of the situation in Japan was realistic. Some analysts have concluded that surrender would have occurred shortly under any circumstances. Others have found that Soviet entry into the war was the critical factor. And there is evidence that the atomic bomb played a major role.

In the days prior to Hiroshima, the Japanese armed forces had continued to prepare to defeat an American invasion. They correctly anticipated the planned date of the invasion and the beaches on which the Americans were to land. Ammunition had been stockpiled, thousands of planes for kamikaze raids were prepared, all civilians except the elderly had been conscripted for the final defense effort, and some training of civilians on how to assist in the fighting had been undertaken. When Hiroshima was destroyed, this news was not made public. The armed forces rejected initial reports on the destruction as exaggerated and expressed doubt that it was an atomic bomb. It was suggested that the bomb was only effective on the surface, that shelters would provide protection.

In the Supreme Council for the Direction of the War, a kind of inner cabinet, the premier, the foreign minister, and the navy minister constituted the peace faction, while the war minister, plus the army and navy chiefs of staff resisted surrender. All agreed the emperor must remain, but the war faction insisted on surrender only if three more conditions were met: that Japan would not be occupied, would disarm its own forces, and would try any war criminals itself. This division persisted *after Hiroshima* and it continued on August 9, the day after the Russian entry and after the council heard the first reports about Nagasaki. The cabinet also met that day and was similarly divided.

Late in the evening the Supreme Council met in the emperor's presence, reviewed the issues, and remained deadlocked. Then the premier, evidently by prearrangement, took the extraordinary step of asking the emperor to decide. In remarks that reduced everyone to tears, the emperor ordered a surrender message prepared. He thereby removed the responsibility for the decision from the armed forces, which could therefore accept it. When broadcast, the surrender message clearly implied that the emperor would remain, and the American response said the emperor and all others would be subordinate to the supreme allied commander. In this fashion the unconditional surrender formula was skirted sufficiently to end the war. Even then, however, fanatical army officers attempted a coup to forestall a surrender, with some loss of life.

Thus it is possible to say that the bomb made no difference in the attitude of the military leaders, that the key was the retention of the emperor. It is also possible to say that the bomb created such a terrifying prospect that the emperor could finally act and get the armed forces to accept his decision. In view of the military attitude even after the two atomic bombs and the fact that it took an extraordinary intervention by the emperor to bring surrender, it is hard to conclude that the American assessment of the situation within the Japanese government was unrealistic, that there were no grounds for believing the bomb was necessary to force a surrender.

As for the actual use of the bombs, this strategic surprise had been years in the making. In some ways the Manhattan Project could be traced back to 1939, to Albert Einstein's letter to Roosevelt warning of German interest in nuclear research. The administrative structure for the project began to take shape in October 1941. The B-29s for delivering the bomb were picked out in the fall of 1943; Colonel Paul Tibbets was named to head the crew in the summer of 1944 and the training flights for delivering atomic bombs were initiated in the fall. After July 20, 1945 the bomber crews even made several practice runs with dummy bombs over Japanese cities. The attack was a very long time in preparation by almost any definition.

The Japanese were totally vulnerable to the attack, more so than the Americans knew. By the summer of 1945 Japanese air defenses were minimal. The Americans not only had the bomb and a suitable delivery system, they also had developed a proximity fuse that set off the bomb at a predetermined altitude for maximum effect. By sending only a few planes to each target, the Americans, inadvertently, did not trigger air raid warnings and the populations of the two cities were then totally unshielded. The final casualty levels came as a shock to Oppenheimer and others. Stimson had been appalled at earlier estimates of 20,000 fatalities, and of course the two bombs killed far more than this in each city.

Japan was also vulnerable because it knew nothing about the planned attacks before they occurred. Brief consideration had been given to nuclear energy during the war, but it was not considered possible for anyone to make a bomb. American security precautions had been elaborate, and included informing very few officials about the project. Truman learned about it after Roosevelt's death. Eisenhower first heard of the project at Potsdam, MacArthur was not told until late July, and Secretary of State Stettinuis was never told. The surprise on August 6 was complete.

MANCHURIA 1945[17]

On August 9, 1945 the Soviet Union launched a massive three-pronged invasion of Manchuria and overwhelmed the Japanese Kwantung Army in little more than a week. Although Japan moved to accept the Potsdam Declaration the next day, regular fighting continued in Manchuria for 5-6 days and sporadic hostilities lasted until August 20. Foreign Minister Molotov had officially notified the Japanese ambassador of war on August 8, but the latter's telegram to Tokyo was "mislaid" in the Soviet telegraph office and thus Soviet forces struck without warning.

This Soviet action has received little attention in the West. Coming after the first atom bomb, it has been dismissed as Stalin's last-minute grab for all he could get before Japan collapsed. As Japan was clearly beaten and the course of the war not markedly altered by the attack, we might conclude that it was not a meaningful strategic surprise. However, several aspects of the campaign make it worthy of further examination. The attack took a number of months and much effort to prepare, and was mounted in anticipation that the war might last three months or longer. In other words, it was not a last-minute operation in its conception. Next, the campaign has many of the classic elements of a strategic surprise. Finally, the Russians regularly cite it as a prime illustration of modern Soviet military operations. It is a case study in the Soviet approach to strategic surprise and of considerable interest as such.

The Soviet government had a number of incentives to seek this surprise attack. We can dismiss short-term defensive concerns and objectives as the primary motivation. Prior to and during World War II Japanese units in Manchuria had been a persistent military threat, but now Japan was desperately seeking assistance to end the war by way of numerous concessions to entice Soviet cooperation. Hence Moscow's goals were entirely offensive, political, and territorial in nature. At Yalta Stalin specifically asked, and was granted, as his price for entering the war:

1. the southern half of Sakhalin Island
2. the Kurile Islands
3. access to/control over Port Arthur, Darien, and the Manchurian railroads, which together would provide a dominant position in Manchuria
4. confirmation of Mongolia's independence from China, i.e., its status as a Soviet protectorate

Stalin also hoped to have a hand in the occupation of Japan and may have sought to absorb all of Korea within his sphere of influence.

The first three goals were aimed at reversing the results of the Russo-Japanese War. After the attack Moscow emphasized what it described as the treacherous and imperialistic nature of Japan's conduct in that earlier struggle. Thus these goals tapped a streak of Russian nationalism and resentment, not just a great power appetite for more territory. The fourth goal had long been sought in Russian dealings with China (and remains a serious point of contention in Sino-Soviet relations today).

As for the attractions of surprise, this new war would come at the end of a long and terribly devastating one, making a quick and relatively cheap campaign appealing. In addition, by estimates in Moscow and Washington, the Japanese had significant military strength remaining and could well fight on into 1946. To shatter a major portion of Japan's remaining forces would be a significant contribution to shortening the war. Thus the attack was planned along blitzkrieg lines—sweeping attacks on numerous fronts, neutralizing enemy men and equipment in short order, and rolling up the entire Kwantung Army.

Certain other factors, one speculates, were probably at work as well. Soviet military leaders had gone to school on the painful capacity of the Germans to mount sudden coordinated armor and air power strikes to shatter an opponent, and using the rapid mobility of one's forces to exploit the resulting advantages. Now they had a last professional opportunity to display what they had learned, a kind of postgraduate exercise. The other factor, suggested earlier, was the legacy of painful conflicts with Japan, an old and arrogant opponent since before the turn of the century. These historical experiences seem to have shaped Soviet incentives much more than such factors as elite values, the personalities of key leaders, or cultural preferences.

A final consideration was that the war would certainly not be popular with the public, which turned out to be the case. There was no widespread, deeprooted hatred of Japan such as Germany had (eventually) evoked and no spontaneous enthusiasm when war was announced. Of course, the nature of Stalin's rule precluded signs of opposition either in the government or elsewhere.

On balance, Moscow had strong incentives both to enter the war and to do so via a surprise attack. The Japanese were well aware of this and offered substantial concessions (described later) in hopes of keeping the Russians neutral. Thus the chief disincentive was these Japanese concessions, for they offered the possibility of significant gains at little or no cost. But this would have meant associating with a nation certain to lose in the end, alienating the victors in the process, and there is no sign the Soviets ever seriously contemplated accepting the Tokyo offer. The Soviet assessment of Japan's true military capabilities at that point was in error, but this was an error shared and reinforced by American estimates. Achieving strategic surprise came to be the central feature of the campaign, the basis for all the planning. Yet the incentives for attacking were such that the effort would almost certainly have been mounted even if the opportunity for surprise had been lost.

Having outlined Soviet incentives, we must explore the conditions that provided the opportunity for a strategic surprise. One was a considerable

Soviet capacity for large operations. As early as October 1943 Stalin was telling Western leaders his country would enter the war, and orders to assess the forces and supplies needed went to the Soviet general staff in September 1944. The resulting estimates provided the basis for requests for lend-lease and other assistance. Even before this planning, however, Stalin and his military leaders had the general dimensions of the Soviet effort in mind, telling the Allies that about three months after Germany's surrender would be required to sufficiently enlarge Soviet forces in the Far East to enter the war. The figures on what the Soviets would bring to bear were quite close to the actual forces eventually involved.

The government then orchestrated an impressive buildup. The Trans-Siberian Railway was used to the fullest. In addition, to reach the key front in Mongolia, the mechanized units traveled up to 750 miles on their own, while the troops marched as much as 300 miles. They passed over forbidding desert terrain in blazing summer heat, with movement mainly in the mornings and evenings to cope with daytime temperatures as high as 112 degrees. At the end of 1944 the Soviets maintained about 750,000 men, 1,000 tanks, and 1,000 aircraft in the theater. The buildup began in February 1945, accelerated after April, and by August 8 there were nearly 1.6 million men (including 1,059,000 in combat units), over 5,500 tanks and self-propelled guns, more than 5,300 aircraft, and some 27,000 artillery pieces and mortars. This provided a marked quantitative and qualitative military superiority. The campaign was apparently expected to last up to eight weeks, but it is unclear whether this was an acceptable error on the side of caution or a considerable miscalculation of the Kwantung Army's capabilities.

To manage these forces an organizational innovation was employed. A special high command for the forces in the Far East was set up under the former head of the general staff, Marshal Vasilevsky. This permitted the conduct of operations with less direction from Moscow than was the case in the war with Germany. Lower level units were also assigned greater flexibility than usual. This larger degree of command autonomy is apparently one of the features that makes it appealing for the armed forces to this day.

Added to military superiority were numerous elements of deception and surprise. To disguise the preparations, unusual regrouping and logistical arrangements were used, and activities along the borders were kept as normal as possible up to the attack. Soviet commanders moving east travelled under false names, and after they arrived many personally reconnoitered the attack locations so as not to rely on aerial surveys or reconnaissance efforts that might compromise surprise. Plans were detailed on commanders' maps with little other documentation, and the maps were kept in locked safes. Few were told of the plans for the attack on each front, and orders were communicated orally to avoid radio traffic. Deployments were carried out secretly (often at night) and linked to training exercises wherever possible, with some air units not brought up until just before the attack. A bogus force concentration was constructed along one front to mislead the Japanese, while stringent efforts to prevent Japanese reconnaissance were made at most points.

The Soviets then sought to gain further advantage via tactical surprise. The attack was mounted during a rainy season and, on one front, in the midst of a severe thunderstorm. The initial attacks came at night and were not preceded by the long bombardments that the Soviets believed the Japanese would expect. The main effort was led by a tank army for the first time in Soviet history, and the rapid advance via massed armor was designed to contradict Japanese experience and expectations. The Soviets threw in the use of advance mobile detachments and some airborne units at various points to multiply the pressures on Japanese perceptions and reactions.

Even more surprising, in intent and effect, was the strategic plan behind the invasion. The Soviets attacked along 5,000 kilometers of borders, inviting the continued dispersal of Japanese forces. The Russians then sliced through those forces along several attack avenues. In the past, major Japanese and Russian units had been concentrated along the maritime region, where there were extensive Japanese fortifications. This constituted the First Far Eastern Front, where a thrust to the west was mounted. The Soviets also attacked in the northeast, the Second Far Eastern Front, across the Amur and along the Sungari Rivers. On August 10 the Soviets added an attack on southern Sakhalin Island by land and naval units.

The real shock came in a third attack along the Transbaikal Front, in which Soviet forces poured out of Mongolia in an arc stretching from north China to upper Manchuria. Major Soviet forces (some 650,000 men) were concentrated there, particularly mechanized units, far more than the Japanese anticipated. The territory before them was desolate, stretching to the Great Hsingan Range. The Soviet plan anticipated, correctly, that a massive attack from this quarter would be unexpected and that resistance would be minimal. The plan called for bounding the 500 miles from Mongolia to Mukden without pause, racing through the mountains before Japanese forces could fortify them; in all there were two days to get to the mountains, three days to cross and secure them, and five days to seize Mukden and Changchun. Manchuria was to be seized through the back door.

The plan worked exceedingly well. On the first two fronts Soviet forces made headway but ran into stiff opposition at times. On the Transbaikal Front opposition was minimal and the major obstacles soon came to be logistical in nature. Progress was so rapid that the commander, Marshal Malinovsky, altered the timetable. As supplies dwindled, particularly of fuel, he had the advance units charged with the missions formerly assigned to their parent forces, gave them priority on supplies, and sent them off to race through the country. His forces covered up to 700 miles in some eleven days, taking Mukden on August 20 and Changchun on the 21st, averaging over fifty miles per day for the campaign.

Success was enhanced by the vulnerability of the opponent. Despite Soviet efforts to hide the preparations, Tokyo accumulated evidence that an attack was quite possible. From mid-1944 the Soviet press was increasingly unfriendly in its references to Japan. Official cordiality toward Japanese diplomats also declined, and in November Stalin referred to Japan as an "aggressor." By late February, Japanese intelligence was receiving reports of Soviet troop movements to the Far East. In March it learned that at Yalta Stalin had promised to enter the war three months after Germany's defeat.

In April the Soviet Union gave the required one-year notice it was renouncing the USSR-Japan Neutrality Pact of 1941. Initially this was taken as a sign the Soviets planned to attack about when the Americans invaded the home islands, which the Japanese then believed would be in late spring 1946. But soon it was decided that a fall campaign was planned, particularly since the Japanese noted the lack of winter clothing and equipment for the Soviet troops coming east. Japanese consulates along the Trans-Siberian Railway were now reporting the passage of twenty troop trains or more per day. Further suspicion was aroused by a *New Times* travel article in June which referred to Port Arthur as a Russian city (!), and by the visit of Chinese and Mongolian envoys to Moscow in July.

A serious Japanese intelligence failure occurred in predicting the exact date, however. By mid-May Imperial General Headquarters had settled on August or September, but Kwantung Army Intelligence still expected the attack to come in 1946. Soon all agreed on early fall, the best guess being late August. A key reason the attack came sooner than expected was another intelligence failure, in which the Japanese underestimated the size of existing Soviet forces, then did the same on the capacity of the Trans-Siberian Railway and the rate of the Soviet buildup. While the Soviets were moving over 30 divisions, the Japanese thought they had shifted only 20–25. In the belief the Russians had some 45 divisions on hand and would gather at least 60 before attacking, the Japanese put off the date of the attack several weeks—when in fact there were 80 Soviet divisions plus other units already in place.

However, there is a possibility that the Japanese had the original date for the invasion roughly correct, and that Stalin forced his troops to attack sooner than they had wished or planned. Stalin's negotiations with the Chinese government to put a seal of approval on the territorial concessions granted Moscow at Yalta were still going on when the attack occurred. Several Soviet commanders have written that Stalin personally pushed the attack date forward from early September to early August. What caused the change? Marshal Vasilevsky recalled Stalin acting just after being told about the atomic bomb

at the Potsdam Conference in July. Other Soviet memoirs say the shift came
after Stalin returned from Potsdam. Raymond Garthoff believes the catalyst
was Hiroshima. If any of these versions is accepted, this becomes a case in
which a structural factor aided in the achievement of strategic surprise—
namely a change in the timetable coming so late that it would have been very
difficult for the Japanese to have detected it in time.

Certain additional political/psychological considerations inhibited Japanese
anticipation of an attack. With the loss of Saipan, many civilian leaders
realized the war was lost and began searching for a way to end it. As early
as July 1943 some thought had been given to the Soviet Union as mediator,
and during 1944 Japan sought to entice them into better relations. In the spring
of 1945 Tokyo launched a major diplomatic effort to renew the Neutrality
Pact, secure Soviet mediation, and keep the Soviet Union out of the war.
Tokyo offered to renounce certain fishing and mineral rights on Soviet land
or in Soviet territorial waters, to withdraw from Manchuria, and to look with
favor on Soviet interests there. For the Japanese, Soviet mediation would
have supplied a way around the unconditional surrender formula cherished
by the Americans. Also it would have helped solve the problem of the armed
forces resistance to surrender. The Russians stalled, endlessly requesting
clarification and delaying meetings, while hurrying their preparations. Thus
top officials in Tokyo were still desperately hoping for Soviet help, not looking
for a Soviet attack, and when the attack came it was a shock.

Military leaders in Manchuria had less reason to be surprised, but their
preparations and postattack strategy left much to be desired. In the preceding
year important units of the Kwantung Army had been moved to the home
islands and others had been sent to China. One-third of the available ammunition stocks in Manchuria had been shipped to Japan in the summer and
there were serious shortages in all units. Nominal Japanese strength was about
one million men in 24 divisions, plus 1,200 armored vehicles and 1,800
aircraft. But nearly one-quarter of the troops were Manchukuo and Mongolian
satellite units. Most divisions were at half strength or less, or were filled out
with poorly trained men, often too old or very young, with no combat experience. Available fighter planes were obsolete and the best air defenses
were in southern Manchuria to meet B-29 raids. Only about one-fifth the
number of the Soviets' artillery pieces were available.

Realizing an attack could come soon, the Japanese ordered a crash mobilization, but too late to meet the actual invasion. Eight of their Manchurian
divisions were mobilized just ten days before the attack. Planned reinforcements from China never had time to arrive. Realignments of troops to fit a
new defense plan had not been completed. Most top officers on one front
had gathered for a headquarters war game when the attack occurred. As a
result of this generally low level of preparation, Japanese military leaders had
rated the real value of their 24 divisions at more like seven or eight.

Finally, the Japanese adapted badly to the Soviet strategy, as things turned out. To meet the thrust from Mongolia, the high command sought to move units into position to harass Malinovsky's forces, in keeping with a previously prepared contingency plan. But General Ushiroku wished to withdraw, to let the Soviets become overextended and outrun their supply lines, and then to counterattack. The general simply pulled back to the Dairen-Mukden-Changchun Railway, ignoring Kwantung Army headquarters, and the honor of all concerned required that this fait accompli be accepted. It might not have been a bad strategy, except that Tokyo surrendered before the counterattack was ever mounted. The 44th Army saw no significant fighting; its units were mostly in Mukden when hostilities ended, and Malinovsky's forces were never really challenged.

In terms of its results, the campaign had mixed or uncertain results. Sizable Japanese forces were overwhelmed and nearly 600,000 prisoners were hauled off to the Soviet Union for several years of forced labor before repatriation. But disagreement persists as to the degree to which the attack forced the Japanese surrender. The following are the alternatives:

1. the atom bomb played the major role (the major American view)
2. the Soviet attack was crucial (the Soviet view)
3. both, together, forced the surrender[18]
4. the key was permitting retention of the emperor—given this, Japan would have surrendered before either the bomb or the attack[19]

As to its larger objectives, the attack brought incorporation of southern Sakhalin and the Kuriles plus the settling of Mongolia's status. But the Soviet presence in Manchuria was eventually eliminated by pressures from Mao's government. Soviet hopes to join in the occupation of Japan were thwarted by American resistance.

The attack is interesting as an illustration of two types of strategic surprises that may be sought. One is the surprise designed to strike where the enemy isn't—to achieve great success by nullifying his major forces. The other is the surprise attack designed not to avoid the enemy's major forces but to overwhelm and shatter them. The Russians used the former in the operations on the Trans-Baikal Front; the latter was the overall objective of the campaign. Both were successfully achieved, albeit against a gravely weakened opponent.

NOTES

1. Major sources for this case study included: David Walder, *The Short Victorious War, The Russo-Japanese Conflict 1904–5* (London: Hutchinson and Co., 1973); Edwin Falk, *Togo and the Rise of Japanese Sea Power* (London: Langmans, Green and Co., 1936); Edwin Falk, *From Perry to Pearl Harbor* (Garden City, New York: Doubleday, Doran and Co., 1943); Morinosuke Kajima, *The Emer-*

gence of Japan as a World Power 1895–1925 (Rutland, Vermont: Charles E. Tuttle Co., 1968); Ian Nish, *Japanese Foreign Policy 1869–1942* (London: Routledge and Kegan Paul, 1977); Sidney Tyler, *The Japan-Russian War* (Philadelphia: P. W. Ziegler Co., 1905); Shumpei Akamoto, *The Japanese Oligarchy and the Russo-Japanese War* (New York: Columbia University Press, 1970); Denis and Peggy Warner, *The Tide at Sunrise* (New York: Charter University Press, 1970); Tatsuji Takeuchi, *War and Diplomacy in the Japanese Empire* (Chicago: University of Chicago Press, 1935); Nagayo Ogasawara, *Life of Admiral Togo*, trans. by Jukichi Inouye and Tozo Inouye (Tokyo: Seito Shorin Press, 1934); Georges Blond, *Admiral Togo*, trans. by Edward Hyams (New York: Macmillan, 1960); R. V. C. Bodley, *Admiral Togo* (London: Jarrolds, 1935); John R. White, *The Diplomacy of the Russo-Japanese War* (Princeton: Princeton University Press, 1964); *The Russo-Japanese War, the Ya-Lu*, trans. by Karl Von Donat (London: Hugh Rees Ltd., 1908).

2. The Russian view is that Japan merely entered the negotiations to cover its plans for war and help justify its initiation of the fighting. See Andrew Malozemoff, *Russian Far Eastern Policy, 1881–1904* (Berkeley: University of California Press, 1958), pp. 237-47.

3. The admiral was mindful of the fact that Japan could not build capital ships in its existing shipyards, and that while the Russians had ships in European waters on which to draw, Japanese losses could not be replaced.

4. Denis and Peggy Warner, *The Tide at Sunrise*, p. 11.

5. Major sources for this account included: Roberta Wohlstetter, *Pearl Harbor: Warning and Decision* (Stanford: Stanford University Press, 1962); John Toland, *The Rising Sun* (New York: Random House, 1970); Nobutaka Ike, ed., *Japan's Decision For War* (Stanford: Stanford University Press, 1967); Robert J. C. Butow, *Tojo and the Coming of the War* (Princeton: Princeton University Press, 1961); Dorothy Borg and Shumpei Okamoto, eds. *Pearl Harbor as History* (New York: Columbia University Press, 1973); George Waller, ed., *Pearl Harbor, Roosevelt and the Coming of the War* (3rd ed.; Lexington, Mass.: D. C. Heath, 1976); James Herzog, *Closing the Open Door, American-Japanese Diplomatic Negotiations 1936–1941* (Annapolis: Naval Institute Press, 1973); Christopher Thorne, *Allies of a Kind; the U.S., Britain and the War Against Japan 1941–1945* (London: Hamish Hamilton, 1978); U.S. Congress, Joint Committee on the Investigation of the Pearl Harbor Attack, *Investigation of the Pearl Harbor Attack* (Washington, D.C.: Government Printing Office, 1946); A. Russell Buchanan, *The United States and World War II*, Volume I (New York: Harper and Row, 1964); Bruce Russett, *No Clear and Present Danger* (New York: Harper and Row, 1972); Charles Neu, *The Troubled Encounter: The United States and Japan* (New York: John Wiley and Sons, 1975); Saburo Ienaga, *The Pacific War: World War II and the Japanese 1931–1945* (New York: Pantheon Books, 1978); James Morely, ed., *Dilemmas of Growth in Prewar Japan* (Princeton: Princeton University Press, 1971); John Deane Potter, *Yamamoto: The Man Who Menaced America* (New York: Viking Press, 1965).

6. Richard Storry, *A History of Modern Japan* (New York: Barnes and Noble, 1962), p. 185.

7. Stephen Pelz, *Race to Pearl Harbor* (Cambridge: Harvard University Press, 1974), p. 221. See also pp. 217–26.

8. Paul Dull, *A Battle History of the Imperial Japanese Navy 1941–1945* (Annapolis: Naval Institute Press, 1978), p. 7 argues that Japanese naval leaders knew about Rainbow 5, but attacked at Pearl Harbor to try to force an early U.S. decision to

quit so as to avoid a long war. The weight of the evidence seems to suggest, however, that the Japanese were more concerned about a U.S. offensive naval reaction.

9. On domestic pressures see Donald Friedman, *The Road From Isolation: The Campaign of the American Committee for Non-Participation in Japanese Aggression 1938–1941* (Cambridge: Harvard University Press, 1968).

10. S. E. Smith, ed., *The United States Navy in World War II* (New York: William Morrow and Co., 1966), p. 4.

11. Ibid., p. 4

12. Besides those cited on the Pearl Harbor case study, some additional sources consulted on the section included: Louis Allen, *Singapore 1941–1942* (London: Davis-Poynter, 1977); S. Woodburn Kirby, *Singapore: The Chain of Disaster* (London: Cassell, 1971); S. Woodburn Kirby, *The War Against Japan, Volume I, The Loss of Singapore* (London: Her Majesty's Stationery Office, 1957); Lionel Wigmore, *The Japanese Threat* (Canberra: Australian War Memorial, 1957); Stanley Falk, *Seventy Days to Singapore* (New York: G. P. Putnam's Sons, 1975); Kate Caffrey, *Out in the Midday Sun* (New York: Stein and Day, 1973); Raymond Callahan, *Burma 1942–1945* (London: Davis-Poynter, 1978); Raymond Callahan, *The Worst Disaster: The Fall of Singapore* (Newark: University of Delaware Press, 1977); Tim Carew, *The Longest Retreat, the Burma Campaign 1942* (London: Hamish Hamilton, 1969); Masanobu Tsuji, *Singapore, the Japanese Version* (New York: St. Martin's Press, 1960); Noel Barber, *A Sinister Twilight, the Fall of Singapore 1942* (Boston: Houghton, Mifflin, 1968); Charles Bateson, *The War With Japan* (East Lansing, Michigan: Michigan State University Press, 1968); Basil Collier, *The War in the Far East 1941–1945, a Military History* (New York: William Morrow and Co., 1969).

13. Major sources for this case study included: Martin Sherwin, *A World Destroyed, the Atomic Bomb and the Grand Alliance* (N.Y.: Vintage Books edition, 1977); Paul Baker, ed., *The Atomic Bomb, the Great Decision* (N.Y.: Holt Rinehart, and Winston, 1969); Henry L. Stimson and McGeorge Bundy, *On Active Service in Peace and War* (N.Y.: Harper and Row, 1947); Gar Alperovitz, *Atomic Diplomacy: Hiroshima and Potsdam* (N.Y.: Simon and Schuster, 1965); William Manchester, *American Caesar, Douglas MacArthur 1880–1964* (N.Y.: Dell, 1978); Herbert Feis, *The Atomic Bomb and the End of World War II* (Princeton: Princeton University Press, 1966); B. H. Liddell Hart, *History of the Second World War* (London: Cassell, 1970); William Craig, *The Fall of Japan* (N.Y.: Dial Press, 1967); Stephen Ambrose, *Rise to Globalism*, revised edition (N.Y.: Penguin Books, 1976); Thomas Paterson, *The Origins of the Cold War*, 2nd edition (Lexington, Mass.: D. C. Heath, 1974); Adam Ulam, *The Rivals, America and Russia Since World War II* (N.Y.: Viking Compass Edition, 1971); John Toland, *The Rising Sun* (N.Y.: Random House, 1970); Robert J. C. Butow, *Japan's Decision to Surrender* (Stanford: Stanford University Press, 1954); Louis Morton, "The Decision to Use the Atomic Bomb" in Robert Art and Kenneth Waltz, eds., *The Use of Force* (Boston: Little Brown, 1971), pp. 316–39.

14. Lester Brooks, *Behind Japan's Surrender* (N.Y.: McGraw Hill, 1968), pp. 15–16.

15. This view has been disputed by Walter Schoenberger, who traces the decision to the nature of the international system, and to some deeply rooted traits in American culture. See Walter Schoenberger, *Decision of Destiny* (Athens, Ohio: Ohio University Press, 1969), pp. 285–93.

16. Henry L. Stimson, "The Decision to Use the Atomic Bomb" in Paul Baker, ed.,

The Atomic Bomb, the Great Decision (N.Y.: Holt, Rinehart and Winston, 1969), p. 10.

17. In addition to some of the sources cited earlier, important sources for this section included Lilita Dzirkals, *"Lightning War" in Manchuria: Soviet Military Analysis of the 1945 Far East Campaign* (Santa Monica: Rand Corporation, 1976); Raymond Garthoff "Marshal Malinovsky's Manchurian Campaign," *Military Review,* XLVI (October, 1966), pp. 50–61; Raymond Garthoff, "Soviet Intervention in Manchuria, 1945–56," *Orbis,* X (Summer, 1966), pp. 520–47; Raymond Garthoff, "The Soviet Manchurian Campaign, August 1945," *Military Affairs,* XXXIII (October, 1969), pp. 312–36; George Lensen, *The Strange Neutrality* (Tallahassee, Florida: The Diplomatic Press, 1972); David James, *The Rise and Fall of the Japanese Empire* (London: Oxford University Press, 1953); William Craig, *The Fall of Japan* (New York: The Dial Press, 1967); Louis Allen, *The End of the War in Asia* (London: Hart-Davis, MacGibbon, 1976); John Despres, Lilita Dzirkals, and Barton Whaley, *Timely Lessons of History: The Manchurian Model For Soviet Strategy* (Santa Monica: Rand Corporation, 1975).

18. Analysts taking this view include B. H. Liddell Hart, *History of the Second World War* (London: Cassell, 1970), p. 696; and Richard Storry, *A History of Modern Japan* (N.Y.: Barnes and Noble, 1962), p. 230.

19. Analysts offering this view include Paul Kecskemeti, *Strategic Surrender, The Politics of Victory and Defeat* (Stanford, California: Stanford University Press, 1958), pp. 198–99; and Alexander Werth, *Russia at War 1941–45* (N.Y.: E. P. Dutton, 1964), p. 1043.

CHAPTER FOUR
Endemic Surprise? Strategic Surprises in First World–Third World Relations*

Michael Doyle

The North Korean attack surprised South Korea in June 1950. The Chinese intervention in the Korean War in November 1950 stunned the United States. The United States attempted to surprise Cuba with the invasion at the Bay of Pigs in April 1961. In each of these cases the attacking state intended to surprise the attacked state and in each case surprise (or astonishment) beyond that intended by the attacking state was experienced. The North Koreans seem to have been surprised by the American military response to their attack. Moreover, in the North Korean attack, not just one state but alliances both planned and experienced the surprises. The Bay of Pigs constituted a surprise that failed; the United States did not anticipate Cuban preparedness. The Chinese both intended to warn *and* to surprise the United States.

These attacks are complex and in certain respects unique, but they also share features with the others examined in this volume. Like the other cases we examined, these surprises reflect varying elements and sources. Sometimes the surprise resulted from faulty intelligence or inappropriate preconceptions. Sometimes states failed to anticipate whether an attack would occur; in others, they were surprised by what forces would be employed, and where, when, or why an attack might take place.

But these three cases also share one additional feature. Each involves surprise between a developed, technologically and industrially advanced society and a less developed, less technologically and industrially advanced society. Although occurring in a Cold War context, they are each "First World–Third World" conflicts. The social as well as cultural differences separating these two worlds of development played a role in these surprises. Sources of surprise common to almost all instances of unanticipated attack took on a new and important, increased and altered significance in the special context of relations between the developed and the less developed countries of a markedly differentiated world.

KOREA, JUNE 1950[1]

North Korea's divisions struck in the early morning of Sunday, June 25 and surprised South Korea's armed forces. The more than eight divisions of the North Korean attack smashed into the four divisions of the Republic of Korea Armed Forces stationed along the 38th Parallel. Only one regiment of each division of South Korea's forces was in a forward position when the North Koreans crossed. A number of the South Korean officers and men were on weekend passes in Seoul. The American military advisors were similarly unready for a North Korean attack. Brigadier General Roberts, commander of the American military advisory group in Korea (KMAG), had departed ten days earlier for reassignment. Roberts' deputy, Colonel Wright, was about to leave for a new assignment and was seeing his family off in Japan. A lieutenant colonel was left in charge on this weekend in June.

No greater awareness of impending trouble disturbed Washington. Both Truman and Secretary of State Acheson were away from the capital: Truman at his home in Independence, Missouri; Acheson at his Maryland farm. On the other hand, in Pyongyang the mood must have been one of tense expectation. In late 1949, according to Khrushchev's memoirs, the North Korean premier, Kim Il-Sung, had journeyed to Moscow to request Stalin's approval for an invasion of the South. After Mao Zedong's (Mao Tse-tung) added China's acquiescence, Kim received the go-ahead. But none of the communist powers anticipated a U.S. counterintervention—this was to be a civil, a "class" war—and Kim had promised a rising of South Korean communists to coincide with his attack.[2]

The June attack was a combination of stunning strategic surprises. Neither South Korea nor North Korea accepted the political division of the Korean nation, and as both had threatened to unify the peninsula by force, both were conscious of the possibility of war. But none of the pertinent actors, not even those who planned the attack, fully anticipated the outcome of the first few weeks of the war. The North had expected a different kind of war from the one that ensued. South Korea and the United States, of course, experienced the greater surprise. Their surprises were complex and asymmetrical. Although South Korea made many correct assessments of the North Korean focus and intentions, the United States, on which South Korea depended for its security, demonstrated either faulty or densely foggy perceptions on *whether* an attack would occur on South Korea, *what kind* of attack might take place, and *where, when,* and *why* a strategically significant challenge from the communist bloc would arise. In attempting to unravel the complexity we should examine the forces available to each side, the warnings of an attack that were available, South Korean and American strategic policy that shaped the interpretation of those warnings, and North Korean and Soviet incentives to plan a surprise attack.

Force

The two armies that confronted each other on that morning in June were of quite different caliber. The North Korean army had received extensive support and training from a large Soviet military mission. Following the withdrawal of Russian forces in 1948, a 3,000 man military mission stayed behind to train a rapidly growing North Korean Peoples Army. After a struggle among a Chinese-oriented Yenan faction and Moscow-oriented and domestic factions, the latter two, under Kim, won and began to form a society and army on the Soviet model. The Russian ambassador, Col. General Shtykov, directed both this mission and, after the pattern the Soviets also established in Eastern Europe, much of the rest of the government of North Korea. The creation of a North Korean armed force began with a border constabulary formed in 1945 from Koreans who had fled their country to Soviet territory and had received training there. In 1950 this force numbered approximately 50,000. The second element of North Korean forces was its regular army. The North Korean Peoples Army (NKPA), activated in 1948, reached a strength of 135,000 men by March 1950. These soldiers were far from raw recruits, fully a third having fought with the Chinese Peoples Army throughout World War II. Each of the army's eight divisions was equipped with artillery on a par with the older Soviet divisions that fought in World War II. Furthermore, the Soviets had equipped an armored brigade with 120 T34 medium tanks—a powerful and versatile weapon with a broad tread that made it effective on Korea's often mired roads.

By June 1950 the Republic of [South] Korea forces numbered 98,000 in the army and 48,000 in the national police. The army had grown very rapidly after the establishment of a separate government for the South under Syngman Rhee in 1948. Following the withdrawal of U.S. ground forces in June 1949, a Korean military advisory group (KMAG) of 482 officers and men stayed behind to help form a Korean army. The South Korean Army was organized into eight divisions, but only four of these were at full strength by April 1950. The main objective of the army lay in securing domestic order for the regime Rhee was building. This required suppressing local political committees, many communist-led, overcoming two mutinies, purging the armed forces of 2,000 suspected communists, and crushing a guerrilla insurgency maintained by approximately 70,000 communists in the rural areas of the South. The last effort was not completed until April 1950. Requiring three divisions of Rhee's armed forces, these counterguerrilla wars produced battle-hardened soldiers that earned the respect of their American military advisors. But similar estimations did not extend to the Korean officer corps or to the overall operational readiness at the battalion level. Few battalions were trained, or demonstrated a capability for large-scale operations; exercises at the regimental or divisional level were rarer still. Moreover, by June 1950 equipment was far from adequate. Both South Korean officers and their American advisors were well aware that North Korean artillery outdistanced South Korean artillery and that the North Korean army units were considerably more mobile. Indeed, South Korean forces were short of basic logistical supplies: in June, 15 percent of its weapons and 35 percent of its vehicles were unserviceable.

The rapid defeat of the South naturally followed from the clash of these two unequal forces. The North Korean army crossed all along the parallel, pushing the South's thin line of defense backward. The soldiers of the Republic of Korea did not panic, but their antitank shells bounced off the T-34's. Soldiers then leapt at the tanks trying to dynamite them. Failing to halt the tanks, the South Koreans began to fall back. When it became clear that the main thrust of the invasion was toward Seoul, General Chae, commander-in-chief of the ROK army, ordered two divisions forward to block this thrust. This plan was poorly conceived, one of the divisions being over 120 miles away, and a coordinated counterattack failed to materialize. As the North Koreans drove toward Seoul, Chae and his senior staff blundered again. Rather than set up defenses around the capital, he ordered the bridges that controlled the retreat south of the capital destroyed before the equipment of the divisions defending Seoul could be brought across. Lacking their guns, the South's divisions began the disorganized flight that was not to be slowed until, with the help of U.S. troops rushed from Japan, the defense perimeter at Pusan was established.

Warnings

There were many warnings of an impending North Korean attack—indeed, far too many. The South Korean officer corps repeatedly expressed fears of a North Korean attack, but since the Rhee government also claimed the "South Korean Army could defeat North Korea in two weeks" (which no one in the American Mission believed) the warnings were taken no more seriously than the boasts.[3] General MacArthur's intelligence staff in the Far East Command (which was *not* responsible for gathering intelligence in Korea, but was nevertheless the major source of military information on Korea) warned Washington between June 1949 and June 1950 *1,200* times of an impending attack by North Korea. In one sense, all of these warnings were timely and accurate. North Korea and South Korea had been engaged in a protracted artillery duel across the parallel for years. These artillery exchanges were regularly accompanied by border crossings of military units. Thus, the warnings soon amounted to continued cries of "Wolf!" as far as many in Washington were concerned. When Secretary of Defense Louis Johnson, who was returning from an inspection trip of the Far East at the time, was informed of the invasion, he at first dismissed it as just one more border violation. He commented that North

Korea had violated the border *every* Sunday in the months prior to Sunday, June 25.

However, during the early spring of 1950 a more substantial set of warnings began to arrive. The Central Intelligence Agency (CIA) noted a rapid build-up of North Korean divisions—many with trained soldiers recently returned from China—as well as a marked increase in their equipment. The CIA further warned of a strong possibility of a shift from isolated border raids to a full scale attack.[4] On May 11, 1950, the South Korean Ministry of Defense warned the U.S. Mission that a rapid buildup had occurred in North Korean forces and that these forces now included 155 medium tanks. The U.S. Mission responded by suggesting that the estimate had been deliberately exaggerated. The United States estimated North Korean tank forces at 65 tanks. In fact, the South Koreans were closer to the actual figure, but many of their past estimates had indeed been wildly exaggerated.

With the advantage of hindsight, four pieces of intelligence gathering and immediate assessment of the situation stand out as failures. One problem lay in the channels for disseminating and analyzing intelligence on North Korea and its Soviet patron. Sources seemed to demonstrate systematic biases in the information that flowed to Washington, and these varying sources do not seem to have been critically compared with each other. Just as the CIA was making its warnings of increased military danger from North Korea (May 1950), George Kennan in the State Department stated that he was being assured by the Defense Department that the South Korean Army was vastly superior to its northern opponent,[5] leading him to downplay independent evidence that the communist bloc was about to initiate a military action. Although KMAG and Tokyo demonstrated in their internal memoranda a full awareness of the deficiencies in the South Korean Army, KMAG, responsible for the training and preparedness of South Korean forces, tended in its final evaluations to reflect a positive assessment of its own efforts as much as a hard analysis of the state of the South Korean Army. Second, the importance of the presence of T-34 tanks, apart from their numbers, appears never to have been properly evaluated. Although KMAG was aware of the existence of tanks in North Korea, they were thought to be "light tanks," not the *medium* T-34.[6] Moreover, their significance was downgraded. Only North Korea's air and artillery units were judged fully superior because KMAG, in its refusal to support South Korean requests for tanks, argued that tanks were an inappropriate weapon for the Korean terrain. General Roberts, the KMAG commander, had led a tank division in WWII; the embassy naturally accepted his judgment that tanks would bog down on the muddy roads and rice fields. But his judgment seems to have been based not on an evaluation of the T-34 but on his familiarity with *American* tanks which had a much narrower tread.[7] The third intelligence failure lay in Ambassador Muccio's dismissal of Kim-Il Sung's promise, issued on June 7, 1950, to hold Korea-wide "unification elections" on August 15. Muccio judged this to be a "purely propaganda compaign attempting to offset results of recent elections." (These South Korean elections had produced an anticommunist but also anti-Rhee majority). Nevertheless, Muccio did realize that Kim's promise, or threat, was distinctive: "Noteworthy first time date set for occupation of Seoul, although many previous claims to do so. . . . They conceivably might also serve as preliminary step toward all-out civil war, although seems improbable."[8] For the first time Kim himself had set a *date* for unification that, if he failed to achieve it, would embarrass him politically. The fourth intelligence failure appeared to derive from North Korean deceptions and a misreading of preparations for the attack. In early June, scattered reports of the movement of North Korean troops south of the border reached the U.S. embassy. Accompanying these reports were accounts of the evacuation of all civilians from a five-mile zone just north of the parallel. Both were indications of a prospective attack, although no information concerning a build-up of invasion supplies, a more telling indicator, was available. But both reports were discounted. Indeed, the establishment of the evacuated zone *discredited* reports of the troop movements, for such a zone was regarded as a usual communist, Soviet bloc practice designed to shield an oppressed populace from contact with the "Free World." It thus indicated in the embassy's estimation a stabilization of the 38th Parallel border, not a preparation for the elimination of the border altogether.[9]

Strategic Preconceptions

To see why the various warnings were judged to be "improbable" indicators of an attack, we need to examine the preconceptions imbedded in the American strategic posture toward Korea, the Far East, and the Soviet Bloc. Following World War II, American strategic doctrine rested on two pillars. One was maintaining a defensive-deterrent capability that could meet and defeat global aggression by the USSR against the Western democracies. Avoiding a repetition of World War II by maintaining a monopoly of atomic weapons designed to deter such an attack formed the foundation of this pillar. The key external stake in such a global war was, as it had been in World War II, Western Europe. Since, prior to 1949, a practical American monopoly of atomic weapons was expected to continue at least until 1953–1954 and since the Soviet Union was judged to be preoccupied with domestic reconstruction, American strategic planners did not expect an all-out challenge in the immediate future. The second pillar of United States global strategy consisted of the "Truman doctrine"—a globalized version of George Kennan's containment policy for dealing with a new "totalitarian" threat. The thrust of this policy lay in a strategy of political support aimed at providing economic aid and military assistance to states threatened by communist subversion or domestic instability. It had engendered by 1950 a string of European successes that included the Marshall Plan, the Berlin airlift (1948), and the defeat of communist insurgents in Greece.

The Far East constituted a decidely less important arena of American containment than Western Europe. Strategically it was expected to be a less significant area in a future world war, as it had been in the last. A ground war against communists on the Asian land mass was far from a welcome prospect. The central strategic interest was felt to be, as it had been in World War II, the control of the Pacific. For this purpose the American "defense perimeter," as defined in Acheson's famous address at the National Press Club (January 12, 1950), ran from the Ryukyus to include Japan and the Phillippines. The political situations in China, later Taiwan, Indochina, and Korea were too uncertain and too peripheral to justify a full American commitment.

Acheson's assessment represented a widely accepted policy. MacArthur, the Joint Chiefs of Staff (JCS), the State Department, and a number of congressional leaders had all been consulted in its formulation. Asia was clearly not the Truman administration's crucial concern; Europe remained the American focal point. Of the many "trouble spots" around the world identified by American intelligence reports as potential objects of Soviet attack, Secretary Acheson held that Greece, Turkey, Iran, Germany, and Indochina (due to its importance to France) had a higher priority and represented a *greater* U.S. commitment than Korea. Thus U.S. global strategic policy was conceived in World War II terms: defending the continental United States and its vital European allies against an all-out Russian attack and maintaining a strategic depth through control of the two world oceans. Other areas, such as mainland Asia, were secondary. They would be aided to the extent possible, but their defense was not necessarily America's problem.

The American government viewed South Korea through China-policy lenses. Reflecting their sense of the domestic and peninsular strains to which South Korea was subject, KMAG commented on June 15, 1950 that "Korea is threatened with the same disaster that befell China."[10] American postwar policy toward Korea had replicated a number of the assumptions that guided our policy toward China. At the Cairo Conference, the Allied leaders planned for a four-power trusteeship (US, USSR, China, UK) for Korea designed to lead to its eventual independence. Instead, the rush of events in 1945 produced the American and Russian occupation zones divided along the 38th Parallel. The American-Russian joint commission to effect a unified Korea soon ran into a stalemate. The Russians rejected the American proposal for a national legislature (which would be dominated by the more populous South); the

Americans rejected a Russian proposal for an equal, bilateral commission. The United States in 1947 turned the matter over to a UN Temporary Commission on Korea to persuade North and South Korea to hold a nationwide election. In the meantime, the president had requested a thorough assessment of U.S. interests in the Korean peninsula. The JCS report by General Wedemeyer addressing this question (September 1947) stressed that since South Korea was militarily inferior to North Korea, Korea constituted a "strategic liability" in the event of a future world war that involved operations in Asia. And General Lemnitzer, as late as May 10, 1950, commented: "South Korea was not regarded as of any particular value to the overall American strategic position in the Far East—a point to which the Ambassador [Muccio, to South Korea] agreed." Nevertheless, unless the United States initiated "an elaborate program of economic, political and cultural rehabilitation," U.S. prestige and our cooperation with more important areas (Japan) would suffer.[11] Yet, according to Rusk, inflation, mismanagement, and corruption were wrecking the economy.[12] Ambassador Jessup, on an inspection tour in January 1950, reported that even Rhee saw inflation and the communist insurgency as the key threats. Jessup added that Rhee's dictatorial style threatened both democratic freedoms and the political stability of the regime. Thus South Korea faced, in the view of U.S. policymakers, two threats: first, a world atomic war in which South Korea would be at most a tertiary theater; second, domestic turmoil. The United States could do nothing special to protect Korea from the first. The second had to be confronted locally, by the South Koreans, although with indirect American help. The United States set about providing substantial military and economic aid and using it as a means of badgering Rhee into political (fairer elections) and financial reform, lest Rhee follow the path to disaster Jiang Gaishek (Chiang Kai-shek) had paved in China.

In this context, the lack of eagerness or urgency shown by KMAG and the U.S. Embassy for heavy weapons, including tanks, and the priority they placed on controlling inflation, corruption, and what would later be called political or civic action become quite understandable. South Korea's army had difficulty absorbing the equipment it already had; it needed training. South Korea's economy was caught in a runaway inflation; it needed organization more than it needed dollars. Rhee's forces already had demonstrated an ability to crush his domestic opposition; his government needed consent, local level support, and time to train a professional bureaucracy. None of these apparently pressing threats could have been met by tanks or aircraft or patrol boats.

A Drastic Reappraisal: NSC 68

While American advisors in Korea struggled through 1949 and early 1950 to implement the political and economic "containment" Washington had committed itself to since 1947, global American strategy underwent a drastic reappraisal. This reappraisal was to have few effects on South Korean policy or programs before June 25, 1950, but it would be the source of the unexpected American counterintervention North Korea experienced in the weeks after June 25.

As early as March 1949, the National Security Council (NSC) staff, alarmed by Soviet actions over Berlin, had produced a memorandum on "Measures Required to Achieve U.S. Objectives with Respect to the USSR." It advocated a substantial buildup in armed forces and a stronger set of policies toward the USSR. But State Department disapproval, primarily from Kennan and Bohlen, delayed its acceptance. Following the Soviet explosion of an atomic bomb in August 1949, Mao's victory in China, and mounting domestic criticism, led by the Republicans, of the administration's "failures" to contain international communism and root out domestic "communism," Acheson obtained Truman's approval to begin a more thorough reappraisal and to shunt aside the two leading advocates (Kennan and Bohlen) of a more circumscribed, cautious, and flexible containment policy. [13] NSC-68, the result of the reappraisal, called for a substantial revision of Kennan's containment policy. Military response was placed in the front rank, replacing Kennan's emphasis on political and economic support, and the defense perimeter was globally extended from its European anchor to the very borders of the Soviet bloc, drawing in effect a worldwide line between the "free world" and "Soviet totalitarianism." Truman accepted the report's strategic posture on April 7, 1950, but to extend our perimeter in this fashion, a massive increase in defense spending would become necessary. On this fiscal stumbling block the policy temporarily faltered. There would be no more "losses of China"; Korea too was now on the front lines. Even though Truman, Acheson, and all of the service secretaries had accepted by June 1950 the strategy NSC-68 put forth, no programs had been agreed upon to implement it. Moreover, little awareness of this change in presidential views had spread through the American government. Senator Tom Connally, in an interview in *U.S. News and World Report* (May 1950), dismissed an attack on Korea as "not a casus belli" for the United States. Assistant Secretary Rusk, at the State Department, demurred, but even Rusk failed to make clear how large a change in policy was occurring. [14] John Foster Dulles, on a tour of South Korea, was instructed to help repair the impact of Connally's disavowal by promising the Korean National Assembly that Korea's defense was also ours. Nevertheless, the American decision taken almost immediately by Truman and his close advisor Acheson and confirmed by the Blair House Meetings on June 25 (Washington) came as a surprise to the American public, to the U.S. mission in Korea, and to General MacArthur. It must have been an even more astonishing surprise to the North Koreans and Soviets.

The assumptions behind U.S. global strategy had shifted at the top, but, somewhat ironically, in early 1950 there were substantial signs of success in what heretofore had been the U.S. strategy for meeting the primarily domestic threats to the Rhee regime. Despite the logistical problems of the army, the guerrillas were suppressed in April, freeing units of the army for further training; the Congress had finally passed the stalled Korean aid bill (as a rider to a bill for increased aid to the Republic of China); financial reforms were promised; an election had recently been held with considerably less overt repression than that characterizing the previous one; and the UN Commission was making renewed overtures to North Korea. Nevertheless, in the zero-sum rivalry of the Korean peninsula, these southern successes constituted losses and threats to the North. Containing the domestic threats to the South activated the external threat from the North that had heretofore seemed secondary.

Motives and Opportunities: North Korean and Soviet

Some aspects of American and South Korean intelligence and policymaking prior to the outbreak of the war remain ambiguous. For example, scholars have yet to examine MacArthur's secret intelligence gathering operation in South Korea—from which much of Washington's information derived. Nevertheless, the American-South Korean actions and policies are much an open record in comparison to those of the other side. It is on the matter of who (North Korea, the Soviet Union, China, all three?) planned the surprise and who of the three may have *been* surprised by the attack and the U.S. response that the current debate rages.[15] Less in dispute are the range of motives for the attack and for the use of surprise, and the opportunities both South Korean and American policy must have seemed to offer.

North Korea's Kim Il-Sung had two obvious motives for attack and a third which, although perhaps decisive, remains relatively obscure. One motive lay in a powerful demand for national unity stemming from an awareness of a common Korean culture and from a history of defense against Chinese aggression and resistance to Japanese colonial oppression. The postwar division of the country was a bitter outcome to Northern and Southern leaders; unifying the country would place a fundamental stamp of legitimacy on the government that achieved it. Furthermore, before the war the peninsula had constituted a natural economic unit, the agricultural South complementing the more industrial North. The postwar division created substantial obstacles to the progress of the two economies, intensifying their dependence on outside powers. These motives were enough to make Kim request Soviet support for an invasion of the South. In addition, Kim may have also felt domestic pressures that drove him to decide to attack in late June. Following Rhee's campaign against communists in the South, their leader, Pak Hon Yong, fled to North Korea. This eminent national communist leader was given a prominent position in the North Korean government as well as in the all-Korean communist movement. Pak thus became a sustantial rival to Kim himself. He kept close ties to the guerrilla movement in the South, it being the major source of his influence in the North. When in the spring of 1950, the South Korean guerrillas faced imminent suppression, Pak had a strong incentive to attempt their rescue. Kim had an equally strong incentive to not be outnationalized by Pak.

The South seemed to offer an opportunity for an easy surprise. North Korean leaders were fully aware of the strains in the South's armed forces, economy, and government. They felt that Rhee's repression of a wide range of leftist factions would have left the North with major pockets of support in the South. Rhee's successes in stabilizing his regime in the spring of 1950 may have inspired the Northern leaders to quick and decisive action. A rapid and surprising strike while Rhee's forces were still mopping up the remnants of guerrilla bands in the southern reaches of South Korea carried every prospect of success as well as every sense of urgency.

In late 1949, Kim had secured Stalin's and Mao's approval for his attack on South Korea. Stalin had, according to Khrushchev's later account, been skeptical. After Kim assured Stalin that the "first poke would touch off an internal explosion in South Korea," Stalin raised the objection that the Americans would jump in. Stalin was persuaded that a "swift war" leading to a fait accompli (as Kim argued) and a war fought as "an internal matter" of the Korean people (as Mao believed) would together rule out an American counterintervention. Mao's comments appeared to reflect a close following of the evolution of American Asian policy, including the very ambiguous American commitment to South Korea's security and the Truman administration's experience in the Chinese civil war. Of course, neither Mao nor Kim was aware of the new commitment to militant containment NSC-68 represented. Mao's and Kim's arguments underscored the importance of a surprise attack. Stalin accepted their analysis and stepped up military supplies in early 1950.[16] For Stalin, agreeing to Kim's request represented no grand strategic initiative. South Korea appeared to him as a target of opportunity. The apparent weakness of the South Korean Army, the potential for a guerrilla rising, the element of surprise, and the lack of a U.S. commitment to South Korea all made Kim's request for additional arms and Soviet acquiescence seem a small favor to grant. Embarrassing the United States politically, extending communism, improving the Soviet strategic position vis-à-vis Japan were not of themselves great gains, but the apparent cost of supporting the North Koreans was proportionately low. The Soviets, unlike the Americans, appeared to appreciate the value of "limited war" in a Cold War stalemate.

Then Kim, to further his objective of achieving a surprise, engaged in

deception. He delayed deployments along the parallel until the last moment
to avoid warning the South Koreans or the Americans of the timing of his
attack. But since he also felt a popular rising would greet his troops, he
enunciated the "unification elections by August 15" promise.

However, despite the close supervision Russian military advisors exercised
over the North Korean Army, there is some reason to suspect that the timing
of the June 25 attack came as a surprise to Moscow. The Soviet Union was
completely unprepared to support Kim's propaganda for a "defensive" war
on the days following the attack, and the USSR had not returned to the Security
Council to veto a UN response. Stalin probably had agreed to an attack for
later in the summer. Kim decided—for local, Korean reasons—when the
trigger of the gun the Soviets had supplied should be pulled.

More importantly, all *three* allies seem to have failed to anticipate the
American response. Although the United States was only prepared for (but
had sought to avoid) another "China," Truman's response together with that
of Acheson reflected their very recent acceptance of the premises of NSC-
68. The 38th Parallel was now *within* our effective defense perimeter. MacArthur
was ordered to support the South Koreans.

*   *   *   *

Thus the surprises of June 25, 1950 were complex and asymmetrical. The
four major actors—South Korea, the United States, North Korea, and the
Soviet Union—each had different expectations respecting a possible North
Korean attack on South Korea and the likely South Korean-American response
to such an attack.

Nature of Surprise	**Strategic Surprise** June 25, 1950 *N. Korean Attack*		**Unanticipated Surprise** *U.S.-S.K. Response*	
	South Korea- North Korea	U.S.- USSR	USSR- U.S.	N.K.- S.K.
Whether	+	−	−	+
What	+	−	+	−
Where	+	−	+	+
When	−	−	(−)	+
Why	+	−	−	+

(Structure of table drawn from Alexander George, "Warning and Response: Theory and Practice")

  − indicates surprise
  + indicates no surprise

The South Korean Army and Ministry of Defense did argue in 1950 and earlier that North Korea would attack. They also produced military estimates of North Korean forces closer to the actual figures than those produced by American intelligence. In addition, they accurately sensed the North Koreans' motives, largely because they held the same desire for national unity. But even though they expected an increased threat in the summer of 1950, Kim's concealment of his troop deployments successfully shielded the *timing* of the attack. Moreover, South Korean warnings had become less than credible to their American patrons. Their motives as well as their competence were suspect. On their own, there were few preparations they could take that would have been effective: training could not be greatly improved while an extensive counterguerrilla war raged; their economy could stand no further military expense; a professional army and civic polity could not be fashioned overnight to meet an emergency.

The Americans saw the threat to South Korea from a fundamentally different perspective and even that perspective was fragmented and unfocussed. As the United States perceived it, the threat that North Korea presented was remote, indirect, and derivative of the larger Soviet threat. The United States did not expect the Soviet bloc to initiate a global war against the West. If they were to strike, Korea was not judged to be the most likely spot. The Soviet bloc was not judged to be ready to confront the West in 1950. All these were correct estimations of whether, what, where, and when the Soviets might attack the United States. None were relevant to the events of 1950. The United States did not fully appreciate *why* the Soviets might support North Korea in a *limited war;* the United States felt the Soviets were deterred from a global war by the American atomic arsenal. As importantly, the United States seemed to *hope* that the Soviets would not support a North Korean attack. South Korea truly had enough problems of its own at home. Last, the United States had not resolved whether it would *want* to respond to a North Korean-Soviet attack on South Korea. The Kennan strategy of containment envisaged primarily political threats that should be met by political-economic means; Korea was to show that the USSR would support the use of force in limited wars outside its bloc where expected costs were low. NSC-68 envisaged an aggressive Soviet imperialism expanding by forceful means that should be met by an American, front-line military response. This grand strategy had not become accepted, government-wide policy before June 1950, but it did govern Truman's response following the North Korean attack.

The North Koreans, naturally, planned the attack, the forces it would include, and where and when it would strike. But they also estimated that they faced a purely civil war, one in which leftist South Korean nationalists would rise to welcome them. They too were "surprised" by their lack of support in the South and by the U.S. counterintervention.

The Soviet Union accepted North Korea's proposals for a summer attack after being convinced that strategic surprise would guarantee a rapid victory in what would be accepted as a civil war. They had a rough sense of *what* forces America had available to aid South Korea, but they were as surprised as the American bureaucracy and public by Truman's rapid commitment to support the South militarily. They had naturally assumed that U.S. declared policy—Acheson's defense perimeter, past policy in China—and the public rationale behind that policy ruled out military intervention in a "civil war." Moreover, the timing of the attack, and thus the U.S. counterintervention, caught Moscow unprepared, for Kim Il-Sung appears to have jumped the gun.

These complex and asymmetric surprises may have had special roots in other than the *faulty intelligence, inappropriate preconceptions, poor governmental coordination,* and *successful deception* that in the past have often characterized instances of strategic surprise. These special roots lie in the problems of alliance management and, most especially, in the problems of an *unequal* alliance between a superpower and an economically less-developed, underinstitutionalized state.

In an alliance, perceived threats are rarely identical. Differences in geostrategic position raise asymmetries of concern. The closer the threat to one ally the greater the attention it will tend to devote to it. When security depends on the alliance, these differences tend to produce conflicting assessments of threats and of ways to counter them and thus less than optimal coordination of policy.

However, this general alliance dilemma is overshadowed by the much greater strains produced by an alliance between a developed superpower and a less-developed client state. The alliance between North Korea, China, and the USSR reveals some of these problems. The stakes were vastly different: for North Korea—national unification and survival; for China—regional influence and security; for the USSR—global balances and alliance commitments. The USSR was prepared to support North Korea but not to defend it. Also the USSR probably failed to see the importance of local intranationalist conflicts between Kim and Pak that determined the timing of the outbreak of hostilities. This sort of fundamental factionalism, raising issues of the very nature of the state and of the social system, had not been present in the USSR since the 1920s.

More telling are the misperceptions characterizing the U.S.-South Korean alliance. Compared to South Korea, North Korea was an institutionalized, centralized state. South Korea still represented a faction in pursuit of a "legitimate monopoly of violence." Even *if* the United States had accepted the defense of Korea as a central commitment in U.S. global strategy, South Korea's institutions—its inflation-wracked economy, its political system—were probably incapable of becoming prepared to meet an *external* threat in

1950. Only by commiting U.S. troops specifically to the defense of Korea could Korean security have been enhanced; but South Korea, having recently emerged from colonial oppression, deemed this solution another form of occupation and unacceptable as such. Moreover, the American government wished to avoid embroiling American military forces in the domestic conflict that rocked the highly unstable South Korean polity. The United States was understandably uncertain in these circumstances with respect to what or whom should be protected since South Korea had not yet established a fully legitimate or effective polity in the eyes of its population. The warnings of the Rhee regime were thus considerably discounted by Washington.

June 25, 1950 can thus be seen as a complex and asymmetrical instance of strategic surprises. The events of June 1950 demonstrate many special features, but they also may indicate wider lessons of surprise in alliances between less-developed countries and developed superpowers. The instability of the former when combined with strategic dependence on the wavering attention and commitment of the latter may make susceptibility to surprise an endemic condition of First World-Third World alliances.

CHINESE INTERVENTION IN THE KOREAN WAR, OCTOBER 1950–JANUARY 1951[17]

MacArthur's brilliant surprise attack on Seoul's port, Inchon, enabled the UN command to advance from the port at Pusan to which they had been driven by the North Korean attack. Despite continuing concern over the possibility of intervention by the People's Republic of China or the Soviet Union, MacArthur's mandate was extended to include the reunification of Korea. He began a massive drive north, crushing the North Korean divisions in his path. Alarm mounted in China as MacArthur's soldiers headed toward the Yalu border. Planning for a counterintervention began. Eventually the Chinese Peoples Liberation Army (PLA) intervened in Korea in a three phase movement. The First Phase went from October 14–16, 1950, when Chinese "volunteers" began to cross the Yalu in large numbers, through October 26, when these forces first attacked the South Korean and American units advancing toward the Yalu, until November 7 when all attacks by the "volunteers" abruptly ceased. The PLA paused to absorb the lessons of the first contact with American forces. Confident of their ability to defeat the UN command, the PLA struck again (the Second Phase Offensive) and sent MacArthur's forces on a precipitous retreat to the 38th Parallel. This phase began on November 26 and ended on December 11. Following a pause to permit supplies to catch up with the soldiers, the Third Phase Offensive began on January 1, 1951. When it started the UN command was defending a line just above the 38th Parallel. By the end of this offensive (January 9), the UN command had been pushed back and had evacuated Seoul before finally recovering to and holding a line just south of the 38th Parallel.

PLA OFFENSIVES

First Phase	October 14–16 to November 7	Surprise probe
Second Phase	November 26–December 11	Massive surprise attack
Third Phase	January 1–9, 1951	Drive to the 38th Parallel

The First Phase Offensive constituted a surprise for MacArthur, for the UN command, and for the United States, but it was not a major surprise. Despite numerous threats emanating from Peking that Chinese forces would attack if the UN crossed the 38th Parallel or approached the Yalu border, the United States had discounted these warnings and had assumed that the Chinese would not dare to attack. The presence of Chinese soldiers thus surprised MacArthur and Washington, but their withdrawal from combat after a series of skirmishes so fully conformed to American expectations of China's military capacity that no important lessons were drawn from this episode. MacArthur proceeded with his drive toward the Yalu as planned. The Second Phase Offensive at the end of November was the major shock the UN command suffered. MacArthur expected to encounter additional Chinese "volunteers" but the *scale* and the *mode* of their attack took him and his command completely by surprise. By the time of the Third Phase Offensive, the lessons of PLA warfare had been learned. Ridgway, now field commander of the UN line near the parallel, was pleased to have averted another rout.

Surprises?

MacArthur, in his *Reminiscences,* denied that his command was caught by surprise in the First and Second Phase Offensives. Instead, he argued, his advance to the Yalu constituted a "reconnaissance in force," a necessary strategic gamble.[18] He could not withdraw and still fulfill the objective of unifying Korea set by Washington and the UN. He lacked the troops to hold a line across the most narrow but mountainous section of North Korea, for a roadless mountain chain split the terrain. He planned instead to advance to a defensible line along the Yalu, thereby either overwhelming North Korean troops together with their Chinese volunteers or provoking a counterattack from a possibly large concentration of Chinese forces and then rapidly withdrawing. If the latter, he then anticipated weakening the Chinese counterattack by overextending its supply lines, leaving it vulnerable to defeat further south. This explanation has been challenged on strategic grounds. Critics then and later doubted the wisdom of advancing the Eighth Army (General Walker) up the west coast, the X Corps (General Almond) up the east, and splitting the X Corps into three widely separated thrusts along single file roads in narrow valleys. MacArthur, they seem to suggest, appeared to be springing a trap by putting his foot in it. However, the alternatives recommended—including attempting to hold the narrow waist of North Korea—*did* raise the strategic problems MacArthur noted. Strong evidence indicating that MacArthur, with Washington's reluctant concurrence, conceived of the operation as a mopping-up exercise—a continuation of the rout that followed the landing at Inchon, can be found in MacArthur's statements made in October and November and in the army's reactions to the first news of Chinese attacks.

At the Wake Island conference, which brought MacArthur and Truman together for the first time (October 15), MacArthur replied to Truman's question, "What are the chances for Chinese or Soviet intervention?" with: "Very little. . . . We are no longer fearful of their intervention . . . the Chinese have 300,000 men in Manchuria. Of these probably not more than 100–125,000 are distributed along the Yalu River. Only 50–60,000 could be gotten across the Yalu River. . . . Now that we have bases for the air force in Korea, if the Chinese tried to get down to Pyongyang there would be the greatest slaughter."[19] Truman accepted MacArthur's estimates; JCS Chairman Bradley asked him how soon he could spare a division for assignment in Europe. Beginning on that day and during the next two weeks, 180,000 to 228,000 PLA troops crossed into North Korea.[20] On October 28, General Willoughby, chief of the Far East command's military intelligence branch, issued a daily intelligence summary that read, "From a tactical viewpoint, with victorious U.S. divisions in full deployment, it would appear that the auspicious time for such intervention (Chinese) has long since passed."[21] The PLA's First Phase Offensive had begun three days before.

MacArthur, of course, was aware of the presence of Chinese regulars in North Korea before the Second Phase Offensive began. At first he cautioned Washington against prematurely concluding that a Chinese intervention had occurred, but three days later (November 7) he labelled the First Phase Offensive a "massive Chinese intervention" and requested authority to bomb the bridges across the Yalu. (He was then authorized to bomb the Korean ends of the bridges.) But the Chinese withdrawal between the First and Second Phase Offensives soon restored MacArthur's confidence. He decided to carry out his plan to reach the Yalu and urged his divisions to move as rapidly as possible. He promised the soldiers in the field an "end-the-war" offensive: "The United Nations' massive compression envelopment in North Korea against the Red Armies operating there is now approaching its decisive effort"; further, "Tell the boys . . . they are going to eat their Christmas dinners at home."[22] Neither of these statements suggest a "reconnaissance in force." They suggest an expectation of easy victory following a successful pincer movement, reuniting the 8th Army and the X Corps along the Yalu. If

MacArthur's estimates of Chinese forces had been correct this would not have been a fanciful and ultimately tragic strategy. But they were not. Far East command estimated Chinese forces in North Korea on November 21 at "44,851 to 70,051" facing the 100,000 front line troops of the UN command (440,000 including all support troops). In fact, 180,000 soldiers of PLA faced the 8th Army; 120,000 faced the X Corps; and 65,000 North Koreans (twelve divisions) had recovered sufficiently to take part in the upcoming battle.[23] Furthermore, when word of the first Chinese counterattacks reached MacArthur, Almond, and Walker, their response was not an order to withdraw (the Chinese trap having been sprung), but to press on toward the Yalu.

Nature of Surprise	Chinese Intervention Against The UN (U.S.) Command	
	First Phase	Second Phase
Whether	−	+
What	−	−
Where	+	+
When	+	+
Why	+ −	−

− indicates surprise
+ indicates no surprise

Clearly, there are two surprises to be explained. Why was the presence of Chinese forces not discovered prior to the First Phase? Why was the size and effectiveness of the Chinese forces not appreciated before the Second Phase Offensive sent the UN command reeling back to the 38th Parallel?

Sources of the Two Surprises: Ambiguous Warnings, Commitments, Expectations, Concealment, MacArthur, and Cold War Politics

One of the oft-noted ironies in the surprises the United States suffered is that the Peoples Republic of China (PRC) had made a determined effort in September and October to warn the United States that it would intervene in force should U.S. troops cross the 38th Parallel in pursuit of the crumbling North Korean Army.[24] However, without disputing Chinese intentions to warn the United States, one must note that the warnings arrived in Washington loaded with ambiguity.

The first intimations of the PRC's attitude toward the war in Korea were contradictory. The U.S. consul-general in Hong Kong (Wilkinson) passed a warning, derived from sources inside the PRC, that Foreign Minister Zhou Enlai (Chou En-lai) had indicated China would not "stand by" and wait until

North Korean forces were pushed into Manchuria. The consul-general further noted eight days later (September 12) that Peking was moving 250,000 soldiers from southern China (opposite Taiwan) to northern China.[25] Yet eight days after that, the American ambassador in India reported that the Indian ambassador in Peking, K. M. Pannikar, had reported that "China by herself will not interfere in the conflict and try to pull others' chestnuts out of the fire" unless the UN crosses the 38th Parallel *and* the Soviet Union intervenes, setting off a "WW III."[26] This view was then reinforced by a telegram from Hong Kong (Wilkinson, September 22) reporting that Zhou Enlai had no plans for intervention in North Korea.[27] On September 27, the British Foreign Office conveyed to Washington a new transmission from Pannikar. This indicated an increased Chinese commitment to indirect support of North Korea. However, the British also labelled Pannikar "a volatile and unreliable reporter."[28]

These exchanges preceded the most important warning from Zhou Enlai—his message to Pannikar of October 3 that PRC forces would intervene in North Korea if UN armed forces crossed the 38th Parallel, but that the PRC would not intervene if only South Korean forces crossed the parallel.[29] This was seen as a bluff by the American ambassador in Moscow; Wilkinson, in Hong Kong, judged it to be "propaganda." The Norwegian and Swedish diplomats in Peking reported a somewhat different version of the warnings—one that included a PRC demand for a role in deciding the future of Korea.[30] To compound this confusion, the U.S. ambassador in New Delhi minuted that the government of India had changed its view and now (October 21) thought that their ambassador had been the dupe of an attempted Chinese "bluff."[31]

Nevertheless, these warnings disturbed a number of officials in Washington, among them Edmund Clubb, director of the State Department's Office of Chinese Affairs. But he and others felt these warnings should not, and could not, be heeded. Clubb argued that the United States should not back down from the commitment to the UN to unify Korea on a democratic basis—a commitment that dated back to 1947. MacArthur also argued an "established commitment" position, but less in UN terms than in terms of liberation from communist tyranny, avoiding another "Munich," and fulfilling the objectives of his last great campaign. Chinese warnings were too late and too ambiguous to alter this build-up of aspiration and commitment.

The CIA helped persuade others to discount these warnings for other reasons. In a memorandum written on October 12, 1950, two days before the Wake Island Conference, the CIA estimated that the PRC had the *capability* of intervening "effectively, but not necessarily decisively." But despite Zhou's statements and the evidence of troop movements, the CIA concluded that "there are no convincing indications of an actual Chinese communist intention to resort to full scale intervention." The decisive factors governing American

expectations of Chinese behavior included: supposed Chinese fear of a war
with the United States that would encourage "anticommunist forces" in the
PRC and thus endanger "the regime's very existence," to the loss of prospective membership in the UN, to military losses they would sustain from
American air power in North Korea, to the fact that the best time for intervention had already passed (North Korean forces now being in a precipitous
retreat). These factors, the CIA argued, outweighed the PRC's positive in-
ducements to intervene. These included the enhanced prestige communist
China and world communism would gain from a UN defeat and the retention
of the Yalu power stations. Even if the intervention failed to stop the UN, it
would provide an excuse for domestic failures, add an impetus to Asian anti-
Westernism, and tie up the Western bloc in a costly war. Therefore, covert
action, not overt intervention, could be seen as the likely PRC policy.[32] These
Washington expectations, one should note, are nearly identical to the ones
MacArthur presented at Wake. Thus the ease with which he convinced the
president, General Bradley, and others is understandable. Most of the discussion on Wake concerned postwar reconstruction. Moreover, throughout
these discussions Truman and Acheson assumed the Chinese would realize
that the United States had no aggressive intentions toward the PRC. Each of
these expectations was to prove false.

Although the Far East command's daily intelligence summary (October 20)
estimated that 400,000 Chinese troops were in place along the Manchurian
border and although aerial reconnaissance detected heavy truck convoys in
their vicinity, no positive movements of soldiers were spotted. Accordingly,
on October 20 the Far East command issued its plan for the withdrawal of
U.S. forces that would follow the expected victory.

The First Phase Offensive (October 26–November 7) constituted a surprise
regarding *whether* the PRC would intervene and whether they had forces in
North Korea. It settled the question of whether units of the PLA had entered
North Korea. But the *PRC's intentions* (why), the *scale* of the intervention,
and the *mode* of warfare (what) still remained obscure and subject to contention
during the lull that followed the Chinese attack in late October.

Stronger warnings of a large intervention continued to arrive in Washington
and in Tokyo (Far East command). Wilkinson (Hong Kong) forwarded reports
to that effect on October 31; Rankin (ambassador in Taiwan) reported the
same on November 6, although his warning was not transmitted to the Defense
Department. Both relied on trusted, anticommunist, Chinese sources. The
State Department, assessing Chinese domestic propaganda, noted a war fever
(November 3). John P. Davies concluded that a full scale intervention was
underway and urged that UN forces be prepared for the defensive (November
7). Clubb argued similar points and recommended consolidation rather than
an advance, as did the British Foreign Office. The CIA (*N.I.E. 2*, November

8) weighed in with a revised estimate that 30–40,000 PLA were already in North Korea and that 200,000 more could be brought in rapidly—a force sufficient to push the UN back.[33]

Expectations *were* changing in Washington. On November 8, the JCS, citing previous restrictions should significant Chinese forces be encountered, ordered MacArthur to stop his drive to destroy the North Korean Army by occupying the whole of North Korea.[34] But MacArthur persuaded the JCS to change their instructions in order to avoid injury to the morale of his command and in order to avoid another "Munich" concession to "international lawlessness."

Three factors help account for this reversal: the PLA's success in concealment, MacArthur, and domestic politics. In Acheson's phrase, following the ending of the First Phase Offensive, the PLA "seemed to have vanished from the face of the earth."[35] In fact, the United States still remained unaware of how many PLA forces were in North Korea. The U.S. high estimate for mid-November was 70,000, but actually 300,000 soldiers were hidden in the rugged mountains and steep valleys between MacArthur's forces and the Yalu. Beginning on October 12, PLA armies met North Korean guides at the Yalu who led them under cover of darkness into the forested Korean highlands. Tracks in the snow were brushed over. Transport was limited to Mongolian ponies and rations to what the individual soldier could carry. Weapons consisted of captured American (from Kuomintang forces during 1945–1949) and Japanese rifles and mortars. During the day the armies rested and hid. U.S. air reconnaissance could find no trace of these forces. When daylight marches became necessary in preparation for the Second Phase Offensive, forest fires were set to cover the movement of large columns. Thorough organization, despite primitive equipment and communication (bugles), made these forces disciplined and mobile. Experienced officers inspired by Mao's military doctrine practiced strikingly effective tactics of encirclement, surprise, and the massed charge. On November 24, the Chinese struck the divided UN forces, whose dispositions were known to them from scouting parties.

Nevertheless, Washington *had* become concerned by early November and had sought to impose caution on MacArthur. Its decision to accede (nevertheless) to MacArthur's plan for an all-out offensive reflected the peculiar relationship that had developed between the government and its leading proconsul. Partly because many in the administration were awed by MacArthur's military record—he had been chief of staff of the army while many members of the JCS had been junior officers, by his spectacular success at Inchon despite long odds, and by a reluctance to tamper with the command decisions of a general in the field—Washington's orders took the form of suggestions and positions apparently meant to be negotiated. On top of this, the lull between the First and Second Phase Offensives again seemed to confirm his judgment. The CIA revised its estimate (*N.I.E. 2/1;* November 24) to conclude that a PLA "holding operation" was likely but that a plan for "major offensive operations has not been demonstrated."[36]

Last, the domestic politics of the Cold War *could* have influenced Truman's decisions regarding MacArthur. The Democrats had just (November 7) suffered a marked reduction in their majorities in the House and Senate. McCarthy's attacks on domestic subversion resounded throughout the electorate. Curbing the Republican Right's favorite general and facing the prospect of hearing his "Munich" denunciations could not have been welcome. At the very least, a strong consensus among the JCS against MacArthur's plan would have been needed to relieve this general in apparent full flush of victory. This was lacking, and retaining *this* general also meant accepting his ground strategy.

The Peoples Republic: Opportunity, Motivations, and Surprise

China's opportunity to achieve a strategic surprise lay in MacArthur's strategy, the Korean terrain, and the tradition of the Peoples Liberation Army. Without MacArthur's division of his command—the 8th Army on the west coast, the X Corps on the other side of steep mountains on the east coast, with each unit separated by high ridges between narrow valleys—the PLA's achievement would have been impossible. On a plain their concealment could not have succeeded. Without the experience of years of warfare and guerrilla operations, the PLA would not have been trained into the *coordinated,* mobile "mass-guerrilla" army it had become. However, these mass-guerrilla tactics had certain limitations. With each soldier carrying only three days' rations and with the army lacking adequate motor transport, the Second Phase Offensive was unable to catch the retreating Americans.

More intriguing are Chinese motivations for the intervention and for the use of surprise. Despite the fact that Truman, Acheson, Marshall, and the JCS never contemplated an attack on the PRC, it is clear that China intervened largely to prevent what it thought might be an invasion of China through Manchuria. Zhou Enlai's statements affirming a reluctance to pull "others' chestnuts out of the fire" together with his October 3 warning which specifically excluded a South Korean crossing of the 38th Parallel as a casus belli indicate that it was probably the threat to China, not to Korea, presented by U.S. forces that concerned the Peking leadership. Peking had planned to aid North Korea, to resist American and South Korean arms, but only indirectly. Direct and massive intervention resulted from the threat the UN (U.S.) advances seemed to present to Manchuria. Although the United States assured China that it had no aggressive intent toward the Peoples Republic, Chinese leaders had noted aggressive statements by MacArthur (promising domination of the east Asian coast) and by Secretary Matthews (calling for war against communism to "compel peace"). Even though Truman required each to retract, the Chinese also noted MacArthur's continuing bellicose statements, his seeming ability to expand the war from South to North Korea and override restraints. Would the Americans truly stop at the Yalu? Could they control their general?

Achieving surprise must have then seemed both difficult and important: difficult due to the previous warnings designed to deter the Americans; important due to American military resources and prestige. Concealment and misinformation planted by PLA prisoners taken in the First Phase Offensive were employed. The lull between offensives, when they cautiously waited to see what the U.S. reaction might be, answered their questions—the Americans were advancing; the surprise would work.

*   *   *   *

Among the many interlocking factors that shaped the October and November surprises, two underlying features particularly call for comment. The first was the U.S. misreading of Chinese capabilities. The Peoples Republic, in Washington's view, was wracked by powerful anticommunist movements endangering the existence of the regime; it needed a war to legitimate domestic failures; it was incapable of intervening without Soviet air support. The descriptions bore little resemblance to the army, state, and party, even in 1950, that had spent twenty-five years in continuous struggle, liberated substantial areas of China from Japanese rule, and routed the American-equipped Kuomintang. There appears to have been an amalgamation of Chinese, and apparently of all less technically developed societies, into an image of the less competent. General Almond, commander of the X Corps, attempted to encourage the men of the 1st Battalion (32nd Infantry Regiment, 7th Division) after they had sustained heavy losses from PLA attacks (November 27) near the Chosin Reservoir: "The enemy who is delaying you for the moment is nothing more than remnants of Chinese divisions fleeing north. We're still attacking and we're going all the way to the Yalu. Don't let a bunch of Chinese laundrymen stop you."[37] This was not an instance of simple racism or simple national chauvinism. This sort of military contempt did not apply to the Japanese, and the Second and Third Phase Offensives changed the American soldier's view of Chinese military capabilities rapidly.

The other side of that blinding sentiment led to an overestimate of technical, advanced machinery and organization. MacArthur expressed this best on November 17 in a conversation with Ambassador Muccio: "The general continued he was sure Chinese communists had sent 25,000, and certainly no more than 30,000 (one-tenth the actual number) soldiers across the border. They could not possibly have got more over with the surreptitiously covert means used. If they had moved in the open, they would have been detected by our air forces and our intelligence."[38]

THE BAY OF PIGS: APRIL 1961[39]

The two previous cases represent successful instances of surprise achieved by a less-developed, "Third World" state against a "First World" superpower, the United States. The Bay of Pigs invasion reverses these features. It constitutes an instance of attempted but spectacularly unsuccessful surprise by a "First World" state against a less-developed, "Third World" state.

The origins of the proposal to invade Cuba have been traced back to a three-hour discussion between Vice President Richard Nixon and Premier Fidel Castro during the latter's 1959 visit to the United States, for it was then that Nixon gained the impression that Castro leaned toward communism. Soon thereafter the vice president urged strong action against the Castro regime.[40] Increasingly clear signs of anti-Americanism in Castro's speeches and actions together with his close association with the Cuban communist party brought about Eisenhower's authorization on May 17, 1960 of a CIA plan to train, equip, and organize Cuban refugees as guerrillas to overthrow Castro's government. American officials hoped to repeat the success achieved in the ouster of Arbenz from Guatemala six years before. At the same time, the United States slashed the Cuban sugar quota and took diplomatic measures within the Organization of American States (OAS) to isolate Cuba. Candidate John Kennedy, not cognizant of the administration's plans, criticized the Republicans, in a statement drafted by his speechwriters, for failing to support Cuban "freedom fighters."[41] This caused an uproar. Nixon was chagrined that he could not reveal, and indeed had to deny, such plans. He then urged that the covert operation be conducted before November. Kennedy's liberal supporters were outraged, leading Kennedy to deny he meant military support and to maintain that he only intended moral support. Yet Kennedy, in the campaign as well as earlier, had put himself forward as a vigorous and militant opponent of communism, particularly of its threat to the Third World.

CIA planning was confined to a small group directed by the dazzlingly efficient Richard Bissell, "father" of the U-2 program and chief of the operations branch of the CIA. With the support of Allen Dulles, the guerrilla operations began to grow to a military invasion at brigade scale.

Kennedy was briefed on the program following his election and Eisenhower, thinking the plan was still limited to the refugee-guerrilla operation he had endorsed, gave the operation his stamp of approval.[42] Kennedy expressed his support for planning to proceed but made no commitment to final approval. Soon after the inauguration, at an NSC meeting on January 28, 1961, Allen Dulles and Richard Bissell gave the new administration a well-polished briefing on what was now called "Operation Trinidad." Bissell described plans for an amphibious and airborne assault by Cuban refugees on Trinidad, a town situated on the southern coast of Cuba where the Escambray Mountains meet the sea. The U.S. role was substantial. In addition to providing training and transport and overall direction, the United States was committed to giving air cover to the landing and to resupplying the invasion force by means of parachute drops. After expressing his warm interest in the project, Kennedy ordered a JCS assessment. A special subcommittee of the JCS gave it a "fair chance" in their overall evaluation *if* the invasion achieved complete surprise, *if* the landing by the brigade was accompanied by air strikes and air superiority, and *if* a popular rising against Castro followed the securing of the beachhead. Actually the JCS assessment was more pessimistic than "fair": (the estimated odds of its success were "30/70"), but their exclusion from operational control made their sense of responsibility for the operation less than wholehearted.[43]

Operating with a small and isolated staff, Bissell proceeded to organize a Cuban government in exile (domiciled in a New York hotel), training bases in Guatemala, a naval flotilla to transport and support the landing, and an air force of World War II vintage B-26s. The B-26s were chosen as the brigade's air force because they could be disguised to resemble Cuba's own B-26s (the "Cuban defectors" cover) and, should that cover fail, because they could pass for just the sort of planes Cuban exiles could have obtained from any of a number of Latin American air forces. The project was kept at the highest levels of secrecy in Washington. NSC members were briefed, but neither the State Department Cuban Desk nor the assessment branch of the CIA was informed. Secrecy, Bissell argued, was essential so that surprise would ensure that the landing could be made unopposed and a secure beachhead established. Secrecy was also essential so that the U.S. role could remain indirect, merely supportive, and ultimately deniable. Indeed, Kennedy had become concerned that the operation was appearing "too dramatic"; he vetoed an American parachute-drop to resupply the brigade. The "Trinidad Plan" included no airfield that could eventually accommodate the landings of the B-26s for the purposes of resupplying the brigade and refueling the aircraft. Thus, the invasion site was changed to the Bay of Pigs ("Operation Zapata"). The Bay of Pigs had such an airfield but it was also 80 miles from the Escambray Mountains into which the brigade was supposed to flee should the invasion fail.

However, secrecy began to slip almost from the start. Recruiting in Miami among the Cuban exile community inevitably spread the word of a planned invasion. Accounts flourished of the training camps in Guatemala. Indeed one of the eventual leaders of the brigade, Oliva, left Cuba *after* he heard about the prospect of an invasion by Cuban exiles supported by the United States.[44] American reporters from *U.S. News and World Report* and the *New*

York Times began in March 1961 to print stories of the coming invasion from information they gathered in Miami.

All the president's key advisors gave their approval of the invasion on April 4. These advisors were not unaware that unconventional operations entailed high risks, but many other and seemingly similar operations in the Third World had produced spectacular successes with low costs. The easily engineered collapses of Mossadegh in Iran and of Arbenz in Guatemala lent an aura of credibility to Bissell's vivid prognoses of the success of the operation.[45] Its military fitness had been certified by an impressive Marine, Colonel Hawkins (Bissell's advisor on amphibious warfare and military planning). Its political potential to stir up a Cuban rising had been guaranteed. At a meeting on March 29, and responding to skeptical questions from Kennedy, Bissell and Dulles had assured the White House advisors (according to Schlesinger) that the "active support" of more than a quarter of the Cuban population was likely (the Guatemala coup had appeared far less promising). Air superiority was said to be certain. Castro's MIG pilots were not yet trained; the T-33s he did have were considered to be mere "trainers" (their purpose in the U.S. Air Force). At worst, the operation's deniability in case of failure as well as the brigade's ability to escape into the Escambray Mountains had been assured by Bissell. After listening to a lengthy disquisition by Senator Fulbright, who was invited specially to this meeting to give a doubter an airing, Kennedy polled his top advisors and found them prepared to endorse the invasion.[46]

On April 17, 1961, the 1,400-man brigade moved ashore on the swampy coast of the Bay of Pigs. From the very beginning the plan developed disastrous problems. Rather than being deserted, the Bay of Pigs was occupied by workers (and militia) constructing a seaside resort. Coral reefs blocked the approaches to parts of the bay and later incapacitated one of the ships, many landing craft would not start (their motors had rusted), and the night landing delayed the unloading of the tanks until the next day. Then Kennedy cancelled the second wave of air strikes because the Cuban-defector cover for the B-26s snapped. Castro's T-33s established air control over the beach on the next morning. On the second day the brigade found itself surrounded by 20,000 Cuban soldiers. The brigade fought valiantly and inflicted large casualties on the Cuban militia and on Castro's regular military units, for the brigade had kept up a deadly fire on Castro's troops advancing along the confined roads bordered by dense swamp that were the only approaches to the beach. However, on the third day superior numbers of infantry, artillery, and tanks took their toll. Remnants of the brigade fled out to sea to waiting American ships; the rest fled into the swamps and were captured in the next few days.

A Failure in Surprise:
The U.S.-Sponsored Bay of Pigs Invasion of Cuba

Nature of Surprise	Cuban Perceptions
Whether	+
What	−
Where	−
When	+
Why	+

− indicates surprise
+ indicates no surprise

The costs of the Bay of Pigs to the United States were clear and substantial. The invasion tarnished the new administration's image among Third World nations and put U.S.-Cuban relations on a warlike footing for more than a decade. The flimsy and soon exposed cover story for the B-26 raids ("Cuban defectors") abused the reputation of Adlai Stevenson. Both the attempt and the failure of the invasion weakened the Kennedy presidency. The sources of the failure to achieve surprise and successful invasion, producing instead what Walt Rostow later called "the most screwed-up operation there has been," are complex.

Castro's Preparedness, The Cuban Target

The clearest reasons for the failure were Castro's awareness of an impending invasion and the measures he took to prepare against it. Castro *was* surprised by the *place,* the *size,* and the *disposition* of the invasion force. He had received no information that the Bay of Pigs was the likely target. He judged that the invasion force would be considerably larger—from 3,000 to 10,000. However, even though he did not know the exact date, he had noted the open secret that an invasion was being prepared from Miami and was likely to arrive in the spring. American press accounts beginning in late March placed him on special alert. He had stepped up the training of his regular army and the militia, particularly in the artillery by turning every new artilleryman into an instructor as soon as he completed the training course. He incorrectly judged that a single landing was unlikely (it would be subject to a rapid defeat); scattered beachheads seemed more probable. Therefore, he alerted militia units along the entire coast and stationed larger regular forces near especially likely spots—zones close to mountains such as the Escambray. He ordered his air force dispersed and placed on alert. When news arrived of strange ships off Oriente province (a CIA diversion that miscarried), Castro alerted all his units. They converged rapidly on the Bay of Pigs when the local militia in the area reported the arrival of an invading force.

However, even if Castro *had* been surprised by the landing, its chances of success would still have been low. His army of 200,000 had been well-trained and was deeply loyal to the new regime. No force of 1,400 could have over-awed them. Even effective air cover for the brigade would not have helped change such disproportionate odds, unless large numbers of Cubans had risen in support of the landing. This was far from likely. Although dissidents and bands of insurgents did exist, they were isolated and small. The official CIA estimate developed under Sherman Kent at the CIA's Board of National Estimates on Castro's political support described it as extensive and contin-ually increasing.[47]

Cuba was neither surprised—in ways it could not counter—nor potentially subject to the sort of operation Kennedy and his advisors approved. These, clearly, constitute the major reasons for its failure. Why Kennedy and his advisors approved the plan in the first place thus becomes even more puzzling.

The United States: Experts, Access, Consensus, and the Politics of "Being Soft on Communism"

Kennedy himself blamed his misjudgment on an undue reliance on expert opinion, particularly military opinion.[48] He had been particularly impressed by Colonel Hawkins' (Bissell's military advisor) endorsement and by the JCS's acquiescence. In fact, the "experts" he relied on were far from being so; the truly expert advice he received was accurate and skeptical. Hawkins' previous experience in amphibious night landings of irregular troops consisted of going ashore on Iwo Jima with three American divisions in broad daylight. The JCS heavily qualified their "fair" endorsement stressing the importance of air cover and political support (the projected risings of disaffected Cubans). Bissell had no experience in these matters. The most experienced official present was probably Dean Rusk, who had engaged in similar operations in World War II in the China Burma Theatre. The top advisors did not hear from either people experienced in these sorts of landings (Amory at CIA) or from specialists on political conditions in Cuba.

This constriction of the policy process supposedly resulted from the need to achieve secrecy and surprise. Bissell excluded the analytical branch of the CIA; Rusk excluded his experts in analysis and Cuban affairs. Bissell and Dulles were aware of conflicting views but tried to keep them from surfacing. Kennedy had indicated that Bissell was Dulles' heir-apparent. A success in Cuba would, apparently, guarantee the job Bissell sought. They played the roles of advocates, operators, and analysts of the invasion. Bureaucratic self-interest worked against effective performance of the last role. Rusk and other top advisors were apparently swayed by the secrecy argument and by an atmosphere of snowballing consensus and commitment ("groupthink") that surrounded the evolution of the plan and that called for small group loyalty and mutual reinforcement among the leaders of the new and untried administration.[49]

Nevertheless, Kennedy himself made most of the crucial decisions, many of them alone, and he *was* informed of dissenting analyses of the political assumptions of the invasion-rising scenario.[50] Schlesinger had alerted him to the possible depth of Castro's political support, and Kennedy specifically requested an article on the subject, which he carefully read.[51] Throughout the discussions Kennedy emphasized the deniability, the scaled down U.S. involvement (even to the extent of risking the survival of the brigade by cancelling the second air strike), the escape of the brigade should it fail (here he may have been misled by Bisell), and the political problem that would arise if the invasion was cancelled and the disgruntled Cubans returned to the United States complaining that Kennedy had failed to live up to the commitments made by the Eisenhower administration. Kennedy thought he had slipped into the presidency with too narrow a majority to afford a charge of being soft on communism.

An Underlying Assumption

Peter Wyden concludes his exhaustive study of the Bay of Pigs with an analysis of one underlying assumption that affected the overall quality of the planning and the discussion among Kennedy's advisors. What led these experienced officials to challenge technical issues (such as airfield runways) but accept without question Bissell's and Dulles' assurance of an uprising against Castro and of a disorganized Cuban army, Wyden suggests, was the "gook syndrome." This involved an inability to understand the weakness of certain Third World societies and to perceive the strengths of others, a homogenizing of less-developed societies.[52] The experience in the overthrow of Mossadegh in Iran and of Arbenz in Guatemala was automatically assumed to apply to the Cuban context. These governments had fallen easily. Castro's was judged, without any one at the top asking challenging questions, to be equally susceptible to a coup. This assumption was based on and reinforced by an exceptional lack of awareness of Cuban (and other Third World) conditions. None of the top decision makers noticed that moving the invasion site from the Escambray to the Bay of Pigs placed the brigade in the middle of an extensive swamp, 80 miles from the mountains into which they were supposed to flee should the invasion fail. One cannot help feeling that *equally* uniformed and unquestioned assumptions would not have governed a plan to invade a country whose geography and political system were familiar to American leaders. Such familiarity was largely confined to other First World and certain Soviet bloc states. The Third World truly appears to have been a world apart.

COMMON THREADS IN FIRST WORLD-THIRD WORLD SURPRISES

These three cases of First World-Third World strategic surprise reveal important common threads. First, the common First World assumption of sovereign equality, the political and strategic hard shell of "territoriality" that defines states as similarly defensible political units in an anarchic international system, does not consistently hold in the political *conditions* of the Third World. Indeed, the Third World appears to be an environment of extremes. Mossadegh's Iran and Arbenz's Guatemala illustrate one extreme of political weakness; North Vietnam displays another extreme, that of relative political strength. The first two were regimes that fell under only slight pressure; the third withstood enormous force. South Korea and Cuba, the two Third World states attacked in strategic surprises, do not seem to fall at the political extremes, nor were the forces that attacked them comparable; however, in 1950 South Korea's domestic problems in establishing a legitimate political order rendered it highly susceptible to surprise attack, while in 1961, Castro's successes in establishing fervent domestic political support (revolutionary élan) rendered his regime highly defensible. This degree of political variation as well as the general strains of economic underdevelopment shared by almost all Third World states made the First World assumptions of the defensible "hard shell" of state security much less appropriate. Not taking into account radical differences in the political coherence of Third World states can thus be a significant source of failure in surprise attacks. Some Third World states may be incapable of meeting an external attack; others may be capable of meeting attacks that, relatively scaled, would overwhelm most First World states. This variance could contribute to making surprise an *endemic* condition of First World-Third World foreign relations.

Added to actual differences in Third World conditions are important aspects of the *perceptions* First World states may have of Third World societies. Given the real variations in political effectiveness of Third World governments, misconceptions are likely to result. The CIA in 1950 appears to have interpreted the PRC's domestic "political turmoil" in terms that would have been appropriate for South Korea, but were not for the PRC. Third World states may have, as did South Korea in 1950, only a very small role in the security calculations of the superpowers. Attention to their security needs is thus limited. Occasionally superpowers may assume, as did the Soviet Union in its relations with North Korea, that they have more control than actually exists. And superpowers may be prone to vastly underestimating the effectiveness of unfamiliar methods of warfare, such as the People's Liberation Army's reliance on "primitive" logistics, in unfamiliar environments for which in fact those methods are well suited.

Ethnocentrism frequently creates misperceptions and thus helps account for failure to achieve surprise and susceptibility to it. However, the problem of First World-Third World ethnocentrism is a particularly virulent form of this common problem. The special feature these three instances of strategic surprise seem to reveal to a particularly striking *degree* is a marked inability of officials to interpret and anticipate the *intentions and capabilities* of Third World states, to understand the radically different circumstances dividing the developed and the less-developed societies.

NOTES

* I wish to thank Michael Mastanduno for his help in assembling a bibliography. I am grateful to Dick Betts, Michael Handel, Klaus Knorr, Frank Trager, Nancy Weiss, Hila Rosen, and especially Patrick Morgan for very helpful criticism—both substantive and stylistic—on an earlier draft of this chapter. Richard Immerman and Kenneth Regan also gave this chapter a critical reading and made a number of constructive suggestions.

1. The major sources for the surprises of June 25, 1950 include: Dean Acheson, *Present at the Creation* (N.Y.: New American Library, 1970); Dean Acheson, *The Korean War* (N.Y.: Norton, 1971); Roy E. Appleman, *South to the Naktong, North to the Yalu* (Washington, D.C.: Department of the Army, 1961); Richard Betts, *Soldiers, Statesmen, and Cold War Crises* (Harvard, 1977); Richard Betts, *Surprise and Defense: The Lessons of Sudden Attack for U.S. Military Planning* (Washington, D.C.: Brookings Institution, forthcoming); Wilbur Chaffee, "Two Hypotheses of Asia-Soviet Relations as Concerns the Instigation of the Korean War," *Journal of Korean Affairs*, vol. VI, no. 314; J. Lawton Collins, *War in Peacetime* (Houghton Mifflin, 1969); H. A. DeWeerd, "Strategic Surprise in the Korean War," *Orbis*, vol. 6, no. 3 (Fall 1962); David Detzer, *Thunder of the Captains: The Short Summer in 1950* (N.Y.: Crowell, 1977); Alexander George, "Warning and Response: Theory and Practice" in Yair Evron, ed., *International Violence: Terrorism, Surprise, and Control* (Jerusalem: Leonard Davis Institute for International Relations, 1979); Gregory Henderson, *Korea: The Politics of the Vortex* (Harvard University Press, 1968); Fred Kaplan, "Our Cold War Policy, Circa 1950," *New York Times Magazine*, May 18, 1980; George Kennan, *Memoirs: 1925–1950* (N.Y.: Bantam, 1969); William Manchester, *American Caesar: Douglas MacArthur* (N.Y.: Dell, 1978); Ernest May, "The Nature of Foreign Policy: The Calculated vs. the Axiomatic," *Daedalus*, Fall 1962; Ernest May, *"Lessons of the Past": The Use and Misuse of History in American Foreign Policy* (Oxford, 1973); Harold Noble, *Embassy at War* (Seattle: University of Washington Press, 1975); Glenn D. Paige, *The Korean Decision: June 24–30, 1950* (N.Y.: Free Press, 1968); David Rees, *Korea: The Limited War* (London: Macmillan, 1964); General Matthew B. Ridgway, *The Korean War* (Doubleday, 1967); Major Robert K. Sawyer, *Military Advisors in Korea: KMAG in Peace and War* (Washington, D.C.: Department of the Army, 1962); James F. Schnabel,

Policy and Direction: The First Year (Washington, D.C.: Dept. of the Army, 1972); Robert R. Simmons, *The Strained Alliance: Peking, Pyongyang, Moscow and the Politics of the Korean Civil War* (N.Y.: Free Press, 1975); William Stueck, "The Soviet Union and the Korean War," *World Politics*, vol. 28, no. 4, July 1976; Strobe Talbott, trans. and ed., *Khrushchev Remembers* (N.Y.: Bantam, 1971); Harry S. Truman, *Memoirs*, vol. II, *Years of Trial and Hope* (N.Y.: Signet, 1965); U.S. Congress, Senate, Committees on Armed Services and Foreign Relations, *Hearings, Military Situation in the Far East*, IV, 2nd Cong., 1st Sess., 1951; U.S. Department of State, *Foreign Relations of the U.S., 1950, Vol. VII, Korea* (Washington, D.C.: G.P.O., 1976) (Hereafter, *FRUS*); *U.S. News and World Report*, May 5, 1950; Major General Charles A. Willoughby and John Chamberlain, *MacArthur, 1941–1951* (N.Y.: McGraw-Hill, 1954).

2. S. Talbott, trans. and ed., *Khrushchev Remembers*, pp. 401-02.

3. Rees, *Korea*, p. 16.

4. Truman, *Memoirs*, p. 377.

5. George Kennan, *Memoirs: 1925–1950* (N.Y.: Bantam, 1969), p. 312.

6. *FRUS, 1950, Korea*, pp. 5, 105.

7. Appleman, *South to the Naktong*, p. 11 and Noble, *Embassy at War*, p. 226.

8. *FRUS, 1950, Korea*, pp. 99-100.

9. Noble, *Embassy at War*, pp. 231-32.

10. Sawyer, *Military Advisors*, p. 104.

11. Truman, *Memoirs*, pp. 369-73; *FRUS, 1950, Korea*, p. 79.

12. Ibid., p. 41.

13. Kaplan, "Our Cold War Policy."

14. *U.S. News and World Report XXVIII* (May 5, 1950) 30; *FRUS, 1950, Korea*, p. 64; and "NSC-68" in *Naval War College Review*, 1975.

15. Debates focus on whether the Russians planned, or were informed of, the June 25 *timing* for the attack or were caught by surprise as North Korea jumped the gun and on whether the Soviet Union saw the war as purely an offensive against the West or as also a device to disrupt China's growing influence in East Asia. The latter dispute represented by Wilbur Chaffee's, "Two Hypotheses of Asia-Soviet Relations as Concerns the Instigation of the Korean War," *Journal of Korean Affairs*, vol. VI, no. 314 (Oct. '76/Jan '77), is not of immediate concern for the analysis of strategic surprise in June since the CPR was in this phase of the Korean War a minor actor. The first debate is important. Its chief protagonists are Robert Simmons, *The Strained Alliance*, and William Stueck, "The Soviet Union and the Korean War," *World Politics*, vol. XXVIII, no. 4, July 1976. Stueck successfully casts doubt on some of Simmons' interpretations, but his own explanations, such as for the absence of the USSR from the Security Council (its not wishing to appear involved) are not fully convincing. Participation in the Security Council, even vetoing UN support for South Korea, would constitute little more involvement than that the Soviets were already credited with holding over its North Korean client. Even a highly dependent "ally," such as was North Korea, is capable of jumping the gun on an operation already accepted by its patron. Lacking more direct evidence, Simmons' argument remains, in my view, the more plausible account for the Soviet confusion surrounding the June attack.

16. Talbott, *Khrushchev Remembers*, p. 401.

17. Bibliography for the Chinese intervention draws on the following sources as well as those already cited in note 1: Alexander George and Richard Smoke, *Deterrence in American Foreign Policy* (N.Y.: Columbia, 1974); M. Krasner, "The Decision to Cross the 38th Parallel," *Military Review*, October 1972; Martin Lichterman,

"To the Yalu and Back," in Harold Stein, ed., *American Civil-Military Decisions* (University of Alabama Press, 1963); Douglas MacArthur, *Reminiscences* (N.Y.: McGraw-Hill, 1964); S. L. A. Marshall, *The River and the Gauntlet* (N.Y.: Wm. Morrow, 1953); James S. McGovern, *To the Yalu* (N.Y.: Wm. Morrow, 1972); Richard Neustadt, *Presidential Power* (N.Y.: Wiley, 1960); Allen Whiting, *China Crosses the Yalu* (Stanford: Stanford University Press, 1960); Major General Courtney Whitney, *MacArthur: His Rendezvous with History* (N.Y.: Knopf, 1956).

18. Willoughby and Chamberlain, *MacArthur*, p. 388.
19. Rees, *Korea*, p. 119 and Truman, *Memoirs*, p. 420. The line the unified 8th Army later held under Ridgway's command was further south and the 8th Army, by this time, had been considerably enlarged. Not even the PLA planned cross-peninsula, east-west operations in the rugged North Korean terrain. See Appleman, *South to the Naktong*, p. 746, and Schnabel, *Policy and Direction*, p. 212.
20. Whiting, *China Crosses the Yalu*, p. 52.
21. Quoted in McGovern, *To The Yalu*; p. 52.
22. Rees, *Korea*, pp. 148, 150.
23. Appleman, *South to the Naktong*, pp. 717-18, 754, 768.
24. Whiting, *China Crosses the Yalu*, pp. 110-11.
25. *FRUS*, pp. 698, 725.
26. *FRUS*, p. 742.
27. *FRUS*, p. 765.
28. *FRUS*, p. 794.
29. *FRUS*, p. 839.
30. *FRUS*, p. 903.
31. *FRUS*, pp. 986-87.
32. *FRUS*, p. 933.
33. *FRUS*, p. 1087.
34. *FRUS*, p. 1097.
35. Acheson, *The Korean War*, p. 68, and Marshall, *The River and the Gauntlet*, pp. 1-20.
36. *FRUS*, p. 1220. Truman's version of this memorandum in his memoirs, p. 434, does not capture the tone of the report. Whitney, *MacArthur*, pp. 412–18, better conveys the ambiguity of the assessment.
37. R. A. Gugeler, *Combat Actions in Korea*, p. 69; quoted in Rees, *Korea*, p. 163.
38. *FRUS*, p. 1175.
39. Bibliography for the "Bay of Pigs": Howard Hunt, *Give Us This Day* (New Rochelle, N.Y.: Arlington House, 1973); Irving L. Janis, *Victims of Groupthink* (Boston: Houghton-Mifflin, 1972); Haynes Johnson et al., *The Bay of Pigs: the Leaders' Story of Brigade 2306* (N.Y.: Norton, 1964); Lyman Kirkpatrick, "Para-Military Case Study—The Bay of Pigs," *Naval War College Review*, November-December 1972; Thomas Powers, *The Man Who Kept the Secrets: Richard Helms and the C.I.A.* (N.Y.: Knopf, 1979); Arthur Schlesinger, Jr., *A Thousand Days* (Greenwich, Conn.: Fawcett, 1967); General Maxwell Taylor, *Swords and Plows-hares* (N.Y.: Norton, 1972); *The Taylor Report* (National Security Files/Cuba, Box 61, Declassified: June 2, 1977); Peter Wyden, *The Bay of Pigs: The Untold Story* (N.Y.: Simon and Schuster, 1979).
40. Johnson et al., *The Bay of Pigs: The Leaders' Story*, p. 25.
41. Schlesinger, *A Thousand Days*, p. 75.
42. Wyden, *The Bay of Pigs: The Untold Story*, p. 88.
43. *Taylor Report* (memorandum No. 1), pp. 7-8, 11. Wyden, *The Bay of Pigs: The Untold Story*, pp. 89-90.

44. Johnson et al., *The Bay of Pigs: The Leaders' Story*, p. 41.
45. Richard Immerman, *They Cried Wolf: The CIA in Guatemala* (Austin, Texas: University of Texas Press, forthcoming) makes this connection to Guatemala.
46. Schlesinger, *A Thousand Days*, p. 236. Wyden, *The Bay of Pigs: The Untold Story*, pp. 91, 139, 169. However, Hunt in *Give Us This Day* has asserted that Bissell and Dulles were aware that their subordinates (among them Hunt who arranged contacts with anti-Castro Cubans in Miami) judged that neither the underground nor the populace would be able to play a decisive role in the campaign. They anticipated the establishment of a beachhead and then a "request for aid would provide the U.S. with all the excuse needed to supply and *reinforce* the insurgents" (p. 77). This was also the impression Hunt and others conveyed to the Cubans of the brigade (Johnson et al., p. 75). It was diametrically opposed to what Kennedy had been told and to Kennedy's advisors' conception of the invasion, a conception frequently reinforced by Bissell's and Dulles' assurances of a popular rising and a limited U.S. role. Dulles and Bissell have denied that they assured the White House that a rising was likely. By April 4 the rising had become accepted by the advisors as a fundamental premise for the invasion. Kennedy may have been more skeptical, but then he appears to have been certain that the brigade could not be brought home.
47. Wyden, *The Bay of Pigs: The Untold Story*, p. 93. The depth of Castro's support and the neglect of this crucial factor are the central arguments of Kirkpatrick, "Para-Military Case Study—The Bay of Pigs." Kirkpatrick was a CIA official who conducted a postmortem of the invasion.
48. Schlesinger, *A Thousand Days*, p. 277.
49. Janis, *Victims of Groupthink*, pp. 33-49.
50. Wyden makes this point, *The Bay of Pigs: The Untold Story*, p. 316.
51. Schlesinger, *A Thousand Days*, p. 231. Kennedy also received a critical memo from Schlesinger and engaged in a long discussion with Fulbright.
52. Wyden, *The Bay of Pigs: The Untold Story*, pp. 326-27.

CHAPTER FIVE
Crisis and Surprise in Three Arab-Israeli Wars

Michael Handel

Based on the analysis and comparison of separate case studies, current theories of strategic surprise have largely ignored the learning process associated with a series of closely interrelated surprise attacks. A state that has been involved—either as the initiator or the victim—in successive surprise attacks, will develop a military doctrine very different from that of a state that, at lengthier intervals, has fought against various adversaries. In the Middle East, the same countries have warred with each other four times in less than three decades. Within *one* generation in Israel, almost the same decision makers took part in the War of Independence (1948), the Sinai Campaign (1956), the Six Day War (1967), and the Yom Kippur War (1973). It is therefore possible to use this unique history to examine strategic surprise not as a single, sui generis event—but as a continued, repeated phenomenon.

Furthermore, unanticipated wars in the Middle East, particularly the Six Day War, have resulted mainly from the instability of the region and the mutual fear of surprise attack. A closer look at the relationship between systemic instability and strategic surprise promises to yield some valuable insights and lessons.

Another interesting factor has to do with the powerful impact of a sudden Middle Eastern conflict on third parties. This type of war between Israel and its neighbors, or between other regional states such as the Iraq-Iran war (Fall 1980), the Syrian attack on Jordan (1970), and the Egyptian-Libyan conflict (Summer 1977), can cause a superpower confrontation (as it did in 1956, 1967, 1973), or it can damage the world economy through severe fluctuations in the supply of oil.

The superpowers can be related to war and strategic surprise in the Middle East in yet another way. Given their heavy dependence on the military hardware and support of the super and great powers, Middle Eastern nations would normally hesitate to launch a major attack without some assurance of continued outside support. This "support" would include trying to ensure that the powers would come to their rescue should they be threatened by an all-out defeat. Thus, the superpowers potentially have some leverage in reducing the probability of unexpected wars in the Middle East, although they have yet to make good use of their influence.

This article focuses primarily on three major cases of surprise: the Sinai Campaign, the Six Day War, and the Yom Kippur War; it also reviews a crisis that almost culminated in another war because of the mutual fear of surprise attack prevailing in the Middle East. The War of Independence and the War of Attrition (1968–1970) have been omitted, as most of the surprise attacks during these wars were on the tactical level.

A combination of geopolitical conditions can create a highly unstable regional environment in which an unexpected move from peace to war can occur very rapidly; even a seemingly trivial crisis may easily escalate into a major confrontation and spill over into the international system. Such was the impact, for example, of the Balkan region on the European system on the eve of World War I. The geopolitical vulnerabilities of some states in a region of high tension and radically opposing interests will only further reduce regional stability, and the fear of being suddenly attacked will become a self-fulfilling prophecy of a preemptive or interceptive war.[1] Such vulnerability is the cornerstone for the development of a state's political-military doctrine. The need to compensate for geographic weaknesses will be dealt with by transferring the war to enemy territory, by launching a preemptive attack, and by building a hair-trigger mobilization system; mobility and speed will be crucial for the ability to quickly shift the military effort from one front to another.[2]

Israel's geographic vulnerability following its establishment in 1948 is well known.[3] It lacked strategic depth or naturally defensible borders, and was encircled by hostile neighbors. These factors, compounded by its demographic inferiority, scarce natural resources, and political isolation, led to the evolution of a political-military doctrine similar in many respects to that of Germany before World War I. Unintentionally—but inevitably—Israel's doctrine had a destabilizing impact on the Middle East.

For the student of strategic surprise, the Israeli War of Independence (1947–1949) is of limited interest. The overwhelming Arab military capability and numerical superiority in every possible aspect completely eliminated their incentive to launch a carefully planned surprise attack in the opening phase of the war. Their forthcoming attack was advertised and openly discussed months in advance. Having thus deprived themselves of the element of surprise (much like the catastrophic Italian offensive against the Greeks in 1940), their attacking forces utterly failed to translate their superior capabilities into concrete gains on the battlefield.

On the other hand, the Israelis, whose superior intelligence was fully aware of Arab capabilities and plans down to the exact timing of attack, could carefully prepare their own defensive surprises. The invading Arab forces, who lacked adequate intelligence regarding the Israelis, were frequently caught off guard by what turned out to be "defensive surprises." Most Israeli surprises during the early phases of the war were on the tactical-doctrinal level. The Israelis continuously resorted to unexpected tactics dictating their own rules of the game. For example, the Arab forces were surprised by the following:

- The Israelis chose to fight at night whenever and wherever possible. The Arab armies were not well trained for night fighting and were thus tactically surprised by Israeli night operations and deep raids on Arab positions. Under cover of darkness, the Israelis, who lacked artillery and air support, could achieve better results with lower casualties.
- The Israelis preferred to resort to the offensive whenever possible despite the traditionally accepted wisdom of the superiority of the defense. For them, the best defense was the offense. The choice of high risk, maxi-max tactics proved to be highly successful, and was a major factor in Israeli defensive surprises. Taking the initiative, combined with greater mobility and the advantage of interior lines of mobility, helped to compensate for their inferior capabilities.
- Another serious Arab miscalculation was their estimation of the Israeli military potential and its capacity to expand. While the Israeli Defense Forces (IDF) were, at the outset, inferior to the Arab forces in every possible respect, the Israelis later made better use of the time and the two truces agreed upon during the war. A large influx of Jewish refugees from the European concentration camps as well as the Czech (Russian) supplies of military equipment radically altered the balance of power between the two opposing sides. By the end of the war, the IDF included some 90,000 soldiers and artillery, tanks, and aircraft that had been unavailable at the beginning of the war. Although not lacking in money or equipment, the Arabs could not train the necessary manpower for a larger army and a longer war in such a short period of time.

An obvious although important lesson in strategic and military surprise is that the weaker side has a very strong incentive to compensate for his weakness by resorting to the use of strategem and surprise as a force multiplier. The powerful, stronger side conversely lacks the incentive to resort to surprise and thus not only sacrifices an important military advantage but also plays into his enemy's hands. We shall see below how this simple but often forgotten lesson appears again and again in our story.

The problem of strategic surprise, both in its *defensive* and *offensive* manifestations, has always occupied a major portion of Israeli military thinking.[4] From the defensive point of view, the two major problems were (a) how to secure warning of a surprise attack, and (b) what to do if the warning systems failed. The solution to the first problem was the development of an extremely effective intelligence organization. Perhaps in no other army in the world has the intelligence system acquired such a central role. This system, which includes air reconnaissance photography and early warning systems built in later years, has been allotted a relatively large share of high quality manpower and a budget priority comparable to that of any combat organization.

Israel also established an extensive system of defensive measures to safeguard against strategic surprise in the event of an intelligence failure. It included the development of a peripheral defense line based on armed civilian settlements; a well-organized reserve system that could be quickly mobilized while the regular army and civilian settlements held the line; a variety of passive defenses such as shelters for military aircraft, tanks, and other equipment as well as minefields and antitank ditches; heavier investment in those regular military units that could maintain a high degree of alert (such as the air force); and the preparation of detailed contingency plans for operations under conditions of surprise attack. On a more general level, it was hoped that projecting an image of military strength would lessen the temptation for Arab countries to attack.

Although all of these defensive precautionary measures had a *stabilizing* effect on the regional system, the Israelis were never fully convinced that their country would be safe in an emergency. Until 1967, they preferred to emphasize the offensive uses of strategic surprise—and this had a *destabilizing* impact on the Middle East.

The emphasis on strategic surprise as an offensive tool in Israeli political-military doctrine can be explained as follows:[5]

1. Because of the lack of strategic depth, a surprise attack would threaten population centers and inevitably cause considerable destruction. To avoid this, the Israelis felt that it was better to fight on enemy territory from the beginning—something that could only be accomplished if they launched the first attack.
2. Strategic surprise was considered the optimal way of compensating for overall quantitative inferiority in manpower and major weapons systems.
3. The skillful use of strategic surprise was instrumental in reducing the duration of a war. This was vital for Israel because its economy was not geared for, and could not support, a prolonged conflict; equally important, Israel wanted to be able to emerge victorious and achieve its major goals before the great powers intervened on behalf of the Arabs. If the Arabs attacked first (as in 1948 and 1973) the war would last much longer, and the intervention of the great powers in favor of a ceasefire would either help the Arabs to consolidate their gains or prevent the Israelis from restoring the antebellum status quo.
4. The potential need to fight simultaneously on more than one front required a quick victory on one front so that additional forces could be concentrated

at other key points. A preemptive surprise attack on one front meant that a speedy decision could be reached at a much lower cost.

THE SINAI CAMPAIGN AND THE SUEZ OPERATION[6]

Until 1956, Israel was almost completely isolated in the international arena and did not have the support of any of the great powers.[7] But by the mid-1950s, its interests converged with those of France and—to a lesser extent—Great Britain, both of whom wanted to overthrow Nasser's regime in Egypt, control the Suez Canal, and counter Nasser's pan-Arab aspirations.

These common interests undoubtedly strengthened Israel's willingness to join an attack on Egypt; yet French and British backing was only a necessary and not a sufficient condition for such a move. The Israelis also harbored a number of grievances against Egypt that reinforced their desire to participate in the French initiative.[8] The military balance had recently shifted in Egypt's favor following the Egyptian-"Czech" (i.e., Russian) arms deal made public by Nasser in September 1955. Surprising Israel and the Western powers, this deal represented a quantum jump in the quantity and quality of weapons available to the belligerent countries of the Middle East. Modern tanks, fighter and bomber aircraft, artillery, and even submarines were introduced for the first time in large quantities, thereby threatening "the delicate balance of armaments" that the Western powers had tried to maintain in the region since 1950.

October 1956 brought signs of increasing coordination of military planning and command between Egypt, Syria, and Jordan. On October 21, pro-Nasser elements won a majority in Jordan's parliamentary elections, and three days later, Egypt, Syria, and Jordan signed a military agreement consolidating their armed forces under the direct command of Egypt's Ministry of War. In addition, there were rumors of Iraqi troops moving into Jordan.[9] It is worth noting that similar circumstances recurred in 1967, when King Hussein concluded a treaty with Egypt that placed the Jordanian Army under Egyptian command.[10] Thus, a radical shift—or an anticipated shift—in the balance of forces may create the incentive for a preemptive surprise attack.

The Egyptian closure of the Straits of Tiran to Israeli shipping off and on since 1953 (including the air corridor of the straits) was a major obstacle to the development of Israel's economy, particularly its shipping industry, the port of Eilat, and the Negev. In contravention of numerous international conventions and a unanimous United Nations Security Council decision (September 1, 1950), the Egyptians also closed the Suez Canal to *any* shipping to and from Israel.[11]

In April 1955, the Egyptian intelligence organization established a special unit, the Fedayeen, for making terrorist raids deep into Israeli territory. These raids caused heavy casualties and serious demoralization in Israel. Israel's retaliatory raids against Egypt (and Jordan) were only partially successful since they failed to prevent the Fedayeen attacks and soon became too costly to be continued.

Nevertheless, none of these problems had been sufficient to induce the Israeli government, under the cautious leadership of Prime Minister David Ben-Gurion, to take the offensive. The decisive factor was the position of the French and British governments, whose planned operation against Egypt would benefit from Israeli participation. The Israelis did not need much pressure to be convinced that they should take part in the operation.[12] They hoped to exploit the unique circumstances in order to redress the above-mentioned grievances and to firmly reestablish their position on the map of the Middle East.

* * * *

Despite the impossibility of completely concealing the preparations in Israel, Malta, and Cyprus for the two interrelated campaigns, there was no alert in the Egyptian armed forces when the campaign opened, and Nasser was at a birthday party for his five-year-old son.[13] The achievement of strategic surprise resulted from a combination of factors such as secrecy, deception, and the preconceptions of the surprised parties (Egypt and the United States). The primary factor was the great secrecy surrounding the decisions of the three states. The meetings in France, first between the Israelis and the French, then the French and the British, and finally involving all three countries at Sèvres, were effectively hidden from public view. The meeting at Sèvres (October 22–24, 1956) was confined to the smallest possible number of top leaders and their closest aides on a "need to know" basis. There were no leaks.[14] The top diplomats of these countries were *not* informed of the plans, and only a few military leaders knew about all of the agreements involved.[15] In Israel, knowledge of the agreements, and of the meetings at general headquarters for planning the Sinai operation, was strictly limited to the military commanders participating in the operation. (Dayan, for example, asked Rabin, who was then the commander of Israel's northern military district, to leave the room when the details of the Sinai Campaign were being discussed!)[16] Israel's ambassadors, most of the ministers, and other top officials were not briefed on the plan to attack Egypt. On the day the war broke out, Abba Eban, Israel's ambassador to the United States, met with William Rountree, assistant secretary of state for Middle Eastern affairs, in order to emphasize Israel's defensive posture and desire for peace. During their conversation, a message concerning Israel's attack in the Sinai was given to Rountree, who read it aloud. Rountree then turned to the embarrassed Eban and sarcastically said, "I am certain, Mr.Ambassador, that you will wish to get back to your embassy to find out exactly what is happening in your country."[17]

According to Ben-Gurion's memoirs, even when he finally discussed the military plans with his Cabinet members on October 28, 1956, he presented the move not as a full-scale war to be coordinated with France and Great Britain, but only as a large military raid. Some leaders of the opposition (such as Begin, but *not* the communist members of the Knesset) were informed, under an oath of secrecy, of some of the details one day after the campaign had already begun.[18]

Israeli mobilization plans were delayed until the last possible moment to avoid undermining the chance of achieving surprise. During the discussions at Dayan's headquarters on October 7, 1956, it was suggested that the reserve units, i.e., the bulk of the Israeli army, be mobilized a week before D-day to be prepared for battle. (At that time, Israeli reservists did not have adequate training and performed very poorly in the campaign as compared with regular army units.) Dayan rejected this proposal outright. "Under no circumstances could I accept this recommendation. It would mean a general mobilization throughout the country about a week before the start of the campaign, nullifying our plan to surprise the Egyptians. We finally decided that only the officers would be called up a few days before D-day, and that armored units would be mobilized on D-day minus 3. All other units—D-day minus 2."[19] Other units of the IDF, which were needed to defend the borders with Syria and Jordan, were mobilized only at D-day plus 1 on the assumption that the Syrians and Jordanians would not be able to take action without some preliminary preparations.

The Israelis also executed an elaborate deception plan. On the night of October 10, following the murder of Israeli civilians by infiltrators from Jordan, Israel launched a massive retaliatory attack against Jordan—the Kalkiliah raid. The raid heightened the tension between Israel and Great Britain when King Hussein invoked the Anglo-Jordanian Defense Treaty. There were even rumors that the British might bomb Tel Aviv. The deteriorating Anglo-Israeli relationship also made it difficult for the Americans and Egyptians to believe that these two nations could, at the same time, be partners in a plan to attack Egypt.[20] To divert attention to the Jordanian border, the Israeli general staff concentrated all of the active operations there during the three months preceding the Sinai Campaign. Israel deliberately abstained from taking any action on the Egyptian border. The deception plan was aided by the entrance of an advance Iraqi force into Jordan on October 14 (reported by Israeli intelligence on October 16).[21] Iraqi movements supported by the British government drew attention further toward the east. Israel explained the partial mobilization as a precautionary move against the threat on its eastern front. In *Diary of the Sinai Campaign*, Dayan says:

As the reason for their call-up, reservists were told that a clash was likely with
Jordan because of the entry into its territory of Iraqi forces and because of its
joining the Egypt-Syria command. This deceptive explanation ties in with the
news and articles which have been appearing in the press in the last few
days. . . .[22]

Some of the troops to be used in the attack on Egypt were actually based
closer to the Jordanian border, and had to start their move toward the Sinai
from that region—an additional distance of some seventy-five miles.

The deception plan was so successful that some of those who were fully
aware of it were afraid that it might inadvertently touch off a war with Jordan.[23]
The plan certainly deceived the United States, as is evident from President
Eisenhower's two urgent messages (October 28 and 29) to Prime Minister
Ben-Gurion, stating that no Iraqi troops had entered Jordan, and warning
Israel not to take any military initiatives.[24] When Abba Eban, Israel's ambassador, met with Dulles on October 28, Dulles asked him to explain what
was happening on the Israeli-Jordanian border. (Large maps of Israel and
Jordan were hanging on the walls of his office.)[25] On the afternoon of October
29, Ben-Gurion avoided making a promise not to go to war in his reply to
Eisenhower's message; his answer was phrased in such a way as to imply
that the situation on the Israeli-Jordanian border was the main problem on
his mind. In his memoirs, *Waging Peace,* President Eisenhower admits that
he was surprised not only by the attack itself, but particularly by its direction.

There was no dearth of signals to indicate what was happening. Israel and
its allies could not hide their mobilization and concentration of troops in
Malta, Cyprus, and Israel—even though they did their utmost to present those
concentrations as defensive in nature. The fact that a mobilization of troops
occurred simultaneously should have indicated the possibility of collaboration
between three nations, whose only common interest was their desire to get
rid of Nasser. Certainly Israel was not going to attack Jordan, which had a
defense agreement with England. Other examples of major signals (and "noise")
occurring at the time are enumerated in Table 5.1.

Other preparations—such as the Sèvres conference, decisions concerning
military operations, and schedules for the attack—were less easily detectable
than the aforementioned signals, but they could have been at least partially
discovered by more efficient clandestine intelligence efforts. In allowing themselves to be caught unaware, the United States and Egypt had made a major
blunder. Evidence on the American side indicates that top political leaders
(i.e., Eisenhower and Dulles) were more to blame than U.S. intelligence
(particularly the CIA), which apparently made a correct assessment some
twenty-four hours before the attack.

How can this failure be explained? First, Eisenhower and Dulles were busy
campaigning for the presidential elections on November 6. They may have

also clung to the idea that the British and French would not take any action before the elections—although no promise to this effect was ever given. There are indications that Eisenhower and Dulles had complete faith in Prime Minister Eden and simply believed that he would not take any action, particularly in an election year, against major American interests. "How could Eden do this to me?" was Eisenhower's immediate reaction upon being informed of the British and French ultimatum to Egypt and Israel—an act which finally confirmed the collusion between England, France, and Israel.[26] The Americans may have also assumed that London and Paris would at least give prior notice, since all three nations were members of NATO. Soon after, the British and French were themselves surprised to discover that being members of the alliance did not guarantee American support or even neutrality. Each side overestimated the other's loyalty to the alliance, not realizing that when a serious conflict of interest occurred, each would choose its own interest first. Finally, the outbreak of the Hungarian revolution also created a serious distraction for the Americans.

Why were the Egyptians surprised? In the first place, it seems that their intelligence service did not receive enough information; it was not able to detect the preparations in Malta, Cyprus, and Israel and predict their direction. Also, the Israeli deception plan probably convinced the Egyptians that if any action was going to take place, it would be on the Israeli-Jordanian border. The Egyptians may have seen their military strength and numerical superiority as a deterrent to—not a target for—an Israeli attack. Given the force ratio, an Israeli attack would have appeared irrational. (The Israelis made the same mistake in 1973 when they decided that an Arab attack was unlikely because of its poor chances for victory.) The Egyptians failed to discover the Anglo-French-Israeli collaboration, which had increased Israel's ability to attack without being attacked in return. (The British and French might have promised to make a preemptive attack on the Egyptian Air Force; French aircraft were to protect Israeli population centers, and French destroyers were to protect Israel's shores.) Egyptian intelligence was probably not aware of the secret French arms shipments to Israel during the summer and autumn of 1956.

*   *   *   *

The original Israeli version of Operation Kadesh included a plan to open with an attack on Egyptian airfields. Inferior in number of aircraft, the Israeli Air Force had planned, since approximately 1953, that if war broke out the Egyptian Air Force should be destroyed on the ground. According to Ezer Weizman, who was then chief of operations:

> Before the 1956 war, we were ready on a few occasions to knock out the Egyptian Air Force on the ground. This was the case on different occasions

Table 5.1
A Partial List of Major Signals and Noise Preceding the Sinai and Suez Campaigns

SIGNALS	NOISE
The British mobilize reservists in August 1956 and prepare an expeditionary force scheduled to attack either Alexandria or the Suez Canal area on September 15. The attack is delayed to September 19, postponed again to September 26, then delayed again without a specific date.	*October 10*—Dulles meets with the French and British foreign ministers in New York. He asks about their troop and aircraft concentrations and is told these are only for "deterrent" and "precautionary" purposes.
	October 11—The British chargé d'affaires in Tel Aviv tells Ben-Gurion that an Iraqi division is about to enter Jordan. He warns that if Israel takes further military action, Britain will go to Jordan's aid. British bombers are put on alert for a possible attack on Israel.

From the middle of October until the outbreak of hostilities, there is a blackout of news and information exchange between the French and British governments and intelligence services and their American counterparts.[27]

SIGNALS	NOISE
October 15—Eisenhower is informed that U-2 flights have discovered about 60 French Mysteres fighter aircraft at Israeli airfields.	
October 16—Prime Minister Eden and Prime Minister Mollet meet in Paris.	
October 19—Jacques Chaban-Delmas, minister of state, tells the American ambassador, Douglas Dillon, that the British and French are negotiating with Israel to coordinate an attack against Nasser. Dillon urges delaying the action until after the American presidential elections, and Chaban-Delmas replies that the action is scheduled to take place immediately after the elections. Dillon reports this conversation to U.S. intelligence.[28]	
	October 22—The Hungarian revolt begins.
	October 23—Street fighting in Budapest. Soviet troops enter Budapest.
October 23 (8PM)—Pineau arrives in London and confers with Eden and Lloyd	*October 23 (afternoon)*—Lloyd tells the House of Commons that "for the British people, force will always be the last resort."
	October 26—A rumor is spread in Paris that King Hussein has been murdered. This is the major topic of discussion at a U.S. National Security Council meeting.

Table 5.1 Continued

October 27—Three British aircraft carriers sail from Malta to the eastern Mediterranean. Other ships sail as well, and British troops continue to embark at Malta on convoys to the eastern Mediterranean.

October 25—28–U.S. intelligence monitors increased coded radio traffic between Paris and Tel Aviv.

October 27—A new government under Imre Nagy is formed in in Budapest. Fighting continues.

October 28—The U.S. ambassador in Great Britain asks Foreign Minister Selwyn Lloyd about the rumor of an imminent Israeli attack on Egypt. Lloyd replies that he has no information concerning this and is more worried about an Israeli attack on Jordan.

---

and in different circumstances, and so were the instructions cancelling these planned operations. As the commander of Ramat David, I was scheduled to lead twelve "Mustangs" to knock out Kabrit. The cancellation order caught us in the final stages of preparation. . . . I believe that had we attacked the Egyptian airfields and the planes parked in them in 1956 . . . both along the Canal and deeper in Egypt . . . that we would have achieved results similar to those achieved eleven years later during the Six Day War.[29]

Israeli chief of staff, Moshe Dayan, and above all Prime Minister Ben-Gurion, did not believe the Air Force could simultaneously decimate the Egyptian Air Force on the ground and protect Israeli air space. For that reason, Ben-Gurion refused to sign the agreement at the Sèvres conference unless the French promised to protect Israeli air space. However, his attempts to secure a British and French preemptive attack failed. On October 25, Dayan changed the original plan.

The second change I made, concerning the employment of the Air Force, is that *it will not open the campaign with the bombing of Egyptian airfields but will confine itself in the first two days to providing air support* to our ground forces and protection to Israel's skies. . . .

There is naturally some risk in basing ourselves on my assumptions, and if they should prove wrong and the Egyptian Air Force reacts to our seizure of Mitla by bombing Israel's cities, we shall pay dearly for having *passed the opportunity of surprise* and failing to knock out the Egyptian planes while they are still on the ground.[30] (Emphasis added)

This, then, was an Israeli surprise that did not take place in 1956. But Dayan had, in the above statement, given an important clue to Israel's strategic thinking and had, in fact, warned Egypt well in advance of 1967 what Israel's tactics would be if it should have to act alone. Dayan's *Diary of the Sinai Campaign*, published in 1965, evidently was not carefully perused by the Egyptians.[31] As for the 1956 war, the Egyptians had other immediate warnings of a preemptive air attack. The first was the appearance of Israeli fighter aircraft—*which could have destroyed all of the Egyptian aircraft on the ground*—over their airfields on the evening of October 29. In his memoirs, Weizman writes:

> Benny Peled, the Israeli Air Force Commander-in-Chief of today, was ordered to take off with four Mystères and patrol over Kabrit airfield (a large Egyptian airfield near the Suez Canal). He was strictly forbidden ''to attack, damage, or bomb!''. . . . He returned frustrated. The Egyptians had been totally surprised by the whole operation. Using the element of surprise, he could have completely destroyed the Egyptian ''Vanpires'' and ''Meteors.'' Benny recalled, ''The surprise was complete! The Egyptian aircraft were organized in a long line. It would have been possible to ignite them all. Only following our arrival was an order given and the planes began to disperse, but were all left exposed without protection.''[32]

Despite warnings by leaflets and radio on October 31, which left the Egyptians more than enough time to disperse and evacuate their aircraft (or alternatively to intercept the attackers), not much was done. When the British bombing raids began, there was no blackout over Egyptian airfields, although the war with Israel in the Sinai had begun two days earlier.[33] Egyptian unpreparedness was the same a day later, when Egyptian aircraft parked on the runways of at least eight different airfields were destroyed.[34] By November 2, the Egyptian Air Force was virtually nonexistent. Even more noteworthy is the fact that following this debacle, their failure to take steps to protect the aircraft led to a greater disaster in 1967. The Israelis, however, began in 1957 to build concrete underground shelters for all their fighter aircraft.

Although the British and French achieved a strategic surprise in the opening of the war and their attacks on Egyptian airfields, they failed to achieve surprise at lower levels. This was, in part, the result of the repeated warnings given to the Egyptians concerning the area of the scheduled attacks, and the considerable delays (mainly caused by the British) in beginning the assaults on Port Said and Port Fuad. The British, and to a lesser degree, the French, took the Egyptian armed forces too seriously; they prepared as if they were going to face the German Army on the beaches of Normandy. This attitude caused serious delays which prevented them from exploiting their initial successes.[35] Ultimately, they were unable to accomplish any of the goals set for their part of the operation.

OPERATION ROTEM—THE SURPRISE THAT NEVER WAS

On the night of January 31, 1960, the IDF launched its first large-scale raid since the Sinai Campaign on Syrian military positions at Twafiq. This was in reprisal for continuous Syrian shelling of Israeli settlements along the border. Syria and Egypt were, at that time, officially unified as the United Arab Republic (UAR). Egypt, Syria, and the Soviet Union apparently suspected that the Israeli government, acting on behalf of the United States and the other Western powers, was trying to pressure the UAR and undermine the ongoing unification process. This was not the case.

A few days later, following another incident, the IDF concentrated a small number of troops on the Syrian border as a precautionary measure. Between February 14 and 19, Nasser visited Syria for consultations. In the meantime, the Soviet Union had been supplying the Syrians and Egyptians with "reliable evidence" that the Israelis were planning to attack Syria. (A similar Soviet ploy in May 1967 triggered the crisis which led to the Six Day War.) On February 17, a high state of alert was declared in the Egyptian armed forces, and Nasser notified the UN Emergency Forces in the Sinai that hostilities could break out at any time.[36]

On February 18, the Egyptians secretly began to move troops across the Suez Canal into the Sinai. First to cross were the Second, Fifth, and Seventh Infantry Divisions, which were followed by the Fourth Armored Division. The first evidence of these moves was received by Israeli intelligence about four days later.[37] Ending a long break in such activities, the Israelis sent a reconnaissance airplane to photograph the Suez Canal on February 23; this flight failed to discover the Egyptian task force, but by that time most of the Egyptian Army was already in the Sinai. In fact, it was deployed close to the Israeli border in the El Arish area. Between 400 and 500 Egyptian tanks— an enormous number by the standards of that time—were facing the surprised Israelis, who had only 20 to 30 tanks to meet the threat.

Until Israel could move more tanks to the south, it was completely dependent on the air force for protection. During a meeting at general headquarters on February 24, Chief of Operations Rabin passed a note to Ezer Weizman, commander of the air force, telling him, "Ezer, until further notice, our land forces were caught with their pants down and everything depends on the air force."[38] Within two days, the IDF moved some 100 to 130 tanks down to protect the Egyptian-Israeli border.

The crisis was not publicized during that period, which may partially explain why it did not result in war. With the help of the United States and the careful avoidance of provocations, the crisis was defused; by March 1, most of Egypt's troops had been withdrawn from the Sinai.

The failure of Israeli intelligence to discover the Egyptian entry into the Sinai at an early stage was immediately perceived as a serious blunder. Recalling measures taken to improve the Israeli warning system, Rabin writes:

> We carefully examined all the aspects of warning and observation, and also improved the photographic reconnaissance capability of the Air Force. We took great care to improve our intelligence capabilities and activities in all areas, so

that every Egyptian movement into the Sinai in the future would be immediately brought to our attention as soon as possible.

As the head of operations at that time, Operation Rotem (the code name given to Israeli preparations to meet the Egyptian threat once it was discovered) was imprinted on my memory. Some of the lessons which I learned were later useful on the eve of the Six Day War.[39]

Operation Rotem is a rare case of a *potential* strategic surprise whose traumatic impact led to the constructive reorganization of intelligence working methods, and the improvement of an early warning system and mobilization program. By the time Nasser sent his troops into the Sinai in May 1967 (this time in broad daylight), Israel was ready to meet the challenge.

THE SIX DAY WAR

The details of the May-June crisis preceding the Six Day War are well known and need not be retold here. Instead, we will retrace the development of the crisis on the Israeli side, examining the steps taken by the Israeli general staff from the very beginning. Each escalatory step on the Egyptian and Arab side was met by an Israeli defensive countermove, and we will see how Israel finally decided to initiate a surprise because of its unique security dilemmas.

The devastating Israeli surprise attack that opened the war reflected the lessons of the Sinai Campaign and Operation Rotem; the Egyptians and their Soviet advisors, for unknown reasons, did not learn these same lessons. Perhaps they believed that because the military and political circumstances prevailing in 1956 had been unique, Israel alone would not dare to attack Egypt. These were, however, political assumptions irrelevant in a situation in which a small country had its back to the wall.

Ironically, the May-June 1967 crisis again came as a surprise to the Israelis; intelligence and military leaders had developed the conception that as long as Egypt was involved in the war in Yemen, there was no danger of an Israeli-Arab war until 1969 or thereafter.[40] They had concluded that even if Egypt withdrew its 50,000 troops from Yemen, it would require at least a year and a half to prepare its armed forces for a confrontation with Israel. As it turned out, Egypt's war in Yemen was unsuccessful and highly unpopular, so Nasser was looking for an excuse to withdraw his troops.

It was the Egyptian chief of staff's visit to Syria on May 13 and 14, a higher level of alert in the Egyptian Army, which first focused Israeli attention on regional developments.[41] Between May 11 and 13, the Russians supplied the Syrians with false information, which reported the presence of approximately twelve Israeli brigades on the Syrian border; the Syrians, in turn, transmitted the information that Israel might be planning an all-out attack on

Syria to Egypt's chief of staff, who initiated measures to alert Egyptian troops and send them into the Sinai. A few early warning messages were promptly received by Israeli intelligence and handed to Chief of Staff Rabin on the night of May 14.[42] The next morning brought the news that Egyptian troops were openly moving through Cairo toward the Sinai.

No one assumed that the Egyptians intended war, but to be on the safe side Rabin, in consultation with the government, decided to put the regular army on alert and to intensify air and ground reconnaissance in the area. Because of the lessons of Operation Rotem, the IDF had kept enough armored units in the south to deal with any emergency. By May 16, Israel had concentrated some 200 tanks in defensive dispositions in the Negev. On the previous day, Israel had informed the U.S. ambassador and the French military attaché that it had no troop concentrations in the north and no offensive intentions.

Israeli intelligence in the meantime estimated that the Egyptians were simply repeating the Operation Rotem exercise, and would soon withdraw their forces from the Sinai. On May 16, additional information confirmed that these forces did not yet pose a major threat. Israel increased the level of alert for all its armed forces and, as additional precautions, the men of two reserve tank brigades were notified that they might soon be mobilized, and some minefields were laid along the border with Egypt.

Later that evening, Israeli intelligence reported that the Egyptian Fourth Division had not yet advanced into the Sinai; the whereabouts of that elite division were important because it was expected to play a central role in any Egyptian war effort. The Israelis had decided that the presence of the Fourth Division in the Sinai would require a partial mobilization of reserves. A few hours later at general headquarters, Major-General Yariv, head of Israeli military intelligence, pointed to some recent danger signals; Egyptian IL-28 bombers were moving to an airfield in the Sinai, and Iraq had moved some of its MiG-21 fighter aircraft to Syrian air bases. Therefore, the general staff beefed up antiaircraft defenses by placing HAWK surface-to-air missiles around sensitive targets.

May 17 brought the Radio Cairo announcement that General Mourtagi had been appointed commander of the Sinai front. A more serious escalatory step was Egypt's request that the United Nations Emergency Forces be evacuated from its border with Israel. The director of Israeli intelligence asserted that Egypt now appeared to be attempting to deter Israel from attacking Syria. Moreover, Egypt's prestige in the Arab world would be enhanced by the demonstration that it could save Syria from an impending Israeli attack. Egyptian dispositions were still considered primarily defensive. Nevertheless, Rabin feared that Nasser might change his mind and move to an offensive posture. That afternoon, Rabin appeared before the Knesset Foreign Relations and Defense Committee and suggested that Egypt might (a) put general pressure on Israel as in Operation Rotem, (b) close the Straits of Tiran, or (c) attack sensitive targets in Israel. In the course of the briefing, Rabin received a report that Egyptian MiG-21 fighters, for the first time since 1956, were flying reconnaissance missions across the Negev from Jordan to Israel. It was quickly decided to disperse Israeli aircraft on the ground, strengthen antiaircraft units, and mobilize more reserves for the air force. As Egyptian troops continued their move into the Sinai, Israel began a limited mobilization of reserves, which was completed in four or five days. The level of alert in all IDF units was correspondingly increased.

On the morning of May 18, there were reports of euphoria in the streets of Cairo at the prospect of certain victory over Israel. Ezer Weizman, the chief of operations, reported that 400 Israeli tanks were now concentrated in the Negev, and the commander of the air force reported that all planes, including trainer aircraft, were being readied for action. That afternoon, it was learned that Egypt's foreign minister had formally requested the evacuation of all UN troops from the Sinai. For the Israelis, this meant that Egyptian intentions would henceforth have to be considered offensive. Israeli intelligence added the news that the Syrian Army had been placed on alert. The call-up of Israeli reserves was increased, although care was taken to mobilize only the most essential units in order to avoid increasing the tension. While Rabin was meeting with Prime Minister Eshkol that day, they learned that the Egyptian Sixth Division had crossed the Suez Canal.

Rabin's account of the events of May 19 does much to illustrate the prevailing atmosphere among Israeli military leaders.

> May 19. A discussion of all heads of military branches. The picture is clarifying. The political and military reality that existed so far has completely collapsed. The UN forces are gone. A formidable Egyptian military force is already concentrated in the Sinai, although Egypt's Fourth Division has not yet entered the area. The chief of intelligence estimates that Egyptian dispositions will now enable offensive operations. We decide to send further reinforcements to the south, north, and central regions.

> The same evening. Discussion at G.H.Q. Head of intelligence: "There is no doubt that the latest Egyptian moves constitute an extremely radical shift of the line accepted so far by Egypt." Yariv adds that since inter-Arab collaboration has not yet been established and not all the Egyptian forces have been sent to the Sinai—it is difficult to assume at this point that the Egyptians have changed their basic evaluation that the time for a struggle with Israel has not yet arrived. Nevertheless, the latest steps indicate an Egyptian readiness to move toward such a confrontation and perhaps even initiate it.[43]

Rabin presented four possible options which Egypt could choose: (1) not take any further steps, declare victory, and assert that Egypt had saved Syria from an Israeli attack; (2) provoke Israel into a reaction, with the assumption that it would result in failure and Egypt would make strategic gains; (3) initiate a surprise attack—should this be the Egyptians' choice, their primary targets would be Israeli airfields and other vital areas; (4) engage in a prolonged war of attrition that would force Israel to keep its reserves mobilized for an extended period of time, while Egypt waited for an opportune time to attack (after having withdrawn its forces from Yemen.) It was assumed that Syrian movements would be in accordance with Egyptian plans.

Rabin then analyzed each of these possible strategies *according to the risks involved for Israel.* He considered the third option to be the most dangerous, especially if coordinated with other Arab states and opened with an all-out air attack. He therefore ordered the IDF to prepare for this contingency, regardless of its low probability. The other options, although more likely, would not threaten Israel's existence—but a surprise attack would pose a mortal danger.

For many years the IDF had been prepared for this situation. It had detailed plans for two types of operations: the first was a defensive plan to be implemented in reaction to a full-scale Arab attack (Operation Anvil); the second (Operation Pitchfork against Egypt, Operation Scourge against Jordan, and Operation Sledgehammer against Syria) was a preemptive offensive that could only be implemented if the IDF had ample warning and the appropriate political circumstances.[44]

In his memoirs Rabin states that by May 19 he believed war was unavoidable, for the new reality brought about by Nasser's moves (i.e., the collapse of Israeli deterrence) could only be changed by the use of force. Yet Egypt still had not given Israel a casus belli, although intelligence sources strengthened the estimates that Egypt planned to go to war. It was therefore decided to mobilize more units and carry out additional reconnaissance flights over the Sinai.

On May 20, Yariv reported that the Fourth Armored Division had not yet moved into the Sinai, but that the Egyptians were returning three infantry brigades from Yemen and hastily moving into the Sinai amid great confusion and disorder. During this period, the Israeli government emphasized the need to solve the snowballing crisis via political means. The general staff feared that (a) the Egyptians or the Arab coalition would attack before the Israeli army could gain the initiative, thereby leaving the IDF to fight in the worst possible situation; (b) even if the Israeli government finally gave the green light, it would be too late because the Arabs would be on the alert. As the number of Egyptian troops in the Sinai grew (finally reaching seven divisions)—so did the pressure of the IDF commanders to launch a preemptive attack before it was too late.

On May 21, the Israeli government convened for its usual weekly meeting.

Rabin reviewed the preparatory measures which the IDF had taken, pointing out that the IDF was strong enough to allow a few more days of negotiations as advocated by the U.S. government. Intelligence reports that day brought more bad news. A general mobilization had been declared in Egypt—and Jordan's chief of staff flew to Cairo to coordinate Jordanian and Egyptian military plans. Yet there was still no sense of urgency on the Israeli side since there were no indications that the Egyptians planned to block the Straits of Tiran and the sea lanes to Eilat. But the next day, an unexpectedly large number of Egyptian troops was sent to Sharm el-Sheikh, which controlled the Straits of Tiran. In the meantime, it was estimated that, given the lack of international support, the IDF would have no more than twenty-four to seventy-two hours to achieve its operational goals before being pressured by the superpowers to end the war.

At 3:45 on the morning of May 23, the Israelis learned that Egypt had formally announced its decision to block the Straits of Tiran to all ships traveling to and from Israel. Additional reports told of a Syrian decision to stop all movements of the UN observers in the Golan Heights and of Syrian reinforcements along the border.

That afternoon, Rabin explained the IDF's plans to the government, emphasizing that it would be impossible to confine military operations to the Sharm el-Sheikh area. The most effective way to open the war would be with an attack on Egyptian airfields, regardless of their high state of alert. It was, he continued, preferable to act as soon as possible, but a delay of forty-eight hours would not be too detrimental. The government then decided to take an additional forty-eight hours to solve the crisis by diplomatic means. Rabin and the other top military leaders acquiesced, but they felt that a much longer time would be needed if the government was going to examine all of the diplomatic options for avoiding war. To Rabin, much more than freedom of navigation in the Straits of Tiran was at stake.

> Nasser has deliberately and provocatively challenged us. He has thrown us a glove. If Israel wants war—*ahalan wa-sahalan* (''welcome'' in Arabic). If we do not take up the glove thrown, the deterrent capacity of the IDF will be meaningless. Israel will be humiliated. What power in the world would then be interested in supporting a small state that had ceased to be a military factor and whose neighbors were pinpricking it humiliatingly from all directions? . . . Nasser has threatened Israel's position, and in a later stage his army will threaten our very existence. Even though I don't want war, we cannot escape it if the American diplomatic efforts fail.[45]

War became inevitable that day. Even if diplomacy had succeeded, it would have created the impression that Israel had been saved by the efforts of the great powers and was incapable of defending itself; therefore, heartened by Israel's apparent weakness, the Arabs would have attacked sooner or later anyway. During that day and the next, Ezer Weizman urged an immediate preemptive air and ground attack. Weizman's certainty that such an attack would succeed encouraged Rabin, but in his memoirs Weizman claims Rabin did not have complete faith in the IAF's capacity to execute the attack.

The IDF general staff issued additional orders on May 23 for the continuation of reserve mobilization, although it was obvious that no military operations would take place within the next three days. A deception plan intended to induce Egypt to send more troops to the Sharm el-Sheikh area was also scrapped. Chief of Staff Rabin suffered a nervous breakdown and was out of the decision-making process until May 25.

May 25 brought mounting pressure from top military commanders (especially Weizman and Yariv) to resort to a preemptive attack as soon as the next morning; Yariv added that there was a possibility that Soviet intelligence had informed the Egyptians of Israel's plan to destroy Egypt's air force on the ground, which might give the Egyptians a reason to attack that night. The commander of the IAF said that an Egyptian attack was possible, but the IAF would nevertheless have to wait until morning before any action could be taken.

This was indeed a classic case of the reciprocal fear of surprise attack. It is not clear what led Yariv to expect an Egyptian attack at that time. Perhaps the Israelis had projected their own plans on the enemy. In any event, Chief of Staff Rabin ordered a full defensive alert for that night as well as the final mobilization of all Israeli reserve units. By that time, the Egyptians had concentrated as many as four infantry divisions and an armored force equivalent to two divisions in the Sinai; among these was the division by which Egyptian intentions were gauged. (In all, the Egyptians had over 800 tanks in the Sinai.)

The debate between the government and the IDF general staff now intensified. Most of the ministers were still seeking a political solution, or at least an American commitment to open the Straits of Tiran; they did not believe the military leaders' assurances that the war could be won without external support. The military leaders insisted that every passing day enabled the Egyptians to strengthen their positions in the Sinai. Why should Israel, they argued, sacrifice the element of surprise, or even worse, allow itself to be attacked first by the Egyptians? Prime Minister Eshkol nevertheless maintained that the IDF should not attack until all political alternatives had been exhausted; he was still waiting for the results of Foreign Minister Eban's conversations with President Johnson and U.S. State Department officials. Rabin now believed that the American response would be unsatisfactory, and that Israel would have to go to war on Saturday, May 27, or on Sunday, May 28.

On May 26, the Israeli government received contradictory messages from the United States. First it was reported that the U.S. Sixth Fleet would participate in opening the Straits of Tiran, and the president would warn the Egyptians that if they attacked Israel the United States would come to its aid. A second report poured cold water on the Israelis; Secretary of State Dean Rusk, it said, had told Eban that the United States had no information concerning any Egyptian offensive intentions, and President Johnson could not give Israel assurances without first obtaining congressional approval. If Israel attacked first, the Americans would find it difficult to lend any support. The president, the report continued, planned to establish an international naval force to break the blockade of the Straits of Tiran.

The general staff recommended that Eshkol convene the Cabinet in order to approve a decision to go to war the following morning (May 27). Eshkol refused, saying no decision would be taken until Eban had returned to report on his conversations. That night, the Russian ambassador requested an immediate meeting with Eshkol, where he accused Israel of being responsible for the crisis and warned it not to attack. After this conversation, Eshkol called Rabin to discuss the possibility of sending an Israeli ship to the Straits of Tiran, and letting the Egyptians fire the first shot so the United States would not be able to complain that Israel had begun the conflict. Rabin felt such a move would only warn the Egyptians of Israeli intentions, needlessly compromising the element of surprise.[46]

Intelligence reports on the morning of May 27 indicated that an Egyptian armored division had taken up a position from which it could cut the Negev in half in a thrust to Jordan. Weizman again urged that the IDF be permitted to at least launch its planned attack on the Egyptian Air Force; he assumed that following an air attack, fighting would also break out on the ground, thus forcing a decision on the government.[47]

Intelligence reports from the United States suggested that the CIA did not believe the Egyptians had offensive intentions at that stage. But bad news came when Eban cabled the contents of his conversations with President Johnson. If Israel took action on its own initiative, Johnson warned, it would be left in isolation, with the United States unable to provide support. A subsequent report included some of the demands Nasser presented to UN Secretary-General U Thant; Israel would have to recognize the Gulf of Aquaba as Egyptian waters, as well as agree to other (equally unacceptable) conditions.[48]

In the Cabinet meeting that evening, Rabin pressed for a decision to go to war, while Eban reported that President Johnson had warned, "Israel must not take action first! I need two to three weeks to implement our political plans that will bring an end to the crisis."[49] The Cabinet's first vote on whether to go to war ended in a draw; nine ministers for, nine against, with some of those voting against threatening to resign if the government's decision was otherwise.

On May 28, Yariv suggested that the following day would be excellent for launching an attack, since Egypt's best task force on the central front could be caught off guard as it took up new forward positions. Another Cabinet meeting indicated that most members favored delaying a decision on war for two or three weeks, as President Johnson had requested.

Realizing how difficult it was for Israel to maintain a full mobilization, Rabin and other top military leaders were dismayed. Israel is forced to base most of its army on the mobilization of reserve units in wartime, and during a crisis every male citizen between the ages of 18 and 55 is called to service. Under such circumstances, the Israeli economy is completely paralyzed, and a prolonged war or crisis can lead to its collapse. This has introduced a destabilizing element into Middle Eastern crises; after a certain period of full mobilization, the Israeli government must launch a preemptive attack to avoid its slow economic destruction. This was not fully understood by its Arab neighbors and the great powers.

Nasser's perception of the Israeli leadership was an important factor in his calculations. Israel was deep in an economic recession and the morale of the population was visibly low. An effective leader in many ways, Prime Minister Eshkol lacked charisma and had no heroic image. He was generally thought to be hesitant and indecisive. Chief of Staff Rabin was known as a competent, analytical, and technocratic officer—and not as a courageous or heroic leader (like Dayan). The impression of a weak Israeli leadership certainly undermined the credibility of the nation's deterrence posture, perhaps encouraging Nasser's belief that he could achieve an easy victory without war.

When Eshkol turned to the Israeli public in a radio speech on the evening of May 28, he was depressed and tired after a prolonged governmental debate in which the religious ministers and Abba Eban had threatened to resign if Israel went to war instead of trying to negotiate for two or three more weeks. His speech was abysmal—Eshkol had not read the speech before, is said to have lost his glasses, and delivered a hesitant message that caused serious demoralization in Israel. It may also have inadvertently reinforced Nasser's image of a weak Israeli government.[50] What Nasser misunderstood was the internal dynamics of Israeli politics.

After the speech, Eshkol met with the military leaders and insisted it was still too early to take military action. The generals responded angrily, arguing that no other country was going to help Israel, which was meanwhile losing all ability to deter its enemies. War was necessary to guarantee Israel's survival. Eshkol defended his position, but the arguments in favor of military action must have eroded his belief in the desirability of further delay.

The government's indecision forced the IDF to wait; no deadline was established for how much longer the government was willing to delay. It was decided that 30,000 nonessential reservists should be released. This may have caused Soviet and Arab intelligence organizations to conclude that Israel was not planning on war.

On May 30, history repeated itself when King Hussein signed a mutual defense agreement with Egypt. The two countries agreed to coordinate their military plans, and an Egyptian commando task force was sent to Jordan. Because of Israel's vulnerability to an attack from Jordan, the IDF decided to change its military dispositions along the Syrian and Jordanian borders. Jordan was now ranked as the second most dangerous threat, with Egypt first and Syria third. All plans related to a war against Jordan were brought up to date, including the possible occupation of Jerusalem. Hussein's move strengthened Israeli fears and lent credence to the argument that a preemptive surprise attack was the best way to win an unavoidable war.

On June 1, Prime Minister Eshkol learned that President Johnson had no specific plans for breaking Nasser's blockade of the Straits of Tiran. Realizing that there was no more reason to delay, he agreed to create a National United Front government. Dayan was appointed defense minister and Begin also joined the government. Eshkol now had both the justification and the political support necessary to go to war. That same day, Yariv reported to the new government on the latest developments and summarized the situation. No specific decision was made, but, in Rabin's words, there was no doubt that the moment of decision was near.

The IDF presented its plans for war to the Cabinet Committee on Foreign Affairs and National Security on June 2. As expected, the military leaders recommended that Israel attack as soon as possible in order to minimize casualties and guarantee a successful outcome. They were supported by Dayan. Eshkol, Eban, Allon, Dayan, and Rabin secretly decided not to attack *before* Monday, June 5, 1967. This was a negative decision, in that it did not specify a date for opening the war, but for the first time, diplomacy was relegated to the background. That afternoon, Dayan told a British journalist that it was both too late and too early for Israel to begin a war. He repeated this statement during a news conference on June 3: "It is too late for a spontaneous military reaction to Egypt's blockade of the Tiran Straits . . . and still too early to learn any conclusions of the possible outcome of diplomatic action. The Government—before I became a member of it—embarked on diplomacy and we must give it a chance."[51]

As part of the plan to disguise Israel's intention to attack, a number of reservists were released during the weekend.[52] Meanwhile, Dayan and Rabin put the final touches on the plan to attack Egypt. All participants assumed Israel would have no more than 72 hours to accomplish its goals; after that, international pressures such as UN Security Council ceasefire resolutions and Soviet threats of military intervention would force Israel to slow or even halt its operations.

On June 3, Amit, the director of the Mossad, returned from the United States. After lengthy conversations with U.S. officials, he had concluded that the United States would do nothing to help open the Straits of Tiran—but would also not interfere if Israel should attack the Egyptian Army. It was determined that a final decision would be taken the next morning by the ministers' committee on national security. The meeting included Eban's presentation of the latest reports on the fruitless diplomatic efforts. Intelligence reports concluded that the Egyptians believed a military confrontation was inevitable. A special command had been established in Jordan under an Egyptian general, who ordered the Jordanian forces to take up positions along the Israeli border. Two Egyptian commando battalions had also been sent to Jordan. All reports indicated that the Arabs would soon attack. Dayan then presented his views, devoting most of his speech to the dangers of sacrificing surprise, especially when Israel was faced with the probability of a two-front war. Dayan's second point was that if Israel did not strike first, it would have to fight according to the enemy's dictates.[53] After his suggestions were put to a vote and approved by the government, Dayan instructed Rabin to prepare the attack for the next morning.

The course of the Six Day War has often been described in detail. Therefore, this chapter only briefly discusses the Israeli surprise attack from the air at the beginning of the war, and summarizes some explanations for the Arab failure to anticipate it.

The time chosen for a surprise attack reflects many considerations, but is frequently either at dawn or dusk. The Israelis chose 8:45 a.m. Egyptian time. The air force and intelligence service had long kept a close watch on the Egyptian Air Force's daily routine—especially during the last two weeks of the crisis. They found that the Egyptians habitually sent out hour-long patrols with the first light of dawn, after which the pilots ate breakfast between eight and nine o'clock. This gave the Israelis an hour during which the high level of alert maintained at dawn would be relaxed. Another advantage of this timing was that most senior and medium-ranking Egyptian officers would be en route from their homes to the base. Once the dangerous early morning hours had passed without incident, the Egyptians would be expecting another routine day of training and work.[54]

The choice was ideal for the Israelis. It enabled the pilots to get plenty of sleep and to fly in daylight, therefore more easily maintaining radio silence. They would then arrive at their targets after the early morning mists had dispersed, yet it was early enough to allow for the exploitation of initial success by repeating the attacks as many times as necessary.

The attack was a maxi-max high risk strategy, where almost all of the Israeli Air Force was sent in the first wave; out of 196 aircraft available, 183 participated, leaving only a dozen or so to defend Israeli skies in an emergency.

(Weizman claims only four were left to defend Israeli airspace.)[55] The simultaneous arrival of the planes over Egyptian airfields called for a complex plan, which coordinated factors such as the travel time to each airfield and the various speeds of different types of aircraft.[56] Radio silence was total. Even a pilot who had to bail out on the way to the target could not report his position. Flying at treetop level, all aircraft simultaneously arrived over their targets undetected.[57] Executed in three waves, the attack concentrated on Egyptian aircraft, runways, radar, and control stations. The first wave attacked 11 airfields, destroying 197 Egyptian aircraft (189 on the ground, 8 in the air). Six airfields were paralyzed and 16 radar stations were destroyed. A second attack according to almost real time information did not allow the Egyptians to regain their balance. While the first attack had been planned to the last detail, the second included many improvisations tailored to the results of the first wave. The second wave of 164 aircraft attacked 14 airfields and destroyed 107 Egyptian planes. A third and final wave finished the Egyptian Air Force;[58] the Egyptians had lost three-quarters of their air force, or 304 out of 419 aircraft. Despite their incredible success, the Israelis lost ten percent of their aircraft: Weizman reports that 19 out of 196 aircraft were ruined.[59]

The success of this surprise attack reduced the threat to the Israeli hinterland as well as to its advancing forces in the Sinai; it gave an enormous boost to Israeli morale and enabled the IDF to enjoy air support, while the Egyptian Army in the Sinai was left exposed to Israeli air attacks.

Approximately three hours after the war broke out, Syrian, Jordanian, and Iraqi aircraft attacked targets in Israel. The commander of the IAF instructed some of the third wave aircraft en route to Egypt to change course and attack Jordanian, Syrian, and Iraqi airfields. These attacks proved highly successful even without the advantage of surprise. The Jordanian Air Force was completely decimated, half of the Syrian Air Force was destroyed, and one airfield in Iraq was attacked. Israeli losses were 10 aircraft.

The spectacular success of the air force was achieved not only through the excellent performance of its pilots, but—more importantly—by meticulous intelligence work. Israeli intelligence apparently knew the number and location of all Arab aircraft, and knew of all radar installations and antiaircraft defenses, as well as the routine at each airfield. The role of intelligence organizations is critical both in warning against a surprise attack and in preparing one; yet while their failures draw universal condemnation—their successes are often taken for granted.

*   *   *   *

Why did Egypt fail to anticipate the attack? There is no simple answer. A variety of explanations can be offered, although it is difficult to evaluate the relative importance of each.

1. Perhaps the most important explanation lies in their perception of Prime Minister Eshkol's indecisiveness and weakness. His bland style combined with what appeared to be an uninspired military leadership under Chief of Staff Rabin, and an economic recession, probably nurtured the idea that this Israeli government would be incapable of deciding to go to war. The government's slow response to the developing crisis, its emphasis on diplomacy, and Eshkol's unfortunate speech may have reinforced Nasser's conviction that he could win the crisis either without war, or in a war begun at his own convenience.

2. The Arab intelligence services probably had very incomplete information on Israel's real military strength. They also apparently underestimated the level of Israeli training (in particular, that of pilots and tank crews), and the very low turn-around time of Israeli aircraft—factors that magnified the size and efficiency of the Israeli Air Force. (On the average, each Israeli plane could be put into action 4 or 5 times a day.) Egypt's intelligence service may therefore have focused on the quantitative rather than the qualitative aspects of the balance of power—a common but dangerous error. The inclusion of the Syrian, Jordanian, and Iraqi forces in Egyptian planning as the crisis progressed must have strengthened the belief that Israel would not attack first against such odds, especially because it had already lost the element of surprise. Israel's military achievements during the Sinai Campaign were either forgotten or attributed to British and French aid.

3. The Egyptians did not understand the Israeli "Massada" or "Holocaust" complex and the sensitivity of the Israeli military doctrine concerning the need to preempt whenever Israel felt sufficiently threatened by Arab troop concentrations. Nasser also did not realize that by closing the Straits of Tiran—a declared Israeli casus belli—he left Israel no choice, since its leaders considered that loss of deterrence worse than war. They preferred war on their terms to a delayed war on Nasser's terms.

4. As the crisis unfolded, Israel was isolated and without the strong support of any great power. The Soviet Union had triggered the crisis and then sided with Egypt and the other Arab states. France, Israel's major weapons supplier, and Great Britain imposed an embargo on weapons shipments to Israel. Preoccupied by the Vietnam War, the United States refused to help Israel open the Straits of Tiran, even though the Americans had previously guaranteed Israel's right of passage in exchange for its withdrawal from the Sinai in 1956–57. Nasser may have concluded that Israel would not dare to attack without the support of at least one great power.

5. Egypt may have been misled by comparing the May-June 1967 crisis with Operation Rotem—the February 1961 crisis which was defused without the outbreak of hostilities. The circumstances were, however, radically different; in 1967 there was the blockade of the Straits of Tiran and the growing involvement of Syria, Iraq, and Jordan. Above all, Operation Rotem was not conducted in public, while the 1967 crisis involved public commitments and an invoked casus belli.

6. Israeli deception also played an important part—particularly Dayan's June

3 statement that the crisis must now be resolved by diplomatic means because it was too late to go to war. Reported by the international press, the "release" from service of many Israeli soldiers on the eve of the war must have helped allay Egyptian suspicions. It is possible that additional deceptions were used and not made public after the war.

7. Because of the unusual length of the crisis, the Egyptian Army developed a new routine and reached its peak level of alert in late May.

8. Often armies that are involved in the preparation of an offensive, as the Egyptians were in the Sinai, tend to concentrate on their own planning ("planning in a vacuum") and ignore similar preparations being made by the enemy. (The German surprise attack in the Battle of the Bulge occurred when the American and British forces were preoccupied by their own plans for a new offensive.)[60]

Thus, the Israelis went from being surprised, to surprising their adversary. Benefiting from the lessons of Operation Rotem, the reformed Israeli intelligence service had performed extremely well. After the Egyptian Army moved into the Sinai with great publicity and fanfare, Israeli intelligence was able to follow precisely the Egyptian build-up, enabling the IDF high command and the government to know at what point the Egyptian troop concentrations posed a threat. Nevertheless, to rely completely on intelligence estimates under such circumstances is tricky; as we have seen, Israeli intelligence did not have sufficient information on Nasser's intentions.

The gradual development of the crisis helped Israeli intelligence to avoid yet another blunder. The Israelis had time to countermobilize, prepare their forces in the Negev, and adjust their perceptions. They moved from an estimate that war was not likely in the next two years—to Egyptian defensive concentrations in the Sinai—to an Egyptian move to military dispositions that implied offensive intentions.

Any situation involving the possibility of a surprise attack by either of two sides at the same time is a touch-and-go predicament. For all we know, the Israeli decision to attack barely beat the Arabs to the punch. The asymmetry of dangers and fears made the Israelis attack first—a situation not fully appreciated by the Egyptians.

The Six Day War later shaped Egyptian and Israeli behavior in the Yom Kippur War in 1973. The Egyptians learned the correct lessons and opened the 1973 war without a prior political move or crisis; the Israelis learned the wrong lesson and expected that the next war would also be preceded by some kind of political crisis to serve as a warning.

THE OCTOBER 1973 WAR[61]

By 1973, experience had taught the Arab countries that strategic surprise was a key element in military success. Earlier, the Arabs had been confident that their overwhelming numerical military superiority guaranteed an easy victory; no effort was made to conceal their preparations for war. In contrast, their plans for attack in 1973 were made under the strictest secrecy and concealed by elaborate deception; great efforts were made to maintain a facade of routine activities.

From Arab reports, it is clear that the *planning* and *timing* of the attack were meticulous. Early October was chosen as the best time to attack for a variety of reasons. In the first place, the autumn climate was most suitable for the attacking forces. Secondly, it coincided with the Jewish high holidays—on the assumption that the Israeli level of alert would be lower, that more than the usual number of soldiers would be on leave, and that the closure of all businesses on the day of atonement would slow down Israeli mobilization.[62] A third factor was the approach of Israeli elections in early November, which diverted the attention of Israeli leaders from security matters and foreign affairs to domestic affairs and political campaigning.[63] Furthermore, in 1973 the holiest of the Arab holidays—Ramadan—fell in October; and it was hoped the Israelis would assume that no Moslem country would initiate a war during that month. (So far as is known, this last ruse did not have any effect on Israeli intelligence estimates.)

Purportedly in preparation for the well-advertised war games that were to begin in early October, the Egyptians and Syrians readied their troops over a period of four months. This undoubtedly misled Israeli intelligence, creating an opportunity for the Arabs to concentrate their troops without starting an international crisis. When Israeli intelligence grasped the real intent of the troop concentrations, it was too late for Israel to muster sufficient political and military counterpressure by belatedly activating its own mobilization process. On the morning of October 6, when Israeli intelligence concluded that the Syrian-Egyptian war games were only a ruse, much valuable warning time had been lost. The government had always been promised a warning time of at least 48 to 76 hours, but in October 1973, it was cut to 12–16 hours, which did not allow a full-scale mobilization. To maintain secrecy for as long as possible, Egyptian and Syrian soldiers were not told—until the attack itself—that their war games were the first phase of a real war.[64]

Other deception plans included, for example, the demobilization of 20,000 Egyptian soldiers 48 hours before the war and the spreading of rumors over a long period of time concerning the shortage of spare parts for Soviet military equipment, the low maintenance level of Egyptian antiaircraft batteries, and other indications about the low level of preparedness for war and the weakness of Egyptian and Syrian material capabilities. On the political level, Egyptian Foreign Minister Zayat arrived in the United States at the end of September 1973 to reactivate Washington as a mediator and to give peace another chance. At the last moment, the attention of Israeli decision-makers was drawn to a

Palestinian terrorist action in Vienna, which Syrian intelligence claimed to have planned.[65]

Major General Hassan el Badri calls the Egyptian deception plan "an overwhelming success" that "misled foreign intelligence service bodies including the CIA, as well as Israeli intelligence."[66] Yet it seems the only part that was truly effective was the "war games." Otherwise, the Egyptians simply added noise to a system already overloaded with contradictory information. While the attack was indeed devastating, it was technically only a partial surprise.[67] When it began, partial mobilization had already been declared and Israeli troops were supposed to be fully alerted.

The Egyptians and Syrians surprised the Israeli Army not only in the timing of their attack but also in two other important areas, namely in technology[68] and in their military doctrine and goals. The effectiveness of some of the Arab coalition's weapons—in particular Soviet antiaircraft missiles, antitank missiles, bridging equipment, and night fighting equipment—came as a great surprise to Israeli troops on the battlefield.[69] Both Arab armies had introduced these new weapons on a *massive scale*—the condition necessary for making a powerful impact with new weapons systems. Moreover, the effectiveness of the new weapons enabled Egypt and Syria to design a new military doctrine which proved to be more appropriate for the quality of their manpower. Some of the Israeli doctrine's greatest advantages were neutralized; and the Israeli troops, initially thrown off balance, lost a number of important battles. By the time adequate countertactics had been improvised, the Israelis had suffered heavy material losses, lost ground that had to be regained, and suffered a blow to their morale and self-confidence.

The innovative Egyptian doctrine was strategically offensive but tactically defensive. It was the opposite of the Israeli military doctrine which was strategically defensive, but highly offensive on the tactical level. The Egyptians were able to develop such a modern version of Wellington's tactics only because of new weapons that gave the defense the advantage. The highly effective and mobile antiaircraft missiles (the SAM-6, and the infantry-fired SAM-7) combined with the deadly rapid-firing ZS4-23-4 antiaircraft guns, imposed considerable limits on the performance of the Israeli Air Force; and the Soviet antitank missiles (the SAGGER and SWATTER) again combined with the RP6-7 and hand-held short-range infantry nonguided type of bazooka blunted, at least for the first few days, the offensive superiority of the Israeli armor.

In the years preceding the war, Israeli intelligence *had* obtained all the technical data on the performance of the newly acquired Egyptian and Syrian weapons. This information was duly passed along to the Israeli armed forces on all levels but was not taken seriously. Neither Israeli intelligence nor the general staff and various branches foresaw the impact those weapons would have on the battlefield, and they failed to recognize the new tactical opportunities that were created. In short, they did not see that the pendulum in the development of modern weapons had swung in favor of the defense. As a result, no effort was made to modify the Israeli military doctrine accordingly. The Israelis made a mistake that can be found in many other failures to anticipate a surprise attack: they projected their own military doctrine on the enemy. The cardinal assumption of the Israeli doctrine was that without air superiority or at least parity, one could not expect to win a war; furthermore, the offensive power of the tank dominated the battlefield on the ground. In both types of warfare the Israelis had a big advantage over their adversaries. Through the projection of their own reasoning on their adversaries, the Israelis felt that since the Egyptians and Syrians had no chance of winning the war militarily, they would not consider taking military action until their air power and the performance of their tank crews had been improved. To all this the Israelis added one more projection: their first defeat would also be the last one, so they would never dare to start a war they did not expect to win. The Israelis therefore incorrectly assumed that the Egyptians and Syrians would not open a war in which they would lose, particularly because of the 1967 debacle and what the Israelis perceived as the Egyptian defeat in the war of attrition.

Assumptions of symmetry are dangerous. While the Israelis were thinking positively, their enemies were thinking negatively. The Arabs set limited goals rather than a clear-cut military victory, and did not plan to achieve air superiority or to defeat Israeli tanks in huge tank battles. Instead, new technology enabled them to limit Israeli air superiority from the ground and blunt Israeli tank power with infantry. Significantly, Egypt and Syria could lose the war on the battlefield and win it politically (as they did), a strategy which was never open to, or feasible for, the Israelis.

This was a case in which there was no doubt concerning the adversaries' intentions. The Israelis had always assumed that whenever the neighboring Arab states had the capability to attack—they would. The Israelis' major mistake was to focus on the Egyptian and Syrian capabilities. Having concluded that the Arabs did not have the capabilities to wage a full-scale war, the Israelis believed that this would, in the short run, also affect their intentions. Had the Israelis instead focused more attention on Arab political intentions, they might have more seriously considered the possibility of a limited war or of a total war whose outcome was uncertain.

There are other important explanations for Israel's surprise and the decision not to preempt when the government became aware of the Arabs' plans in the last hours before the war broke out. Confident of their superior capabilities, top Israel commanders overestimated the defensive value of the Suez Canal and the Golan Heights on the one hand, and underestimated Arab capabilities on the other. They misjudged the impact that leaving the first move to their adversaries would have on their own plans. This weakened their incentive to preempt (although the Israeli Air Force was prepared to stage a preemptive attack at around 12:00 noon). As it turned out, knowledge of the timing of the attack did not prevent many other, no less damaging surprises from occurring in terms of the attackers' methods, doctrines, and new weapons. The Israeli high command temporarily lost control over the direction and pace of the battle, and could not implement its original plans, while the rate of attrition of manpower and matériel was much higher than anticipated.

There were, however, *political reasons* that reduced the incentives to preempt. Having been branded as aggressors and occupiers following the Six Day War, the Israelis were reluctant to risk this again. After preempting, it would be impossible to prove that the enemy had indeed been poised to attack. Moreover, since there is never a one hundred percent certainty that the enemy will attack—only a higher or lower probability—the Israelis were afraid that a preemptive attack would be a self-fulfilling prophecy. The Israeli government warned the Egyptian and Syrian governments, through the United States, not to attack. Israel naively thought that the Arabs would cancel their plans when they realized that they had lost the element of surprise as far as timing was concerned. A partial alert and mobilization in Israel, known to the Egyptians and Syrians, was to imply that there was no use in beginning a war, since Israel was ready to defend itself. An earlier partial alert and mobilization declared by the Israelis in May 1973 had *not* ended in conflict. Prime Minister Golda Meir and Defense Minister Dayan later admitted that the Israeli government decided not to preempt for fear of losing the backing of the United States, Israel's only ally. American officials (Henry Kissinger in particular) had threatened to withdraw American support if Israel attacked first.

The propensity to use strategic surprise is directly related to the general stability of a regional system. In an unstable system such as the Middle East, conflicting political, religious, and ethnic interests combined with a highly militarized system continue to provide a powerful incentive to resort to surprise attack. The military experience of nations in the area has demonstrated that a successful surprise attack can be the key to victory, sometimes even to the future of a nation. It is therefore to be expected that in the future, strategic surprises, such as the recent Iraqi attack on Iran, will recur more frequently in the Middle East than in any other region.

NOTES

1. Thomas C. Schelling, *Arms and Influence* (New Haven: Yale University Press, 1966), chapter 6, pp. 221-59.
2. See Gerhard Ritter, *The Schlieffen Plan* (London: Oswald Wolff, 1958); L. F.

Turner, "The Significance of the Schlieffen Plan" in Paul M. Kennedy, ed., *The War Plans of the Great Powers 1880–1914* (London: Allen and Unwin, 1979), pp. 199-221.

3. Michael I. Handel, *Israel's Political-Military Doctrine* (Cambridge: Harvard Center for International Affairs, 1973).

4. See in particular Yigal Allon, *Masach Shel Chol* [A curtain of sand], rev. ed. (Tel Aviv: Hakibbutz Hameuchad, 1969); Moshe Dayan, *Story of My Life* (New York: Warner Books, Inc., 1977).

5. Handel, *Israel's Political-Military Doctrine*; Edward Luttwak and Dan Horowitz, *The Israeli Army* (London: Allen Lane, 1975).

6. The section on the Sinai and Suez Campaigns is based on the following books: A. J. Barker, *Suez: The Seven Day War* (London: Faber and Faber, 1964); Michael Bar-Zohar, *Ben-Gurion: Biographia Politit* [A political biography], 3 vols. (Tel Aviv: Am Oved, 1977), vol. 2; André Beaufre, *The Suez Expedition—1956* (New York: Praeger, 1967); David Ben-Gurion, *Israel: A Personal History* (New York: Funk and Wagnalls, 1971); Moshe Dayan, *Diary of the Sinai Campaign* (London: Widenfeld and Nicholson, 1966); Abba Eban, *An Autobiography* (New York: Random House, 1977), p. 211; Dwight D. Eisenhower, *Waging Peace: 1956–1961* (Garden City, N.Y.: Doubleday and Co., 1965); Herman Finer, *Dulles Over Suez* (Chicago: Quadrangle, 1965); Kenneth Love, *Suez: The Twice-Fought War* (New York: McGraw-Hill, 1969); Nadav Safran, *From War to War* (New York: Pegasus, 1969); Hugh Thomas, *Suez* (New York: Harper and Row, 1967); Ezer Weizman, *Lecha Shamaim Lecha Ha'aretz* [To you the sky, to you the land] (Tel Aviv: Maariv, 1975), pp. 153-54; the abbreviated English translation is Ezer Weizman, *On Eagles' Wings* (Tel Aviv: Steimazky's, 1976).

7. Handel, *Israel's Political-Military Doctrine*, pp. 21-37; Michael Brecher, *The Foreign Policy System of Israel* (New Haven: Yale University Press, 1972), pp. 542-65.

8. See Ben-Gurion, *Israel: A Personal History*, pp. 482-502; Dayan, *Diary of the Sinai Campaign*, p. 4; Safran, *From War to War*, p. 209.

9. Dayan, *Diary of the Sinai Campaign*, p. 58; Ben-Gurion, *Israel: A Personal History*, pp. 502-04.

10. The Pact of Amman between Egypt, Jordan, and Syria was signed on October 24, 1956. On the eve of the Six Day War, King Hussein repeated the 1956 mistake and signed a defense pact putting the Jordanian Armed Forces under Egyptian command; see Dayan, *Avnay Derech* [Milestones] (Jerusalem: Edanim Publishers, 1976), pp. 420, 424, 426.

11. Dayan, *Avnay Derech* [Milestones], pp. 10-15; Ben-Gurion, *Israel: A Personal History*, pp. 437-38.

12. Ben-Gurion was reluctant to join the Suez Campaign, but finally agreed under the pressure of Dayan and Peres from within, and French promises from without. The best account is in Michael Bar-Zohar, *Ben-Gurion: Biographia Politit* [A political biography], vol. 4, pp. 1207-09.

13. Love, *Suez: The Twice-Fought War*, p. 481.

14. The names of the thirteen participants in the Sèvres conference are listed in Bar-Zohar, *Ben-Gurion: Biographia Politit*, pp. 1232-61. The protocol containing the agreement was typed in only three copies, and has never formally been published or mentioned at all by Ben-Gurion in his writings.

15. Love, *Suez: The Twice-Fought War*, p. 472.

16. See Shabtai Teveth, *Moshe Dayan: Biographia* [A biography] (Tel Aviv: Shocken Press, 1972), p. 456.

17. Abba Eban, *An Autobiography*, p. 211; Herman Finer, *Dulles Over Suez*, pp. 353-54.
18. Ben-Gurion, *Israel: A Personal History*, pp. 503-05.
19. Dayan, *Diary of the Sinai Campaign*, pp. 37-38.
20. The misconception here is that two countries in conflict over one issue cannot collaborate on other issues. The American involvement in Vietnam implied to most observers that the United States could not simultaneously negotiate a rapprochement with China, which supported the North Vietnamese. Similarly, communist Russia and Nazi Germany, which were deep in ideological conflict in 1939, surprised everyone when they concluded the Ribbentrop-Molotov agreement. The fact that the United States was involved in a conflict with Iran over the American hostages does not mean that it would not respond to an Iranian call for help should that country be invaded by the Soviet Union.
21. Dayan, *Diary of the Sinai Campaign*, p. 58.
22. Ibid., p. 70. The articles published in Israel's daily newspapers were encouraged by the Israeli general staff. Although the press in Western democracies is not systematically manipulated as in totalitarian states, it can be influenced—perhaps with even greater success. The government does not require the active collaboration of the press—it simply releases information selectively. Also, soldiers participating in a mobilization may not be aware (a) that they are preparing for war but are being told until the last minute that they are participating in an exercise, (b) of the true direction of the attack.
23. On October 25, the U.S. State Department received news from military intelligence that Israel was beginning to mobilize. The U.S. ambassador cabled late in the afternoon of October 28 (Israeli time) that the Israeli mobilization was now total. Finer, *Dulles Over Suez*, pp. 148-49.
24. Dayan, *Diary of the Sinai Campaign*, p. 71.
25. Finer, *Dulles Over Suez*, p. 353; Bar-Zohar, *Ben-Gurion*, pp. 1258-59.
26. Eisenhower, *Waging Peace*, pp. 56, 72.
27. Love, *Suez: The Twice-Fought War*, pp. 471-72; Finer, *Dulles Over Suez*, pp. 335, 352.
28. Love, *Suez: The Twice-Fought War*, p. 472; Finer, *Dulles Over Suez*, p. 334.
29. Weizman, *Lecha Shamaim Lecha Ha'aretz*, pp. 153-54; see also Handel, *Israel's Political-Military Doctrine*, pp. 28-29, p. 81, notes 18-20.
30. This information may have slipped unnoticed through the hands of the Israeli censors when the book was published; see Dayan, *Diary of the Sinai Campaign*, p. 63.
31. In an appendix, Dayan included an Israeli intelligence report detailing Egyptian Air Force dispositions on the eve of the campaign (pp. 218-19). He also gives the Kadesh Planning Order No. 1 (October 5, 1956) but *not* the plans of the Israeli Air Force (p. 209).
32. Weizman, *Lecha Shamain Lecha Ha'aretz*, p. 156.
33. Barker, *Suez: The Seven Day War*, p. 99.
34. Ibid.; Beaufre, *The Suez Expedition 1956*, pp. 87-88. All in all, 260 Egyptian aircraft were destroyed, most on the ground; see Thomas, *Suez*, pp. 68-69.
35. Beaufre, *The Suez Expedition 1956*, pp. 68-69.
36. See Yitzhak Rabin, *Pinkas Sherut* [Memoirs], 2 vol. (Tel Aviv: Maariv, 1979), 1, p. 107. The American edition of Rabin's memoirs is abbreviated and omits many important facts; Yitzhak Rabin, *The Rabin Memoirs* (Boston: Little, Brown and Co., 1979).
37. According to Zeev Schiff and Eitan Haber, eds., *Lexicon Lebitachon Israel* [The

Israeli defense dictionary] (Tel Aviv: Zmora, Bitan, and Modam, 1976), pp. 482-83, Israeli intelligence was first informed of the Egyptian troop concentrations by U.S. sources.

38. Weizman, *Lecha Shamaim Lecha Ha'aretz*, p. 256; Rabin, *Pinkas Sherut*, p. 107.
39. Rabin, *Pinkas Sherut*, p. 108.
40. In a lecture at Harvard University in April 1967, Dayan said that he did not envision a war between Israel and Egypt for the next ten years; cited in Teveth, *Moshe Dayan*, p. 560; see also Rabin, *Pinkas Sherut*, 1, p. 133; Weizman, *Lecha Shamaim Lecha Ha'aretz*, p. 254.
41. Rabin, *Pinkas Sherut*, p. 134. In writing on the Six Day War, I have primarily relied on Yitzhak Rabin, *Pinkas Sherut*, but also on Dayan, *Avnay Derech*; Spectator [Major General Shlomo Gazit], "Moscow's Circle of Mistakes," *Ma'arachot* 209 (August 1970), pp. 2-7; Weizman, *Lecha Shamaim Lecha Ha'aretz*. The best detailed summary of the diplomatic background of the crisis and the decision-making process of the Israeli government is Michael Brecher, *Decisions in Israel's Foreign Policy* (London: Oxford University Press, 1974), chapter 7, pp. 318-453.
42. Rabin, *Pinkas Sherut*, p. 134.
43. Ibid., p. 139.
44. Rabin discloses in his memoirs for the first time that Israel's offensive planning was based on the operational defensive plans of the Egyptians (Al-Kahir), Jordan (Al-Hussein), and Syria (Al-Jihad). He adds that Israeli intelligence did not obtain their offensive plans—if indeed they existed. According to Rabin, the number of Egyptian troops sent into the Sinai was larger than their own original plans called for, which may indicate haste and lack of careful thought invested in Nasser's decisions.
45. Rabin, *Pinkas Sherut*, p. 158.
46. Ibid., p. 167.
47. Ibid., p. 168.
48. Ibid., p. 169; see also Brecher, *Decisions in Israel's Foreign Policy*, chapter 7; and Eban, *An Autobiography*, chapters 12-14.
49. Rabin, *Pinkas Sherut*, p. 170. Abba Eban's account of this conversation in his memoirs is different. I chose, however, to present Rabin's summary of the reports received, since it more accurately reflects the atmosphere in Israel. The Israeli government suspected that Eban's reports of his conversations were inaccurate—so much so that the head of the Mossad (the Israeli DDO), Meir Amit, was sent to Washington, D.C. on May 30 to determine the truth. The government's suspicions were correct; Eban, probably out of a desire to avoid war or to appear as if he had saved Israel at the last moment, had been sending back overly optimistic reports. See also Rabin, *Pinkas Sherut*, pp. 177-78; Brecher, *Decisions in Israel's Foreign Policy*, pp. 412, 414, 417.
50. Dayan, *Avnay Derech*, p. 419; Rabin, *Pinkas Sherut*, pp. 171-72; Brecher, *Decisions in Israel's Foreign Policy*, p. 401.
51. Quoted in Barton Whaley, *Stratagem: Deception and Surprise in War* (Cambridge, Mass.: MIT Center for International Studies, 1969), p. 575.
52. Ibid., p. 575.
53. The problem of gaining time to achieve decisive results before being stopped by external pressures was central to Israeli planning. Dayan suggested that everything possible be done to stretch the time available, delaying as long as possible the release of information that would clarify the situation. It was assumed that Arab

vanity, by refusing to admit defeat and boasting about nonexistent victories, would contribute to the political confusion on the international level, between Arab states, and between headquarters and field commands.

The Israelis assumed that as long as the Arabs were thought to be doing well, no one would interfere. It was therefore decided to open the war with a vague statement and to delay wherever possible the news of Israeli success on the battlefield. The Israeli deception plan worked extremely well. It may have worked too well by convincing Jordan to join the war.

Dayan proposed that this general statement be published after the attack on Egyptian airfields had taken place. The announcement was made at 8:15 a.m. on June 5, at least half an hour after the attack had occurred: "From the morning heavy battles are taking place in the southern area, between Egyptian armored and air forces and Zahal (the Israeli Army). The Egyptian forces opened air and land attacks this morning. Egyptian armored forces advanced at dawn across the Negev and our forces went out to meet them. At the same time, many Egyptian jet fighters which were approaching the coast of our country were seen on radar screens. A similar effort was made in the Negev area. The Israel Air Force went out to meet the enemy and air battles were begun which are continuing at this minute" (Whaley, *Stratagem: Deception and Surprise*, p. 581-A). No announcement was made about the successful air attack on Egyptian airfields, although Egyptian propaganda declared the destruction of many attacking Israeli aircraft; see Dayan, *Avnay Derech*, p. 424. Egyptian troops in the field were temporarily unaware that they had to operate without air cover and support. King Hussein of Jordan was convinced, partly by Nasser and partly by his own army, to enter the war at noon, after the war was almost certainly lost for Egypt. Poor intelligence work, Egyptian propaganda, and Israeli silence misled the Jordanians. The Egyptian, Jordanian, and Syrian governments and high commands were always taking decisions at least a step behind the Israelis, thereby contributing to the success of Israeli plans.

A similar ploy was used during the opening phase of the Sinai Campaign, when a carefully worded Israeli announcement left the impression that the Israeli air drop at the Mitla Passes was only part of a reprisal raid—not a war.

54. Dayan, *Avnay Derech*, p. 427; Weizman, *Lecha Shamaim Lecha Ha'aretz*, p. 267.
55. Weizman, *Lecha Shamaim Lecha Ha'aretz*, p. 266; Dayan, *Avnay Derech*, p. 433; Rabin, *Pinkas Sherut*, p. 187.
56. Weizman, *Lecha Shamaim Lecha Ha'aretz*, p. 266.
57. The Israelis employed one more little-known deception plan. Early in the morning before the attack, the Israeli Air Force sent a few training aircraft for a routine flight so that the Egyptians would believe that this was the beginning of another routine day; see Major-General Chaim Herzog, *The War of Atonement* (Jerusalem: Steinmatzky's, 1975), p. 251.
58. Dayan, *Avnay Derech*, pp. 433-34; Rabin, *Pinkas Sherut*, p. 188.
59. Weizman, *Lecha Shamaim Lecha Ha'aretz*, p. 269; Dayan, *Avnay Derech*, p. 433.
60. Michael Handel, *Perception, Deception and Surprise: The Case of the Yom Kippur War* (Jerusalem: The Leonard Davis Institute of International Relations, 1976), p. 20.
61. For books and articles on the October 1973 War see: Agranat Commission, *Commission of Inquiry—Yom Kippur War: Partial Report* (Jerusalem: Government Printing Office, April 1975); Hassan el-Badri et al., *The Ramadan War*

1973 (Dunn Loring, Virginia: T. N. Dupuy Associates, 1978); A. J. Barker, *The Yom Kippur War* (New York: Ballentine, 1974); Hanoch Bar-Tov, *Daddo*, 2 vol. (Tel Aviv: Maariv, 1978), vol. 1 (in Hebrew); Avraham Ben Zvi, "Hindsight and Foresight: A Conceptual Framework for the Analysis of Surprise Attacks," *World Politics* 28 (April 1976), pp. 381–95; Richard K. Betts, *Surprise and Defense: The Lessons of Sudden Attacks for U.S. Military Planning* (Washington, D.C.: The Brookings Institution, 1981); Dayan, *Avnay Derech*; Handel, *Perception, Deception and Surprise: The Case of the Yom Kippur War*; Herzog, *The War of Atonement*; Mohamad Hassenein Heikal, *The Road to Ramadan* (New York: Quadrangle Books, 1975); Edward Luttwak and Dan Horowitz, *The Israeli Army* (London: Allen Lane, 1975); Golda Meir, *My Life* (New York: Putnam's, 1975); *Military Aspects of the Israeli-Arab Conflict* (Tel Aviv: University Publishing Projects, 1975); Amos Perlmutter, "Israel's Fourth War, October 1973: Political and Military Misperceptions," *Orbis* 13 (Summer 1975); Anwar al Sadat, *In Search of Identity* (New York: Harper, 1979); Zeev Schiff, *October Earthquake: Yom Kippur 1973* (Tel Aviv: University Publishing Projects, 1974); Avraham Shlaim, "Failures in National Intelligence Estimates: The Case of the Yom Kippur War," *World Politics* 28 (April 1976), pp. 348-80; Sunday Times Team, *Insight On the Middle East War* (London: Andre Deutsch, 1974); Weizman, *On Eagles' Wings*.

62. Actually, this was the worst possible day to attack, since the roads in Israel were completely empty and mobilization could proceed more quickly. Israelis were at home, and could be easily reached by a radio call-up of reserves.

63. The government party campaigned under the slogan of bringing stability and peace and was therefore reluctant to mobilize Israeli troops and undermine its own campaign rhetoric. Preoccupation with elections appears in other surprises, i.e., the German reoccupation of the Rhineland came close to French elections, and Eisenhower was in the midst of an election campaign in October 1956.

64. The Syrians benefited from an incident which inadvertently helped them to decieve the Israelis. On September 13 in a large-scale air battle the Israeli Air Force shot down 13 Syrian fighters. Following the incident, Israeli intelligence tended to interpret Syrian troop movements as preparations for a reprisal operation, not for all-out war.

65. See Handel, *Perception, Deception and Surprise*.

66. El Badri et al., *The Ramadan War 1973*, p. 47.

67. Total surprise or full warning can rarely be found. They can be seen more realistically as two extreme ideal types. Surprise is almost always relative. The possible intensity of surprise can be presented on the following type of spectrum.

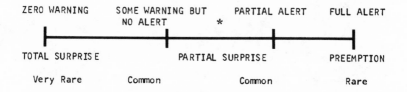

At the time of the attack, the Israelis were somewhere in the middle of the spectrum at point *. (For the sake of comparison, Pearl Harbor and Barbarossa found the United States and the Soviet Union much closer to total surprise.)

68. Handel, *Perception, Deception and Surprise,* p. 50-52.
69. Israeli military intelligence obtained almost complete information about the new Russian weapons in the Egyptian and Syrian arsenals. This information was distributed to the air force, tank corps, and other headquarters, but nothing was done about it nor was it properly distributed to lower field echelons. In other words, the "technological surprise" was not inevitable, and it was not the result of an intelligence failure. The quantities and performance of antitank and anti-aircraft missiles (including the SAM-6) were known.

CHAPTER SIX
Strategic Surprise for War Termination: Inchon, Dienbienphu, and Tet

Richard Betts

Tactical military surprises within wars are common, more expectable, and usually less consequential than sudden attacks that begin wars. Such surprises are more often of interest to professional soldiers than to political analysts. An exception is the sort of surprise, like the German blitzkrieg against France, that radically transforms the nature of a war. This chapter discusses three cases of this sort which have little in common with each other, except one point: they were surprise attacks conceived and initiated by the weaker party in the conflict,[1] and designed to bring about the end of war in a situation where attrition was either an unattractive or impossible alternative strategy. A sharp shock, reversing the momentum of the war in a *coup de main,* was to substitute for mass and superiority in forces. Most often, political leaders assume that an eroding position deters the enemy from apparently reckless expenditure of assets. But weakness, if not matched by willingness to accept defeat, can be an incentive to resort to high-rolling risk, to wager the war on one bold throw of the dice.

These cases are notable also for the linkages between tactical surprise and political determinants of strategy and commitment to prosecution of the war. Boldness by an opponent believed to be on the ropes is not likely to drive the surprisee from the field, but it can demoralize his leadership. Dienbienphu is the only case where the surprise was an unambiguous success, because military victory crystallized demoralization and war-weariness in the stronger enemy's councils of war. Inchon was an immediate military success, but not a longer-term political success, because after defeat of the North Koreans was assured it prompted an escalation of goals (reunification of Korea under a noncommunist regime) that soon led to unanticipated widening of the war (Chinese intervention) and another American defeat. The Tet Offensive was a long-term political success, since it provoked decisions in Washington to cap U.S. involvement, negotiate, and withdraw gradually. But because it was not a military success, it took a long time—almost seven years—for the attack to bear fruit in terms of the initiator's goal: reunification of Vietnam under a communist government. All three cases, though, are distinguished from "normal" intrawar tactical surprises by the quick reversal of fortune and grasp of the initiative from the stronger enemy.

THE INCHON LANDING, 1950[2]

When North Korea struck across the 38th Parallel in June 1950 the United States was unprepared tactically, strategically, and politically. Not having envisioned war in Korea as a contingency apart from general war (in which case it was to be conceded to the communists while U.S. forces went to other theaters), American manpower, readiness, and logistics were abjectly unable to cope with the attack. The massive U.S. war machine of 1945 had been largely demobilized, and what was left was understrength and underequipped.

Moreover, the weight of the North Korean strike was greater than anticipated. Early hopes that the invasion could be blunted with the troops under Douglas MacArthur's command in Japan were dashed several times during the summer of 1950, as United Nations forces continued to reel southward. In July MacArthur planned to launch an amphibious operation in the enemy's rear—code-named Operation Bluehearts—but had to abandon the idea because all forces were needed to keep General Walker's front from being routed. By August North Korean forces had overrun most of the peninsula and UN troops had been pushed into a pocket around the post of Pusan. With few units available for reinforcement from outside the Far East, and not enough time to let the normal mobilization process provide them, the prospect of defeat in Korea was no longer unthinkable.

Turning the Impossible into the Advantageous

MacArthur decided to turn the situation around with a daring gamble, and made the decision on political as well as military grounds. He reasoned that a bold stroke that would recapture South Korea's capital would be a stunning propaganda victory, restoring Asian populations' shattered belief in Western power and resolve, reversing what he saw as the global tide of communist success.[3]

Given the bleak tactical situation, this was impossible. Therefore MacArthur had to do the impossible. Surprise had to compensate for the traditional American advantages in combat of mass and materiel. MacArthur picked the west coast port of Inchon as the site for an amphibious operation to be launched on September 15, 1950, to cut North Korean army supply lines and recapture

Seoul. Opinion within the rest of the professional military was almost unanimous that such an operation was infeasible. Inchon was far to the rear, making a link-up with Walker's forces in the south problematic. Tricky tides and channels, allowing few options for direction and timing of an approach in daylight, shallow depths in the harbor, dangerous mud-flats, rocks, shoals, a sea-wall around the city (rather than more easily traversable beaches), a fortified island in front of the landing areas, urban congestion at the landing site that would restrict troops' ability to fan out and secure the beachhead, port facilities apparently insufficient for resupply of a corps-sized contingent even if it managed to stay ashore and move inland, and other barriers as well all indicated that an operation there would be disastrous.

The choice of Inchon contradicted the precepts for amphibious doctrine learned in World War II. Major General Oliver Smith, commander of the 1st Marine Division in the operation, at first considered the proposal "preposterous"; a naval staff planner of the attack said, "We drew up a list of every natural and geographic handicap—and Inchon had 'em all." Even the navy lieutenant who secretly scouted the area just prior to the strike radioed back, "Inchon not suitable for landing either troops or vehicles." But what made the choice of Inchon so apparently reckless enhanced the chances for successful surprise. And military planners came up with ways to find silver linings in the cloud of dread. For example, fire support ships would have to cope with treacherous currents in the channel at Inchon by dropping anchor, which would make them "sitting ducks" for North Korean gunners in the fortress on the island of Wolmi-Do. As tempting targets, however, the ships would draw fire that would make it easier to pinpoint uncharted artillery positions in the fortress, which could then be destroyed with counterbattery fire.

Obstacles at the site were only half of the "impossibility" of the idea. The other half was lack of time and resources to mount the attack. The planning process for Operation Chromite (the code name for the landing), which the tactical challenges would suggest should have been even longer and more careful than for operations under less exacting conditions, was compressed to an unprecedented extent. And to marshall the men, equipment, and transport that were necessary, military leaders had to pluck forces almost out of the air.

When Inchon was picked, only thirty days were available for planning, because of tidal conditions. (Other major amphibious landings had taken at least half a year to prepare.) Officials then discovered that all of the records and information on the site were boxed in uncertain locations in a St. Louis warehouse, and six months would be needed to dig them out. With these sources foreclosed, navy planners scoured the ranks of personnel in Japan, searching for individuals with any knowledge of the area. Subsequently, the

1st Marine Division had only twenty days in which to plan its part of the attack. Moreover, the pressing schedule required concurrent, rather than sequential, planning by the separate navy, marine, army, and air force elements involved. This precluded careful coordination, and allowed even less time for subordinate units to devise and distribute their own detailed plans. It also allowed no time for rehearsal or joint training of the disparate forces earmarked for the invasion. This was particularly perilous because joint operations are always more difficult and subject to foul-ups than are those undertaken by a single service or command.

The planners had little to work with. Much larger forces than were available had been committed to much smaller and less dangerous objectives in the preceding Pacific war. In contrast to practice during the island-hopping campaign, the navy would be unable to isolate the site from reinforcement. At Saipan, where three divisions (with one in reserve) were used, there had been no city or hydrographic constraints, and American flanks had been completely protected. Inchon was so far beyond the Pusan perimeter that the necessary turning movement after successful assault would be over two times greater than at Anzio—and there the link-up had taken four months.

To gather even the dangerously limited force that was to hit the objective, the U.S. command had to quickly execute what General Lemuel Shepherd called "an expansion, augmentation, and movement without parallel in American military history." This required completely stripping the negligible central reserve—no more troops would be available for Korea for a minimum of four months—at a time when uncertainties still existed about the tenability of the position at Pusan. To fill out participating marine units, personnel had to be scrounged from all over the globe. (Some were rounded up, for instance, from a battalion dispersed on several ships in different parts of the Mediterranean. To maintain security this unit stopped only once—to take on fuel at Ceylon—in transit all the way around the world to the Far East.) To get enough ships for the landing an odd jerry-rigged collection had to be assembled, only half of which were even commissioned naval vessels.

By the end of July the situation at Pusan had become even worse. Staff planners despaired that use of the army's 7th Division for the Inchon attack would be "visonary and impractical," and recommended delaying the strike for a month. MacArthur rejected the warning. As the Pusan perimeter weakened further shortly before the September 15 target date, General Walker resisted releasing a marine unit for Inchon, but after a dispute MacArthur told Walker he would have to hold without it. (So tenuous was the battlefield situation that as the armada was assembled to move to Inchon a regiment of the 7th Division was held offshore at Pusan as a *floating reserve,* ready to land if the removal of the marine unit caused a breach in the perimeter!)

For the American military, often criticized in modern times for overreliance on extravagant resources and firepower, and plodding attrition rather than bold maneuver, MacArthur's preparations to attack the North Korean rear were unprecedentedly risky, ad hoc, and adventurous. Not surprisingly, other military leaders did not like the idea.

Risk, Doubt, Faith, and Luck

One man dominated the Inchon decision: General of the Army Douglas MacArthur. In few other American military operations in this century was the commander's character so central a determinant of decision. MacArthur was a national hero, charismatic, legendary, and senior to his nominal superiors (the Joint Chiefs of Staff) by two decades. As a five-star general he also, anomalously, outranked those superiors. Not surprisingly, despite grave doubts about MacArthur's plan, the Joint Chiefs gave him great leeway. Since civilian leaders, including the president, deferred to the military on the specific campaign decisions in war planning (none of the major civilian memoirs, such as Truman's or Acheson's, refer to any deep discussion of the Inchon plan at the level of the National Security Council), the Joint Chiefs' deference to MacArthur left the critical decisions almost within his hands. There was, however, enough anxiety in military circles about the high risks involved that MacArthur had to work to convince his colleagues.

The Chromite plan raised objections even within MacArthur's own staff, but most important was the alarm of the Joint Chiefs. At the end of July, in view of deterioration in Walker's position, the Joint Chiefs questioned whether the Inchon plan was still wise. JCS Chairman Omar Bradley had long considered amphibious operations obsolete. Army Chief of Staff J. Lawton Collins was concerned about dividing the meager forces in Korea and worried that the X-Corps designated to land at Inchon might be pinned down by enemy reinforcements as happened at Anzio. Indeed, MacArthur had no evidence to substantiate his estimate that the North Koreans had weak defenses at Inchon and were fully committed against Pusan. Reconnaissance did show that many gun emplacements at the site were unmanned, but U.S. intelligence had no knowledge of North Korea's defensive plans or doctrine, since the only experience to that time had been with its offensive moves. In contrast to the stereotypical military penchant for excessive prudence in estimating enemy capabilities, Chromite appeared to be a blatant example of *"best-case"* planning.

Admiral James Doyle, commander of the amphibious forces, and General Shepherd preferred a landing twenty miles further south at Posung-Myon, where there were beaches and a shorter route to Seoul and the main North Korean artery of supply. Such a change, though, would delay the operation. Collins favored an attack at Kunsan, but this would not envelop the North Korean army as completely as a move at Inchon. MacArthur dismissed both recommendations. The critical point of decision occurred at a conference and briefing in Tokyo on August 23, where Collins, Chief of Naval Operations Forrest Sherman, and other skeptical military leaders were present. "As the briefing went on," Sheldon recounts, ". . . . It seemed that every aspect of the plan was hung with one or more little bells of discord. They were all beginning to ring with an annoying clamor." Nervousness about the astronomical risks began to bubble up among the assembled brass.[4]

At this point came the famous monologue by MacArthur which all accounts cite as the turning point. For 45 minutes, in the captivating rhetorical style for which he was reknowned, MacArthur stated his case. "The very arguments you have made as to the impracticabilities involved," he said, "will tend to ensure for me the element of surprise. For the enemy commander will reason that no one would be so brash as to make such an attempt." He went on to cite the schoolbook example of Wolfe's "impossible" maneuver against Montcalm at Quebec, scaling cliffs considered an impassable barrier, which ended the French and Indian War in 1759. Finally, he presented the argument that there was no acceptable alternative. "To fight frontally in a breakthrough from Pusan will be bloody and indecisive. The enemy will merely roll back on his lines of supply and communication. . . . Inchon . . . will save 100,000 lives."[5]

Impressed by this performance, the JCS grudgingly agreed to the plan. But they had misgivings even later and a week before D-day, much to MacArthur's disgust, they raised the question of rethinking the operation again, and MacArthur again brushed their doubts aside. He was committed to the high-risk/high-payoff course despite its heavy dependence on luck. And a great deal of luck there was. Systematic mining of the approaches to the harbor, for instance, might have foiled the assault. In July the Soviet Union began shipping mines to the North Koreans, who began sowing them in several places in early August. U.S. naval commanders did not detect this initial mining. But apparently the North Koreans, as MacArthur predicted, agreed with the American doubters that the obstacles at Inchon precluded an attack there, so they concentrated their mining efforts at other ports. U.S. luck held out as minelaying was held up in late August by a shortage of parts, and was begun too late at Inchon to keep ships out on September 15.

Deceptions and Diversions

The cloak of apparent impossibility was not enough to assure North Korean unreadiness to counter the Inchon stroke. Security was sieve-like in Japan, which was alive with enemy agents (who could easily observe the marshalling of troops and loading of ships) and lacked normal wartime censorship. In Tokyo the Inchon plan was ruefully referred to as "Operation Common Knowledge." A week before the landing a Japanese spy for Pyongyang was caught with the plans in his possession. To cover such vulnerabilities, a series of tactical deceptions was launched.

The British light carrier *Triumph* was shifted to the east coast of Korea and destroyers bombarded targets to the north of Inchon. At Pusan a marine brigade was lined up ostentatiously and given a public lecture, easily over-heard, on hydrographic conditions at Kunsan, far to the south of the real objective. The air attack plan for the peninsula was designed to keep Pyon-gyang guessing. The air force especially plastered lines of communication and stationary targets around Kunsan from September 5 onward. A few days before the attack a diversionary American-British commando raid was launched against Kunsan. On the day of the Inchon assault South Korean guerrillas were landed on the east coast, where the USS *Missouri* also undertook shelling operations.

In the early stages of planning Chromite, before General Smith got the marines involved, army staff officers wanted to maximize surprise by dis-pensing with gunfire support against Inchon's fortifications until the last minute. (Naval planners thought ten days of shelling might be necessary for the reduction of Wolmi-Do.) "The crux of the problem, therefore," as Heinl writes, "was to balance out opposed considerations of surprise and of guar-anteed destruction of enemy targets which could jeopardize the assault by shooting landing craft out of the water and raking the beaches."[6] As a com-promise, and covered by the concurrent diversions to confuse Pyonyong, heavy bombardment of Inchon was postponed to the last days before the landing.

On September 15 the X-Corps assaulted Inchon with complete surprise and negligible losses. There were only 196 total casualties—including no more than 22 dead—on the decisive first day of the operation. The attack was a complete success, the North Koreans were routed, and within a short time U.S. and South Korean troops were plunging across the 38th Parallel into North Korea. MacArthur's stunning success led to the march to the Yalu River which, however, provoked Chinese intervention and another massive defeat for UN forces. MacArthur's successor as commander in Korea, General Ridgway, remembered MacArthur's rationale that Inchon would succeed be-cause Pyongyong would consider such an attack to be crazy, and noted: "It is ironical that MacArthur would himself, before the year was out, discount the chances of the Chinese commander's committing sizable forces across the Yalu—because 'no commander in his right senses' would do that."[7]

DIENBIENPHU, 1954[8]

The French defeat at Dienbienphu in early 1954 was a symbolic turning point in postwar international relations. While the loss did not destroy the

French military position in Indochina, the shock and demoralization it produced led directly to French withdrawal. This marked the first major military defeat of a colonial power by indigenous forces. This single unexpected coup, in a situation where assumptions of Western military superiority had prompted a major commitment of French troops to the position at Dienbienphu, had political and strategic ramifications far beyond the objective military significance of the battle itself.

Political Prologue: Optimism, Hubris, and the French Gamble

By late 1953 France and its Vietnamese allies had been fighting the communist Vietminh for seven years. After previous periods of pessimism, the outlook appeared quite bright. New Vietnamese recruits were pouring into the French Union forces and the Vietminh were seemingly off balance, incapable of more than small local nibbling actions, and certainly not ready to stand up to decisive battle. The commander in Indochina, General Henri Navarre, had inherited a favorable military situation from his predecessor, General de Lattre, and Navarre opposed negotiations because he believed that for the first time victory by the French Union was in sight. The Laniel government in Paris, however, wanted to end the war.

The Vietminh at this time was threatening Laos, which Navarre was required by treaty to defend. (An earlier Vietminh threat to Laos, in 1950-51, had failed.) Navarre's strategy was to establish several fortified airheads—the principal one being Dienbienphu—in the northwest part of Vietnam, and to suck the Vietminh into a "meatgrinder" set-piece battle. Such was their optimism about which side would prevail in such an encounter that the French military leaders' greatest fear was that the Vietminh might *not* attack Dienbienphu. On January 25, 1954, General Vo Nguyen Giap (commander in chief of the Vietminh military) took his forces away from Dienbienphu, headed for the Laotian city of Luang Prabang, found it too well fortified, and cancelled his attack. This reinforced the French command's optimism.

In February French Defense Minister Pleven, and General Ely, toured the battle zone. They agreed, as did numerous American military advisors, that Navarre's optimism was warranted. Navarre announced that Giap's offensive had peaked and been blocked. The American chairman of the Joint Chiefs of Staff, Admiral Arthur Radford, told Congress that "a few months should insure a favorable turn in the course of the war."[9] Tired after seven years, but buoyed by such predictions, Paris began initiatives to schedule negotiations in Geneva in late April.

All on the side of the French Union seemed to assume that the French had the initiative, that Dienbienphu represented an active pressure against the communists rather than a defensive vulnerability. General Giap, however, had other ideas. He too was frustrated with seven years of war, and by the fact that large and growing French Union forces—backed by massive American financing—could not be defeated by countrywide attrition. He was smart enough to know there was no advantage to be gained from fighting on the terms the French wanted and expected. For a Marxist with a higher opinion of his own people's potential than the Westerners, who viewed the Vietminh as a militarily primitive rag-tag collection of guerrillas or nonprofessionals, the situation was an invitation to design around Navarre's strategy. Giap resolved to pursue a course that would produce a political shock, and "provoke a new crisis in the enemy's ranks, to create a new military situation."[10] He decided to take extra time to marshal capabilities and perfect the conditions for this jolt.

Underestimates and Overestimates: French Imprudence in Planning

Navarre worried too little about limitations on French capabilities and expected too little of the Vietminh. On the first point, the French overestimated their capacity to supply Dienbienphu with sufficient ammunition and artillery, or to divert enough men to implement a contingency plan for withdrawal from the position. The commander on the scene also had to rely on an unrealistic estimate of the perimeter frontage (31 miles) that the number of men at Dienbienphu (originally 5,000, increasing ultimately to 17,000) could defend in such bad terrain (prior experience showed that a 700-man battalion could normally hold only about 1,500 yards). This misestimate was all the more telling since plans called for half the garrison to be on patrol, because the rationale for the base was that it would serve an offensive purpose.

On the second point, Navarre suffered in the early stages from poor use of his intelligence organization. Although many particular intelligence estimates were correct, and some indeed predicted Vietminh activity months in advance, the command discounted many of the accurate reports and relied on ones later proved to be erroneous. By his own account Navarre anticipated Vietminh augmentation, but not the overwhelming extent of augmentation that occurred. He believed the garrison could cope with a threat two or three times greater than was estimated, but the essential surprise came when the threat turned out to be very much larger than that. Defending himself later against the charge of failing to foresee the worst, he argued that "a commander who foresees only the worst condemns himself to inaction. And inaction . . . involves more risks that action." This reasoning echoed Clausewitz. And Navarre's gamble was far less breathtaking than MacArthur's at Inchon. But Navarre lacked MacArthur's luck. As a result, he recounted, his command at Dienbienphu was faced by "error in estimation of the adversary's capability, provoking a complete tactical surprise from the first hours of the assault."[11]

The first disastrous misestimates concerned logistics. The French were overly confident about their own capacity to support Dienbienphu, but they had a more realistic view of these limitations than of their enemy's. Conscious that Dienbienphu was uncomfortably far from aviation bases in the Tonkin Delta, the French reasoned that distance hampered the Vietminh to a comparable extent. A May 1953 study by General Salan, concluding that Giap could not deploy heavy weapons in quantity because of transport difficulties, had established such assumptions. Only gradually did it begin to dawn on them that the end of the Korean War and consequent shift of Chinese supply efforts to Indochina invalidated this conclusion. Navarre still believed when he inserted the garrison at Dienbienphu that Giap's supply limitations would preclude him from sending more than two divisions against the position for more than a short time. Giap recognized immediately that success would depend on solving the logistics problem. His memoir of the battle is replete with references to the primacy of *"ravitaillement."* He brought all the Vietminh's resources to bear in setting up a steady flow of supplies. Even before the battle began the French received numerous intelligence reports of coolie columns transporting massive amounts of food and materiel toward Dienbienphu. On March 10, 1954, three days before Giap opened fire on the base, Vietminh messages were intercepted revealing a plan to supply rice for 70,000 men in the area, and intelligence detected twenty 105mm guns, many other smaller artillery pieces, and 100 antiaircraft guns. Yet the French were not tempted to try a withdrawal. Hit-and-run small unit tactics seemed the strong suit of the communists. How could they really hope to prevail in a fight on the terms most favorable to a modern Western military establishment—a sustained conventional frontal engagement?

The second set of misestimates concerned artillery and airpower. The French command had believed Giap would have time to get artillery and antiaircraft (AA) batteries from China soon enough to weigh in the battle. They estimated that mountainous terrain would preclude movement of pieces larger than mortars or 75mm guns, which would not permit concentrated or sufficiently damaging barrages against French shelters. But as the battle later developed this premise was disproved. Vietminh guns interdicted the airfield at Dienbienphu and withering antiaircraft fire forced planes to drop supplies from much higher altitudes (which caused losses of materiel as many parachute packages fell outside the perimeter). Again, intelligence provided warnings before the onset of the seige. By mid-February 1953 a prisoner had been captured with blueprints for novel configurations of reinforced underground artillery positions, whereby only the aperture for the firing tube would be unprotected. Yet although the French garrison was itself understrength in artillery, Colonel Charles Piroth told Navarre, *"Mon Général,* no Viet-Minh cannon will be able to fire three rounds before being destroyed by my artillery."[12]

In selecting the position at Dienbienphu the French had violated the fundamental infantry principle "take the high ground," conceding the surrounding hills to the communists. They did this despite a sobering experience at the prior battle of Na Sam in late 1952 where they did hold the high ground and were saved from a mauling by their own artillery. Again, however, French generals could not bring themselves to take the Vietminh seriously as a first-rate conventional threat. "Just give us a set-piece battle," the French said. "We'll beat them every time."[13]

Artillery commanders told Navarre that Vietminh guns would be observed while being emplaced and neutralized by counterbattery fire and air attack, which in fact turned out to be insufficient and ineffective. Giap not only camouflaged and dug in his pieces, but constructed numerous dummy positions to divert the limited fire-missions the French were able to mount. Navarre blamed the "too great optimism of the technicians who, attributing their own conceptions to the enemy, underestimated his possibilities." In not anticipating how Giap could use camouflage and reinforcement, the technicians had assumed he would—according to standard post-Napoleonic practice—have to set up his pieces out of sight on the reverse sides of the slopes (where the height of the crests would preclude trajectories that could reach the center of the basin) rather than on the sides facing Dienbienphu. They were disabused of this presumption shortly before the battle started, but by then it was too late. The French were already committed to the position at that point, which enhanced wishful thinking and hoping for the best. Thus the sudden and stunning artillery onslaught on the first day of battle, according to Navarre, had a demoralizing shock effect on the psychologically unprepared defenders.[14] (The Vietminh had sighted their artillery one piece at a time over many days, firing only about 150 rounds each day. Then when they began the barrage, about half of their pieces were used to pin down French artillery, while the other half softened up targets for assault.)

A visiting American mission from Korea early in 1954 shared and supported French confidence that Dienbienphu's security could be maintained by air. But the French had little capacity to mount air strikes in the area. They had fewer planes in Indochina than a single U.S. battalion would have at its disposal in Vietnam fifteen years later. No more than 80 strike aircraft were ever available to support Dienbienphu, and distance prevented them from carrying maximum loads. The density of Vietminh AA fire disoriented air force planners, who found themselves scrambling for ways to adapt to a challenge unprecedented in the war. Including transports, 48 of the limited inventory of aircraft were lost over Dienbienphu, and sixteen on the ground. So desperate was the situation, and so well dug-in were Giap's guns, that when the time came for the French to plead with the United States to mount air strikes to relieve Dienbienphu (the abortive "Operation Vulture" plan), consideration was given to use of nuclear weapons.[15]

POLITICAL EPILOGUE: TACTICAL DEFEAT, STRATEGIC WITHDRAWAL

For almost two months the French Union forces held on at Dienbienphu, but were overrun on May 8, leaving thousands of casualties and thousands of POWs. The very next day the Indochina portion of the Geneva Peace Conference began. The French losses in the battle were smaller than those the United States had suffered in the retreat from the Yalu at the end of 1950, as Bernard Fall pointed out, "But their cumulative effect on the outcome of the war had farther-reaching consequences . . . because the French political structure was a great deal shakier than that in the United States." General Ely noted that "success is contagious," the *attentistes* (fence-sitters) in Vietnam turned toward Ho Chi Minh, and "this psychological disequilibrium . . . the morning after Dienbienphu" had a profound impact on Geneva. (General Navarre bitterly attributed the defeat to the prior decision to proceed with the conference, without which, he asserted, the Vietminh would not have taken such high risks and gambled so much on the battle: "On the day when the Geneva Conference was decided, the fate of Dienbienphu was sealed.")[16]

Devastating as it was, the Dienbienphu debacle did not cripple the French militarily. It would have been physically quite feasible to carry on the Indochina war. A U.S. National Intelligence Estimate the week before the battle ended concluded that defeat there "would not in itself substantially alter the relative military capabilities of French Union and Viet Minh forces," but "The political consequences . . . would be considerably more adverse than the strictly military consequences."[17] Symbolic significance of the defeat overrode objective military significance.

Contrary to Navarre's expectations, the Vietminh did not take time to rest after the victory and gave French forces no respite. In late May General Ely reported to the French Committee of National Defense that the generals supported a call-up of reserves. Coupled with the American decision, soon afterward, not to intervene without "united action" (meaning British participation, which Winston Churchill foreclosed), this meant that the French—undergoing domestic political turbulence—were faced with a more costly war and above all an apparently endless one. The Laniel government fell in early June. Accommodation at Geneva, with an agreement to partition Vietnam, followed. Ho Chi Minh's message of congratulations to his troops after Dienbienphu, turned out to be quite prescient: "This victory is big, but it is only the beginning."[18]

THE TET OFFENSIVE, 1968[19]

During the Tet holiday truce at the end of January 1968, Hanoi and the National Liberation Front (or the Viet Cong [VC]) launched sudden attacks against a large number of cities and towns in South Vietnam, including a dramatic but unsuccessful raid on the U.S. embassy compound in Saigon. For several days the strength of the attacks and resulting chaos left much of the world in doubt about whether the South Vietnamese government would survive the onslaught. Intense combat continued long after the surprise, and the communists held onto the imperial capital city of Hue for weeks. When the dust settled the southern communist VC had suffered astronomical losses of troops and cadres, and failed to consolidate any of their initial gains. But where they lost militarily they won politically. The Tet shock catalyzed a change in American policy leading to negotiations, the end of the bombing of the DRV, and gradual withdrawal of troops. Tet did not end the war for the communists, but it created the necessary conditions for eventual victory. As Dienbienphu had prompted the fall of the Laniel government in 1954, Tet prompted the abdication of Lyndon Johnson—or at least his decision not to seek reelection—in 1968.

Sources of Surprise

Late 1967 was a period of mild optimism in Washington about the course of the Vietnam War. While estimates within the government of how long it would take to reduce the conflict to low levels were pessimistic—ranging up to many years—there was a widespread presumption that the *direction* was not in doubt. Attrition was gradually wearing the enemy down. Although domestic opposition to the war was growing strong, there was little public doubt that U.S. and south Vietnamese (GVN) forces held the upper hand on the battlefield.

Some analysts have argued that faulty or falsified estimates of communist military strength led to the surprise at Tet. This is uncertain. There was indeed a debate within the government about statistics on the Order of Battle (OB), and there is evidence of concern about the political sensitivity of estimates that would suggest enhanced VC strength—concern which may have pressured some analysts developing the statistics. But it is not clear that the OB data were corrupted; the debate involved disputes about counting some local VC community and youth organizations that embodied modest military capabilities at best. And it is unlikely, even if the statistics were misestimated, that they account for the unanticipated communist success in the first days of the offensive, because (1) the disputed units were not involved in the attacks, and (2) not even all the units that *were* counted were involved. Finally, the Special National Intelligence Estimate just prior to the offensive did not cover up the dispute about data; it explained what the categories of VC forces were and why some were excluded.[20] Yet it was undeniable that the scale and intensity of the Tet attacks were so shocking because they did not accord with the essential *impression* of flagging communist capability. The intelligence post mortem concluded:

> . . . most commanders and intelligence officers, at all levels , did not visualize
> the enemy as capable of accomplishing his stated goals as they appeared in
> propaganda and in captured documents. Prevailing estimates of attrition, infil-
> tration, and local recruitment, reports of low morale, and a long series of defeats
> had degraded our image of the enemy. . . . [observers] saw his generalized
> calls for a "general uprising" as merely exhortatory, and not as a blue-
> print. . . . Moreover, in the past many "great offensives" had blossomed in
> Communist propaganda but had not materialized on the ground.

Tactical surprise (within the operation as a whole) was enhanced by taking
advantage of the holiday truce and by disciplined VC stealth, infiltrating
troops into cities by mingling with crowds of holiday travelers. In Saigon
weapons and ammunition were smuggled in funeral processions, vegetable
trucks, and false-bottomed sampans. Plans were highly compartmented and
final attack orders were disseminated only one to three days before H-hour.
Tet truces had become routine since first declared by the communists six
years earlier, and most of the South Vietnamese Army (ARVN) was home
on leave. Because of the festivities, many ARVN soldiers did not listen to
the radio and thus did not return to their units when an alert was broadcast
at the first sign of attack.

The U.S. command (MACV) and South Vietnamese leadership were preoccupied with other threats. General Westmoreland believed Hanoi was preparing the principal thrust—another Dienbienphu—at the marine garrison of
Khesanh. A week before Tet the North Vietnamese Army (NVA) surrounded
that position with 35,000 troops and began shelling the airstrip. (Three weeks
after the Tet Offensive began Westmoreland still believed the attacks on the
cities were a diversion from Khesanh.) Crises in Korea had also absorbed
American leaders' attention. A week before Tet the U.S. intelligence ship
Pueblo was seized, and a few days later North Korean commandos attempted
to storm the Blue House (the president's residence) in Seoul. Domestic political intrigue had diverted the attention of some GVN principals. So worried
was President Nguyen Van Thieu about Vice President Nguyen Cao Ky that
he first thought the initial firing in the VC attacks in Saigon came from Ky's
troops marching against his palace.

Most fundamental, as in many other cases of strategic surprise, was the
tendency not to expect an attack of the scale and boldness that was launched
because it seemed to be an irrational gamble for the enemy to contemplate—
as indeed it turned out to be in narrow military terms once the battlefield
verdict came into focus weeks afterward. The two top U.S. commanders
admitted, "It did not occur to us that the enemy would undertake suicidal
attacks in the face of our power. But he did just that." Westmoreland later
claimed, "The only surprise was in its rashness. . . . inviting great casualties . . . [in] areas where superior firepower could be brought against them.

The dispersal of his forces across the broad front incurred further risk against superior concentration of Allied Forces.'' Elsewhere, in his memoirs, Westmoreland noted that his intelligence chief at MACV, General Davidson, told him: ''Even had I known exactly what was to take place, it was so preposterous that I probably would have been unable to sell it to anybody. Why would the enemy give away his major advantage, which was his ability to be elusive and avoid heavy casualties?''[21] Thus there were powerful reasons for MACV and Washington not to appreciate sufficiently the intelligence warnings that they had before the event.

Uncertain Warnings, Partial Preparedness

The Tet attacks were far from a complete surprise to American officials. They were, however, almost a complete surprise to the press and public and this contributed to the psychological and political impact, which was ultimately more important than the severe military setbacks the VC suffered by the time the offensive had run its course. While MACV had predicted an offensive, its timing and intensity were not anticipated. This facilitated the evanescent but stunning communist military success of the first few days which created the shock and fixed the popular images of the battle as a defeat for the United States and GVN.

The underlying reasons for the degree of surprise the VC did achieve against MACV and ARVN, as noted, lay in the assumption that Westmoreland's attrition strategy was keeping them on the defensive, leaving the initiative with allied forces. There were also general strategic indicators that served to cast doubt on the tactical intelligence pointing to a massive offensive. In September 1967, for instance, General Giap affirmed in a journal that the DRV and VC intended to conserve forces and wage a protracted war of attrition. In retrospect this appears to have been a deception. At least one captured document said the decision for a general offensive was made in Hanoi two months earlier. It also was inconsistent with several VC attacks in the months before Tet that were puzzling because they were atypically large and tenacious, against objectives the VC could not hope to hold, and yielded high losses to little apparent purpose. Captured documents suggested they were consciously designed (1) to lure U.S. troops to peripheral areas, and (2) to practice large coordinated attacks.

Another problem, so common in strategic surprise, was the cry wolf phenomenon. Spring offensives were a staple of communist strategy, though previous ones were nowhere near as broad and intense as the 1968 case. The official U.S. intelligence community post mortem noted, ''We have little doubt that at some level of the intelligence apparatus low-level reports could be found forecasting many of the attacks made at Tet; we have equally little doubt that similar reports could be found alluding to attacks on many other cities and on many other dates.''

Unlike the classic case of Pearl Harbor, failures in data correlation, co-ordination, or communication did not play a substantial role in the Tet surprise. Compartmentation of intelligence, for example, did not hinder warning. There were, in fact, numerous and mounting warnings from intelligence—many of which were revealed publicly in some form—prior to January. On November 27, 1967 the CIA station in Saigon reported that the communists were planning ''a political and military offensive utilizing all VC assets.'' That fall General Earle Wheeler, chairman of the Joint Chiefs of Staff, said in an unnoticed speech that the communists might make a ''thrust similar to the desperate efforts of the Germans in the Battle of the Bulge.''[22]

MACV had rejected the November 27 CIA warning, but a month later Westmoreland was convinced that something big was indeed in the wind. On December 20 he reported a probable change of VC policy, ''a crucial decision concerning the conduct of the war . . . to undertake an intensified country-wide effort, perhaps a maximum effort, over a relatively short period of time.'' The next day President Johnson told the Australian Cabinet that he expected ''kamikaze'' attacks in Vietnam.[23] While these warnings existed, however, it is not clear how prominent they were in the view of the principals, or how seriously they were taken. Pike Committee staffers who examined the president's daily briefings from this period claimed that they did not hint of anything like what eventuated.

The fact remains, though, that an unprecedented communist effort of some sort was predicted internally and announced publicly. ''For the first time in history,'' Oberdorfer writes, ''the attack order for a major offensive was publicized in advance as a press release by the side to be attacked.'' On January 5, 1968, MACV issued a press release on a captured document concerning a projected general offensive and uprising. But then the release itself depreciated the plausibility of the revelation, suggesting that it may have been designed as morale-boosting VC internal propaganda. ''The very boldness of the plan generated antibodies against belief. . . . Outlandish claims of strength and achievement had been made before.''[24] Given the cry wolf problem, and incentives to hedge against the danger of later appearing ridiculously alarmist, this was understandable. Not surprisingly, then, the American press did not accord much attention to such announcements.

Communications intercepts, in the weeks just before Tet, began to indicate unusual urgency and secrecy in VC planning, but they did not reveal *when* the big push would come. Officials in Saigon did not believe it would happen during the holiday truce. Moreover, while MACV was alert and worried, according to the intelligence post mortem, ''The urgency felt in Saigon was not, however, fully felt in Washington in the pre-attack period. . . . finished intelligence disseminated in Washington did not contain the *atmosphere* of crisis present in Saigon. . . . atmosphere is not readily passed over a teletype circuit.''[25]

Nevertheless, warnings in Vietnam did lead Saigon to undertake a few preparations that, while insufficient, mitigated the success of the initial attacks. American intelligence had only one agent within the VC, according to a CIA analyst, but that one handed over plans for the attack on Danang—the second largest city in South Vietnam—which allowed the U.S. Marines there to redeploy for a successful defense of the city. General Frederick Weyand also convinced Westmoreland to pull some troops in closer to Saigon from outlying areas. Finally, through an apparent failure of communist coordination, VC units in the northern part of South Vietnam launched their attacks a day early. Monitoring of activities in that zone had already led the U.S. command to cancel the truce in that region and bring U.S. and ARVN units there close to full readiness. Units further south, however, did not react as quickly, and were almost totally surprised when the rest of the countrywide offensive broke. The assaults hit 90 percent of the provincial capitals, five of six of the "autonomous cities," over a quarter of the district capitals, and about 50 hamlets.

TURNING CLAUSEWITZ ON HIS HEAD:
SUCCESS FROM DEFEAT

Whatever the North Vietnamese politburo's rationale for the Tet Offensive—perhaps the most intriguing and uncertain aspect of the whole event—it failed militarily. In the very short term it succeeded, smashing the GVN pacification program, and holding Hue for almost a month. But while U.S. and GVN forces reeled for a few days and suffered heavy casualties themselves, they recovered quickly and in the course of the next weeks eviscerated VC main force units and decimated their cadres. The VC never recovered. Therefore, until the communist victory seven years later, it was the North Vietnamese Army (most of which was not committed in the Tet period) that took over the military burden of the war. In the several years after Tet the Saigon government's control of the countryside increased substantially and was not seriously threatened until after U.S. combat forces had been withdrawn from Vietnam. But Tet was still the crucial ingredient in communist victory, because it brought the U.S. government to the decision, long and hesitant as its implementation was, to disengage, negotiate, and eventually leave the GVN as the only military opponent to the North. For Hanoi after 1968, politics *itself*, to the American public, was a more important determinant of the war's outcome than the military results of the surprise.

Bernard Brodie pointed out that if General Giap really intended the political outcome of the Tet venture he was a genius, and if he expected actual tactical victory he was stupid. Brodie believed that the DRV did not really expect the general uprising and disintegration of the GVN that most anlysts assert was the goal of the offensive. The communists did announce a general uprising as their goal, however, and a profusion of new front groups, committees, federations—political tactics consistent with such an aim—sprang up in the weeks the offensive raged (and they withered as the VC lost hold of the towns). Some observers who believed the general uprising strategy was serious speculated that Ho Chi Minh may have been misled by overoptimistic reports about the fragility of the GVN from his own intelligence service, or "can-do" confidence by his field commanders about their capacity to destroy the cohesion of ARVN. (American critics saw this type of overoptimism in our own ranks.) The crucial point turned out to be that while the GVN did not crumble under the shock of the surprise, public support within the United States for the war effort did.

The main reason the VC offensive did not achieve more decisive military results, aside from greater than anticipated resilience of the ARVN, was the failure to exploit fully the surprise of the first days. Many main force units were withheld too long, while sappers and small units that had infiltrated and struck in the cities were gradually dislodged, and the surprised allied forces were able to recoup and pass over to offensive action. As a result, VC ranks were drastically depleted, the GVN was jolted into a higher degree of national mobilization (via universal conscription for the first time, and large scale arming of villagers and city dwellers in People's Self Defense Forces), and fighting drove more people out of disputed areas and into the cities where security—after the initial communist strikes—was greater. VC military activity was subsequently reduced to harassment actions, and the war became much more conventionalized—U.S. and ARVN units against the NVA—because, as Blaufarb writes, "the political link between the enemy and the population withered away, and forces which were largely foreign to the area conducted operations which more and more resembled incursions from outside."[26]

Ironically the U.S. and Saigon government in large part won the *counterinsurgency* war in 1968–72. The biggest subsequent communist military push, in spring 1972 after all U.S. ground combat units had been withdrawn, was a conventional armored invasion across the Demilitarized Zone, which was defeated (at great cost) by ARVN conventional tactics and U.S. airpower. But as Tet had damaged popular support for the VC and DRV within South Vietnam, so had it crippled American popular support for continued prosecution of the war with U.S. forces. Opposition to U.S. policy by both hawks and doves had been building steadily through 1967, and was crystallized dramatically by the Tet surprise, which also created an opening in intragovernmental debate for officials who favored deescalation. Awareness that costs of the war were far exceeding the gains, which earlier could be constrained by optimism about the attrition strategy, was reinforced as Tet threw the contradictions in policy into high relief. "It was not until the Tet Offensive of 1968," as Thompson and Frizzell point out, "that the disparity between Hanoi's and Washington's views of 'unacceptable losses' was highlighted."[27] Americans understandably did not focus, as Westmoreland did, on the astronomical communist losses; they focused on the lesser but unforeseen and dramatic U.S. losses—over 500 casualties a week at the height of the offensive. During the offensive 20 percent of Americans surveyed by a Gallup poll switched from being hawks to doves. And more hawks began to demand that the United States *either* commit decisive amounts of force to win quickly, or withdraw. If Tet was a victory for the United States, it was a Pyrrhic victory.

As at Dienbienphu, the communists struck when conditions for negotiations had congealed. On December 30, 1967, DRV Foreign Minister Nguyen Duy Trinh finally agreed that Hanoi would engage in talks once American bombing of the North stopped. In his March abdication speech President Johnson cut the bombing back to the southern part of North Vietnam's panhandle. (Wheeler's message to Sharp directing the halt of operations north of the 20th Parallel explicitly cited the decline in popular support and the neutralization of hardliners within the bureaucracy produced by the Tet attacks.) By November the bombing had ended, negotiations began, and the process leading to the accord of 1973—which, together with unilateral U.S. legislation, ended direct American military support to the GVN—was set in train.

LIMITED WAR AND DECISIVE SURPRISE

Strategic surprise as a device by the weaker party to bring his enemy to terms can be effective in a limited war only when the stronger party's interests are not absolute and his commitment not open-ended, but are revealed to him—in the shock of surprise—as less worth the cost of perseverance than his opponent's interests are. At Dienbienphu it became inescapably evident that French colonialism or global containment of communism were not worth continued high costs to Paris, while national independence was a goal for which the communist Vietnamese were willing to bleed profusely and, most important, indefinitely. Less dramatically and less immediately, but eventually just as decisively, the Tet surprise forced the same recognition in Washington. What unites these two cases is the function of surprise in shocking the stronger party into admission of the fact that the unfavorable *political* asymmetry in commitment was more salient than the favorable military asymmetry in capabilities.

The Inchon case does not fit this mold because the United States was weaker only in the immediate and temporary sense of number of forces available. The surprise achieved would have had successful consequences in the end had the United States sought only to restore the status quo ante, and not to threaten fundamental interests of the enemy. But the escalation of goals following the Inchon success led, after Chinese intervention, to another situation where endless expenditure of blood and treasure was less acceptable to Washington than to Beijing (Peking) and Pyongyang who had unremitting rather than limited interests in preservation of the North Korean communist regime. Surprise as a psychological rather than strickly operational stratagem for war termination requires, in short, (1) a clear linkage of immediate tactical gains to a mechanism for negotiating a settlement, and (2) a disparity in interests so that the stronger party has a greater incentive than the weaker to settle, compromise, or deescalate rather than persevere at a level guaranteed to frustrate the surpriser.

Without such conditions, stunning surprises by the weaker side are only a dent in the curve toward victory by the stronger. This was the problem with the German thrust through the Ardennes at the end of 1944. The Battle of the Bulge might have been a strategic coup had the Allies been tired of war and willing to consider a conditional surrender. Hitler seems to have harbored some hopes that this might be the case. General Von Manteuffel recounts the Fuhrer's rationale:

> "In the whole of world history," he [Hitler] went on, "there has never been a coalition which consisted of such heterogeneous elements with such diametrically opposed objectives. . . . Ultracapitalist states on the one hand, ultra-Marxist states on the other. On the one side a dying world empire, that of Great Britain, and on the other a 'colony,' the United States, anxious to take over the inheritance. . . . The Soviet Union is anxious to lay hands on the Balkans, the Dardanelles, Persia and the Persian Gulf. Britain is anxious to keep her ill-gotten gains and to make herself strong in the Mediterranean. These states are already at loggerheads, and their antagonisms are growing visibly from hour to hour. If Germany can deal out a few heavy blows, this artificially united front will collapse. . . ."[28]

When some of Hitler's commanders argued that his plan for the Ardennes was too ambitious, and recommended instead a more modest attack aimed at straightening out the line at Aachen, perhaps pushing as far as Liège, Hitler dismissed them on the grounds that such an action would not stun the Western Allies enough to induce them to negotiate. He believed that the shock to Western public opinion could force abandonment of the unconditional surrender policy, or at least that if the tactical offensive succeeded in taking Antwerp it would force the Allies to stop and confer, delaying military initiatives, thus gaining time for development and deployment of the new superweapons that became Hitler's fixation for salvation in the final months of the war.[29]

But of course the Allies did not view the war against national socialism as limited, and the temporary shock did not catalyze a reassessment of the acceptable price for continuing to prosecute their campaigns toward unconditional victory. Thus the Battle of the Bulge represented no more than an impressive but not very consequential tactical surprise. (The lack of political preconditions that might have made the attack a reasonable strategic gamble, in fact, contributed to the success of the surprise. An intelligence analyst who detected anomalies and argued that the Germans had a reserve and were concentrating forces was disregarded because to others the logical conclusion was that it would not pay Hitler *militarily* to attack in the West given the bad situation on the Eastern Front. No one considered that he might have a political gambit in mind to obtain a separate peace in the West.)[30] Where potential for political compromise exists, either because of war weariness or constraints of the international system (such as pressure from allies), it may be rational for a surpriser to be willing to lose the battle for he may win the war by invalidating the opponent's confidence in the durability or acceptability of the status quo. Although he almost certainly did not foresee the complete rout of the Egyptian Army, this is what Egypt's President Sadat intended and accomplished in 1973. Over six months before Egypt and Syria attacked, Sadat previewed his limited war strategy in a *Newsweek* interview mentioning the Tet Offensive as his model.[31]

If contradictions or questions about resolve are not already latent in the victim's decision-making system, tactical surprise by the weaker opponent will only prolong the war and hasten the surpriser's demise. If such contradictions or questions are indeed present, unadmitted but lurking and waiting to be thrown into the center of debate by a catalytic event, then intrawar tactical surprise may accomplish its strategic purpose. In these cases it is the fact of surprise itself and its subjective effect on the wavering victim, rather than the objective military results of the surprise on the battlefield, that is decisive.

NOTES

1. I refer to weakness in the sense of relative capabilities at the scene of battle. In the Inchon case the United States was not, obviously, weaker than North Korea in a general sense. On the battlefield at the time, however, American forces *were* weaker: North Korea had almost completed the conquest of the peninsula, and U.S. and South Korean troops with their backs against the sea at Pusan could not expect massive reinforcements from CONUS for quite some time.
2. This section is based on: Roy E. Appleman, *South to the Naktong, North to the Yalu: June–November 1950* (Washington, D.C.: Department of the Army, Office

of the Chief of Military History, 1960); James F. Schnabel, *Policy and Direction: The First Year* (Washington, D.C.: Department of the Army, Office of the Chief of Military History, 1972); Malcolm W. Cagle and Frank A. Manson, *The Sea War in Korea* (Annapolis: Naval Institute Press, 1957); Lynn Montross and Nicholds A. Canzona, *U.S. Marine Operations in Korea, 1950–1953*, vol. II: *The Inchon–Seoul Operation* (Washington, D.C.: Headquarters, U.S. Marine Corps, G-3, Historical Branch, 1955); James A. Field, Jr., *History of United States Naval Operations: Korea* (Washington, D.C.: Government Printing Office, 1962); Walt Sheldon, *Hell or High Water: MacArthur's Landing at Inchon* (New York: Macmillan, 1968); Robert Debs Heinl, *Victory at High Tide: The Inchon–Seoul Campaign* (London: Leo Cooper, 1972); David Rees, *Korea: The Limited War* (New York: St. Martin's, 1964); Walter Karig, Malcolm W. Cagle, and Frank A. Manson, *Battle Report: The War in Korea* (New York: Rinehart, 1952); Robert Leckie, *Conflict: The History of the Korean War, 1950–53* (New York: Putnam's, 1962); Douglas MacArthur, *Reminiscences* (New York: McGraw-Hill, 1964); Michael Langley, *Inchon Landing: MacArthur's Last Triumph* (New York: Times Books, 1979); J. Lawton Collins, *War in Peacetime: The History and Lesson of Korea* (Boston: Houghton Mifflin, 1969); Dean Acheson, *Present at the Creation: My Years in the State Department* (New York: Norton, 1969); Matthew B. Ridgway, *The Korean War* (Garden City: Doubleday, 1967); Courtney Whitney, *MacArthur: His Rendezvous with History* (New York: Knopf, 1966); and Harry S. Truman, *Memoirs*, vol. II: *Years of Trial and Hope, 1946–1952* (Garden City: Doubleday, 1956).

3. MacArthur's goal was "to salvage the reputation of Allied arms, to bring into sharper focus the colossal threat of imperialist Mongoloid pan-Slavism [sic!] under the guise of Communism, and to smash its current challenge in one great blow." Charles Willoughby, quoted in Rees, *Korea: The Limited War*, p. 78.

4. Sheldon, *Hell or High Water*, pp. 46, 109-10, 115.

5. Ibid., pp. 117-19; MacArthur, *Reminiscences*, pp. 349-50.

6. Heinl, *Victory at High Tide*, pp. 57, 59.

7. Ridgway, *The Korean War*, p. 40. The secretary of state recalled, "One must understand the tremendous risks assumed by General MacArthur at Inchon, and the equally great luck that saw him through, to understand the hubris that led him to assume even more impossible chances in his march to the Yalu at a time when his luck—and, unhappily, the luck of the United States also—ran out." Acheson, *Present at the Creation*, p. 448.

8. This section is based on: Vo Nguyen Giap, *Dien Bien Phu*, 3rd edition (Hanoi: Editions en Langues Etrangères, 1964); Henri Navarre, *Agonie de l'Indochine (1953–1954)* (Paris: Plon, 1956); Paul Ely, *Memoires: L'Indochine dans la Tourmente* (Paris: Plon, 1964); Bernard Fall, *Hell in a Very Small Place: The Siege of Dien Bien Phu* (New York: Lippincott, 1967); Bernard Fall, *Street Without Joy*, 4th edition (Harrisburg: Stackpole, 1967); Bernard Fall, ed., *Ho Chi Minh on Revolution: Selected Writings, 1920–66* (New York: Praeger, 1967); Jules Roy, *The Battle of Dienbienphu*, Robert Baldick, trans. (New York: Pyramid, 1966); Joseph Laniel, *Le Drame Indochinois: De Dien-Bien-Phu au Pari de Genève* (Paris: Plon, 1957); John Keegan, *Dien Bien Phu* (New York: Ballantine, 1974); Stewart Menaul, "Dien Bien Phu," in Noble Frankland and Christopher Dowling, eds., *Decisive Battles of the Twentieth Century: Land-Sea-Air* (New York: McKay, 1976); Melvin Gurtov, *The First Vietnam Crisis: Chinese Communist Strategy and United States Involvement, 1953–1954* (New York: Columbia

University Press, 1967); U.S. Department of Defense, *The Senator Gravel Edition: The Pentagon Papers* (Boston: Beacon Press, 1971), vol. I; Robert F. Randle, *Geneva 1954: The Settlement of the Indochinese War* (Princeton: Princeton University Press, 1969); Jean Lacouture and Philippe Devillers, *End of a War: Indochina 1954*, Alexander Lieven and Adam Roberts, trans. (New York: Praeger, 1969); Jean Renald, *L'Enfer de Dien Bien Phu* (Paris: Flammarion, 1955); Robert Shaplen, *The Lost Revolution: The U.S. in Vietnam, 1946–1966*, 2nd edition (New York: Harper Colophon, 1966); Denis Warner, *The Last Confucian: Vietnam, South-East Asia, and the West* (Baltimore: Penguin, 1964); Denis Warner, *Certain Victory: How Hanoi Won the War* (Kansas City: Sheed Andrews and McMeel, 1978); and Robert B. Asprey, *War in the Shadows: The Guerrilla in History* (Garden City: Doubleday, 1975) [Book Club edition, vol. II].

9. Gurtov, *The First Vietnam Crisis*, p. 76.
10. Giap, *Dien Bien Phu*, p. 85 (my translation).
11. Navarre, *Agonie de l'Indochine*, pp. 254, 295 (my translation). See Karl von Clausewitz, *On War*, O. J. Matthijs Jolles, trans. (Washington, D.C.: Combat Forces Press, 1953), pp. 51-52.
12. Roy, *The Battle of Dienbienphu*, pp. 162-63.
13. Warner, *Last Confucian*, pp. 73-74.
14. Navarre, *Agonie de l'Indochine*, pp. 196, 251, 253 (my translation).
15. Some American officials denied this, but the point is affirmed by French Foreign Minister Georges Bidault, U.S. Air Force Chief of Staff Nathan Twining, and SAC commander Curtis LeMay. See Richard K. Betts, *Soldiers, Statesmen, and Cold War Crises* (Cambridge: Harvard University Press, 1977), pp. 21, 106, 253.
16. Fall, *Street*, p. 313; Ely, *Memoires*, pp. 97-98 (my translation); Navarre, *Agonie*, p. 255 (my translation).
17. NIE 63–54, "Consequences Within Indochina of the Fall of Dien Bien Phu," April 30, 1954, in *Pentagon Papers*, I, pp. 482-83; see also p. 97.
18. Ho Chi Minh, "Congratulatory Letter to Armymen, War Service Workers, Shock Youth, and People in the Northwest Area Who Have Won Brilliant Victory at Dien Bien Phu," May 8, 1954, in Fall, ed., *Ho Chi Minh*, p. 270.
19. This section is based on: U.S., Congress, House, Select Committee on Intelligence (cited hereafter as HSCI), *Hearings, U.S. Intelligence Agencies and Activities*, 94th Cong., 1st sess., 1975, Part 2: *The Performance of the Intelligence Community*, and Part 5: *Risks and Control of Foreign Intelligence;* "Intelligence Warning of the Tet Offensive in South Vietnam (Interim Report), " April 11, 1968, declassified December 3, 1975 (The intelligence community official postmortem), reprinted in HSCI Hearings, Part 5, Appendix IV; SNIE 14.3–67, "Capabilities of the Vietnamese Communists for Fighting in South Vietnam," November 13, 1967, declassified December 1, 1975, reprinted in HSCI Hearings, Part 5, Appendix III; Draft Report of the House Select Committee on Intelligence, reprinted as "The CIA Report the President Doesn't Want You to Read," *The Village Voice* vol. XXI, no. 7 (February 16, 1976); U. S. G. Sharp and William C. Westmoreland, *Report on the War in Vietnam (As of 30 June 1968)* (Washington, D.C.: Government Printing Office, n.d.); Department of Defense, *Pentagon Papers*, vol. IV; Don Oberdorfer, *Tet!* (Garden City: Doubleday, 1971); Peter Braestrup, *Big Story: How the American Press and Television Reported and Interpreted the Crisis of Tet 1968 in Vietnam and Washington* (Boulder: Westview Press, 1977), 2 vols.; Bernard Brodie, "The Tet Offensive," in Frankland and Dowling, eds., *Decisive Battles;* Victoria Pohle, *The Viet Cong in Saigon:*

Tactics and Objectives During the Tet Offensive, RM-5799-ISA/ARPA (Santa Monica: Rand Corporation, January 1969); Samuel Adams, "Vietnam Cover-Up: Playing War With Numbers," *Harper's*, May 1975; Herbert Schandler, *The Unmaking of a President: Lyndon Johnson and Vietnam* (Princeton: Princeton University Press, 1977); Lyndon B. Johnson, *The Vantage Point: Perspectives of the Presidency, 1963–1969* (New York: Holt, Rinehart and Winston, 1971); Maxwell D. Taylor, *Swords and Plowshares* (New York: Norton, 1972); William C. Westmoreland, *A Soldier Reports* (Garden City: Doubleday, 1976); U. S. G. Sharp, *Strategy for Defeat: Vietnam in Retrospect* (San Rafael: Presidio Press, 1978); Townsend Hoopes, *The Limits of Intervention (An Inside Account of How the Johnson Policy of Escalation in Vietnam was Reversed)* (New York: McKay, 1969); Leslie H. Gelb with Richard K. Betts, *The Irony of Vietnam: The System Worked* (Washington, D.C.: Brookings, 1979); W. Scott Thompson and Donaldson D. Frizzell, eds., *The Lessons of Vietnam* (New York: Crane, Russak, 1977); Frances Fitzgerald, *Fire in the Lake: The Vietnamese and the Americans in Vietnam* (Boston: Atlantic-Little, Brown, 1972); Douglas S. Blaufarb, *The Counterinsurgency Era: U.S. Doctrine and Performance, 1950 to the Present* (New York: Free Press, 1977); Allan E. Goodman, *Politics in War: The Bases of Political Community in South Vietnam* (Cambridge: Harvard University Press, 1973); Douglas Pike, *War, Peace, and the Viet Cong* (Cambridge: MIT Press, 1969); Guenter Lewy, *America in Vietnam* (New York: Oxford University Press, 1978); Joseph A. McChristian, *The Role of Military Intelligence 1965–1967*, Vietnam Studies Series (Washington, D.C.: Department of the Army, 1974); and National Security Study Memorandum-1, reprinted in U.S., *Congressional Record*, vol. 118, Part 13, 92d Cong., 2d sess., May 10, 1972.

20. Lewy, *America in Vietnam* p. 75; R. W. Komer, "'Self-Serving Accusations' Over the '68 Tet Offensive," *Washington Post*, September 26, 1975, p. A-27; IC Post Mortem (HSCI Hearings, Part 5), pp. 2000, 2008–9; SNIE 14.3–67 (HSCI Hearings, Part 5), pp. 1989–1990. This estimate did, though, emphasize that "Communist strategy is to sustain a protracted war of attrition."

21. Sharp and Westmoreland, *Report on the War*, p. 158; Westmoreland letter, reprinted in HSCI Hearings, Part 5, p. 2009; Westmoreland, *Soldier*, p. 321.

22. IC Post Mortem (HSIC Hearings, Part 5), p. 2000; HSCI Hearings, Part 2, p. 686; Braestrup, *Big Story*, vol. I, p. 60.

23. Oberdorfer, *Tet!*, pp. 120–21; Johnson, *The Vantage Point*, p. 381.

24. Oberdorfer, *Tet!*, pp. 117, 118–20. The captured document read in part, "The central headquarters has ordered the entire army and people of South Vietnam to implement general offensive and general uprising . . . use very strong military attacks in coordination with uprisings of the local population to take over towns and cities. . . . Troops should move toward liberating the capital city, Saigon, take power, and try to rally enemy brigades." Quoted in Braestrup, *Big Story*, vol. I, p. 71.

25. IC Post Mortem (HSCI Hearings, Part 5), pp. 1997–98.

26. Blaufarb, *The Counterinsurgency Era*, pp. 261–68.

27. Thompson and Frizzell, eds., *The Lessons of Vietnam*, p. 107. 107.

28. Hasso Von Manteuffel, "The Battle of the Ardennes 1944–5," in H. A. Jacobsen and J. Rohwer, eds., *Decisive Battles of World War II: The German View*, Edward Fitzgerald, trans. (New York: Putnam's 1965), p. 401. Soviet historians, with a tendency to embrace such dialectics and to cast aspersions on Western good faith in the antifascist alliance, are fond of quoting this monologue. See for example

Nikolai V. Sivachev and Nikolai N. Yakolev, *Russia and the United States,* Olga Adler Titelbaum, trans. (Chicago: University of Chicago Press, 1979). See also Hugh M. Cole, *The Ardennes: The Battle of the Bulge* (Washington, D.C.: Department of the Army, Office of the Chief of Military History, 1965), pp. 1–2, 12.

29. Von Manteuffel, "The Battle of the Ardennes," pp. 396–97, 401–02.
30. Donald McLachlan, "Intelligence: The Common Denominator/1," in Michael Elliott-Bateman, ed., *The Fourth Dimension of Warfare,* vol. I: *Intelligence/Subversion/Resistance* (New York: Praeger, 1970), pp. 57–58.
31. Zeev Schiff, *October Earthquake: Yom Kippur 1973,* Louis Williams, trans. (Tel Aviv: University Publishing Projects, 1974), pp. 6–7.

CHAPTER SEVEN
Strategic Surprise: The Incentive Structure*

Klaus Knorr

Our case studies, as well as case studies by other authors, offer (excepting a very few cases) extremely little empirical information on how governments and their military establishments get motivated to inflict strategic surprise on an opponent. We assume that the relative neglect in the literature—relative in particular to the opportunity for effecting surprise—reflects the impression that the motivation is obvious, too obvious to invite and reward study. In addition, relevant decision-making in the communist countries is for the most part shrouded in secrecy, and even in many recent cases featuring more accessible societies, much information is yet to be placed in the public domain. While the authors of case studies in the present volume were instructed to examine the incentive as well as the opportunity structure, they uncovered relatively little on the former precisely because the primary and secondary literature on which they depended had little, or not enough, to say on the subject. Painstaking monographic work, which we were unable to undertake, would probably unearth much of interest even if not a complete record of most cases. (The modest contribution of our case studies concerning incentives, and their operation in decision-making, results also from the fact that in some of the cases of states suffering surprise, the effect was not produced by its opponent attempting to plan it, but by his having done other things, such as the invention of a novel form of warfare, that caused surprise [e.g. the Prussian wars against Austria and France]).

These empirical and analytical limitations have determined the approach selected in this chapter. The choice in analyzing a problem after individual case studies have been completed is either to arrive at theory inductively, i.e., from what can be inferred from the cases, or to deduce a theory at the outset from what a rational actor is likely to do, and then check and complicate the resulting propositions against what the case studies reveal, however fragmentarily. The limitation of the case material makes the second approach more attractive even though the checking and complicating of deduced behavior suffers inevitably from the dearth of information. In this chapter, indeed, we cannot hope to do more than raise pertinent questions and speculate about possible answers. Even this limited effort, however, seems worthwhile in view of the profound gaps of knowledge in this problem area.

HYPOTHESES

Interest in staging surprise presupposes, of course, a willingness to fight, even if only under certain contingencies. The present study is not about the incentives that govern this willingness which, we are aware, may be affected by the perceived opportunity of benefiting from surprise. The utility of achieving strategic military surprise inheres in its military consequences and these, in turn, depend upon several factors, including the degree and mode of surprise, the coping ability of the surprised state, and possibly the reactions of third actors. But if the foreseen utility is substantial, to seek to use surprise is obviously desirable. It is indeed this obviousness, we surmised, that has minimized analytical interest in motivation. If surprise appears to have promising effects and you can do it, you are seriously interested. In fact, the interest to do so may often be so plain to the government and military concerned that they spend little thought on pros and cons, and hence leave only a meager record of other than implementing decision-making.

Yet the problem is not so simple. The obvious attractiveness of inflicting strategic surprise has foreshortened analytical effort too much. The attempt to inflict it can fail and, even if it succeeds, may not entail a favorable outcome of the conflict; the attempt, and perhaps even the achievement of surprise, may incur disadvantages. The attractiveness of attempting it must be thought of as a matter of degree ranging all the way from overwhelming to zero. Whether to attempt it or not is a question of choice, not a foregone conclusion. Once this is recognized, the actor's structure of incentives and disincentives is revealed as an important subject for study in this area of statecraft.

Three factors determine the attractiveness of an attempt at achieving strategic surprise: the estimated chances of achievement; the anticipated advantages, short-term and long-term, of achieved surprise; and the expected costs or disadvantageous side affects of the attempt, including its preparation.

Clearly, any attempt at inflicting surprise risks failure to some degree. The attempt may succeed as planned, fail completely, or succeed only in part. Unknown to the attacker, the target state may learn of the plan in time to make last-minute preparations, e.g., the plan may leak through carelessness or betrayal, signals may be decoded, the intelligence services of the target state may deduce the opponent's plan from various bits of information, etc. Or the target state proves unexpectedly capable of improvising effective countermeasures, once the attempt is underway, more quickly than anticipated.

Or the target state takes an unexpected offensive of its own that changes the military circumstances to which the surprise attempt was adapted. Or chance and nature intervene, e.g., unexpected good or bad weather may prove troublesome, or a key commander may die, etc. Thus, a large number of conditions crucial to a successful outcome are not, or are not fully, under the control of the state planning strategic surprise. Even at best, its planners must face an irreducible degree of uncertainty.

The perceived advantages of achieved surprise, as of going to war at all, are likewise subject to uncertainty. What precisely will be the military and political consequences of a successful attempt, a partly successful attempt, or a failure over the shorter and longer range? Will complete success insure military victory, or stave off defeat at the hand of a stronger opponent, or bring about a less costly war? The ultimate consequences even of successful surprise depend on the opponent's reaction which, in turn, depends on his military, political, economic and moral resilience, his capacity for coping. They may also depend on the responses of third parties, whether prospective enemies or actual or potential allies. And how are all these consequences apt to vary if the attempt to use surprise succeeds only in part or fails utterly? None of these outcomes, short term or long, can be estimated with accuracy and complete confidence. Uncertainties may be reduced, but cannot be eliminated.

Finally, the attempt at achieving strategic surprise is apt to be demanding and costly in various ways other than the risk of failure. These costs are additional to those involved in precipitating war at all. Regarding components that are demanding, the question arises of whether the demands can be met; and inherent costs must be absorbed. For instance, the plan may be demanding and costly in terms of preserving secrecy and deceiving the adversary. Can the necessary secrecy be assured? Are deception capabilities up to requirements? Even if such requirements can be met, what costs are incurred? For example, insuring secrecy by restricting information to very few people, even perhaps keeping it from some of one's own political leaders and military, from diplomats and allies, may entail costs in terms of (1) defective estimates of the chances of success and the consequences of the attempt, whether successful or not; (2) inadequate military and diplomatic preparations; and (3) offending national leaders and allies abroad, or perhaps bypassing constitutional arrangements.

In addition, the political and military leaders involved may differ in their estimate of the plan's risks, costs, and other consequences, and it may go forward only by overcoming resistance in ways that are politically or militarily debilitating. Important actors may have to be browbeaten, offended, bribed, or ignored. Furthermore, the execution of the plan may divert military forces from other assignments. Some other front may be exposed to hostile attack. Or certain new military capabilities may have to be disclosed prematurely whose first use might have made surprise possible subsequently and elsewhere. Finally, the attempt at surprise may require the infraction of legal and moral norms, and its execution may thus engender some loss in the state's moral and legal posture internationally and domestically. Clearly, there are many kinds of risks and costs that may impinge. If they do, they must not only be borne as they materialize, their perception and evaluation ahead of time is also subject to uncertainty and error.

The questions we have raised make it clear that the incentive structure is fundamentally complex although the actor in the real world may simplify it or ignore some considerations impinging on it. In considering an attempt at inflicting strategic surprise on another actor, he faces—as in the decision to go to war at all—a problem of tradeoffs centering on the basic question of whether the attempt is worthwhile in the light of carefully evaluated benefits and drawbacks. The rational actor will decide against the attempt if the anticipated advantages are small or very uncertain and do not promise to exceed expected disutilities. He will decide for it if expected net benefits are substantial. It may also be possible for him to straddle the choice, hoping for surprise but foregoing certain risky or costly operations that, if adopted, would maximize the chances of success. In this case, strategic surprise would be considered a desirable but not indispensable component of the operational plan.

Decisions will be more difficult to make when uncertainties dominate on one or all the evaluative perspectives and a positive decision amounts essentially to a gamble, perhaps a poor gamble. When it comes to gambling, we must distinguish between the considered gamble and the pure gamble. A considered gamble is based on a calculated risk and is decided upon only after careful evaluation of all pros and cons in the light of prevalent uncertainties. A pure gamble occurs when an actor is inclined to gamble as a matter of personality, or because he perceives viscerally that there is no acceptable alternative (e.g., Japan in 1941), and will plunge without a careful prior evaluation of the problems or when the calculated risk would be forbidding to the purely rational decision-maker. The predisposition to accept a pure gamble operates on the preconscious level. In the real world, of course, considered and pure gambling may occur in various mixtures. In any case, the disposition to gamble strengthens the incentives to use risky surprises.

We have already suggested how the absence of a unitary decision-maker further complicates the planning process by pointing out that, operating under conditions of pluralistic decision-making (a matter of more or less), decisions may be more difficult to make and to implement, and that these difficulties per se can be regarded as a cost. On the other hand, pluralistic decision-making may also bring more experience and expertise to bear on the evaluation of pros and cons, and, in addition, is apt to reduce the influence of the pure gambler. Dropping the assumption of actor rationality introduces various complications. The following possible deviations from rational decision-making require notice:

1. Failure to address and evaluate, in the light of available and procurable information, all questions of pro and con relevant to the outcome, e.g., not recognizing or considering all important consequences, including risks and costs, and ignoring or belittling uncertainties in these respects;
2. Propensity to act on pure gamble;
3. Bureaucratic behavior which, even if rational in protecting the interests and procedures of particular bureaucracies, leads to irrational decisions in terms of the interests of the state or society.

In principle, irrational decision-making may lead either to the foreclosure of an opportunity to benefit from strategic surprise or to a go-ahead decision that is poorly considered or amounts to a pure gamble. Again, rational and irrational decision-making in the real world may occur together in various blends.

WHAT THE CASES TELL: ANTICIPATED ADVANTAGES OF ACHIEVED SURPRISE

Resort to strategic surprise is obviously meant to achieve a more favorable outcome of war than would result without it. In six of twenty cases shown in Table 7.1, the state resorting to surprise was clearly inferior to its opponent.

- In 1904, Japanese leaders, reluctantly preferring war to the expansion of the Russian empire at the expense of Japanese interests, could not hope to defeat Russia, vastly superior in manpower and industrial resources, in a protracted conflict that would allow the tsar to deploy additional forces in the Pacific regions. A quick victory against local Russian forces that were relatively weak and in no state of alarm seemed feasible. Strategic surprise would decisively contribute to this result.
- In 1941, the Japanese elite groups, dominantly military, in power felt war with the United States to be inevitable sooner or later and were aware of the vastly superior material resources of that country. By knocking out the U.S. Pacific Fleet in a surprise attack, and making Japanese defenses in the western Pacific strong, they hoped that the United States, distracted by the conflict raging in Europe, would not muster the will to subdue a

Japan which, exploiting the resources in newly conquered areas, would be growing in strength.

- With his military means on hand in the shrinking Pusan sector insufficient to drive back the North Korean armies in head-on battle in 1950, General MacArthur resorted to the surprise landing near Inchon in the rear of the North Korean forces, in order to turn the tide of that war.
- The small irregular force available for the CIA-directed invasion of Cuba in 1961 needed an unopposed landing and secure beachhead—as well as a subsequent Cuban uprising against Castro—before it could take on Castro's army with hope of success. Surprise was a prerequisite.
- In 1968, the North Vietnamese and Vietcong were facing bleak prospects if they continued to fight the forces of the U.S. and the Saigon government by means they had tried for several years. A new mode of warfare, the Tet Offensive, launched with surprise, appealed as a superior alternative.
- In 1973, Egypt and Syria were, at least in the judgment of experts, militarily outclassed by Israel. Assisted by strategic surprise, they could hope, probably not to win, but to do well enough to force their grievances in the attention of the great powers and the world at large.

In each of these cases, only surprise could compensate for inferiority. The incentive to use surprise was very strong. It enhances the military effectiveness of available forces relatively to those of the enemy.

The incentive was apparently also strong for countries that were only marginally superior or marginally inferior to their opponents.

- The Prussian general staff designed in the early 1860s a new strategy and mode of warfare in order to cope in any conflict with the two great military powers Austria-Hungary and France.
- Prior to World War I, Germany was regarded as possessing the strongest army in the European continent. German planners, however, were worried about a two-front war against Russia in the east and France in the west. They tried to solve their strategic problem by a plan that would concentrate the bulk of available forces for a surprise march through neutral Belgium in order to force a quick decision in the west before Russia was fully mobilized.
- In the face of overwhelming British superiority at sea, and unable to divert more than a small force for the purpose, Hitler ordered the occupation of Norway in 1940 but saw his only chance to do so by resorting to surprise and the quick achievement of a fait accompli.
- A few months later, the German blitzkrieg in the west, profiting from strategic surprise in the mode of warfare and in the choice of an apparently unsuitable sector of the front for the decisive breakthrough, was expected to knock out the French, which it did, and compel Britain to negotiate for peace, which it did not.
- With the British remaining at war, Hitler became afraid of a prolonged

war of attrition in which the United States and the Soviet Union were likely to intervene against Germany. Fearing that he could not win against such a coalition, he decided to crush the USSR in order to forestall its intervention and to obtain control of its oil and other material resources. Strategic surprise was to be a vital means to achieving a quick victory over the Red Army.

- The government of North Korea was aware of its military superiority over South Korea, but speedy success of reunification by force was deemed important to present the United States with a fait accompli and thus preventing its intervention. Attacking by surprise was likely to accomplish this end.
- When the Chinese intervened in the Korean War, they resorted to deception in the hope that surprise would compensate for their perceived weaknesses vis-á-vis the world's greatest superpower.
- In 1954, the Vietminh wanted a salient victory over the French army in order to impress on the war-weary French government that the loss of its Indochina empire was inevitable. A large concentration and relentless commitment of force, wholly unexpected by the French command, led to the spectacular victory at Dienbienphu and the desired strategic outcome.
- When the Israelis joined the Anglo-French attack on Egypt in 1956, they had already formed a strategic concept that, in view of Israel's small size and vulnerability to attack, placed a high premium on striking first and by surprise in order to make sure that any military conflict would be conducted on the opponent's territory and achieve all objectives very quickly.

There remain the cases in which strategic surprise was planned by an actor clearly superior to its enemy.

- The United States dropped atom bombs on Japan—an extraordinary technological surprise in the mode of warfare—wholly or primarily in order to spare itself the large casualties expected from a conventional assault on the Japanese islands. (If, as some historians have argued, the United States also or primarily wished to enhance its deterrent power vis-à-vis the Soviet Union by demonstrating the destructive power of its new weapon, surprise was not needed for that purpose.)
- Greatly superior Soviet forces launched their blitzkrieg on the Japanese Army in Manchuria in the same year. The Soviets—who would have won in any event—planned to act with surprise in order to make the campaign short, principally because it was assumed to be unpopular in their war-weary country.
- Israel again acted on its favorite strategic doctrine in 1967. When hostilities seemed unavoidable, it preempted and, using surprise, its forces crushed enemy air forces at the outset, carried the ground war to enemy territory and acted to win with devastating effect, in part in order to gain its objectives before the great powers were able to intervene.

Although the incentive to profit from strategic surprise was strong in all cases, the ultimate decision-maker estimated the attempt to be feasible (with the possible exception of the Bay of Pigs), and apparently perceived the expected benefits to exceed the risks and costs. The question remains of whether the chances of success and the associated risks and costs were always properly evaluated. In only one case, to be sure, did the attempt at inflicting surprise fail (The Bay of Pigs).

Even in the cases in which achieved surprise is associated with a favorable outcome of war, it can be asked whether the relevant estimates concerning feasibility, risks, and costs were actually realistic. Success could have resulted from the intervention of fortuitous circumstances unforeseen by the planners. In nearly all instances, the attempt at using strategic surprise succeeded only because of the unwilling cooperation of the target state or states. While such cooperation usually obtains, there is always a chance that the target state suddenly becomes more alert to its danger. Only in four instances—the Austrian-Prussian War, the Franco-Prussian War, the use of atom bombs in Japan, and the Soviet invasion of Manchuria—is it clear that the target state, once subjected to surprise, had no choices that would have altered the outcome, although the intervention of third powers might have done so in a few cases, e.g., what if France had intervened in the Austro-Prussian War or Austria in the Franco-Prussian War? In other instances of long-term success, something could have gone wrong that would have precluded this outcome. What if Russian intelligence had been more alert in 1904? What if the United States had decided to push the Chinese back into Manchuria in 1950? What if the United States had offered to help France after Dienbienphu to retain control in Indochina? What if the U.S. public, led by the media, had perceived the outcome of the Tet Offensive as a heavy military defeat of the adversaries?

Not all of such possible intervening factors are foreseeable or easily factored into estimates to the extent they are identified. Achievement of surprise and a favorable outcome in the long-run may therefore be attributable to correct estimates or to luck, wholly or in part. Conversely, bad luck may account wholly or in part for uses of surprise that fail to achieve ultimate objectives of costs, risks, and consequences; defective planning; or pure gambles that did not pay off. In the cases listed on Table 7.1 as failures in terms of the outcome of war, only in one—the North Korean invasion of South Korea—can ultimate failure be attributed to ill luck because the estimate of North Korean planners that the United States was unlikely to intervene had been reasonable in the light of the information they possessed.

It is also worth asking how the incentive to use strategic surprise is related to whether the attacker's objectives were acquisitive/aggressive (i.e., out for more territory, resources, and power) or defensive (i.e., protective of the status quo). In most cases, the attacker was moved by both sorts of incentives,

Table 7.1
Some Characteristics of the Cases
(A = state using surprise; B = state experiencing surprise)

	Year	Surprising[5] Initiation of War	Surprising Mode of Warfare	A clearly superior to B	A clearly inferior to B	Failure to Achieve Surprise	Success in terms of outcome of war	Failure in terms of outcome of war
Austro-Prussian War	1866		X				X	
Franco-Prussian War	1870		X				X	
Russo-Japanese War	1904	X	X		X		X	
World War I	1914	X						X
German Occup. of Norway	1940		X					X
German Blitzkrieg	1940	X						X
German Invasion of Russia	1941	X						X
Pearl Harbor	1941	X	X		X			X
Jap. Attack on Philippines and Malaya	1941	X						X
U.S. Atom Bombs in Japan	1945		X	X			X	
Soviet Invasion of Manchuria	1945	X	X	X			X	
N. Kor. Invasion of S. Kor.	1950	X		?[2]				X
Inchon Landing	1950	X	X		X[3]		X	
Chin. Intervention Korean War	1950	X	X				X	
Dienpienphu	1954		X				X	
Bay of Pigs	1961	X			X[4]	X		X
Tet Offensive	1968		X		X		X	
Israel Attack on Egypt	1956	X		X			X	
Six-Day War	1967	X					X	
Yom Kippur War	1973	X			X		X	

[1] Some cases involve more than one surprised state
[2] North Korea clearly superior to South Korea, but inferior to the U.S.
[3] U.S. forces in theatre inferior
[4] U.S. sponsored force inferior
[5] Surprise because war is initiated at all or is initiated at an unexpected time or place

but in a good many cases—at least in eleven—the defensive objectives appear to have been the more important. This defensive motivation is often coupled with a sense of a deadline approaching, of time being on the side of the opponent, of a fear that before long it will be too late to act.

- In 1904, the Japanese acted to forestall Russian domination in the Far East and before the Russian military buildup in the region was completed.
- In 1914, the Germans wanted to forestall a prolonged war on two fronts and before Russian mobilization and deployment were complete.
- The Germans occupied Norway in 1940 in order to preempt British control of that country.
- Hitler decided on the invasion of the Soviet Union in 1941 because he was apprehensive of American and eventually Soviet intervention against Germany.
- In 1941, the Japanese leaders acted out of fear that a war with the United States was unavoidable and wanted to fight on better terms while war was raging in Europe.
- In 1945, the United States resorted to the atom bomb because it wanted to avoid the costly invasion of the Japanese isles.
- In 1950, General MacArthur wanted to relieve pressure on the inferior U.S. forces around Pusan and eventually avoid large casualties required by a counterattack straight up the Korean peninsula.
- The Chinese intervened in order to prevent a Western power from reaching their border.
- In 1956, the Israelis wanted to forestall an Arab military buildup and, in 1967 to avoid war on Arab terms.
- The Tet Offensive was intended to reverse the unfavorable course of war in Vietnam.

CONSTRAINTS ON DECISION-MAKING

While in many, if not most of the cases, not enough is known about the decision-making process prior to the infliction of strategic surprise, there is enough to illuminate some of the problems, including deviations from rational behavior and multiple decision-makers. Regarding Prussia's wars against Austria and France, the redesign by Moltke and his staff of their country's military strategies and force structure was unproblematic to them. Prussia would be obviously better off if its capabilities were improved vis-à-vis the other European powers. But the emerging design was, prior to the war with Austria, not readily accepted by important figures among Prussia's commanders to whom the new strategy seemed untested and risky and who felt their own decision-making power curtailed. It was only the King's strong backing that made the new design prevail. He had the authority to settle the issue personally.

The Japanese leaders who decided on attacking the Russian empire by surprise in 1904 were not very confident in their ability to win. But war with Russia was assumed to be inevitable and leaders opposed to a preemptive war had been forced out of the government by the time the final decision was made. The decision was a calculated gamble if the assumption on the unavoidability of war is taken as given. (That assumption, like all such assumptions, was itself an estimate based on the definition of Japan's interests and a projection of Russian behavior into the future.)

The Schlieffen plan, designed some years before World War I in order to seize the initiative in a two-front war, was too bold for Schlieffen's successors. The concentration of overwhelming force for a surprise offensive through neutral Belguim meant accepting the risk of a French penetration into southern Germany. Schlieffen and his planners were willing to accept this disadvantage in order to achieve a quick victory on the western front. Subsequently, these costs were deemed too high and Schlieffen's plan was gradually diluted. The right wing of Germany's forces deployed in the west—on which the chances of a knock-out blow rested—was weakened in order to bolster defenses elsewhere. This compromise may well have precluded a Germany victory in 1914. The compromise suggests that a truly daring attempt at surprise runs the risk of emasculation in any decision-making system that is collegial even if elitist, and accords veto powers to cautious minds. The contrast with the bold German strategies in World War II is stark and clarifying in this respect. In these cases, it was pluralist decision-making that was emasculated by Hitler's decisive intervention.

While the German navy was largely lukewarm or skeptical about the surprise attack on Norway, the high command of the German army strongly resisted the idea on the grounds that it would divert forces needed for the war in the western front and that it was unduly risky. Unless the various German force elements coming by sea and from the air arrived simultaneously, exactly as planned, the Norwegians and British would be warned in time to mount formidable resistance. The Germans also needed fog to conceal their approaches, and the weather could have failed to cooperate. Conservative leaders and staffers surely were on fairly solid ground in opposing this audacious, if finely calculated, gamble. But Hitler embraced it and set up a new command structure in his own headquarters in order to bypass the obstructive army high command. He established himself as the unitary actor. Again, when the blitzkrieg in the west was being planned, the cautious and conservative army high command opposed the strategy that was finally adopted. They thought blitzkrieg—with reckless Panzer columns leaving their flanks exposed—too risky, and the Ardennes, the area chosen for the principal breakthrough as unsuitable for the quick advance of large armored forces. Their own plan called for an offensive that would have foregone strategic surprise. Again Hitler opted for the daring strategy that promised the achievement of a stunning surprise. And Hitler had become commander-in-chief in fact as well as form. His fiat was final. Yet the way by which Hitler was apprised of the war-winning strategy was so much the result of uncertain chance that one is tempted to speak of a bureaucratic miracle.

There was virtually no open opposition in high army circles to Hitler's plan for crushing the Soviet army in a swift campaign in 1941, again with help of surprise. Previous resistance to bold and risky strategies had been useless and Hitler had been proven right in Norway and the west. Yet this time the gamble did not pay off in the end and, as a result, Germany lost the war and Nazi rule collapsed. On this occasion, therefore, effective resistance to ruthless gambling, and a decision-making-system affording scope for thorough vetting would have been useful. Given the huge depth of Soviet territory, the long distance to Moscow, and that there were only a very few months before the severe Russian winter set in, the chances of success were objectively speaking too slim to justify so consequential an attack, including the acceptance of the risks of war on two major fronts. There is no evidence of worst-case analysis which would have compelled more realism in strategic planning. All the actual planning was "best-case" analysis based on estimates of Soviet military strength that were seriously mistaken. The risk was underrated and the incentive driving Hitler to open war against the USSR prevailed. The gamble failed disastrously.

When the Japanese planned their surprise coup against Pearl Harbor, decision-making was the monopoly of a small military group which, acting out of a peculiar substructure, evaluated strategic choices with the martial values embedded in it. War with the United States was regarded as inevitable, an assumption rooted largely in projected American reactions to Japanese conquests in Asia which, in turn, were considered essential to giving Japan control over material resources to insure her survival over time. But how inevitable was such a war, and were the Japanese conquests really necessary to Japan's survival? Japanese planners were also aware of the material superiority of the United States, but pinned their hope on American reluctance to mobilize the resources for a protracted war across the Pacific Ocean. In retrospect, it is clear that these hopes were illusory. Once the decision to go to war had been made, there was considerable skepticism about initiating a surprise attack on Pearl Harbor. Highly placed navy officers deemed that plan too risky and preferred a more conservative alternative to defending the expanding Japanese empire in the western Pacific. But Admiral Yamamoto, who wore down the opposition, preferred reckless and risky moves. He believed in fate and was ready to gamble. Stung by Pearl Harbor, the United States did mobilize the resources for defeating Japan even though it was simultaneously engaged in the war in Europe.

As the decision approached on exploding atomic bombs in Japan, some Americans in the know (which were not many outside the laboratories), nursed doubts about the wisdom of launching this utterly new mode of warfare. But these doubts did not prevail. The argument that the first employment of atomic weapons was likely to incite a nuclear arms race and lead to nuclear proliferation lacked sufficient persuasion because this arms technology could not be undone or its existence kept secret, and the Soviet Union, fearful for its security, could hardly have been expected to forego this new technological development. The infliction of dreadful losses on the Japanese population could be justified in view of the fact that conventional bombing caused massive casualties as well, and because a conventional attack on the Japanese homeland was expected (perhaps wrongly, for the Japanese might well have surrendered without American troop landings) to cost many hundreds of thousands of American lives. In the end, the American decision was virtually unanimous. It is to be noted, however, that this decision-making was limited to relatively few officials. And whether the moral costs of atom-bombing Japanese cities were properly estimated remains an open question. Was the alternative of staging a test explosion and using it as a threat against Japan dismissed too easily? Would the Soviets have been more amenable to radical nuclear arms control if the bombs had not been used? Was the bomb perhaps used because it had been developed? Does the invention of any new mode of warfare create a momentum toward its employment that difficult to arrest? These and similar questions cannot be answered conclusively even now, and they invite the counterquestion of whether deterrence between the great powers would have worked as well as it has since World War II.

The only risk North Korea faced when planning its surprise attack on South Korea on June 25, 1950 was that the United States would not accept the forcible reunification of the Koreas and intervene. Previous statements of the U.S. government justified this risk to be estimated as extremely small, especially if the North Koreans created a quick fait accompli. In fact, the United States was in the process of changing its mind as NSC 68 was formulated. NSC 68 was delivered to President Truman on April 7, 1950. But even though opposition in the administration delayed its formal acceptance by several months, the strategy of a forward defense against Soviet bloc advances had been fully accepted by him. The North Korean government had probably no inkling of this development and was scarcely in a position to anticipate it. They could not exclude some risk of American intervention, as Stalin apparently did not, but they regarded it as low and acceptable.

The decision on General MacArthur's landing at Inchon in September 1950 reflected unusual circumstances in American decision-making. The military risks looked stupendous and military leaders outside MacArthur's staff were deeply impressed by them. They were inclined to caution against the proposed strategy. The landing would probably not have taken place, had it not been for MacArthur's charismatic personality, power of persuasion, and political following in the Congress and the public at large. These factors gave the general much more control over strategic decision-making regarding his command than is customary in the American system. MacArthur argued that the very riskiness of the planned operation would assure the achievement of surprise and, with it, of victory. The greater the risk of a strategic move, the more it will be discounted by the opponent, which tends to reduce the risk.[1] MacArthur won approval even if reluctantly conferred. In the normally pluralistic setting of the United States, MacArthur thus approximated the unitary actor.

We know next to nothing about the decision-making that preceded the North Korean invasion of South Korea in 1950, the Chinese intervention in the Korean War, the Vietminh attack on Dienbienphu, and the Tet Offensive. Regarding the latter, the risks run by Hanoi and the Vietcong were, as seen retrospect, clearly very high. The forces committed to the offensive were crushed in most places. And could the planners have realistically envisaged the favorable political consequences that entailed the military defeat, or was the ultimate outcome largely a matter of luck?

Planning for the disastrous invasion at the Bay of Pigs suffered from serious misestimates regarding the likelihood of achieving surprise and the popular uprising against Castro that was to be touched off by the landing. The capabilities of Castro's forces were greatly underestimated. Indeed, in retrospect, it seems improbable that the operation would have succeeded even if surprises had been achieved. Yet all of President Kennedy's advisors gave some sort of approval, even if not given wholeheartedly by the military; it should be noted that the group of officials engaged in making the decision was kept small by its planners in order to preserve secrecy, and perhaps to avoid searching criticism and bureaucratic rivalry that might have halted the plan. Thus, the advice of the Directorate of Intelligence, the CIA's Board of Estimates, and of the Cuban desk in the Department of State was not solicited, and it is virtually certain that they would have expressed serious criticisms of the assumptions on which the officials in charge had based their analysis of risks and probable consequences. The military approved only on condition that sufficient aircover was provided for the operation. One of the additional reasons why a high degree of secrecy was established and President Kennedy called off an air strike was to make a denial of U.S. involvement credible in the event the operation failed. The elimination of the air strike, however, contributed to the invasion's failure, and the high degree of secrecy that restricted important advisory resources failed to deceive Castro. One wonders whether President Kennedy genuinely favored the operation and whether it was considerations of domestic politics that kept him from calling it off.

Facing daunting numerical odds in 1948, the Israelis designed a mode of warfare, i.e., in doctrine and tactics, calculated to surprise their opponents, that made the most of their qualitative assets in terms of skill and discipline. They fought persistently in ways unexpected by the Arabs. There were no great risks in this. The strategy was the only one that promised success. In 1956, the Israelis took few if any risks, aligned as they were with France and Britain in the attack on Egypt. Israel was no longer isolated diplomatically. Its small air force would have been vulnerable to a surprise attack by Egypt, but Israeli intelligence on Egypt was good and the Israelis painstakingly masked their belligerent intentions against Egypt, thus avoiding excessive provocation of Nasser and preparing their own surprise attack.

When the 1967 Arab-Israeli crisis deepened as Nasser undertook successive diplomatic and military steps that provoked the Israelis and indicated to them the probability of war, they were already united on a strategy, once war seemed unavoidable, of attacking preemptively and doing so by surprise. It was the only way, as they perceived it, of compensating for Israel's geographic vulnerability and small population. The possible risks and costs of preemptive war in 1968 were, however, substantial and fully understood by the government. The primary costs derived from the country's international isolation and from U.S. pressure to stick to attempts at a diplomatic solution of the crisis. Washington threatened that it would be unable to come to Israel's aid if she initiated war. For several weeks Israeli civilian and military leaders argued about the comparative risks of defying American wishes and leaving to Nasser the decision of precipitating hostilities. While the civilian leaders were sensitive to American pressure, they eventually changed their minds in the absence of good prospects for a peaceful solution of the crisis. Eventually the Israelis became united in the decision to attack, and to attack by surprise.

Little is known of Egyptian planning before the war of 1973. We can only speculate. If Arab planning was reasonably realistic, the leaders must have reckoned with the possibility of eventual defeat even if Israel was subjected to strategic surprise. But Arab objectives were apparently not so much military victory as upsetting the status quo and of mobilizing the outside world on behalf of the Arab case against Israel. They ran the risk that they might provoke an Israeli preemptive strike. But that risk was small as long as their opponent remained only partly mobilized and also because, with strong Soviet support for Egypt and Syria, U.S. support for Israel would probably be problematical should Israel strike first. In fact, it was precisely because it wanted to avoid any appearance of threatening war that the Israeli government maintained only a skeleton mobilization.

CONCLUSIONS

Our conclusions are formulated along two dimensions of the problems presented by strategic nuclear surprise: first, the key conditions affecting the incentive structure; second, the problem of warning for states that might be subjected to surprise by a hostile actor.

In all the cases in which we have sufficient information the advantages expected from resorting to strategic surprise (or to strategies surprising the opponent) loomed large to those planning it. The perceived benefits attract all kinds of actors; small, medium, and large states; militarily powerful and relatively weak states; states that are highly developed industrially and technologically, and states that are not; Western and non-Western countries; countries with democratic and nondemocratic regimes. Size of country and population need not matter because a small state may plan to inflict surprise on another small state (e.g., North Korean invasion of South Korea) or on a larger state that has deployed only a fraction of its forces in the theater of operations (e.g., Dienbienphu, Tet). Regarding the actual or imputed balance of military strength, actual or potential, a relatively powerful state may seek to use surprise because it had not mobilized or deployed sufficient forces in the theater of conflict (e.g., Inchon) or wants to win without incurring large casualties (e.g., atom bombs on Japan, Soviet invasion of Manchuria); and a relatively weaker state may use surprise against a basically stronger opponent in order to compensate for its inferior force strength (e.g., Israelis in 1956, Tet) or to create a fait accompli before the stronger had deployed larger forces in the theatre (Japan in 1904, Pearl Harbor). There are, however, two ways in which one can hypothesize the position of the relatively strong state as differing from that of the relatively weak one: first, the stronger state is less in need of the advantages of surprise and second, the stronger state runs a lesser risk in attempting it. It can recover from the failure of the attempt. States relatively undeveloped technologically may plan strategic surprise against an opponent that is underdeveloped as well (e.g., North Korean invasion of South Korea), or because it sees the opportunity of exploiting imported or captured sophisticated arms (e.g., Dienbienphu, Egypt and Syria in 1973), or because it can choose a surprising mode of warfare not requiring technological superiority (e.g., the Chinese intervention in the Korean War, Tet). Incentives can apparently be strong in states differing greatly in culture and form of government.

Opportunity and large looming advantages will, of course, generate strong incentives toward using surprise only if the perceived chances of success are deemed good and associated risks and other costs are estimated to be overshadowed by the anticipated benefits. However, surprise may also be used by an actor who faces daunting military odds, sees no better alternative than to fight, and is moved by despair. The relationship between opportunity and incentives is reciprocal. Once perceived, opportunity may generate incentive (e.g., atom bombs on Japan, Soviet invasion of Manchuria, Yom Kippur War), and felt incentive may lead to a search for opportunity (e.g., Schlieffen plan, German occupation of Norway, Inchon landing). Both factors may be present at once and mutually supportive.

What sorts of factors tend to engender or support strong incentives?

Realistic and unrealistic estimates of chances of success and consequences that indicate the probability of substantial if not dramatic net benefits on the outcome of war. Six cases in which the attempt at achieving surprise failed or in which the successful attempt failed to bring about a favorable outcome of the conflict indicate that estimates can be faulty because they underestimated the opponent (e.g., Bay of Pigs, German invasion of the Soviet Union, the blitzkrieg in the west which did not cause Britain to negotiate for peace), because success in one theater of war did not affect the ultimate outcome of war (e.g., German occupation of Norway), or because the possible intervention of a third power was misjudged (e.g., North Korean invasion of South Korea). Incentives will also tend to be strong when, or to the extent that an actor is disposed to accept a pure gamble rather than a carefully calculated risk (e.g., Hitler's invasion of Russia, Pearl Harbor). Faulty estimates or the inclination to gamble can, of course, maintain strong incentives also in cases in which the long-run consequences turned out to be beneficial (e.g., Inchon, perhaps Tet). Bureaucratic momentum and the associated effect of a favorable mindset also are apt to play a role in sustaining high incentives. It must be noted, however, that the decision to gamble that involves a pure gamble may be defended despite eventual failure to result in a favorable outcome of war. Hitler seems to have concluded that he would lose the war if he did not attack the USSR, and Admiral Yamamoto might have defended his Pearl Harbor plan on the same ground. If they were correct in their conjectures (which need not be assumed), they could have regarded their gambles as the only chance to win.

Once an idea for using strategic surprise is conceived, the incentive to go ahead depends on the nature of the decision-making process. As appeared from deductive hypothesis, the cases demonstrate that the closer decision-making approximates the unitary actor, the more likely resort to strategic surprise, especially in a bold and risky manner. Autocratic rulers evidently enjoy an advantage in this respect (e.g., Hitler and Stalin). So do small elite groups that constrict participation in the process (e.g., Japan in 1904, Japan in 1941, North Korea in 1950, China in 1950, Dienbienphu in 1954, Tet in 1950, Egypt and Syria in 1973). More participants with different expertise and different dispositions to gamble tend to make for more realistic estimates on likely success, costs, and consequences. But the more actors with veto power, or powers of persuasion, are admitted to the process, the more opportunity will there be for risks and disadvantages to be emphasized, and for compromises to preclude bold attempts at strategic surprise, although this tendency may be contained if "groupthink" develops and falls in behind a dominant leader who favors a bold strike. One would, therefore, expect democratic societies to find strategic surprise more difficult to use than is the case with more tightly structured governments. Indeed, our twenty cases represent fourteen nonpluralistic governments and only five democratic societies; and two countries, the United States and Israel, account for the latter cases.

While democratic countries seem less likely than others to resort to a surprising initiation of war, their constitutional handicap lessens once war has started, when strategic decisions are apt to be left to relatively few leaders and the need for secrecy restricts participation. This explanation fits the American decision to employ atom bombs against Japan. In the case of the Inchon landing, moreover, other American leaders deferred to General MacArthur for special and abnormal reasons. The unitary actor can come about by circumstance as well as constitutional form. Tight decision-making and secrecy were also practised in the planning of the Bay of Pigs landing and, as an instrument, involved not the armed services but the CIA whose clandestine activities received a special status. Tight secrecy also restricted participation in Israel's decision-making in 1956. The 1967 case, however, suggests that a democratic state can initiate war by surprise when its entire leadership is extremely sensitive to matters of security and survival, and when the outbreak of war is regarded as unavoidable. As a result of Israel's short and difficult history, the issue of survival unites the vast majority of the population as well. On the other hand, while autocratic or otherwise tight decision-making facilitates decision on resorting to strategic surprise, they will do so only, of course, if the top leader or leaders possess imagination and daring.

The reader must be alerted to one weakness of our list of cases. We lack cases in which recourse to strategic surprise was considered but decided against either because estimated risks and costs counseled against it or because the nature of decision-making obstructed it. While we did not discover such instances, they may well exist. They may be hard to find. It is also possible, however, that there are few, if any, and that it becomes difficult to forego the attempt once the opportunity is recognized and the incentive generated.

What has been learned about the incentive to resort to strategic surprise is ominous from the viewpoint of possible victims. The historical record should put such states on the alert whenever dangerous conflicts seem to be brewing. This holds for the surprising initiation of war. Indeed, as several cases show, to be alert in threat perception is prudent even when conflict situations do not look alarmingly dangerous (the Japanese attack in Russia in 1904, the German occupation of Norway and Denmark in World War II, North Korean invasion of South Korea in 1950). Proper threat perception is also called for regarding new modes of warfare that might cause strategic surprise. This is a daunting conclusion, for a posture of alertness is costly in many ways and states therefore cannot stay on continuous alert to cover contingencies that happen rarely; intelligence services are uneager to cry "wolf" too often regarding dangers that usually do not materialize.

It does not seem to matter how states differ on various differentiating dimensions; all kinds of actors have proved capable of planning to inflict surprise on opponents. Strong incentives to do so seem to develop readily in all of them. On three dimensions, however, states differ in this respect.

First, although states with superior military resources find resort to surprise attractive, governments aware of their country's vulnerabilities can be assumed to have specially potent incentives. Vulnerability may derive from weaker force structures or military potential (e.g., Prussia before 1866, Japan in 1904, Japan in 1941, MacArthur in 1950, North Vietnam before Tet, the Israelis in their war of independence, and Egypt and Syria in 1973), from the fear of having to fight on more than one major front (e.g., Germany before 1914, Hitler before invading the Soviet Union,[2] Israel in 1967), from small size of territory and its vulnerability to air attack (Israel in 1956 and 1967); from the risk of attracting the intervention of a great power (North Korea in 1950); or from the fact that only small and irregular forces were chosen for an attack (Bay of Pigs). Two motivations stand out: to compensate for relative military weakness overall, and to win quickly. The latter consideration is especially important: when the attacker can win only before the defender has mobilized and deployed all his resources; when victory must be achieved before other states intervene in the conflict either in order to affect its outcome or to stop it; and when a government cannot count on popular support in a prolonged war.

Second, form of government and of decision-making structures affect the probability of plans for resorting to strategic surprise. Interest in such planning presupposes an interest in waging war or at least in accepting the necessity of fighting; modern democracies have been less prone to initiate hostilities than were less pluralist regimes, if only because of pluralist decision-making. This constraint tends to reduce interest in designing a strategy of surprise even though, in principle, there is no good reason why a defender should not plan to achieve surprise, should war be forced upon it, for surprise may facilitate defense, and even though opportunities for using surprise may exist and be seized upon by the defender once war is under way. Furthermore, this constraint disappears if the democratic defender chooses, as Israel did in 1967, to initiate preemptive war when the opponent's attack seems imminent.

In addition, democratic or, more generally, loose decision-making systems lend themselves less to staging surprise attack than do dictatorships or, more generally, tight systems because they find it more difficult to insure secrecy in planning and preparations, and to issue disinformation for the purpose of deceiving enemies.

Finally, the far from rare incidence of deviations from rational decision-making through the predisposition to gamble in a bold and reckless manner, suggests that rulers known or knowable for such predilection require special attention in matters of threat perception.

The reader should appreciate these conclusions in the light of the analysis presented in the following chapter on opportunities. Because the perception of opportunities for staging strategic surprise may prompt the adoption of a surprise strategy, or even the determination to go to war, it is clear that states perceiving such opportunities—whether supplied by special vulnerabilities of the opponent or by suitable capabilities for attack (e.g., forces capable of swift movements)—have strong incentives to consider plans for inflicting surprise.

Because resort to strategic surprise has attracted many states during the last hundred years, one wonders why others were not. Some of our cases are instructive from this point of view. The Japanese in World War II surprised the United States before being surprised by the United States and the Soviet Union toward its end; and North Korea had surprised South Korea and the United States before the Inchon Landing. The Germans occupied Norway by surprise just before the British were about to land troops there. Prior to the Japanese attack in 1904, the Russians, seeing themselves vastly superior to Japan, the upstart oriental power, did not expect war. Austria before 1866 and France before 1870, assumed themselves to be militarily superior to Prussia and did not possess general staffs expected or able to discern possibilities of inflicting strategic surprise on the adversary. Similarly, the French before 1914 were set to rely on attack with irrestible élan without designing particular plans for doing so, let alone looking for opportunities to surprise Germany. Prior to the blitzkrieg in the west, the French were rigidly fixed on a wholly defensive posture, hoping to win a prolonged war of attrition. Stalin's obsessive preoccupation in 1941 was to avoid war with Germany. The Egyptians in 1956 do not seem to have expected war and, in 1967, they and the Syrians moved toward war apparently in a manner and against an opponent that precluded resort to surprise. In 1973, the Israelis dismissed recourse to strategic surprise because they did not expect to be attacked and —if it should come to war—wanted to demonstrate to the world that they were not the aggressors.

The following tentative hypotheses may be ventured in conclusion. Countries that are less likely than others to generate the incentive to resort to

'
strategic surprise are those that do not expect war, that regard themselves as decidedly superior in military strength, that loathe war and are wholly given to a strictly defensive posture, that want to avoid war, and that lack capable and effective bureaucracies for identifying opportunities to inflict surprise on opponents. Finally, as already mentioned before, pluralist democratic countries, in which resort to war must rest on broad consensus, are less likely than others to initiate hostilities, and do so in a surprising manner. States characterized by the opposite qualifications are more likely to use strategic surprise. The readiness with which incentives are generated does, of course, depend on the objective conditions that determine the opportunities for effecting strategic surprise.

Notes

*   This chapter has benefitted from comments on a first draft received from the other contributors to the book.
1. Michael Handel called my attention to this seemingly paradoxical tendency. As he put it: "The greater the risk, the smaller it becomes."
2. Although this invasion started a war on two fronts, Hitler hoped to knock out the USSR and be secure from the attack in the east while expecting a protracted and gathering conflict in the west.

CHAPTER EIGHT
The Opportunity for a Strategic Surprise

Patrick Morgan

It might seem odd that states are periodically jolted by a strategic surprise. After all, it is often said that international anarchy drives statesmen to a degree of suspicion bordering on paranoia. States probably overestimate each other's hostile intent,[1] but history lends support to their fears; attacks do occur and some threats to security are real. This leads to much scanning of the environment on the expectation that opponents are up to no good, spurred on by fears they will resort to deception and surprise. Then there is the fact that a strategic surprise almost never comes out of the blue. Typically, the states involved have been at odds for some time, or are even at war. Surely under such circumstances it should be hard to catch a government flat-footed. Yet nearly all attempts at strategic surprise are initially successful; they strike the victim unprepared and inflict serious harm. How can this be?

This chapter examines the conditions that constitute an *opportunity* for strategic surprise. Such an opportunity has two components: the relevant capacities of the attacker and the pertinent vulnerabilities of the defender. Both have received attention in prior studies, and we shall attempt to link earlier findings with the case studies in this book. Reference will also be made to other examples or to cases which resemble a strategic surprise in important respects, such as the Soviet invasion of Czechoslovakia in 1968, the Sino-Indian border conflict in 1962, the Cuban Missile Crisis, or the Battle of the Bulge.

The broadest question to be considered is whether opportunities are constantly available or are largely the result of impermanent, fleeting circumstances. If the former is true, then threat perception can be only marginally improved by the study of opportunities. But if it takes special conditions to make a strategic surprise possible, then the study of opportunities might pay more dividends.

THE CAPABILITIES OF THE ATTACKER

Four kinds of capabilities compose a state's resources for inflicting strategic surprise. One is *informational*: the state must be able to gather information on where, when, and how a surprise attack could be attempted, often by appropriate intelligence work, reconnaissance, etc. Another is *political/organizational*: a state must be able to make the necessary decisions and then be up to managing the complex effort required. A third is *military*: the state must have appropriate forces for the objective. Finally, there is a *secrecy/deception* dimension. Secrecy is passive, the hiding of intentions and plans. Deception is active, involving efforts to mislead the victim.

Detecting an Opportunity

It appears that in many cases the basic intellectual appreciation of an opportunity occurs at a rather high level. We know too little about some cases to conclude that this is always true, but one often sees the pivotal role of a Moltke, Schlieffen, Hitler, Manstein, Yamamoto, MacArthur, Rabin and Dayan, or Giap in initiating consideration or dominating the planning of the attack. Often detection of the opportunity blends with military contingency planning which has, some time before, outlined what an attack might look like.

Perception of the defender's specific vulnerabilities may well take place after the initial desire to attack has arisen and after a possible opportunity has been detected. Japanese interest in driving the Western powers from Asia was of long standing before specific studies were ordered on where to land and how to fight in Malaya. Yamamoto raised the possibility of attacking Pearl Harbor, then commissioned studies of its feasibility. This seems to have been the pattern in the strategic surprises Hitler inflicted, and the Chinese attack on MacArthur's forces. That is, the initial impetus need not arise due to a particular vulnerability of the opponent; instead that vulnerability may be detected because someone already wishing to attack has been looking for it. Uncovering a specific vulnerability then enhances the appeal of attacking, strengthening the case for deciding to do so.

Next, in the historical examples we consistently find the attacker having adequate but far from perfect intelligence about his target. At the *tactical* level, the attacker displays a good grasp of the disposition of the opponent's forces and their vulnerabilities plus a fairly realistic sense of what his own forces can initially achieve. The Bay of Pigs is a glaring exception in the case studies. Otherwise, the attackers had the necessary understanding, based on good intelligence, of the attack situation. Thus a defender cannot, indeed must not, count on successfully hiding his dispositions and weaknesses.

However, this intelligence is never complete. This may mean that the true scope of the initial opportunity is not perceived, as with the Japanese at Port Arthur. More often, the attack produces some unexpected early results, and a change in plans is then required if all the possibilities are to be exploited.

The Russian attack in Manchuria is a good example. Japan's initial successes in 1941 exceeded her expectations. So did those of the Egyptians in 1973 and they were slow to exploit them. Guderian's panzers outran the nerve and adaptability of his superiors in 1940. Cases where the initial outcome was unfavorable include the Bay of Pigs and the Tet Offensive. Those who would employ a surprise attack had best anticipate being surprised themselves at how events proceed.

More significant is the fact that attackers are frequently burdened with serious *strategic-level misperceptions*. Regardless of how the attack goes, the broader assessments behind it are often badly flawed. Hitler and other German officials sharply underestimated existing Soviet forces in 1941. That same year the Japanese miscalculated the probable course of the war in Europe and the Americans' willingness to fight. Apparently Hanoi, in launching the Tet Offensive, underestimated Saigon's forces and overestimated the Viet Cong's political strength. Washington's assessment of Castro's political and military strength was abysmal. The rapidity with which Hiroshima would be followed by a Russian atomic bomb was poorly appreciated in Washington. North Korea expected a popular uprising in the south to support its attack.

All this leads to the following conclusions. Adequate—not perfect—tactical intelligence is all that is required for achieving surprises and doing considerable harm, and it is unlikely the attacker can be denied sufficient intelligence of this sort. Next, the attacker may have unrealistic assessments and serious misperceptions at the strategic level.[2] Thus in assessing the possibility of an attack, the defender should not count on the opponent being consistently "rational." Often a strategic surprise is attempted on the basis of major misperceptions on the strategic level combined with relatively good assessments of a tactical sort.

Finally, it takes an initiative on the part of powerful decision-makers— military or civilian—to push beyond ordinary contingency planning into active appreciation of an opportunity and the delineatiion of the victim's vulnerability. Such an initiative arises most often from the unacceptability of the status quo vis-à-vis the opponent. Strategic surprises originate in certain broad policy preferences of major decision-makers that are thwarted by the opponent in some fashion.[3]

Political/Organizational Capability

An interesting aspect of strategic surprise is that it is frequently associated with conditions that make the attacker something like a unitary actor. One of these conditions is the secrecy involved, so that few officials participate in deciding on the attack. Then political or organizational factors can work to limit the number still further and, within this smaller group, produce a tendency to defer to an individual or a few key people even when the plan to attack is quite controversial. Hitler played this role in the attacks on Norway, France, and the USSR. MacArthur, Yamamoto, Dulles and Bissell, and Moltke come to mind here. Stalin and Giap probably were in this position in the Manchuria and Dienbienphu cases. Some are leaders with supreme, dictatorial power while others have such status and position their views cannot readily be rejected; either way, any high level reluctance or dissent can be overridden. A final factor is a tendency toward shared images; the decision-makers typically see the world in much the same way, so the real question becomes a more instrumental one—is strategic surprise the best way to solve our problem, and will it work? Given a shared sense of the problem, even a fair number of officials can come round to accepting (while not endorsing) a surprise attack (e.g., Israel in 1967).

Here are some of the implications of this. Generally speaking it should be more difficult for pluralist political systems to mount a strategic surprise, for the process of developing the sufficient consensus for taking such a radical step should be more complicated. However, if the number of decision-makers involved is very limited, pluralist systems look much more like authoritarian ones when it comes to agreeing on a strategic surprise. Therefore, the best conclusion appears to be that pluralist systems are marginally less likely and less able to resort to strategic surprise than authoritarian governments. Next, if only a few officials are involved, major misperceptions need not be widely held to have a profound effect. In the same way, few officials need be inclined to take the risks involved for the attack to be attempted. Finally, this heightens the defender's difficulties in detecting a planned attack; the fewer officials involved, the less likely there will be leaks.

Next, it is not uncommon for attackers to pursue a *two-track policy* in moving toward a decision, planning the attack while trying another alternative. Japan did this in 1904 and 1941—conducting negotiations while preparing for a strategic surprise. The Israelis did the same in 1967. In Korea, Peking signalled its intention to intervene while organizing to attack if the signals were ignored. The Americans offered the Potsdam Declaration while putting the finishing touches on the atom bomb. More broadly, Hitler offered peace during the "phony war" winter of 1939–40 while preparing what became the occupation of Norway and the attack in the west.

Such a policy complicates matters considerably for the defender. While still uncertain about whether to strike, the attacker may send out sharply contradictory signals that are therefore confusing or misleading. There is also the possibility that what seems like a two-track policy is really a deception, the negotiations being just a ploy. Examples include the Soviet diplomatic conversations with Tokyo in 1945 and the Japanese talks with the Dutch in late 1941 (reopened by Tokyo as a ruse); the last Soviet negotiation with the Hungarian rebels in 1956 also belongs here. Or, the defender may deceive himself by treating the opponent's military preparations as a bluff, since states often threaten coercion to gain leverage in confrontations.[4] Of course, the military preparations might alert the prospective victim instead and foreclose the possibility of achieving surprise. However, since surprise is nearly always achieved when seriously attempted, the advantages of a two-track policy lie almost entirely with the attacker, and a potential victim would do well to be sensitive to this fact.

Another important aspect of the decision to attack is that often there is considerable opposition to the decision or the specific plan. This was true for Moltke; Hitler's plans for Norway, France, and Russia; Yamamoto's Plan Z; MacArthur's Inchon landing; and the Israeli strike in 1967. In other cases we have too little information to be sure. The opposition nearly always reflects a *traditional* view—of the proper military strategy or of the virtues of not attacking. (The atom bomb was an exception; using it fit traditional views, and it was the opponents who offered a radical departure in thinking.) Later we will review ways in which traditional thinking is responsible for the victim's being vulnerable to attack. Thus an opportunity for a strategic surprise often exists because *those advocating the attack are better able to overcome standard ways of thinking in their government than are officials in the target state.* As suggested earlier, the opposition is circumvented, ignored, or repressed via conditions which have the effect of creating a unitary actor.

Concerning the organizational capacities involved, several points can be made. A strategic surprise usually took several months or more to prepare. In getting ready attackers consistently displayed organizational skills of high caliber—irrespective of their level of development and technological sophistication, or the scale of the operations. Strategic surprises are models of complex planning and execution including careful training, mastery of new techniques, elaborate timetables, and detailed coordination.

Many cases follow this pattern. In 1866 the Prussians orchestrated the convergence of separate forces on the battlefield; the Germans speedily mobilized in 1870 and 1914; the German buildup in Eastern Europe in 1941 was paralleled by the Soviet buildup in the Far East in 1945; Giap surmounted major logistical problems to envelop Dienbienphu; the Arabs' coordination and operations in 1973 were impressive. Such efforts take time, as they are not mounted on short notice.

The importance of this pattern can hardly be overstated. Much of the literature on decision-making depicts government as a blunt instrument, unsuited to complex fine-tuned actions, particularly if those actions require substantial departures from the norm in policy, strategy, and organizational routines. Strategic surprises are examples to the contrary. And the capabilities displayed are not only military; often there are interlocking scientific, communication, and transport successes involved.

However, exceptions to this pattern of long preparation and elaborate organization are also significant. A strategic surprise can sometimes be generated out of capabilities that were (more or less) already present. Inchon is one, the Israeli air strikes in 1967 another. Today's military technology and forces make this kind of strategic surprise more plausible now and in the future. Long true of strategic nuclear forces, this is increasingly the case with Soviet forces in Eastern Europe, and has been a persistent feature in the Middle East. With nuclear proliferation and many kinds of conventional arms transfers, the victim's problem of declining available time for detecting an impending attack can only grow. This suggests that factors pertaining to *opportunity* will be of declining relevance compared with those related to *incentive* in shaping a decision for a surprise attack.

Military Capabilities

Most strategic surprises do not result from a crucial new weapon used on an unsuspecting opponent with devastating effect, i.e., the atom bomb. What we do find in many cases is the use of existing weapons and forces *in new and different ways*, as in a new mode of warfare or a new wrinkle on existing weapons. The Japanese stretched the combat radius of the Zero for the Phillipines, and used elaborate training to prepare pilots for Pearl Harbor and soldiers for Southeast Asian jungles. Even better than the British at Taranto, they found a way to run torpedos in shallow water. The Arabs mastered new equipment for their 1973 attack. The devastating impact of a new mode of warfare is well known—the German general staff and its utilization of railroads and communications in 1886, 1870, and 1914; blitzkrieg warfare against France and the USSR; the Vietminh shift to a set piece conventional battle in 1954; the Vietcong coming out in the open in the cities for the Tet Offensive; the Egyptians turning to a new way to control the air over the battlefield in 1973. Thus the ''new'' mode of warfare may be historically unique, or simply a departure from the attacker's previous pattern.

From the defender's perspective, this means the attacker has a *greater than anticipated military capability*. He may have some new weapons; more likely he has found a new way to fight, or has—by gambling or in some other fashion—succeeded in getting more out of existing weapons and forces. The attacker exploits this via a strategy that provides him with a *very substantial military superiority at the point and time of attack*. He may achieve this in several ways, singly or in combination: a secret concentration of forces, striking where the defender's forces are weakest; employing forces better trained and more ably led, or using his forces in a quite unexpected fashion.

This degree of superiority is usually made possible and enhanced in its effects by surprise, and it can readily be attained when the attacker lacks overall military superiority—as was true of Japan in 1904 and 1941, Egypt in 1973, Hanoi in 1968, the Vietminh in 1954, and the Germans attacking Norway and France in 1940—although a weaker state is less likely to be able to arrange the appropriate degree of superiority, and presumably more reluctant on this score to try such an attack. Of course, if the attacker is militarily superior across the board achieving superiority at the point of attack may well be easier, but it is still vital. This was the principle violated at the Bay of Pigs, with disastrous results, and in the Tet Offensive. Both attacks were crippled when inferior initial forces were not supplemented by anticipated internal uprisings.

This superiority is different in scale from the use of surprise and concentration of forces to win individual engagements against a superior enemy, a frequent occurrence in military history. The goal in strategic surprise is a critical breakthrough—crushing or enveloping the opponent's major forces, reversing the military relationship between the two sides, or sharply altering the course of a war. To do this the attacker needs a considerable military superiority at the point of attack, for the attack itself and to exploit it thereafter. Thus the "surprise" is not just that the enemy attacks and where, but that he has the military power to attack in such a devastating way.

This leads to a final point, which is that these are military operations the success of which, in the view of the attacker, requires surprise. The atom bomb might have had a shattering effect even if Japan was forewarned, but the Americans thought the shock would be lost by prior warning. In many other cases, if the target state had realized what was coming, the attacker's plans would have been seriously upset. This suggests the central importance of secrecy, for if the attacker believes surprise is vital, then the best way for the defender to prevent the attack is to find out about it in advance.

The Capacity to Hide and to Deceive

Our cases typically involved efforts at secrecy, and many included attempts at deception. Steps to maintain secrecy included notifying just a handful of officials, circulating very few documents or orders, bringing the necessary forces forward at the last minure, making key dispositions at night or in bad weather, and so on. Deception efforts ranged from formal communications that were false, to circulation of elaborate incorrect rumors, to making seemingly "hard" but misleading facts available to the victim.

Evaluating the value of secrecy and deception as tactics is difficult. On the one hand, in terms of keeping important clues from the defender, secrecy and deception are far from completely successful. The Japanese had no inkling of the atomic bomb, which was really unusual. In the other cases, and in those examined by other analysts, the attacker's security arrangements were imperfect and a good deal of suggestive information was available to the defender.[5] Thus one possible "cause" of defender vulnerability we can eliminate is that the attacker is totally successful in concealing his plans. On the other hand, several studies have concluded that secrecy and deception nearly always work in that, as earlier noted, the defender is surprised and badly so.[6] How do we reconcile these two positions?

The proper conclusion is that secrecy and deception, though almost never perfect, are quite relevant to achieving surprise. The nature of their contribution is to hold down the quantity and visibility of the correct information that leaks out, keeping it sufficiently submerged in irrelevant or misleading information to be below the threshold at which it would be effectively perceived and acted on by the defender.

As to the relative importance of the two, secrecy has become progressively more difficult to sustain in the face of improvements in monitoring and surveillance, which suggests that deception may be growing in significance. Ideally, deception causes the defender to seize on an incorrect interpretation. However, this is most likely when the deception coincides with defender preconceptions and biases, and these may be difficult for the attacker to ascertain. Thus deception is more apt to achieve its effects by contributing to the ambiguity and noise in the environment, and our cases seem to confirm this.[7]

Finally, it is hard to conclude that a capacity for secrecy and deception is markedly greater in some kinds of states than others. Our cases display the same pattern—secrecy and deception measures are imperfect, yet surprise is achieved—whether the states are democratic or authoritarian, developed or not, and with states from various cultures and with quite different historical traditions.

THE VULNERABILITY OF THE DEFENDER

In studies of strategic surprise, defender vulnerability has received far and away the most attention. Attacker incentives are usually only briefly considered. Attacker capabilities draw more attention, but the analysis typically moves briskly on to examining where the defender went wrong. There is an undeniable fascination with people misreading the facts and stumbling into disaster, and in addition most studies of strategic surprise have been done in states that were victims, where the defender's failures naturally arouse the most interest.

In these studies strategic surprise is depicted as a perceptual-analytical problem, and suggested solutions concentrate on ways defender perception and analysis might be improved. In the preceding chapter we explored attacker incentives and here we have discussed attacker capabilities. These are important elements of strategic surprise, irrespective of defects in the victim's perceptions, and are equally appropriate to consider when seeking remedies. In other words, prior studies have been too narrow in defining the problem and outlining solutions.

Nevertheless, the defender's vulnerability is an important aspect of strategic surprise and the cases must be reviewed to see what we can learn about it. We can begin with the following framework. There are four types of factors which create vulnerability to strategic surprise:

- Informational: The defender has a limited amount of correct information, much of it is ambiguous, and it is immersed in irrelevant, erroneous, and misleading information.
- Cognitive: Standard human processes of perception and explanation work to inhibit an accurate analysis.
- Organizational: Patterns of organizational behavior can cripple a state's perceptions or undermine implementation of effective responses to threats.
- Political: Receptivity to warning and adequacy of response can be undermined by political conditions and concerns, domestic and international.

Next, threat perception and response in a government involves several stages, and the impact of the types of factors listed above varies from one stage to another. Analysts differ as to how to define these stages,[8] but here is one useful typology:

- Information Availability: Vulnerability is related to the amount and kind of information available about an impending attack.
- Information Collection: Vulnerability is related to the degree to which the available information is collected in a timely fashion.
- Perception: Vulnerability is related to the degree to which the information collected is accurately interpreted and understood.
- Response: Vulnerability is related to the degree to which a state, having interpreted the information it has gathered, selects an appropriate response.

The rest of this chapter explores the effects of informational, cognitive, organizational, and political factors within each stage in producing vulnerability to strategic surprise, and certain qualifications must be kept in mind. The most important is that the phases of a threat perception/response process are only distinct analytically; within a government they overlap. Each has a time dimension, and they overlap here as well. They also interact. To illustrate, efforts at collecting information may be sharply reduced if the initial conclusion from the early data is that nothing important is being uncovered.

Or, the defender's initial response to a warning may lead the attacker to tighten security, limiting the availability of information in the future about the planned attack. Thus for purposes of analysis we are segmenting what is a fluid and dynamic process and simplifying a very complex matter, at the risk of some distortion.

First Phase: Availability of Information

The simplest explanation for a state's vulnerability would be that it receives no warning—no information about the attack is available in advance. Information may be unavailable for three reasons: (1) secrecy, (2) time—the information may become available too late to act on it, and (3) the information may simply not exist. We will consider each in turn.

The effects of secrecy are not well understood in existing studies of strategic surprise. Analysts have noted that the secrecy surrounding a planned attack is often breached. Since surprise is achieved anyway, the importance of secrecy is downplayed. This is unfortunate , for secrecy is an important ingredient.

The frequent observation, in retrospect, that the defender had enough information available to correctly predict what would happen has tended to obscure the fact that detecting a strategic surprise in advance *remains, at bottom, a problem of having too little information*. As Klaus Knorr has pointed out, "threat perception is a matter of 'estimates' that would not be needed if all the pertinent information were unambiguously on hand. One estimates when one does not know.'"[9] Lots of the information the defender would like is often missing because of secrecy. As a result the defender resembles someone doing a crossword puzzle with no clues for every third word. Secrecy denies him key data that would constitute an unambiguous warning, making him guess and thereby allowing preconceptions and other sources of misperception to have more of an effect.

Our cases, and others, offer many examples of the uneven availability of information. Washington knew Japan would probably attack somewhere in late 1941 but secrecy shrouded the location. The Japanese learned of the Soviet buildup in the Far East in 1945, but the main theater and true size of the Soviet forces remained hidden. The French were aware of the Schlieffen plan, but not about how use of reserve units would permit a German sweep through the heart of Belgium. The British and French knew that an attack was coming in May 1940, but not where the main thrust would come or how Guderian's tanks would operate. The scale of Chinese troop movements into Korea was kept hidden. In short, secrecy may play an important part just by hiding the attacker's intentions, or his specific plans, or the exact nature of his capabilities.

Some information may appear too late to assist the defender.[10] Consider the following situations:

1. There is internal disagreement about whether to attack until a relatively short time before the event. Israel in 1967 and Japan in 1941 are examples.
2. The attacker is uncertain on when, where, or how to attack until not long before it does so. The German thrust in the west in 1940 fits here. Possibly the North Korean attack in 1950 is another example.
3. The attacker's military capability is augmented at the last minute. The atom bomb was first tested the same month it was used; the fins for torpedos for Pearl Harbor arrived as the fleet was leaving to cross the Pacific.

In each instance the intelligence "failure" stems from the timing of events. The controversial nature of a decision to go for a strategic surprise can cause this, with disagreements among officials delaying a final clearance until not long before the attack. This is exacerbated in situations where military technology or forces in place provide a constant opportunity to attack. When both sides possess that opportunity they face a situation of reciprocal fear of surprise attack, as in 1967 between Egypt and Israel and in 1940 (over Norway) between Britain and Germany. In these circumstances the victim is ill advised to count on timely warning.

Finally, some information valuable for detecting a possible attack does not exist. Since it does not exist it cannot be collected. This can happen because of the *interdependence of information*. It is well known that hard information about an opponent's intentions is very difficult to obtain. Less often appreciated is the fact that his military capabilities cannot be measured with complete accuracy apart from these intentions. How strong is A? It depends on who A attacks and how. And with limited information on enemy intentions and accordingly imprecise information on enemy capabilities, it is impossible to quite accurately assess one's own military capabilities. The answer to too many questions becomes: "it depends."

Information may be unavailable in another way. In the face of incomplete or ambiguous information, one recourse is to examine the opponent's past behavior (or that of others in similar situations) to determine his normal course of action. This leaves the defender surprised when the opponent does the unusual; he lacks sufficient information to accurately estimate the probability of the unusual happening because there are too few cases. For the victim, the problem is that states have not engaged in strategic surprises very often; the entire universe of cases in the past 150 years is limited, and for any one state it is very limited. The data for developing an estimate with high confidence do not exist. The most singular example is the (fortunate) impossibility due to lack of cases, of computing the probability of a surprise nuclear attack.

In summary, informational factors are significant in phase one of a process of threat perception, analysis, and response. Cognitive, organizational, and political factors do not begin to have an effect until the second phase. Yet we can already partially explain the vulnerability of states to strategic surprise, just by referring to limitations on the data available to the victim.

Second Phase: Collection of Information

Let us assume enough correct information about a planned strategic surprise is available. Possibly the victim is vulnerable because he fails to collect it. Case studies, reported here or elsewhere, shed little light on this. In retrospective analysis, a sense of the information that was available is primarily obtained by sorting through what was collected; no thorough review of what was available but not collected is normally undertaken. This skews the analysis towards highlighting defender mistakes in assessing the data on hand. Still, our cases are somewhat instructive here and we will glean what we can.

Roberta Wohlstetter refers to chance, accident, and bad luck in impeding the collection of information in October 1962 and prior to Pearl Harbor:

> It was bad luck that September-October is the hurricane season in the Caribbean, so that reconnaissance photography was unclear and certain flights were canceled. It was bad luck that the Red Chinese shot down a U-2 on September 9. In 1941, it was bad luck that we had cut all traffic on the Northwest Passage to Russia, and thereby made visual observation of the Pearl Harbor task force impossible. It was bad luck that there was a radio blackout in the Hawaiian Islands on the morning of December 7, and that Colonel French of the Communication Room then decided to use commercial wire instead of recommending the scramble telephone for the last alert message.[11]

Intelligence coups due to luck occur; presumably the same is true of intelligence failures. Such factors fall in our *informational* category.

Under the heading of *cognitive* factors, we are interested in how a defender's expectation can drive his collection of information.[12] Given their approach to war, the Austrians did not think it necessary to inform themselves in detail about Prussia's military resources in 1866, a mistake the French repeated in 1870. In 1940 the French high command was not really curious about German military thinking, and the British and French staffs had no serious interest in military intelligence. MacArthur's confidence the Chinese would not intervene probably sapped the vigor of American reconnaissance, and in 1973 a disparaging view of the Arabs discouraged careful Israeli investigation of how well they had mastered their new Russian weapons. George and Smoke believe preconceptions (that the Soviets were most unlikely to send missiles to Cuba) helped delay U-2 flights over the island.[13]

Deception also enters in here. Deception can be designed to manipulate the victim's search patterns, much like a magician misdirects the attention of his audience. For instance, it may be employed to confuse the defender as to where an attack will occur. The Russians did this in the Manchurian attack; in 1956 the Israelis focused Arab attention along the Jordanian border (not Egypt); and in 1950 the Americans scattered clues concerning landing sites other than Inchon.

When it comes to *organizational* factors we must consider the fact that while there are routines or cycles for the collection of information, valuable information will only be intermittently available, and there may be a poor fit between the two. Nearing the Yalu, American aerial reconnaissance was a daytime effort, while much Chinese infiltration came at night. In 1967 the Israelis arrived over Nasser's airfields just after Egyptian pilots had completed their early morning patrols. Many reconnaissance efforts were adjusted by natural conditions, a fact some attackers exploited. The Japanese used the annual winter monsoon to cover their landings in Malaya and Thailand, while the Germans planned on the cloud cover and dark nights of late spring over Norway. The Battle of the Bulge used winter weather to offset Allied superiority in many areas. (It should be noted that as surveillance technology changes, so does the specific source of vulnerability. Contemporary technology has, for a few states, overcome many of the limits formerly imposed by weather or darkness—but it has also made those states vulnerable to information overload, with raw data outrunning the processing routines.)

A search for information is also shaped by other routines that reflect bureaucratic jurisdictions (and jurisdictional disputes).[14] At Pearl Harbor, organizational priorities and missions were never reconciled sufficiently to produce complete surveillance; the services imperfectly allocated surveillance missions while hoarding skilled people and equipment for training purposes. A struggle between the CIA and the air force over control of U-2 flights helped delay photography over western Cuba in the fall of 1962 for several weeks. Other examples would turn up from a much more detailed look at the cases.

Certain *political* considerations may contribute to a state's vulnerability in this phase by curbing the gathering of data. Political leaders may order restrictions on reconnaissance to avoid being provocative. Elements of this affected British aerial intelligence against Germany in the last months before World War II, and contained Soviet efforts to learn more along the front lines on the eve of Barbarossa. In September 1962 a U-2 flight over Cuba was cancelled because one had just been shot down over China and the administration feared the political repercussions of having the same thing happen in the tense situation in the Caribbean.[15]

Clearly, a government cannot collect all the available information about everything. Choices must be made and they may be the wrong ones. But we can conclude this discussion by pointing out that information collection, like information availability, is not the crucial phase in which the defender fails in cases of strategic surprise. The history of such attacks indicates that, despite less than perfect information gathering, the victim usually has on hand a good deal of valuable information that, if properly understood, would produce a correct assessment of his situation. Thus much of the responsibility for threat perception failures must be assigned to the difficulties involved in assessing that information and to the defender having drawn incorrect conclusions in spite of it.

Third Phase: Perception

We have reviewed the possiblity that information on an impending attack is not available or not collected. Both contribute to vulnerability to strategic surprise, but neither appears to be crucial. The next possibility is that the information gathered is misread. In studies of strategic surprise, more propositions and hypotheses have been offered on defender misjudgments than on any other facet of the subject. Exploring them in the light of the case studies will involve a lengthy and often intricate discussion.

We can group factors that inhibit accurate perception of warning into the same four categories: informational, cognitive, organizational, and political. However, it is impossible to weigh precisely the relative impact of these factors. We lack sufficient access to the inner workings of many governments that have suffered strategic surprises to do this. Another constraint is the fact that the dependent variable, a distorted view of reality, looks much the same regardless of the combination of factors that produced it. Added to this is the bias inherent in retrospective studies, where the perspective of the observer is shaped by his knowledge of the outcome and, in turn, influences selection of the cases.[16]

1. Defects in the Information on Hand

Our case studies confirm other findings to the effect that warning signs of a surprise attack are very often *inherently ambiguous,* and are enveloped by other information—correct and incorrect—which greatly complicates the task of correctly assessing them.[17]

The ambiguity of information on hand is of two sorts. One is the ambiguity of the correct warning signs themselves, either because the information is insubstantial or the source is of doubtful reliability. The other is the ambiguity of the total available information, warning signs plus other data. The latter has come to be referred to as "noise." It can consist of irrelevant information (not pertaining to a pressing matter but requiring processing nonetheless), false information, or information bearing on other important matters. These various facets of ambiguity work, usually in tandem, to cripple the target state's perceptions.

In the spring of 1940, the British received many reports of German plans to attack Norway, but the signals were ambiguous; they fit alternative explanations, such as that the Germans were planning a naval foray into the North Atlantic or were spreading rumors to unnerve their opponents. Similarly vague information arrived in Oslo, where the government was preoccupied with "noise" concerning a possible British attack. The stream of reports Moscow received about German preparations for Barbarossa suggested an attack but also fit an alternative hypothesis—that Hitler was bluffing to extort major concessions.

The overwhelming number of signals that Japan would take a major step in December 1941 fit several possible explanations as to where the blow would fall, while Washington was preoccupied with events in Europe and the Atlantic. As Japanese convoys approached the Malay Peninsula in 1941, it was still unclear just where they would land, paralyzing British decision-making. For Tokyo in 1945 it was hard to know if the Soviet military buildup was simply to prepare for the collapse of Japanese power, backstop a Soviet demand for concessions, or make ready for attack.

The last warnings of a North Korean attack were part of a long series that had previously been wrong, often coming from South Korean sources prone to exaggeration. The Chinese signalled they would intervene in Korea, in part, through an Indian diplomat considered unreliable by the Americans, the British, and at times his own government; then by openly attacking UN forces and pulling back, the Chinese sent an ambiguous message. Prior to the Tet Offensive, the U.S. command was preoccupied with Khesanh, Washington was wrestling with the Pueblo incident, and Saigon worried about a military coup; the warnings clashed with other information suggesting the enemy was on the run. There are similar patterns in connection with the 1956, 1967, and 1973 wars in the Middle East.

We are interested not only in explicit warnings but in general information about attacker intentions and capabilities. In our cases the defender frequently underestimated the attacker's willingness to take risks and relevant military strength. Such misestimates are interrelated. Information on a government's readiness to accept risks is unavoidably vague since governments rarely undertake high risk actions. As the risk depends on the defender's readiness, it cannot be accurately calculated, much less be calculated exactly as it will appear to the attacker. Next, the attacker's capabilities for inflicting a strategic surprise cannot be fully gauged apart from his objectives; where the latter are vague, the former must remain uncertain. Those capabilities are also hard to estimate correctly because surprise will have a multiplier effect. Even the attacker often miscalculates how surprise will enhance his attack, so it is hard to expect the defender to do well at this. And the defender's assessment of his ability to thwart an attack is directly dependent on his view of the attacker's resources for mounting it.

Thus vague information about the attacker's intentions and objectives plus corresponding uncertainties about his exact capabilities cannot help but induce misestimates by the defender as to his own military strength. There is a cascading series of informational deficiencies that contribute to the defender's vulnerability. In one case after another, the defender is surprised not just by the attack but by how well it goes, how strong the enemy appears, how badly his own forces do.

There are other factors involved. Reiterating an earlier point, secrecy limits the salience of the correct signals, making noise a more potent distraction. Secrecy works to keep those signals "soft" by restricting their confirmation from numerous sources, helping confine the origin of the information to indirect sources or ones of dubious validity. Where deception is used, this multiplies the false information available.

The attacker may also save resources useful for a surprise until the stakes are very high. For attacking Norway and the Soviet Union, Hitler departed from his familiar pattern of preceding the opening of hostilities with extreme demands, increasing those two governments' doubts about reports war was coming.[18] The Americans chose to forego air and naval bombardment of Inchon until shortly before the operation to maximize surprise, and the Soviets did the same on certain fronts in Manchuria. This makes the prior behavior of the attacker even less useful as a guide and may be one reason nations so often are overconfident about their ability to predict the actions of opponents.[19]

Then there is the "cry-wolf" syndrome. Correct signals will appear ambiguous if earlier warnings proved incorrect. Sources of correct signals will be partially or fully discredited if earlier they provided incorrect warnings. Thus a cry-wolf pattern can discredit both the correct information and its source. One sees this at work in various cases such as the North Korean invasion, the Tet Offensive, the German attack on France in 1940, the attacks on Norway and Pearl Harbor, and the Yom Kippur War.

Given these elements that undermine the quality of the victim's information, one might conclude that it is impossible, other than in retrospect, to distinguish signals from noise—all the information at the defender's disposal may be imprecise, unclear, or unreliable.[20] If we accept this view, we could almost stop here; defender vulnerability would be primarily the result of defects in information collected. Cognitive, organizational, and political factors would be of secondary importance, contributing to the defender's problem but not being the essence of it.

However, this does not cover all the facts. What usually happens in a strategic surprise is that not everyone is surprised. Often a correct view emerges among lower level diplomatic, intelligence, or military officials close to the incoming information. MacArthur's headquarters remained confident the Chinese would not intervene, but a marine commander on the spot found the signs so ominous he constructed an airfield for emergency evacuation and delayed carrying out orders to advance, thereby saving many of his men.[21] Various lower level Soviet officers were alarmed by the possibility of a German attack in 1941 and tried, via alerts and troop dispositions, to anticipate it as best they could; similar events occurred in the Israeli armed forces on the eve of the 1973 war.[22] A successful prediction of the Egyptian attack in 1973 was made several days before it occurred by an Israeli intelligence officer. The French military attaché in Berlin prior to the war in 1870 and Russian military officers in Tokyo before the Port Arthur debacle supplied good information on Prussian and Japanese capabilities. In 1940 the British ministry in Copenhagen reported the Germans would attack Norway and Denmark, while Norwegian officials in Berlin described German preparations and suggested to their government that an attack was coming.

In other words, there are many cases in which, at the tactical level, "the presence of confusing 'noise' did not obfuscate or eliminate the relevant warning signals . . ."[23] There are also some instances where senior officials were on the money in their reading of the situation. The director of the Indian Intelligence Bureau in 1962 offered a correct estimate of the Chinese threat, and the directors of both the CIA and DIA correctly suspected the Russians were sending missiles to Cuba. Some admiralty officers accepted the reports of an impending German move against Norway as accurate, and not all senior officials in Washington discounted Chinese signals that they would act in Korea.

Obviously flaws in defender threat perception cannot be ascribed solely to ambiguous information. Other factors—cognitive, organizational, or political—must be at work. Doubtless, the ambiguity permits other factors to have a significant impact, such as by allowing incorrect estimates to flourish. But the power of these additional factors is obvious when we consider instances where lower level personnel and senior officials alike failed to get it right even with seemingly incontrovertible evidence pouring in. The Russian destroyers that spotted elements of the Japanese fleet approaching Port Arthur did not frantically raise an alarm. On December 7, 1941 American vessels pursued a Japanese submarine near Pearl Harbor and a radar station detected the approaching Japanese planes but no general alarm was given, while reports from Pearl were not enough to fully alert U.S. forces in the Philippines. In the Norway invasion the Germans were certain surprise was lost when a troopship was torpedoed and survivors were picked up by the Norwegians, but this plus further evidence did not alert Norwegian defenses. Initial contact with the invading Germans in 1941 did not provoke suitable responses at the front lines or back in Moscow.

Another sort of warning occurs when a defender's analysts describe in detail what a future attack by a particular enemy might look like, or when the enemy actually demonstrates it. We might call this "hypothetical warning," and it should build into the defender's threat perception process certain valuable intellectual categories for analyzing the information collected. With such hypothetical warnings the defender should be much better prepared to recognize an impending strategic surprise, having taught himself what some of the possibilities are.

Yet this often does not help much either. Excellent descriptions of a possible Japanese attack on Pearl Harbor were worked out by American officers well before the real one occurred; several officials called attention to the British attack on the Italian fleet at Taranto as an example. A careful prediction of how the Japanese would invade Malaya was drawn up by British officers in the latter half of the 1930s. The Israelis flew reconnaissance missions over totally vulnerable Egyptian jets in 1956 and Dayan referred in his 1965 book to how they could have attacked instead; yet Egypt was no better prepared in 1967. The French held maneuvers in 1938 that paralleled the German thrust through the Ardennes in 1940, and a Soviet war game less than half a year before Barbarossa outlined how successful the Germans could be.[24] The French had an excellent opportunity after 1866 to appreciate the new Prussian mode of warfare, having just seen its results. The French and British need not have been quite so unprepared for blitzkrieg warfare in view of good staff studies that were available on the possible uses of tanks, the nature of German armored units, and the Wermacht's Polish campaign.

II. Cognitive Defects

It is clear the defender can be in trouble even with very good information on hand. Thus nearly everyone who has studied strategic surprise has concluded that governments are caught unprepared primarily because of the ways people, individually and collectively, think.[25] That is, standard processes in perception and the formation of judgments are held responsible for the misuse of warning. However, in this connection analysts have outlined a bewildering variety of propositions and explanations. We must attempt an orderly presentation of their views and evaluate them in terms of salient features of the historical record on strategic surprise, beginning with the intellectual framework these analysts have employed.[26]

Careful studies have made it clear that perception involves categorizing and evaluating stimuli by means of cognitive structures already present in the mind. The mind is not a passive receptor of data about reality. Instead, it is an energetic, active agent that vigorously employs what it "knows" to guide its search for information, the selection of stimuli to be given attention, the sorting and labeling of information received, and the making of judgments.

Cognitive structures are of various sorts. The most fundamental are powerful *assumptions and beliefs* about important aspects of reality, i.e., are people rational, is there an underlying order to things or are they random in character, etc.? These are deeply ingrained and so are seldom explicitly examined and tested against possible alternatives. Other cognitive structures are *values*, subjective preferences as to what one would like important aspects of reality to be. These, too, are deeply ingrained and thus rarely made explicit and subject to challenge.

More elaborate structures, the product of the interplay among assumptions and values with considerable amounts of past information, are often referred to as *images*. These can be quite complex, though their effect is to greatly simplify portions of reality. They are more readily identified and consciously examined, but in many ways they are employed in a reflexive, habitual fashion. Much more consciously designed and articulated are *hypotheses and theories*. Hypotheses and theories emerge from an often only dimly perceived network of assumptions, values, and images; often they are vaguely stated and not completely understood; once embraced they may be employed almost unconsciously or reflexively. Still, in comparison with other cognitive structures, their application is usually more open and tentative. They are more likely to be set out for evaluation against alternatives, and to be understood as tools created to make sense out of reality, to be retained or discarded on the basis of their utility.

Finally, elements of assumptions, values, images, and hypotheses or theories coalesce into *strategies and plans,* which link goals to guidelines for behavior. On this basis perception can be translated into action. Strategies and plans are still more open and tentative, subject to critical evaluation and revision on the basis of incoming information. However, they are far from entirely so, particularly when they have become well established.

This list of cognitive structures applies to groups and collectivities as well as to individuals. The only difference is that various social processes are required to establish and maintain group cognitive structures. Individuals come to subscribe to and internalize many of the cognitive structures of the groups to which they belong, while groups are always something of an amalgamation of cognitive structures of their members.

These cognitive structures are abstractions and simplifications. To encompass all potentially relevant aspects of all possible stimuli would mean chaos and confusion. Perception is always selective. There is also a powerful tendency toward balance or consistency in cognitive structures so as to minimize confusion and uncertainty and to supply an orderly, reliable, and efficient treatment of stimuli. Satisficing is also employed; selection and interpretation of stimuli proceed by trying out possibilities until a seemingly satisfactory fit emerges between stimuli and cognitive structures, rather than until the best possible one is uncovered. The mind "makes do" with what seems to work.

How flexible are these cognitive structures and the perceptions they dictate, particularly in the face of contrary evidence? The answer is that they are resistant to change, sometimes extremely so, for the following reasons (among others). First, cognitive structures embody prior experience and learning, and have emerged as comfortable and useful. This makes it costly and disturbing to change them. Second, cognitive structures are an integral part of an individual's or group's self-identity. To alter them is to alter that identity. This is not easily or comfortably done, nor should it be since a stable identity is an important resource for dealing with the world.

Third, since perception involves selective sampling from available stimuli, the sampling will be biased in ways that conform to the cognitive structures and reinforce them. Fourth, much information is ambiguous; thus it is adapted to suit existing perceptions and the underlying cognitive structures. Finally, in seeking out stimuli and evaluating them via existing cognitive structures there is a bias against seeing them as consistent with alternative perceptions as well. We are biased toward seeing what we expect to see, and against seeing different things differently.

Thus people come armed with a battery of cognitive structures for making sense of the world. Let us collectively refer to them as preconceptions or predispositions, preset patterns of perception and analysis. Portions of this mental equipment can be challenged, revised, even discarded; under the right circumstances this can even be done quickly and smoothly. But such changes cannot be continuous and are not normal. The norm is that these things are relatively static, applied routinely and repetitively. Willingness to alter them varies with circumstances, with individuals or groups and their training and experience. It probably varies over time, with health or age, etc. Thus generalizing about the inertia attached to preconceptions is difficult beyond stating that it is always substantial.

It follows that there is a strong tendency to overlook information that clashes with existing views, interpret such information in ways that sustain these views, or reject it, and people employ a wide variety of cognitive mechanisms for these purposes. Where discrepant information cannot be fully managed, they will tend to shift their views to the minimum extent necessary, starting with the most flexible and conscious cognitive structures. It also follows that once cognitive structures and the perceptions that flow from them are well established it takes considerably more and better information to lead to their rejection than their retention, even if they originally emerged on the basis of quite limited or ambiguous stimuli.

Application of the foregoing framework to strategic surprise is relatively straightforward. Individual decision-makers, groups of officials, bureaucratic agencies, and governments are rich in cognitive structures: assumptions and beliefs about the nature of international politics and the wellsprings of state behavior, important values believed to be affected by foreign affairs, images of other states and leaders or of typical situations and relationships, hypotheses and theories for explaining various events and processes, plus strategies and plans embodied in proposed or adopted policies. These predispositions shape perceptions and expectations. Often they are implicit or largely so.

Among these preconceptions are ones pertaining directly to opponents and the possibility they might attack. These will be strongly resistant to change. Thus decision-makers are vulnerable to a particular strategic surprise to the extent that their preconceptions are insensitive to that possibility, shape perceptions and predictions accordingly, and resist changes that would better accommodate the warning signs.

In the literature on strategic surprise, it is frequently asserted that the facts gathered by states about opponents do not speak for themselves, that they take on meaning only within a network of "preconceptions," "cognitive beliefs," or "assumptions."[27] Where the information is ambiguous, the relative importance of cognitive structures is increased, particularly when the pressure of events requires quick judgments.[28] Many kinds of cognitive structures have been listed, including decision-makers:

- ideologies and operational codes
- time horizons
- views as to the costs of vigilance
- judgments on the allocation of resources and attention across problems
- beliefs about the feasibility and efficacy of alternative policies
- images of opponents—their motivation, interests, intentions
- general views of international politics[29]

This brings us to the central proposition in the literature:[30]

1. The primary source of vulnerability to strategic surprise is the defender's adherence to an incorrect set of views that treats being attacked as highly unlikely or impossible, thereby causing a misreading of the available signals.

The defender believes the opponent will not attack, will not attack soon, will not be able to attack effectively, or will not attack in an unanticipated fashion. The defender is wrong on one or more points, despite sufficient intelligence to get it right.

Here is a breakdown of the cases in the earlier chapters as to the importance of predispositions in determining vulnerability:

Predispositions Were of Primary Importance

1967 Middle East War	Yom Kippur War
Austrian-Prussian War	Franco-Prussian War
Outbreak of World War I	German Invasion of Norway
German Invasion of France	German Invasion of the USSR
Port Arthur	Chinese Intervention in Korea
Pearl Harbor	North Korean Invasion
Tet Offensive	Dienbienphu
Inchon Landing?	Bay of Pigs
Japanese Attack on Malaya and the Philippines	

Predispositions Were of Secondary Importance

1956 Middle East War	Soviet Invasion of Manchuria

Predispositions Were Not Important
Atomic Bomb

The question mark by the Inchon case reflects a lack of information. In the 1956 war, secrecy and the limitations of Egyptian intelligence seem more important than anything else. In the Manchuria case, the fundamental Japanese deficiency was in available resources. The Japanese were not crippled vis-à-vis the atom bomb by preconceptions; the key to surprise was American secrecy and total military superiority.

The proposition receives strong support. The most important factor in defender vulnerability is erroneous preconceptions; lack of same accounts, more than anything else, for Castro so handily managing the Bay of Pigs invasion. However, in keeping with the analysis offered earlier in this chapter, we should add the following qualifications. First, preconceptions have such a significant impact because of limitations in available information and, to a lesser degree, inadequacies in the collection of information about potential attackers. Second, those deficiencies in information are an integral part of international politics—due to its competitiveness, widespread secrecy and deception, and the difficulties arising from differences in languages, cultures, historical experiences, political systems, etc. Third, the pace of international interactions often forces decisions and actions "too soon," before a sufficiently accurate grasp of reality is attained, leaving too little time and other resources for a more leisurely search for and analysis of information. We know enough about perception to be aware of its flaws under the best of circumstances. The peculiar circumstances of international politics simply magnify these tendencies.

Now we can examine three related questions: What sorts of erroneous preconceptions are the most common and the most dangerous? What factors work to sustain preconceptions in the face of contrary evidence? At what level in a government are dangerously inaccurate preconceptions most likely to be found. We will take up each in turn.

1a. An important defender error is holding to an incorrect conception of how the opponent sees the situation.[31]

This error takes several forms and has a variety of harmful consequences. One of its forms is seeing the opponent as rational,[32] ignoring the fact that he may be in the grip of serious misperceptions. Thus an attack is seen as implausible because it would be senseless and the opponent would not be so foolish. The Tet Offensive is a striking example; for the enemy to seek a direct confrontation in the cities appeared suicidal, hence it was discounted as a possibility. Reluctance to envision the strike at Pearl Harbor flowed in part from expectations that Japan would be too rational to so blatantly challenge an opponent with roughly eight times its industrial potential.

Frequently the defender ascribes to a potential attacker the defender's own version of rationality. This can result in an underestimation of the attacker's motivation, a mistake in judging how he will calculate risks, or a misestimate of his tolerance for risk-taking—particularly when there is a distinct asymmetry of motivation between the two parties. Thus the defender fails to appreciate how, from the opponent's perspective, an attack is a reasonable solution to grave problems, which makes the risks involved more acceptable. Or he does not discern that the attacker is, by nature, more inclined to take risks; or he neglects the possibility that the attacker expects surprise to sharply reduce the risks. Holst writes that the British and Norwegians "underestimated the degree of risk-taking the Germans were prepared to accept." Jervis argues that "it may be that states that use force to alter the status quo often differ from others less in their willingness to run perceived risks than in the fact that they perceive low risks in situations where others perceive high ones." And there is Handel's paradox: "The greater the risk, the less likely it seems, and the less risky it becomes."[33]

Good examples exist in the case studies. In 1956 and 1967 the Egyptians failed to appreciate how Israel would see an unanswered increase in Arab military power as putting its back to the wall, requiring desperate measures. Many governments discounted signs of the German attack on the Soviet Union by seeing it as more rational for Germany to avoid war on two fronts than, as Hitler saw it, to take the gamble in order to either avoid a long war or immeasurably strengthen Germany's resources for fighting it. In 1973 Israel had little sense of the political desperation of Arab governments, just as in

1941 the United States did not see that for Japan war seemed the only alternative to a humiliating retreat from empire. At the turn of the century tsarist officials missed the intense Japanese preoccupation with staking out a territorial bulwark against advancing Russian power, a mistake the Americans reiterated vis-à-vis China in advancing to the Yalu. And in all of these cases, surprise was a way for the attacker to lower the risks of failure.

1b. The defender is vulnerable because he extrapolates from the attacker's past behavior to make predictions about the future, and is therefore caught by surprise when the attacker attempts something new.

We can begin consideration of this proposition by noting that states and statesmen are alleged to learn badly from history. Robert Jervis, Ernest May, and others have argued that statesmen often overgeneralize on the basis of a very selective scanning and interpretation of history. This leads to misperceptions of current situations and opponents via the misuse of historical analogies. By contrast, the disturbing aspect of proposition 1b is that vulnerability can also be *the result of a careful, systematic analysis of past experience.*

As noted earlier, information takes on meaning only within a conceptual framework. What better basis, then, for predicting an opponent's future behavior than a framework drawn from an intensive review of his past behavior? But this is a perfect recipe for being fooled when the opponent does something drastically different.[35]

The case studies offer several clear examples. Most striking is the Israeli underestimation of the Arabs in 1973 and the interpretation of the Egyptian buildup as yet another of Egypt's annual fall military exercises. When the American navy lost track of the Japanese carriers in late 1941 this was not alarming—in previous situations of that sort they were clustered in home waters and it was assumed that was where they were. The Norwegian foreign minister and Stalin both expected Hitler, in view of his prior behavior, to contrive a crisis and issue preemptory demands as a prelude to attacking, something he did not do. The Israelis in 1973 were looking for signs the Arabs had achieved rough parity or even superiority in the air, as a prerequisite for an Arab attack. The British and French in 1940 expected Germany to repeat its World War I sweep through Belgium; when the first German moves into Belgium and Holland occurred, they were accordingly misread in London and Paris.

Still, there is a larger number of cases where an incorrect expectation based on the enemy's past behavior apparently *was not* a major flaw in the defender's threat perception (or is not readily detectable). It would seem wise to accept the proposition only with the following qualifications: first, victims have not always been overly dependent on stereotypes of their opponents. Second, sometimes those who mount strategic surprises are repeating themselves in important ways—the Bay of Pigs closely resembled the CIA's Guatemala operation, MacArthur's military record in World War II was a textbook on skirting major enemy forces via amphibious assaults, Hitler repeatedly resorted to surprise, and Pearl Harbor was a reiteration of Port Arthur. Then the defender's mistake is more like a *failure to learn enough* from the enemy's past.

The latter qualification applies as well to a major implication of proposition 1b. If states are fooled by overreliance on the opponent's past, it follows that training and experience can be a handicap in detecting an impending attack. The more one knows about what is normal, the less one is prepared to comprehend the abnormal.[36] There are, indeed, cases which support this view, where the experts discarded reliable evidence of attack because it did not fit the opponent's behavioral profile. The Norwegian foreign minister in 1940 was just such an expert, as were leading analysts and officials in Israeli military intelligence in 1973, and U.S. military leaders in Vietnam on the eve of the Tet Offensive. But at other times the experts looked better (or at least some of them did). The China hands in the State Department eventually saw a much greater possibility of Chinese intervention in Korea than did MacArthur. There are also the examples cited earlier of warning signals correctly interpreted by lower level military, intelligence, and diplomatic personnel. Being experienced and very familiar with the opponent does not always hurt, just as it is no guarantee of success.

We may close the discussion by examining the concept of "behavioral surprise," introduced by Klaus Knorr.[37] It occurs when the general pattern of the attacker's behavior is contrary to the defender's image of the attacker, and is distinguished from "technical surprise" where it is some more specific facet of that behavior—such as the enemy's actual military capabilities—that is surprising. We must ask if this is a readily applicable and useful distinction.

Cases Which Display Predominantly Technical Surprise
    Austria's view of Prussia in 1866
    France's view of Prussia in 1870
    France's view of Germany in 1914
    Cuba's view of the United States in 1961 (degree of technical surprise minor)
    France's view of the Vietminh in 1954
    France's view of Germany in 1940
    Japan's view of the United States in 1945
    American/British view of Japan in 1941 (Pearl Harbor, Malaya, Philippines)
    British/Norwegian view of Germany in 1940
    Egypt's view of Israel in 1967

North Korea's view of the United States in 1950 (Inchon)
Egypt's view of Israel in 1956
South Korea's view of North Korea in 1950
Russia's view of Japan in 1904
Soviet view of Germany in 1941

Cases Which Display Predominantly Behavioral Surprise
Israel's view of the Arabs in 1973
U.S. view of North Korea in 1950
U.S. view of China in 1950
U.S. view of the Viet Cong in 1968
Japan's view of Russia in 1945

Assigning cases to one category or the other depended on the answer to this question: Was the fact of an attack in keeping with the defender's general image of the opponent? A few cases, such as the last three listed, are difficult to classify with confidence. It should also be apparent that many cases have involved elements of both kinds of surprise. Also, the nature of the surprise may vary within the target state; when the Russians invaded Manchuria this was largely a behavorial surprise in Tokyo but was more a like technical surprise to the Kwantung Army.

Our conclusions are as follows. Technical surprises have been more common. The infrequency of behavorial surprise probably stems from the general climate of suspicion in international politics referred to earlier, and from the fact that strategic surprises so often involve states already in conflict. On balance, defenders are more likely to be suitably suspicious and to appreciate the possibility their opponents might attack, than to adequately grasp their opponents' options and plans for doing so. Next, the target state can be disastrously vulnerable if either kind of surprise is achieved. Finally, distinguishing between the two is not always easy; this limits the utility of the concepts for analytical purposes.

1c. An important defender error is excessive preoccupation with his current plans and concerns.

In one sense this is the obverse of proposition 1a, the other side of paying too little attention to how the opponent views the world. Here we are interested in misperceptions Jervis discusses under the heading of "the evoked set"—"A person will perceive and interpret stimuli in terms of what is at the front of his mind."[38] There are at least two ways this phenomenon may contribute to the victim's lack of readiness. In one, the opponent is neglected because leaders are much more concerned about pressing matters in which the opponent figures only marginally if at all. In the other, the defender concentrates on the opponent, but is wrapped up in his own plans and fails to carefully consider what the opponent may do.[39]

The case studies illustrate each. Prussia benefited from its opponents' preoccupation with their own approaches to war. In 1914 French dogma on taking the offensive overshadowed attention to how the Germans might do so. British plans to intervene in Norway left too little attention for a possible German invasion. Nasser was so intent on bolstering Egypt's position in 1955–56 and 1967 that he gave too little thought to Israel's reaction. As for being preoccupied with unrelated matters, those matters may be domestic or international. President Thieu worried about a military coup in 1968. In 1904 Russian attention was on Europe and the Baltic. In 1941 the U.S. had an undeclared naval war in the Atlantic on its hands and was alarmed by German triumphs in Europe. The Tet Offensive came just after seizure of the Pueblo. Korea was invaded when the United States was mainly worried about a possible war elsewhere with the Soviet Union.

We should note that these damaging preoccupations were not the result of deception. In fact, secrecy is probably more valuable here than deception. The defender has the wrong things on his mind and secrecy curtails the flow of information that would, if properly attended to, reorient the defender's attention.

1d. The defender is vulnerable because he believes the clarity of his signals to the opponent is greater than in fact it is.

This is another variant on proposition 1a, failing to understand how the opponent sees things. The defender thinks he has sent a clear message when he has not, which can apply to strategic surprise in various ways. A state may see itself as less hostile and threatening than others see it,[40] and thus not anticipate such a hostile response as a surprise attack. Or, a state may mistakenly believe it has established a firm commitment in the eyes of its opponent; the opponent's challenge then comes as a surprise. Various analysts have described the Cuban Missile Crisis in these terms or detected this pattern in other instances.[41]

In our case studies there are few clear examples. The Americans believed Peking had no grounds for apprehension as UN forces marched up the Korean peninsula. The Americans also thought they were just being firm, not provocative, in resisting Japanese expansion in 1941. Otherwise, this is not a frequent pattern in cases of strategic surprise; we can discard this proposition as being of little value in explaining defender vulnerability.

1e. The defender is vulnerable because he underestimates the military capabilities of the potential attacker.[42]

Underestimating another state's military might can contribute to a strategic surprise either by increasing the defender's confidence that an attack will not occur or by instilling the belief that any attack will be effectively resisted. The range of possible errors is enormous: misjudging enemy leadership, training, equipment, morale, logistical capabilities, strategy and tactics, etc.; or misjudging one's own forces in any of these respects.

Such an error appears in virtually every one of our cases of strategic surprise. (The only apparent exceptions are the Bay of Pigs and Inchon, and we lack the information to be certain this did not apply to Inchon as well.) This tells us a good deal. It is extremely difficult to do accurate net estimates of military power (because of the multiplicity of relevant variables and the limited information available); the defender should always regard such estimates with great skepticism. However, the attacker seems less prone to error in assessing his military capabilities (at least in the short run); he is far more likely to get this right than the defender. The reason, to reiterate an earlier point, is that military power cannot be readily assessed apart from objectives. The attacker knows what he wants to do, and his calculations can be in reference to this. The defender can only construct contingency plans, and as there are all sorts of contingencies the quality of his estimates is accordingly reduced.

Defenders seem especially prone to "technical surprise" when it comes to assessing the effects of technological change on military capabilities. The possible consequences of new weapons, new wrinkles on old weapons, new modes of warfare, or shifts in communications and transportation are particularly difficult to comprehend. Consider the following list:

1866—the Austrians are surprised by a new mode of warfare
1870—the French are equally surprised by that mode of warfare
1914—the French do not comprehend the possible scale and rate of a German mobilization and sweep through Belgium
1940—the British and Norwegians fail to see how air power can substitute for sea power in German invasion of Norway
1940—the French miss the potential in blitzkrieg warfare to overcome defenses
1941—the Russians underestimate the potential of blitzkrieg warfare against their forces.
1941—the Americans do not expect aerial torpedos to run in shallow water, misjudge the caliber of Japanese fighter planes and naval craft
1945—the Japanese regard an atomic bomb as impossible to make
1950—the Americans believe tanks will be relatively useless in Korean terrain
1954—the French do not envision the Vietminh's true logistical and artillery capabilities
1973—the Israelis are unprepared for new Soviet weapons employed in a new way by the Arabs

Next, there are examples of defender estimates (and attacker estimates for that matter) being skewed by ethnocentrism or racism. Unflattering racial stereotypes were plentiful in British and American references to the Japanese in the years prior to Pearl Harbor. Russians at the turn of the century regarded the Japanese with contempt. The French saw the Vietminh as just a primitive, unprofessional rabble. Israeli disdain for the Arabs prior to 1973 is well known. Americans had little respect for Chinese military capabilities in 1950. A defender would do well to be alert to this phenomenon.

1f. States are vulnerable to strategic surprise because they overestimate their capabilities for detecting it in advance.

The target state might have a misplaced confidence in the caliber of its intelligence apparatus and other means of gathering information.[43] Or, the defender may incorrectly rely on certain "indices," signals he believes would be clear signs of an attack.[44] The supreme example of the former in our case studies is the unqualified confidence the Israeli cabinet placed in intelligence in 1973. We reviewed examples of overreliance on indices earlier. Another illustration is that the British knew roughly how many divisions Hitler had available for an invasion of Norway, far fewer than they thought necessary, so other signs of the invasion were viewed with skepticism. The Egyptians in 1956 linked a possible Israeli attack to support of Israel by a great power; with no sign of this (due to secrecy) the attack was not predicted. MacArthur's headquarters focused on the best time for a Chinese intervention; when that time passed it was harder for Chinese threats to be convincing.

We must not fail to note, however, that this is not a mistake characteristic of all the cases. In about half, the defender does not appear to have been overconfident *about his intelligence or other detection systems;* about other things, yes, but not these matters.

1g. Defenders are vulnerable due to wishful thinking.

Wishful thinking means having one's preferences for particular outcomes distort estimates as to how likely those outcomes are, and thus leads to overestimating the probability of desired outcomes and underestimating it for undesired ones. For the defender a surprise attack is distinctly unwanted, especially one that leads to a disastrous defeat. It is reasonable to suppose that defenders may be vulnerable because they hope this will not happen and misread the evidence as a result.[45]

This is not easy to detect via a retrospective analysis, and the evidence is spotty. Stalin wished to put off war with Germany until 1942 and was eager to downgrade the possibility of Hitler attacking in 1941. American leaders that same year devoutly wished to stay out of the war until well into 1942 so the U.S. military buildup could continue. The last thing the United States wanted in approaching the Yalu was Chinese intervention and a wider war. It was compelling for the French and then the Russians to believe that blitzkrieg only worked well against inferior forces—their own would do better. Norway was naturally eager to believe it could sustain its neutral status in World War II as it had in World War I. There was probably an element of wishfulness in Austrian and French estimates as to how war with Prussia would go, or in Egypt's view of its military situation vis-á-vis Israel in 1956 and 1967. However, it is not easy to distinguish wishful thinking from other perceptual errors. If there is such a tendency, we cannot say much about how powerful it is under various circumstances.

Earlier we listed three related questions: What sorts of erroneous preconceptions are most common in defenders? What factors work to sustain such preconceptions? At what level are they most likely found? We are ready for the second of these.

The various predispositions that make defenders vulnerable are not readily abandoned even when warnings and other available information suggest they should be. Hence this second central proposition:

2. The incorrect predispositions which lead to defender vulnerability are retained even in the face of a considerable amount of discrepant information.

Our concern here is with cognitive factors which produce intellectual rigidity. Jervis and others have listed many ways the mind resists change, but none of the case studies penetrates deeply enough to allow us to fully analyze their impact. Instead, we will examine factors typically found in strategic surprise situations which contribute to intellectual inertia.

2a. A strongly held view that one will not be attacked, or will be attacked only in a certain way, cannot readily be dislodged because the ultimate evidence to the contrary is the attack itself.

Evidence of the opponent's military preparations can be discounted on the theory that he is bluffing. As Jervis points out, "the conclusion that the other side is bluffing can be disconfirmed only when war starts. All threats, leaks of plans for attack, and military preparations can be accounted for within this image . . . "[46] Or, the opponent's military preparations can be explained as intended to serve some other purpose, i.e., to attack a third party. As for the defender's view that he will only be attacked in a certain way (for which he is adequately prepared), evidence to the contrary can be discarded as an attempt at deception.

There are numerous signs of this in the cases. In 1973 Arab threats were seen by the Israelis as issued for domestic political comsumption and Arab military preparations were discounted as annual maneuvers. German preparations to invade Norway were explained by the British as readying a naval thrust into the North Atlantic; reports and rumors were seen as part of Germany's war of nerves and deception. Stalin discounted Western reports of a coming German invasion as provocations, and treated Hitler's military buildup as an effort at diplomatic coercion. Later that year the Americans interpreted Japan's threats and preparations as either bluffing (a State Department view) or as aimed at Southeast Asia. Many Russian leaders thought the Japanese were bluffing in 1904. In 1968, the Americans were ready for a Viet Cong and North Vietnamese move, but against Khe Sanh. In 1950 American expectations of military struggle with the communist world were well developed, but tensions in Korea seemed like a diversion and the usual North Korean rhetoric. Of course the Chinese were believed to be bluffing later on, a view clung to even after initial engagements with Chinese troops.

In short, the defender may hold to views which, by their very nature, are exceedingly hard to falsify until it is too late. This applies equally well to notions of relative military strength; if the defender is quite confident of his superiority he will not readily be disabused of this because the ultimate evidence is the test of war. Defender misestimates on this score are ubiquitous in cases of strategic surprise.

2b. Preconceptions that discount the possibility of strategic surprise are reinforced by the "cry-wolf" phenomenon.[47]

In Wohlstetter's words, "An excess of warnings which turn out to be false alarms always induces a kind of fatigue, a lessening of sensitivity."[48] Looking over the case studies we find numerous instances. The Israelis had many false alarms, to one of which they responded with a costly partial mobilization, that dulled their readiness to accept warnings in October 1973. Commanders at Pearl Harbor had checked any number of false sightings of Japanese subs, and warnings the Japanese might make a major military move had been issued from Washington several times in 1941. It was a regular feature of the Korean situation in 1950 that South Korean sources would predict an attack and the North Koreans would do something provocative along the border. MacArthur's panic reaction to the first engagements with Chinese troops looked a bit foolish once they withdrew, which reinforced resistance to later alarms. The Tet Offensive came after a series of false reports of planned communist attacks. Detection of the missiles in Cuba was handicapped by the fact that refugee reports that they were there had been received for over a year.

The cry wolf phenomenon is not observable in all cases. However, it is absent mainly from the earlier ones. As intelligence systems have improved and as military technology has placed a premium on speed, what seems to have happened is that states are increasingly able to gather warnings to which they must pay attention. This suggests the possibility of a rising incidence of cry wolf situations; contemporary states may be burdened with more false alarms.

An alternative possibility is suggested by de Rivera. He argues that modern intelligence, military, and diplomatic agencies attach penalties to failure to report warnings and suspicions, but that high level decision-makers penalize subordinates for pestering them with false alarms. Thus incorrect warnings pile up at middle levels, while officials there are reluctant to challenge optimistic viewpoints of national leaders.[49] We are not in a position to confirm or reject this view.

2c. Warning of a surprise attack, an improbable and unwanted event, is burdened with refuting all alternative explanations of the evidence; it is required to pass stiffer tests as to veracity or reliability, or to consist of several sets of information that converge on the same conclusion.[50]

2d. Given ambiguous information and the inertia behind existing views, when discrepant information appears in bits and pieces it is ignored or interpreted so as to sustain those views.[51]

2e. Policymakers' sensitivity to information about a possible strategic surprise that contradicts their views varies inversely with the degree of commitment to those views.[52]

2f. After decision-makers have acted on the view that a strategic surprise will not occur, cognitive dissonance works to sustain it; they will rearrange beliefs to justify their expectations, spread the alternatives, and avoid situations and evidence that suggest those decisions were incorrect.[53]

2g. A defender's initial perspectives drive his analyses; he is biased toward finding his hypotheses confirmed and usually tests only those hypotheses and not others. Confirming evidence is highlighted and disconfirming evidence downplayed. Thus initial feedback confirms the hypotheses, reinforcing them, so that incorrect ones are not readily altered.[54]

Each proposition offers an explanation for cognitive rigidity. Each is intuitively plausible or is a persuasive extension of findings in several fields as to how the mind works. Each is discussed in one or more studies on strategic surprise. However, our case studies do not penetrate into the cognitive processes of decision-makers to the degree necessary to firmly evaluate these propositions. About as far as we can go is the following.

None of these propositions can be rejected on the basis of the case studies, or looks any less plausible. For each there is at least some evidence that could be interpreted as demonstrating that the factor or factors cited were at work. (This is particularly true of proposition 2d.) Thus we are entitled to strongly suspect that those factors contribute to vulnerability to strategic surprise. But we cannot assess the relative accuracy of these propositions, or suggest how often they apply. They illustrate the matters that need further investigation to refine our understanding of strategic surprise, and of intelligence failures in general.

Our final question, of the three listed earlier, was: at what level of the government are dangerously inaccurate predispositons most likely to be found? There are several possibilities:

- the crippling misperceptions are at lower levels of the government;
- the really serious misperceptions are held by high level decision-makers;
- the crucial misperceptions are normally centered in the intelligence apparatus;
- the major misperceptions can be found in the armed forces; and
- there is always a network of interrelated misperceptions found at various levels and in various agencies

It is clear where most analysts lay the blame, as embodied in the following proposition:

3. The most likely location of serious misperceptions, and the most disabling, is at the level of senior officials, the major decision makers in the target state.[55]

Most analysts agree with the following view:

> The ultimate causes of error in most cases have been wishful thinking, cavalier disregard of professional analysts, and, above all, the premises and preconceptions of policy makers. Fewer fiascos have occurred in the stages of acquisition and presentation of facts than in the stages of interpretation and response. Producers of intelligence have been culprits less often than consumers. Policy perspectives tend to constrain objectivity, and authorities often fail to use intelligence properly.[56]

The evidence from the case studies is mixed. First, there are cases where the highest decision makers subscribed to views that discounted the possibility of attack, irrespective of information to the contrary with which they were familiar:

1940—Dr. Koht, the Norwegian foreign minister, and Churchill, first lord of the admiralty, concerning a possible German invasion of Norway

1941—Stalin, on a German invasion threat
1941—All high level decision makers in Washington, on a possible Japanese attack
1973—All high level Israeli decision-makers, on an Arab attack
1962—Menon and Nehru, as to a Chinese attack
1950—All top Washington officials, as regards to a North Korean attack
1950—Most senior Washington officials, on possible Chinese intervention in Korea
1945—Tokyo leaders, on a Russian attack in Manchuria

Though it is hard to be certain, Nasser in 1956 and again in 1957 probably belongs on this list.

There are also cases where the most debilitating preceptions were professional military misjudgments:

1866—Austrian military leaders, on the relative military strength of Prussia and Austria
1870—French military leaders, on the relative military strength of Prussia and France
1914—French military leaders, on how a war with Germany would go
1940—French and British military leaders, on where Germany would attack and the utility of blitzkrieg tactics
1954—French military leaders, on the outcome of a set piece battle with the Vietminh

Then there are a few cases where top civilian and military leaders shared interrelated misperceptions:

1941—the British in Malaya and London, on the defense of Malaya and Singapore
1968—Westmoreland and his staff plus top officials in Washington, on the strength of the Viet Cong and the nature of a possible attack
1950—MacArthur and his staff plus senior officials in Washington, on whether the Chinese would intervene and, if so, at what cost
1904—Russian military and civilian leaders, on how a war with Japan would go

We should also note that even in the first list, political leaders in several instances had their preconceptions and expectations reinforced by military misjudgments (as when the Defense Department assured the State Department of South Korea's military superiority).

As for intelligence officials, there are few cases where they held to what were, in retrospect, the critical preconceptions, at least as far as this can be determined. In many instances one of the following seems to have occurred:

high political or military leaders were not really interested in intelligence findings, or ignored them, or so dominated their intelligence sources that their own views were reflected in the analyses they received. In several other cases we cannot be sure what role intelligence played (North Korea prior to the Inchon landing, or Egypt in 1956 or 1967).

Earlier we discussed the fact that lower level officials have sometimes done quite a good job at reading incoming information and suspecting that an attack was coming. We also noted that they have at times made quite serious errors as well, errors which contributed to vulnerability to strategic surprise.

Thus we must accept proposition 3 with the following modifications. Critical misperceptions leading to vulnerability to strategic surprise have been frequently associated with the highest officials in the government, but in many cases military misjudgments are either of central importance or reinforce the erroneous views of top officials. The misperceptions of intelligence and lower level personnel seem less responsible, though occasionally important.

There is one other proposition on predispositions worth mentioning here, though the evidence will not allow us to sustain or reject it, because it bears on how to reduce vulnerability to strategic surprise. If all perception is selective and shaped by prior inclinations, if everyone resists information which clashes with their views, then we cannot distinguish between people who are "right" and people who are "wrong" in estimates about a strategic surprise on the basis of cognitive competence. Those who are correct merely have more suitable preconceptions to start with.

4. Those who misread the evidence of an approaching strategic surprise are not guilty of major intellectual mistakes in the way they approached the evidence and reached their conclusions.[57]

Jervis believes statesmen who are correct on some issue are often no more open-minded, no less rigid, than others who were not correct. Sometimes they are right in spite of the evidence.

> For this reason those who have reached the right conclusion may be less reasonable and may be treating the information in less justifiable ways than those who are wrong. Hunches, luck and an accurate general analysis of the other and his situation often explain why a person is able to predict correctly what others would do. Those who disagree, far from being blind to the facts, are often truer to them.[58]

From this view, the preceding discussion needs revision so that defenders are depicted not as having made mistakes but as having been so unfortunate as to be mistaken.

We cannot say much of relevance on this, for the case studies concentrate on defenders who were surprised and examine preconceptions that were in error—no comparable review of successes was attempted. However, if the proposition is correct, leaders and governments should have uneven records: able to inflict a surprise yet be fooled themselves, right sometimes and not other times. That is, in fact, what we sometimes find. MacArthur and his superiors were fooled by North Korea, inflicted Inchon, then were fooled by the Chinese. The Japanese pulled off strategic surprises in 1941 but were grievously surprised in 1945. The Israelis used surprise in 1956 and 1967, then were caught in 1973. Perhaps this is also why states do not learn very well from their prior experiences as victims: the French, the British, the Americans, the Russians, and the Egyptians have been fooled more than once.

III. Vulnerability Due to Organizational Factors

Cognitive factors may explain a major portion of defender vulnerability, but they are not the whole story. Next we must consider possible pathologies associated with the complex organizations of which governments are composed. Once again, we draw on the literature on strategic surprise for propositions and consider them in the light of evidence from the case studies. The propositions of interest are of two sorts, those which pertain to how the government is organized, and those which emphasize the nature of bureaucracy in general or one particular kind of bureaucracy.

It has occurred to a number of people that the way a government is structured for the analysis of information might have something to do with its vulnerability to strategic surprise. This had led to the following propositions, some of which overlap, and some of which are contradictory.

5a. Lack of a centralized intelligence apparatus that pulls together scattered information to produce a single objective assessment contributes to a state's vulnerability to strategic surprise.[59]
5b. A centralized production of a single authoritative estimate does not eliminate vulnerability to strategic surprise.[60]
5c. A pluralistic intelligence apparatus can reduce vulnerability to strategic surprise.[61]
5d. Having multiple sources of analysis does little to reduce vulnerability to strategic surprise.[62]

Proposition 5a was a major lesson drawn by Americans from Pearl Harbor. Proposition 5b reflects the fear that formation of a single estimate may increase a state's vulnerability, if it has any effect at all, because the accepted view will not be systematically challenged and the intelligence product will soon come to reflect the predispositions of political leaders. Such fears lead to proposition 5c. This was a major lesson drawn by the Israelis from the Yom Kippur War, and they took steps to multiply agencies doing estimates to provide top decision-makers with several different channels of information. But proponents of proposition 5d disagree, for several reasons. First, for security reasons, a high premium is placed on not recruiting intellectual/ ideological deviants as intelligence personnel, thus under-representing those who do not share the government's dominant perspectives. Multiplying intelligence agencies does not change this, only a narrow pluralism is created. Second, there is only one buyer for the intelligence product, the national leadership; multiplying agencies heightens competition to ingratiate that buyer by reinforcing its biases. Third, it is feared that multiplying agencies leads to hedging or bureaucratic compromises that hide alternative viewpoints. Fourth, creation of truly competing estimates may allow decision-makers to pick the one they find most congenial. Finally, multiple agencies can mean duplication, organizational jealousies, and a tendency to hoard and manipulate information as a weapon in bureaucratic struggles.

In the case studies it is difficult to find any consistent pattern. The nature of the intelligence structure was not always apparent, but it appears that in a number of cases (Pearl Harbor, the British in 1940, the Tet Offensive, for example) the defender had multiple agencies and at times a fragmented structure, while in other cases (the French in 1914, 1940, and 1954, Israel in 1973, the USSR in 1941, for instance) decision-makers employed a single agency or there was strong central direction of the preparation of estimates. Codevilla may be correct in concluding that structure of the intelligence system is not a significant variable:

> . . . fear of disaster (or its obverse, a passionate thirst for victory) can overcome decisions about the focus of analysis, compel critical examination of prejudice, and diminish the relative importance of bureaucratic self-interest. In sum, almost any system for analyzing intelligence can work well if everyone connected with it believes his own life depends on its success.[63]

It has also been argued that one of the key services intelligence can provide is to serve as a counterweight to the incorrect or questionable predispositions of national leaders. This means an intelligence agency should be close enough to the policymakers to understand their needs, concerns, and views yet autonomous enough to prepare its own best assessment of a situation. This leads to yet another proposition.

6. Vulnerability to strategic surprise is increased when the intelligence process is dominated by policymakers, so that their views unduly shape information gathering and analysis.[64]

To fully explore this we would need examples of successful anticipation of strategic surprise to compare with failures. There are certainly examples of policymakers dominating the intelligence process to no benefit—Israel in 1973 is the perfect illustration. But there are far more examples of policymakers or military leaders being uninterested in intelligence or making little use of it. We should also note that many strategic surprises have been mounted by decision-makers who were uninterested in or dismissed relevant intelligence. It seems the critical element is the nature of the decision-makers and their conceptions, and the degree to which they are prepared to act on those conceptions. If they have strongly held views and are determined to act, their organizational relationship with an intelligence structure is not very important in determining how appreciative they are of alternative views or how sensitive they are to discrepant information.[65]

Earlier we called attention to the numerous instances in which military misjudgments enhanced a defender's vulnerability to strategic surprise. It could be that this is due to a typical military approach to planning.

7. Military planning frequently proceeds by preparing operational plans in the abstract, with little detailed consideration given to the enemy and his plans, which enhances vulnerability to strategic surprise.

Kirkpatrick, in presenting this view, suggests that the enemy is often taken into account almost as an afterthought.[66] It must be said that there are a fair number of instances where this occurred: among Austrian and French military leaders in 1866 and 1870; the French in 1914; the British in 1940 who were preoccupied with their own plans to intervene in Norway; plus MacArthur in Korea, Navarre in Vietnam, and Westmoreland in Vietnam. This is the pattern of other cases as well.

While such examples are persuasive, certain qualifications are in order. Such a preoccupation with one's own plans is almost certainly characteristic of all bureaucratic organizations and of governments in general. It may well be incorrect to single out military planning as unusually deficient in this regard. In addition, military organizations may plan for contingencies but receive far from optimal resources to meet their needs, particularly when political leaders think those contingencies are most improbable. Concentration on their own plans would then occur because they lacked the resources to do much else. In addition, there are certainly plenty of examples in military history and in recent years of military organizations and leaders adopting exceedingly "conservative" estimates of an opponent's military capabilities—as the basis for planning, budget requests, training, and giving advice to civilian leaders. In these cases a lack of careful consideration of the opponent is apt to mean erring on the safe side, not increased vulnerability to surprise attack. On balance, then, this does not appear to be a valid proposition.

A final matter under the heading of organizational factors is the possibility that vulnerability to strategic surprise is inherent in the nature of modern government agencies. Still unsurpassed as an expression of this view is Wilensky's *Organizational Intelligence,* with its sobering conclusion that "intelligence failures are built into complex organizations."[67] He cites such elements as hierarchy, specialization, centralization, the stages of organizational development, tensions between superiors and subordinates, preoccupation with immediate problems, and an intolerance for ambiguity as contributing to intelligence failures.

Analysts of strategic surprise concede that there may be something to this, but a thorough analysis along these lines has never been attempted and the case studies in this book cannot help much. A far more detailed exploration of the inner workings of diplomatic, military, and intelligence organizations would be necessary, and for many cases this is simply not possible. All that can be done is to emphasize that the analysis presented here highlights informational and cognitive factors, not organizational ones, though the reader may have noticed that some of this evidence suggests that organizational factors help create vulnerability in the ways Wilensky says they do.

IV. Vulnerability Due to Political Factors

We are still considering failures in perception as a primary source of vulnerability to strategic surprise. We have examined *informational, cognitive,* and *organizational* elements that can be responsible for misperceptions. The remaining category is *political.*

The tendency in analyzing strategic surprise is to depict governments as *learning* systems, gathering and processing information as a guide to, or basis for, action. This directs our attention to governmental perceptual processes in themselves, somewhat apart from their larger context. But we should remember that governments are primarily *action* oriented, aiming to impose on their environment rather more than understanding it. This means that learning about the world is often a second order process and perception is skewed accordingly.[68] To concentrate on a government's perceptual/analytical processes subtly distorts things, for a government is self-centered and action-oriented and it does its perceiving and learning within that narrow frame of reference. Action (and planned action) shapes perception as much as perception guides action. Governments lack the time and inclination to perceive and learn in ways an academic observer normally understands.

This perspective helps clarify why a government's perceptions can be badly flawed; why it is often reflexive and seldom reflective, how it can be so embroiled in its own plans as to ignore even first-rate information about what an opponent is planning. It helps explain why there is often a poor relationship between decision-makers and action agencies on the one hand, and agencies for information gathering and planning on the other. It is reflected in the nature of decision-makers, their insensitivity to ambiguity and to other problems of perception.

> Intelligence consumers are political men who have risen by being more decisive than reflective, more aggressive than introspective, and confident as much as cautious.[69]

This takes us a long way toward answering the question posed at the beginning of this chapter. If perception is frequently an adjunct or extension of governmental decision and action far more than a precursor of it, then vulnerability to surprise because of misperception can hardly be unexpected, and it is understandable why governments do not readily learn from their own and others' past experience on strategic surprise. Vulnerability is linked to the nature of government; the same mistakes recur because the reality of government itself does not change.

In a sense, to possess power is to be in a position where it is less necessary to learn in order to act—it is others without power that have to do so. Governing rests on the accumulation and exercise of power and the need to learn in order to act is accordingly reduced. The consequences are apparent in the behavior of both attackers and defenders in cases of strategic surprise. Officials with power can brush aside information that to land at Inchon is impossible, that Russia is too strong to be invaded, that a war on the U.S. in the Pacific cannot be won, that dropping the atomic bomb will provoke a nuclear arms race. They can order such things done anyway. Their counterparts can refuse to learn what the military capabilities of Prussia or Germany truly are, can reject warnings of a coming German or Arab or North Korean attack, can discount evidence of their military unpreparedness, can concentrate on their own plans to intervene in Norway or unify Korea. That is what having power means.

No wonder vulnerability to strategic surprise occurs across different cultures and political systems, to various sorts of decision-makers, in many kinds of situations, and at all levels of political and economic development. It is not even associated with a specific military technology, or with any particular organizational pattern for intelligence. Yet the basic similarity of the phenomenon across many times, places, systems, and societies seems apparent. It is one variant of the pathology of political power.

This perspective can also be applied to highlight the impact of a standard dilemma in politics on vulnerability to strategic surprise. That dilemma is captured in the following proposition:

8. Decision-makers resist information about a possible strategic surprise that, if accepted, will require reopening an issue earlier decided only with great difficulty or tackling an issue earlier avoided because it was difficult or highly controversial.

Decision and action in a government involve struggles over the definition of the problem, efforts to create a workable consensus or build an effective coalition, and the hammering out of a policy. An unavoidable concern is timing—often problems can be confronted only when the time is right politically. Thus the policymaker has inhibitions on grasping information about a threat quite apart from those deriving from ambiguous data, standard cognitive processes, or organizational factors. He has a stake in continuing with decisions and policies the elaboration of which required a heavy investment in time, political resources, emotional considerations, etc. We might call this the "can-of-worms" syndrome.

George and Smoke find this to have been at work in the American government being unprepared for the Berlin blockade, the North Korean attack in 1950, and the Chinese intervention.[70] Our case studies seldom supply explicit evidence, but the record is often very suggestive. In 1941 Stalin was caught in a quandary—by 1942 he would be ready to face a German onslaught; 1941 was too soon, and to accept evidence the attack was coming would have reopened the question of whether cooperating with Hitler had been wise. In 1973 the Israelis had a huge investment in the policy of sitting tight in the occupied territories; to have opened this policy for reexamination by accepting the early warning signs of Arab military preparations would have been politically most uncomfortable. In 1941 Washington wanted more time before entering the war, but its policy toward Japan could not have shifted to a more conciliatory line without a political uproar, so it was not eager to contemplate the possibility that firmness toward Tokyo was inciting an attack. For Japanese leaders seeking an end to the war in 1945 amidst die-hard military sentiments, Russia's joining the war was a prospect to downplay because that meant having to face a showdown over whether to abjectly surrender. For the French and later the Americans in Vietnam looking too closely at enemy capabilities meant more controversy about how the war was going, with the overall policy under increasing attack yet not politically easy to change. For Napolean III in 1870 and the Norwegian foreign minister in 1940, it was politically inopportune to fully grasp the nature of the threat.

In short, vulnerability often has been associated with policymakers having the power to not learn about an impending attack in a situation where there were political incentives not to do so. In such situations honest doubts and worries will be, even if expressed, not acted upon. We find numerous instances in which the policymakers were not by any means blind to the possibility of an attack but were vulnerable anyway. The tsar cabled instructions dealing with Japan's possibly going to war. Roosevelt raised with his chief advisors the possibility of a surprise Japanese attack, and war warnings went out to U.S. posts in the Pacific. American officials were persistently concerned about a Chinese intervention in Korea. The Norwegian foreign minister and

Stalin could not help but at least consider the notion that the Germans were coming. Napolean III had his doubts about the coming war with Prussia. It was a staple of Japanese military and foreign policy thinking to worry about a Russian attack.

If cognitive and informational factors were the only ones relevant, we would expect to find such doubts and fears expressed only outside the government or at lower levels within it, to find them nonexistent or thoroughly repressed among top officials. Instead we find decision-makers able, to some extent, to surmount those factors and gain some appreciation of discrepant information and warnings, only to be unable to escape from or override the additional political factors that invite disaster.

Fourth Phase: Response to Warning

The culmination of the defender's failure to appreciate warnings is an insufficient response, and as a result the attack occurs and is quite harmful. Yet the damage is usually much greater than it had to be. Though the warnings were discounted, certain precautions typically would have either reduced the likelihood of the attack or the magnitude of its consequences, precautions defenders might have taken, "just to be on the safe side." It is the failure to do so that we are interested in here, particularly since, as we have just seen, national leaders are often not oblivious to the danger and lower level officials are frequently more sensitive to the warning signs than their superiors. What causes this failure?

I. Informational Factors

Our analysis here can briefly refer back to elements discussed earlier. A truly appropriate response has, in most cases, been inhibited by the opponent's use of secrecy and deception to cover the exact nature of what was planned. The defender therefore had only ambiguous information as to where the blow might fall. Even when surprise was not achieved at the Bay of Pigs, Castro was uncertain as to the size of the landing force and the site selected. This means that any contingency planning is done somewhat in the dark. Examples will elaborate this point.

MacArthur's response to clear Chinese threats to intervene was incorrect because the Chinese successfully hid their troop movements. Navarre stayed in the looming trap at Dienpienphu partly because the Vietminh disguised their true artillery capabilities. The Americans anticipated Hanoi's offensive in 1968 but lacked information on Viet Cong infiltration of the cities, so the U.S. response was incorrectly centered on Khe Sanh. The main front chosen by the Russians for the attack on Manchuria was so well disguised that available Japanese forces were improperly deployed.

The overall ambiguity of the available information works to handicap the defender's response because there are always more contingencies than the defender has resources to prepare for. The defender must be selective and noise, plus secrecy and deception, make it very difficult to choose correctly.

II. Cognitive Factors

Predispositions work to make the defender's response inadequate in several ways. Perhaps the most crucial is the military underestimation of the enemy, because it tends to curtail sensible precautions. The fact that China was deemed unprepared for war helps explain MacArthur's willingness to divide and overextend his forces. The French neglected the precaution of taking the high ground at Dienpienphu because the Viet Minh were supposedly no match in a set piece battle. The Israelis did not feel they had to match the Arab buildup in 1973 because they were certain the Arabs were militarily inept.

Along with this comes the confidence that one can manage whatever happens—the enemy cannot do grievous harm. So thought the Americans in Vietnam in 1968 and in South Korea in 1950, and the French in Indochina in 1954. The Russians in 1904 and the British and Americans in 1941 thought they were prepared to absorb Japan's first blow.

There are two clear instances in which misperceptions of intelligence capabilities led to inadequate precautions. The Americans pushing toward the Yalu and the Israelis in 1973 were confident of getting sufficient advance warnings to make the necessary preparations. This may have been a factor in Egypt's vulnerability in 1956 and 1967, or in other cases, but there is too little information to say for sure. Of course, if the defender believes there is one crucial indicator of the enemy's readiness to attack, he will stop short of an adequate response to other warnings.

Finally, the victim's preoccupation with his own plans or other problems can directly inhibit adequate response to warning given limitations on resources. Commanders at Pearl Harbor were training for war, which left few planes and ships for patrolling. Adequate French preparation for the Schlieffen plan would have left insufficient forces for taking the offensive. British needs elsewhere in 1941 meant too little too late for Malaya, Singapore, and Burma.

III. Organizational Factors

In a broad sense, response may be inadequate because of organizational deficiencies, particularly as they pertain to military readiness. While the case studies offer numerous illustrations, this is not a subject that could be studied in detail and such deficiencies may be of greater significance than would appear at first. We can start by noting that victims have often had serious military weaknesses or deficiencies:

1. a hidebound military system, impervious to new ideas and changing times—Austria in 1866, France in 1870, France in 1914, Russia in 1940, and (to some extent) France in 1940
2. inadequate training of officers and men—Russia in 1904, the Egyptians in 1956 and 1967, South Korea in 1950, the Kwantung Army in 1945
3. insufficient forces and inadequate weapons—Japan in 1945, the United States and Britain in the Pacific in 1941, South Korea in 1950
4. poorly deployed forces—France in Vietnam in 1954, Japan in Manchuria in 1945, Russia in 1941, Israel in 1973, the U.S. in North Korea in 1950

In short, strategic surprise is not always a matter of well prepared defenders being fooled—as in the Tet Offensive, the German attacks in the West in 1914 and 1940 and the Inchon landing. It is more often a matter of inadequately prepared defenders being fooled, so that the two sorts of deficiencies reinforce each other.

More specific deficiencies are harder to spot. Bureaucratic rivalries and jealousies, plus poor organization and training, hampered making Port Arthur alert. At Pearl Harbor, three commanders shared responsibility for the islands defenses, and coordination was insufficient. The British command structure for Malaya was inordinately cumbersome, which hamstrung preparations for defense. Japanese resistance in Manchuria in 1945 foundered on problems in coordinating certain forces.

Finally, the cry-wolf syndrome damages organizational responsiveness in at least two ways. Repeated warnings dull the response mechanism—people go to their posts on alerts with no enthusiasm, patrols become routine, reconnaissance lags. This happened to Israel in 1973, the United States in Vietnam in 1968, the United States at Pearl Harbor. Fear of this effect may also lead high level decision-makers to forego alerts until they are certain; the orders that go out are therefore vague, and fail to arouse sufficient alertness at the point of attack. Pearl Harbor illustrates this to an extent.

IV. Political Factors

One of the more intriguing aspects of the case studies is that the defender often neglected an adequate response to warnings because of political considerations, domestic and international. This has received too little attention in prior studies as an important contributor to defender vulnerability.

American decision-makers in 1950 had to live with the fact that the proper response to the Chinese threat to intervene in Korea—halting the advance of U.N. forces while reconsidering the goal of unifying Korea—would pose immense political difficulties at home, particularly since MacArthur was certain to object publicly. The Saigon government in 1968 was in no position politically to withhold leaves for its soldiers for the Tet holiday celebrations, despite threats of some enemy action. The political compulsion behind Nasser's moves in 1956 and 1967 was more than enough to risk Israel's response; going more slowly would have been very difficult to explain. The Roosevelt administration did not relish the allegations of appeasement that would arise if the Pacific fleet was safely berthed at San Diego.

In a number of cases the defender chose to forego last minute military precautions so as not to provoke an attack or due to a deliberate decision to let the opponent bear the onus of firing the first shot.[71] Israel was moved by both considerations in 1973.[72] In 1940 Britain hoped to lure Germany into military moves that would lead Norway to invite British assistance. Meanwhile, the Norwegians avoided mobilizing so as not to provoke Germany. Stalin forbade various military preparations as potentially provocative. Military leaders at Pearl Harbor were ordered to avoid excessive precautions that could provoke Japan, while the British hesitated to seize possible landing sites in Thailand so as not to be seen giving Tokyo a pretext. Russian officials at Port Arthur had instructions to let Japan make the first move.

Other political considerations have sometimes played a part. One possible response to the Schlieffen plan was for French troops to move into Belgium, but that promised to alienate Britain. In 1940, French-British political problems with the Dutch and Belgians made it impossible to fully coordinate defenses against a German attack. Political considerations also hamper effective response to warning when decision-makers find the costs too great. For the defender, "response is never a free good."[73] This can lead to deferring a complete response to warning in hopes the threat will be eased in some other way, or to allocating inadequate resources to defense, or to foregoing costly emergency deployments and mobilizations. Defenses in the Philippines, Malaya, and Pearl Harbor in 1941 were deficient because of political decisions that resources were needed elsewhere. The Israeli government was wary of ordering a mobilization in October 1973, having paid the heavy economic (and political) costs of mounting one earlier in the year. Manchuria was badly prepared for the Soviet onslaught in 1945 after troops and ammunition had been transferred to meet other pressing needs. Napoleon III could not avoid the fact that the proper response to Russia's military might—a mass army based on conscription—would be far too unpopular politically.

Next, if national leaders have committed themselves *to a strategy or posture other than deterence and defense* to fend off a possible attack, this will detract from taking sufficient precautions. Stalin's strategy was appeasement. Norway counted on strict neutrality in 1940. The Japanese thought concessions would entice the USSR into cooperation in 1945. Israel hoped in 1973 that indicating at the last minute that surprise had been lost would lead the Arabs to cancel the attack. Such policies are usually accompanied by military preparations, in case they do not work. The handicap is that such policies seek to avoid the total effort of deterrence and defense—complete mobilization, full-scale alert, etc.—and that one cannot readily communicate appeasement or conciliation, for instance, when aggressively preparing for war. So too little is done.

Finally, it is possible for the victim to decide that the proper response is to accept defeat, that attempting to fight would be futile and too costly. Only Denmark in 1940 fits this situation in the case studies, but Czechoslovakia in 1968 is another illustration. Of course, this is one scenario offered to predict the American reaction to a surprise Soviet nuclear attack.

In summary, defenders have been moved to forego proper precautions out of a desire not to be provocative, a desire to maneuver the opponent into firing the first shot, a commitment to some other strategy than deterrence or defense, or a belief that effective resistance is impossible.[73]

CONCLUSION

At the start of this chapter a broad question was raised as to whether opportunities for strategic surprise are, more or less, constantly available or whether it takes a set of special conditions to make them possible. It now appears that the special conditions necessary pertain entirely to the attacker's incentives and capabilities. The attacker must be sufficiently motivated to consider surprise attack and to decide on it, must detect a particular weakness in the defender suitable for a strategic surprise, and must invest the time and resources to prepare the attack. Except where the necessary military capabilities are already present or constantly in place, these are all exceptional conditions.

On the other hand, the conditions necessary for the defender to be victimized are not really unusual at all—ambiguous information amidst noise, secrecy, and deception; preconceptions and expectations somewhat at variance with reality; organizational barriers to accurate perception and effective response; political constraints on what a government can afford to see and do. They are very much a part of the daily realities of foreign policy decision-making.

Thus defenders are always somewhat vulnerable while their opponents must be converted by unusual circumstances into attackers. This strongly suggests that efforts to reduce any state's vulnerability to strategic surprise will only be marginally or temporarily useful, and will leave the core of the problem untouched. Such efforts will be most beneficial if focused on improving a government's sensitivity to the special conditions that convert opponents into attackers. However, statesmen would be best served by a pervasive understanding that despite their best efforts they can readily be surprised, and by a resulting interest in steps to either reduce opponents' willingness to attack by surprise or to limit the damage if they do.

Notes

1. Robert Jervis, *Perception and Misperception in International Politics* (Princeton: Princeton University Press, 1976) and "Hypotheses on Misperception," *World Politics*, vol. 20 (April 1968), pp. 454–79.
2. Elaboration on this point can be found in Richard Betts, *Surprise and Defense* (Washington: Brookings, forthcoming), chapter V.
3. In their case studies, George and Smoke convey a similar conclusion, namely that a government finds the status quo intolerable and then goes looking for ways to outmaneuver or overwhelm the opponents. Detection of a weak spot comes after the unhappiness with the situation. See Alexander George and Richard Smoke, *Deterrence in American Foreign Policy: Theory and Practice* (N.Y.: Columbia University Press, 1974).
4. Numerous illustrations and a thorough analysis of the mix of coercive and ac-comodative tactics in crisis bargaining can be found in Glenn Snyder and Paul Diesing, *Conflict Among Nations, Bargaining, Decision Making, and System Structure in International Crises* (Princeton: Princeton University Press, 1977).
5. See Richards Heuer, Jr., "Cognitive Factors in Deception and Counterdeception" in Donald Daniel, et al., *Multidisciplinary Perspectives on Military Deception* (Monterey: Naval Postgraduate School, 1980), pp. 79–80. He reviews Barton Whalley's conclusion that surprise was achieved in 68 cases, despite imperfect security.
6. See Donald Daniel and Katherine Herbig, "Propositions on Military Deception" in Daniel, et al., *Multidisciplinary Perspectives on Military Deception* (note 6), p. 17.
7. See Ibid., pp. 8–12, 33–37.
8. An alternative categorization appears in Betts, *Surprise and Defense* (note 2), chapter 4, p. 3.
9. Klaus Knorr, "Strategic Intelligence: Problems and Remedies" (unpublished paper, 1980), p. 9.
10. This possibility is discussed in Klaus Knorr, "Failures in National Intelligence Estimates, the Case of the Cuban Missiles" *World Politics*, vol. 16, no. 3 (April 1964), p. 463; Michael Handel, "The Yom Kippur War and the Inevitability of Surprise," *International Studies Quarterly*, vol. 21, no. 3 (September 1977), pp. 464–65; and Richard Betts, "Analysis, War, and Decision: Why Intelligence Failures are Inevitable," *World Politics*, vol. 31. no. 1 (October 1978), p. 68.
11. Roberta Wohlstetter, "Cuba and Pearl Harbor: Hindsight and Foresight," *Foreign Affairs*, vol. 43, no. 4 (July 1965), p. 705.
12. A very interesting discussion of how ways of thinking—about war or the enemy, or one's own capabilities—can inhibit serious study of opponents' military capabilities appears in Herbert Goldhammer, *Reality and Relief in Military Affairs: A First Draft (June 1977)* (Santa Monica: Rand 1979), pp. 13–30.
13. George and Smoke, *Deterrence* (note 3), p. 437. They point out that Roger Hilsman reached the same conclusion.
14. The impact of jurisdictional concerns on intelligence is one of the major themes in F. W. Hinsley, *British Intelligence in the Second World War* (London: Her Majesty's Stationery Office, 1979).
15. See Wohlstetter, "Cuba and Pearl Harbor" (note 11), pp. 696–97, and George and Smoke, *Deterrence* (note 3), pp. 473–77.

16. See Steve Chan, "The Intelligence of Stupidity: Understanding Failures in Strategic Warning," *American Political Science Review,* vol. 73, no. 1 (March 1979), pp. 171–80.

17. Illustrative statements of this view: Roberta Wohlstetter, *Pearl Harbor, Warning and Decision* (Stanford: Stanford University Press, 1962), pp. 55–56, 391–97; Johan Holst, "Surprise, Signals and Reaction," *Cooperation and Conflict,* no. 1 (1966), pp. 37–40; George and Smoke, *Deterrence* (note 3), p. 435, where they offer the following proposition: "The immediately available indicators of the existence and form of a potential challenge to deterrence frequently do not provide much guidance concerning the opponent's intentions or objectives . . . " See also Richard Betts, "Analysis, War, and Decision" (note 10), p. 69.

18. That a government often will focus on a key index of a potential attack and then be fooled when it does not appear is suggested in Barton Whalley, *Codeword Barbarossa* (Cambridge: MIT Press, 1973), pp. 223, 241–42; Johan Holst, "Surprise, Signals and Reaction" (note 17), p. 39; Avi Shlaim, "Failures in National Intelligence Estimates: The Case of the Yom Kippur War, " *World Politics,* vol. 28 (1976), p. 352; and Handel, "The Yom Kippur War" (note 10), pp. 489–90.

19. Robert Axelrod, "The Rational Timing of Surprise" *World Politics,* vol. 31, no. 2 (January 1979), p. 244.

20. See Handel, "The Yom Kippur War" (note 10), p. 467, where he also cites similar conclusions reached by Whalley, and by Luttwak and Horowitz.

21. Joseph de Rivera, *The Psychological Dimension of Foreign Policy* (Columbus, Ohio: Charles E. Merrill Co., 1968), pp. 55–56.

22. Abraham Ben-Zvi, "Misperceiving the Role of Perception: A Critique," *The Jerusalem Journal of International Relations,* vol. 2, no. 2 (Winter 1976–77), pp. 81–82, 87.

23. Abraham Ben-Zvi, "Hindsight and Foresight: A Conceptual Framework for the Analysis of Surprise Attacks," *World Politics,* vol. 28, no. 3 (April 1976), p. 388. He reviews examples on pp. 388–94. See also Michael Handel, "Avoiding Political and Technological Surprise in the 1980s," in Roy Godson, ed., *Intelligence Requirements for the 1980s: Analysis and Estimates* (New Brunswick, N.J.: Transaction Books, 1980), pp. 104–05.

24. See Betts, *Surprise and Defense* (note 2), chapter 2, pp. 5, 11.

25. The major exception is Abraham Ben-Zvi; see Ben-Zvi, "Hindsight and Foresight" (note 23).

26. The following discussion draws heavily on Jervis, *Perception* (note 1); de Rivera, *The Psychological Dimension* (note 21); Heuer, "Cognitive Factors" (note 5); many of the other sources cited in this chapter that deal directly with surprise attacks; and the evidence and analysis on how states alter their perceptions during crises in Snyder and Diesing, *Conflict Among Nations* (note 4).

27. See Betts, "Analysis" (note 10), p. 63; Wohlstetter, "Cuba and Pearl Harbor" (note 11), p. 706; and Alexander George, "The Case for Multiple Advocacy in Making Foreign Policy," *American Political Science Review,* vol. 66, no. 3 (September 1972), p. 752.

28. Betts, "Analysis" (note 10), p. 70; George and Smoke, *Deterrence* (note 3), p. 435. Also relevant here is Jervis, *Perception* (note 1), pp. 193–96; and de Rivera, *The Psychological Dimension* (note 21), p. 51.

29. See various elements in the analysis in George and Smoke, *Deterrence* (note 3); Chan, "The Intelligence of Stupidity" (note 16), pp. 173, 178; Schlaim, "Failures" (note 18), pp. 361–62.

30. General expressions of this proposition, for illustrative purposes, can be found in H. A. DeWeerd, "Strategic Surprise in the Korean War," *Orbis,* vol. VI, no. 3 (Fall 1962), p. 451; Holst, "Surprise" (note 17), p. 37, 40; Schlaim, "Failures" (note 18), pp. 349, 352–53, 361–62; Wohlstetter, *Pearl Harbor* (note 17), pp. 391–97; and Steven Hoffman, "Anticipation, Disaster, and Victory: India 1962–1971," *Asian Survey,* vol. XII, no. 11 (November 1967), pp. 963–64.

31. Assertions to this effect can be found in, for instance, Benno Wasserman, "The Failure of Intelligence Prediction," *Political Studies,* vol. 8, no. 2 (1960), pp. 166–67; Shlaim, "Failures" (note 18), pp. 363, 373.

32. Jervis, *Perception* (note 1), pp. 319–23, finds that it is quite common for governments to see other governments as more rational than they are, and other governments' actions and signals as more calculated and purposeful than they are.

33. Discussion along these lines can be found in Wohlstetter, *Pearl Harbor* (note 17), p. 354; Knorr, "Failures" (note 10), pp. 464–65; George and Smoke, *Deterrence* (note 3), pp. 120–21, 160–61, 168–69, 212–15, 464–65, 478–79, 488–89, 527–30; Wasserman, "The Failure" (note 31), p. 166; and Ben-Zvi, "Hindsight" (note 23), p. 394.

34. Holst, "Surprise" (note 17), p. 35; Jervis, *Perception* (note 1), p. 52; and Handel, "The Yom Kippur War" (note 10), p. 468.

35. Analysts offering this view include Chan, "The Intelligence of Stupidity" (note 16), p. 172; Knorr, "Failures" (note 10), pp. 457, 461–62; Shlaim, "Failures" (note 18), pp. 358–59, 371; and Wohlstetter, "Cuba and Pearl Harbor" (note 11), p. 701.

36. For assertions to this effect see Jervis, *Perception* (note 1), p. 196; Shlaim, "Failures" (note 18), pp. 370–71.

37. Knorr, "Failures" (note 10), pp. 462–65. See also Shlaim, "Failures" (note 18), p. 364, and Handel, "The Yom Kippur War" (note 10) pp. 485–87.

38. Jervis, *Perception* (note 1), p. 203. See pp. 203–16.

39. Lyman Kirkpatrick discusses this with respect to military operations in *Captains Without Eyes, Intelligence Failures in World War II* (London: Macmillan, 1969), pp. 14–15.

40. Jervis, *Perception* (note 1), pp. 186–87.

41. On the Cuban Missile Crisis see Wohlstetter, "Cuba and Pearl Harbor" (note 11), pp. 700–01; Knorr, "Failures" (note 10), p. 464. Alexander George and Richard Smoke, *Deterrence* (note 3), explain various challenges to American commitments in this fashion.

42. Analysts who cite this as an important defender error include Wohlstetter, "Cuba and Pearl Harbor" (note 11), pp. 706–07; Wohlstetter, *Pearl Harbor* (note 17), pp. 336–37; Handel, "The Yom Kippur War" (note 10), pp. 473, 485–88; Holst, "Surprise" (note 17), pp. 35–36; and Hoffmann, "Anticipation" (note 30), pp. 964–68.

43. See Handel, "The Yom Kippur War" (note 10), pp. 492–93.

44. See Jervis, *The Logic of Images in International Relations* (Princeton: Princeton University Press, 1970) for the distinction between signals and indices. Holst, "Surprise" (note 17), p. 39 and Whalley, *Codeword Barbarossa* (note 18), pp. 198–200, 223,242, describe this error as it was made by the Norwegian foreign minister in 1940 and Stalin in 1941.

45. See Jervis, *Perception* (note 1), pp. 365–81; Shlaim, "Failures" (note 18), pp. 359–60; Wohlstetter, "Cuba" (note 11), p. 699; Hoffmann, "Anticipation" (note 30), pp. 961–62; and George and Smoke, *Deterrence* (note 3), pp. 172, 191.

46. Jervis, *Perception* (note 1), p. 312.
47. For assertions to this effect see DeWeerd, "Strategic Surprise" (note 30), pp. 439–40; Holst, "Surprise" (note 17), p. 39; Shlaim, "Failures" (note 18), pp. 355–56; Handel, "The Yom Kippur War" (note 10), p. 478; and Wohlstetter, "Cuba" (note 11), p. 699.
48. Wohlstetter, *"Cuba"* (note 11), p. 699.
49. De Rivera, *The Psychological Dimension* (note 21), p. 56.
50. This is a proposition advanced in Chan, "The Intelligence of Stupidity" (note 16), p. 172 where he cites Davis Bobrow to this effect; George and Smoke, *Deterrence* (note 3), p. 574. There is an element of it in Wohlstetter, "Cuba" (note 11), p. 695. See also Shlaim, "Failures" (note 18), p. 358.
51. The primary source of this view is Jervis, *Perception* (note 1), pp. 308–10. See also Shlaim, "Failures" (note 18), pp. 357–58; and Wohlstetter, "Cuba" (note 11), pp. 700, 706, where she also cites Roger Hilsman to this effect.
52. See George Poteat, "The Intelligence Gap: Hypotheses on the Process of Surprise" *International Studies Notes*, vol. 3, no. 3 (Fall 1976), pp. 16–17. Also Jervis, *Perception* (note 1), p. 195–96.
53. See Jervis, *Perception* (note 1), pp. 382–406.
54. See Chan, "The Intelligence of Stupidity" (note 16), p. 176; Wohlstetter, "Cuba" (note 11), p. 701; Poteat, "The Intelligence Gap" (note 52), p. 17; Jervis, *Perception* (note 1), pp. 187–88, 192; and Shlaim, "Failures" (note 18), p. 359.
55. Assertions to this effect can be found in Handel, "Avoiding" (note 23), pp. 93, 95–98, 100–02; DeWeerd, "Strategic Surprise" (note 30), p. 451; Holst, "Surprise" (note 17), pp. 37, 40; Shlaim, "Failures" (note 18), pp. 349, 352–53, 361–62; Hoffmann, "Anticipation" (note 30), pp. 963–64; and Ben-Zvi, "Hindsight" (note 23).
56. Betts, "Analysis" (note 10), p. 67.
57. See Jervis, *Perception* (note 1), pp. 176–81; Chan, "The Intelligence of Stupidity" (note 16), p. 174; George and Smoke, *Deterrence* (note 3), pp. 485–88.
58. Jervis, *Perception* (note 1), p. 178.
59. This was the chief lesson many Americans drew from Pearl Harbor. See U.S. Congress, Joint Committee on the Investigation of the Pearl Harbor Attack, *Investigation of the Pearl Harbor Attack* (Washington: Government Printing Office, 1946), p. 254; Roger Hilsman, *Strategic Intelligence and National Decisions* (Glencoe, Illinois: The Free Press, 1956), p. 23. For a more recent statement to this effect see Kirkpatrick, *Captains* (note 39), pp. 150–53.
60. A conclusion offered by DeWeerd, "Strategic Surprise" (note 3), pp. 436–37, 452; and Angelo Codevilla, "Comparative Historical Experience of Doctrine and Organization," in Roy Godson, ed., *Intelligence Requirements for the 1980s: Analysis and Estimates* (New Brunswick, N.J.: Transaction, 1980), pp. 33–34.
61. See Shlaim, "Failures" (note 18), pp. 366–69, 375–76; Alexander George, "The Case for Multiple Advocacy in Making Foreign Policy," *American Political Science Review*, vol. 66, no. 3 (September 1972), pp. 776–78; George and Smoke, *Deterrence* (note 3), pp. 474–77; Handel, "The Yom Kippur War" (note 10), pp. 492–93.
62. See Chan, "The Intelligence of Stupidity" (note 16), pp. 177–78; Wasserman, "The Failure" (note 31), p. 163; Shlaim, "Failures" (note 18), pp. 376–77; Betts, "Analysis" (note 10), pp. 71–73; and Harold Wilensky, *Organizational Intelligence* (N.Y.: Basic Books, 1967), pp. 42–62.
63. Codevilla, "Comparative" (note 60), p. 35.
64. This view can be found in Wasserman, "The Failure" (note 31), pp. 162–63;

Shlaim, "Failures" (note 18), pp. 366–69; Chan, "The Intelligence of Stupidity" (note 16), pp. 178–79.

65. Thus Codevilla, "Comparative" (note 60), p. 34 concludes "The question of whether the role of policymakers in analysis ought to be large or small . . . admits to no single answer."

66. Kirkpatrick, *Captains* (note 39), p. 14. There are elements of this in Alexander George, "American Policy-Making And The North Korean Aggression," *World Politics*, vol. 7, no. 2 (January 1955), p. 225, where he notes that the American armed services were preoccupied with planning potential big wars and in 1950 had no viable strategies on hand for limited wars.

67. Wilensky, *Organizational Intelligence* (note 62), p. 179.

68. This is more or less the perspective offered in Roger Hilsman, *Strategic Intelligence and National Decisions* (Glencoe, Illinois: The Free Press, 1956), particularly p, 58.

69. Betts, "Analysis" (note 10), p. 83.

70. George and Smoke, *Deterrence* (note 3), pp. 129–32, 171–72, 191, 574. See also Chan, "The Intelligence of Stupidity" (note 16), p. 172.

71. Analysts who have cited this as a factor include Whalley, *Codeword Barbarossa* (note 18), p. 216; Chan, "The Intelligence of Stupidity" (note 16), pp. 172–73; Wohlstetter, "Cuba" (note 11), pp. 701–02; and Handel, "The Yom Kippur War" (note 10), pp. 472, 482–83.

72. Betts, *Surprise* (note 2), chapter III, p. 25.

73. A good review of how Israeli officials displayed nearly all of these political concerns in some fashion in 1973 is Janice Stein "'Intelligence' and 'Stupidity' Reconsidered: Estimation and Decision in Israel, 1973," *The Journal of Strategic Studies*, vol. 3, no. 2 (September 1980), pp. 147–77.

CHAPTER NINE
Lessons for Statecraft

Klaus Knorr

The lessons for statecraft to be derived from the study of previous experience[1] with strategic surprise fall into two areas of concern: first, lessons that will facilitate the planning of strategic surprise in the future and, second, lessons that would reduce the chances of being victimized by strategic surprise. The present chapter will address only the second area of concern. This restriction is not dictated by any greater difficulty in drawing lessons favoring resort to strategic surprise. A set of considerations that should govern the search for an exploitation of opportunities for using surprise can be readily distilled from previous experience. Nor do we want to support our choice on a normative moral basis. It is clear that a number of wars would not have occurred without the beckoning advantage of surprising the opponent, and helping to make war less likely is normatively appealing. Other normative considerations have uncertain applicability. While many militarily aggressive states have inflicted strategic surprise on their opponents, even our limited number of cases contains examples of states doing so which were not militarily aggressive, essentially defending the status quo, or were not more so than their adversaries. As long as war cannot be avoided, there is no good reason why states of a defensive posture should not obtain the benefits of surprise if they have the opportunity to do so. Our choice of concern is rather determined by the fact that doing both analyses would be largely repetitive. The set of considerations aimed at facilitating recourse to strategic surprise is essentially the mirror image of the set aimed at minimizing the chances of being subjected to surprise.

The utility of extracting lessons for statecraft from historical analysis rests on the assumption that past experience is relevant to the future. Have recent developments modified the possibility of strategic surprise? Two such developments need examination from this point of view: First, how has new technology affected relevant conditions? Today's technologies are hugely different from those of the nineteenth century or even of World War II.

Second, is the probable incidence of strategic surprise in the future substantially diminished because contemporary statecraft has already absorbed the lessons to be learned from past experience?

IS STRATEGIC SURPRISE LESS LIKELY IN THE FUTURE?

The issue of whether major scientific and technological developments have impinged significantly on the prospects of strategic surprise centers in four problem areas.

The first concerns the balance between offensive and defensive weapon systems. Opportunities for effecting strategic surprise are favored by the superiority of offensive over defensive armament, whether such superiority rests on high mobility or firepower (e.g., Prussia in 1866 and 1870, the German blitzkrieg in 1940 and 1941, Soviet invasion of Manchuria in 1945, atom bombs on Japan in 1945, Israel in 1967). Vast changes have occurred in both nuclear and conventional arms. Strategic nuclear weapons are exceptionally well suited to surprise attack. Fixed-site nuclear weapons and a high proportion of submarine carriers require no deployment that would give warning, and their missiles do not encounter significant defenses. Only aircraft as carriers give appreciable warning and must penetrate defenses. Cruise missiles are designed to evade defenses or saturate them by sheer numbers. Evidently, the technological superiority of offense over defense in the strategic nuclear area is enormous by historical standards. The key question is whether any attack between nuclear powers of approximately equal rank is worthwhile. Conditions of mutually assured destruction (MAD) preclude incentive, except perhaps in the presence of a high propensity to risk in the assumption that the victim will not execute his retaliatory threat. Surprise attack seems worth considering only if one power can confidently expect to disarm the other by striking preemptively, that is, by destroying its retaliatory forces or its will to retaliate. At present, this condition is likely met between greatly unequal nuclear states. Whether it will emerge between approximately equal powers in the future depends on the development of weapons technology, including antimissile defenses, the use countries make of it, and on perceptions of the retaliatory will of the target country.

Regarding conventional armament, a number of experts have proclaimed that the rise of precision-guided weapons, especially for combatting airplanes and tanks, has once again given defense the edge over offensive technology, and that the Yom Kippur War of 1973 has demonstrated this effect.[2] If this thesis is true, this development tends to restrict opportunities for suprise attack depending on quick frontal breakthroughs. It does not, however, eliminate the opportunity. In World War II as in World War I, defensive weapons were basically superior to offensive ones, but by designing blitzkrieg, a new mode of warfare, the Germans ingeniously overcame this handicap, as did the Israelis in 1967. Ways may be discovered for attacking strategically while staying on the defensive tactically, especially when assisted by strategic surprise.[3] The Egyptians did so in 1973.

But the hypothesis that precision-guided systems favor the defense is by no means generally accepted. The Soviet Union seems to express continued belief in a strategy of swift offensive movement relying heavily on armored forces. New technology provokes countermeasures. The criteria for the overall balance of offensive versus defensive arms depends ultimately on the relative costs of the two. The defense will only tend to dominate if defensive countermeasures to a given incremental addition to offensive capability are consistently cheaper.[4] The question of which side wins out in the weapon design race is not susceptible to a general answer,[5] and whichever balance emerges at one time tends to be unstable. Arms, moreover, are only one element in the balance of military forces and will not necessarily dominate the equation composed also of such factors as numbers, troop training and morale, tactics and strategy, command and control, and logistics. For surprise to occur, the relative configuration of forces needs to be favorable only in a particular instant and location.

The impact on surface warfare of tactical nuclear weapons further complicates the picture. Unless highly dispersed or effectively sheltered, these arms are vulnerable to a first strike and, if they are used at all, there is a strong incentive to strike first. Whether their employment favors defense is difficult to predict and no general answer can be confidently supported. To be sure, they favor defense when launched against concentrations of armor and troops characteristic of blitzkrieg. Yet aside from the condition that they must survive to be used in this fashion, the attacker will employ them as well against any concentration of defending forces and behind the battle zone in order to play havoc with the logistical system and morale of the defender.

Overall, we conclude that the bearing of new technology on the comparative effectiveness of offensive and defensive postures is highly uncertain. Its effects are never unidirectional as both postures are being improved, and as few weapons are overwhelmingly of either an offensive or defensive nature; and whatever net effect in favor of defense there might be at any one time, ingenuity can divert or overcome this tendency. Indeed, this is more likely if defensive states place excessive trust in defensive weaponry. Overconfidence tends to breed vulnerability.

Technological progress has also resulted in striking improvements of strategic warning systems, especially the ability of monitoring signal traffic from a distance and visual penetration by means of satellites and reconnaissance aircraft. These data-gathering systems are becoming ever more refined. New visual sensors will increasingly allow the penetration of clouds and darkness.

Associated technology has been developed for decoding radio messages and for rapidly correlating and analyzing numerically increasing data by means of high-speed computers. This technology permits the tracking of military deployment and logistical movements, and procures valuable information on the capabilities of weapons and forces.

These developments no doubt restrict the possibility of strategic surprise. A number of historical cases of surprise would not have happened in the face of such surveillance technolgy. In 1940, the French would have known the area in which the Germans planned to break through their opponent's defenses. In 1941, the United States would have tracked the Japanese fleet approaching Pearl Harbor. The massive deployment of the Chinese Army for intervention in the Korean War would have been known to the United States.

Yet the restrictive impact of modern strategic warning systems is also limited in various ways. First, some of our cases of surprise would have occurred even if the most modern surveillance capabilities had been available (e.g., the Nazi occupation of Norway, before which the British had all the essential informaion on German deployments, and which was staged during a time period of heavy cloud cover). All observable information was available to the Soviet government before the German invasion of 1940. The Tet Offensive would have happened in any case. And the Israelis (and the United States) had fully observed the Egyptian and Syrian preparations in 1973.

Second, at the present time natural obstacles, i.e., cloud cover and darkness, still handicap photographic intelligence. Furthermore, photographic as well as signal coverage must be pinpointed in order to cover areas of nonroutine interest, and unless all incoming information is properly processed and analyzed, important things may be missed or not appreciated in time. It can also be assumed that an opponent, aware of the type of surveillance he is under, will find ways to counteract and obstruct foreign intelligence efforts. Sensors or their vehicles are also becoming more vulnerable, e.g., by means of satellite killers. Technologies of concealment and deception are also being improved. Modern weapons, moreover, are growing more mobile, interchangeable, and indeterminate, and missions of employment become therefore more difficult to predict. As a result of these trends, one expert concludes that the ability of intelligence, however well equipped, to locate, identify and assess the "operational characteristics of adversary weapons with the degree of confidence desired for intelligence purposes, while relying primarily on technical . . . intelligence, will diminish overall."[6]

Third, not all critical components of military capability applied in an attempt at inflicting strategic surprise are physically observable, for instance, generalship and troop morale. Fourth, there are inevitable time lags between the procurement of masses of information, their processing and analysis, and their presentation to decision-makers. These lags can be significant in coping with fact-moving events. In addition, decision-makers require time for absorbing and acting upon intelligence. Fifth, as German preparation for the invasion of the Soviet Union, or Egyptian deployments before the Yom Kippur War demonstrated, even abundant information on deployment for attack does not give unambiguous warning. Deployments for attack may be undertaken for the purpose of threat-making and crisis-bargaining as well as with the intention to attack. Because military exercises require, or can be made to require, a state of readiness that facilitates sudden attack, countries can play the maneuver game, that is, look threatening in order to inflict the political and military costs of countermeasures on their opponents. And ambiguities of threatening postures can be deepened by the infusion of disinformation.

Sixth, modern surveillance technology is not easily developed, and it is costly and kept under the wraps of secrecy. At the present time, only the United States and the Soviet Union exploit these technologies to the full (the former probably more than the latter). Other countries possess lesser capabilities to a variable extent, some of them none at all. Unless they are provided with warning services or information by more resourceful allies, they remain essentially blind from this point of view. There are thus great international disparities regarding the warning function. Finally, the state planning to use strategic surprise may itself employ elaborate surveillance technologies that effectively assist such planning and the execution of attack. In conclusion, even though the new information technologies can give warning that impedes certain forms of strategic surprise, and perhaps limits the degree of surprise, the incidence of these impediments is apt to vary a great deal and does not preclude surprises in the future.

A third way in which advancing technology has touched on the possibilities of strategic surprise relates to battlefield information, to the ability of dispelling what Clausewitz called the "fog of war." Evidently, the success of attempts at inflicting strategic surprise depends on the quickness with which the target state reacts, and this hinges on the availability of timely and complete information, which is essential to effective command and control. In this area, the means of observation and communication have been dramatically improved. At the same time, however, technological progress in weaponry has generated an ever increasing array of arms, many of which are capable of various modes of employment, and capable also of wreaking greater destruction, and of greater mobility. These developments foreshadow formidable problems in anticipating and tracking what will happen on battlefields in future wars, especially wars between great powers. These difficulties will be particularly great if tactical nuclear weapons are brought into play. It is, therefore, doubtful that future battlefields are subject to effective control.[6] Uncertainties will abound and chaos may result. We cannot count, therefore, on new information technology offering an advantage in penetrating the fog of war. If this is so, the implementation of surprise faces no new barrier and the side resorting to surprise should retain the advantage of at least knowing what its forces have been instructed to do.

One can only speculate on whether statecraft has learned from past experience how to minimize subjection to strategic surprise. The conditions that have caused or contributed to such experiences in the past are generally known and have received considerable systematic analysis. To the extent that conditions located abroad are observable, one would expect intelligence services to monitor them, and to the extent that the opportunities for staging surprise are lodged in the intended target state, one would expect properly focused self-analysis to be pursued as a matter of course. Some learning has undoubtedly occurred. Yet this has hardly led to foolproof protection. The experience of Israel in 1973, a state extraordinarily sensitive to matters of surprise, and also not the least deluded about its adversaries' aggressive motives, counsels caution.

As many historical examples indicate, learning from past blunders is far from easy. The tendency is to oversimplify the reading of past events, expecting their causes to repeat themselves in mechanical fashion, and thus to be prepared for the last crisis. Strategic surprise can take many forms and its design is apt to capitalize on specific configurations of circumstances. It is also known from human experience in sundry contexts that learning intellectually from past events does not insure that this knowledge is applied to future conduct because the preference structure of actors may conflict with the implications of this knowledge. If people want to do something badly, they are tempted to ignore the lessons of history or to reinterpret them in ways accommodating their preferences. Finally, the perception of future contingencies will ineluctably come up against the same difficulties that bedevilled it in the past. Available information will be fragmentary, obsolescent, and ambiguous. In conclusion, while modern states are more alert to the danger of strategic surprise, and possess improved capabilities for threat perception, that is, for collecting and for analyzing information, the danger persists.

LESSONS SPECIFIC TO INCENTIVES

The following lessons result from the study of incentives that prompt resort to strategic surprise—derived from empirical case studies or arrived at by deduction reasoning—and they should be committed to the operational knowledge of statecraft. In scanning, analyzing, and evaluating the strategic environment in order to minimize victimization by strategic surprise, governments should not rule out any possible opponent possessing military capabilities for attack and harboring serious conflict of interest, manifest or latent, with that government.

Potential attackers need not possess superior military forces in order to be or become dangerous from this point of view. Their forces may not need to prove themselves against more than a fraction of the capabilities at the disposal of the defending state which, for one reason or another, is unable to deploy all of these capabilities in the relevant theater of operation; and, if the attacker's objectives of war are limited, it may not even need to win a definitive victory. While concern regarding an adversary's motivation to resort to strategic surprise should obviously be assessed as high when relations are in a crisis mode, concern cannot be wholly suspended when conflictive issues are or seem dormant because these can surface quickly, and because, once they do become critical suddenly, little time may remain for deterrence to be vitalized or adequate defensive preparations against surprise attack put in place.

It does not matter under the defined circumstances whether attack—by surprise or not—is perceived to be improbable. Doing the improbable is the very essence of effecting surprise. Systematic worst-case analysis is therefore indispensable if a defender wants to guard himself against what is regarded as unlikely, but may yet happen. Worst-case analysis should not be made routine in order to prompt protective measures that make war more probable, but in order to place on the agenda precautionary moves designed to minimize the chances of attack by surprise or otherwise. Systematic worst-case analysis is not, of course, a very reliable remedy, for it is far from easy to imagine the worst that the opponent is scheming. The chances of surprise can be curtailed, but they cannot be disseminated.

It should be noted that a posture of alertness by these rules still leaves— at any one time—a great many countries beyond the focus of interest either because they lack suitable capabilities of consequence or because they can be considered safely to lack sufficient incentives for contemplating hostilities, and are not allied to states who have dangerous capabilities and incentives. For example, despite its far-flung interests, at this time the United States need hardly worry about Canada, nearly all Latin American countries, the West European states, sub-Saharian Africa, and most Asiatic states, although it is taken for granted that the safe list is always subject to change, whether by addition or subtraction.

It is also clear that, for purposes of alertness to the possibility of being subjected to surprise, expectations of attack cannot be neatly separated from expectations of attack by surprise. To be sure, some potential enemies would not attack unless they can be reasonably confident in achieving strategic surprise. But this is obviously not a necessary condition in all cases of suspicion. To some attackers, the critical question is whether to fight at all, perhaps because war is regarded as inevitable, and resort to surprise thus appeals as a desirable strategy. To the defender determined not to be victimized by strategic surprise, the first question is always whether a potential opponent will fight; whether it will resort to a strategy of surprise is the second question. The second question will merge with the first only when prospects of effecting surprise must be seen as tilting the balance of decisions in favor of resort to war.

Given these ground rules, governments of defending states should understand that certain countries on the list of concern are more likely to plan to resort to strategic surprise than others, and therefore warrant special attention. Some characteristic states are those that

1. are latently, if not acutely, in a crisis mood regarding the frustration of vital interests;
2. are in an acute crisis mode and are desperate because they see no worthwhile alternative to war;
3. have in the past shown a strong predisposition to settle conflicts over vital interests by resort to arms;
4. have attempted to achieve strategic surprise with success in previous military conflicts;
5. are militarily weaker than their adversaries and depend on surprise to compensate for this inferiority;
6. are specially vulnerable to ground, naval or air attack, e.g., because of small size of territory;
7. cannot afford a prolonged war of attrition because they are inferior in military potential (including manpower), and in stocks of arms and fuel (especially if importers of the essentials), or because they fear negative reactions from domestic or foreign public opinion;
8. need a quick fait accompli because they fear the intervention of third powers, including great powers, and even pressures from allies to terminate hostilities;
9. although strong and perhaps superior to their opponent, wish to minimize casualties and their costs, or minimize destruction in an area to be conquered, or avoid a risky diversion of forces from missions in other theaters of operation, actual or potential;
10. want to win without going to war formally by means of using small special forces (e.g., the Bay of Pigs), "volunteers," or proxies;
11. possess tight decision-making structures and a high capacity for maintaining secrecy or practising deception;
12. can act without the cooperation of allies, or the need to inform and to heed any contrary preferences of allies;
13. have leaders known for their propensity to act boldly and to gamble;
14. have negligible or nil domestic costs of using and preparing for surprise;
15. perceive attractive opportunities for staging strategic surprise because of suitable capabilities they have developed or because of suitable weaknesses in the target state's defenses.
16. have leaders known to be contemptuous of the defender's leaders' will, or its nation's capabilities and resolve.

LESSONS SPECIFIC TO OPPORTUNITY

Opportunities to attack with strategic surprise invariably have components located with both the attacking and the defending states. The defender offers opportunity in the form of his vulnerabilities. On the attacker's side, the opportunities consist of: (1) information on the defender's vulnerabilities; (2) military capabilities suitable for exploiting such vulnerabilities; (3) the ability, linking (1) and (2), of matching these capabilities and vulnerabilities; (4) the political-organizational capability to act on the detected opportunity for staging surprise; and (5) the ability to keep operational places hidden and to employ deception for misleading the defender. The presence or absence of these ingredients, in addition to intentions, are the objects with which the defender's intelligence and policy must cope if he wants to ward off strategic surprise.

However, unless war is already underway, when strategic surprise may yet be staged, the defender must cope with the prior question of whether or not an opponent will resort to war at all. The two foci are closely interrelated. Obviously, a state will not become the victim of strategic surprise if war does not break out. It is another thing, however, to be certain that this will not happen, and when the contingency is uncertain, even if deemed improbable, the question of surprise cannot be safely ducked. Indeed, as already noted, it has often been the prospect of inflicting surprise that had led an attacker to precipitate hostilities. Therefore, even the prior question should not be addressed without reference to the possibility of strategic surprise.

Given the opportunity structures identified above, a defender's strategic intelligence should pay particular heed to opponents who:

1. enjoy excellent intelligence facilities and opportunities for procuring military information on the defender;
2. possess military forces, capable of quick mobilization, deployment and redeployment, and are innovative in the development and use of military technology, strategy, and tactics;
3. have displayed a political-organizational capacity for making and executing decisions with dispatch; and
4. have demonstrated a good capacity for keeping plans secret and for designing and disseminating disinformation.

THE WARNING PROBLEM

As our cases indicate, the defender's task of escaping strategic surprise is not a priori hopeless. He should be aware of the opponent's recorded politico-military posture. He can also secure considerable information on the attacker's military forces, on his military organizational capabilities, and on his practices regarding secrecy and deception. The defender's preparations for attack or for using new modes of warfare usually require a great deal of preparation, some of which is observable or cannot be kept completely secret. His preparations ordinarily require a considerable period of time.

Yet the historical record reveals that nearly all known attempts at staging strategic surprise succeeded, at least in the immediate objective of inflicting surprise, and that this has happened even when the relevant information available to the defender was very impressive and touching on all aspects of the attacker's intentions and capabilites, e.g., the Soviet Union before the German invasion of 1942 and Israel prior to the Yom Kippur War of 1973. Evidently, to procure adequate warning of strategic surprise is not only an exceedingly difficult task, it looks to be close to hopeless unless statecraft in this vital area is capable of substantial improvement, in which case the defender would be safe only if he possessed the means of foolproof deterrence of any attack by anyone.

Let us suppose that the defender has a person in charge of the warning function who is perfectly rational, intelligent, and imaginative, and enjoys the full attention and confidence of his government. Let us further suppose that he has been perfectly free in directing the collection of information about the outside world and that he is personally capable of analyzing all of it. This ideal official will still have to put up with information that is fragmentary, obsolescent, contradictory, and ambiguous, which means that it is capable of alternative explanations and of sustaining alternative estimates of the attacker's intentions, capabilities, and operational plans. Retrospectively viewed, these deficiencies of information may be more or less but, looking ahead, he does not even know this. He must estimate against various uncertainties, and will do so with limited confidence in his conclusions. This problem is insuperable and, in the event, his estimate may prove right or wrong. Being aware of this indeterminacy and perfectly rational, this official will base his estimate of attack and of attack by surprise on the analysis of all hypotheses that fit his information, without being sure that he has formulated all possible hypotheses (unless we assume that his powers of imagination are perfect as well, which he will be unsure of nevertheless). In a matter entailing such grave consequences, he will undertake best- and worst-case analyses routinely, and he will advise his policymaker of the full range of supportable possibilities and of the degree of confidence with which he favors one of them. If that policymaker were equally rational and, in addition, powerful or influential enough to decide on any policy he deems necessary, he would hedge his bet, as the intelligence official did, in designing and adopting policy responses. In real life, to be sure, the policymaker falls short of such rationality and power, and the range of supportable possibilities may be so broad as to leave him with the impression that the situation is utterly indeterminate. This may paralyze him, or make him seek refuge in substituting a simplified reading of the situation or hope for the best. Nevertheless, not all leaders are alike, and the value of the attempt to enlighten them in such a laborious way cannot be dismissed as completely illusory.

In presenting this ideal posture, we have so far withheld one complex of information and analysis from our fictitious intelligence official. In order to estimate both the chances that the attacker will seek to inflict strategic surprise and the nature of the surprise—be it an initation of war or a particular mode of attack or warfare—he must also be apprised of his own country's military vulnerabilities. To grasp the opportunities that are beckoning the attacker, he must be able to relate the attacker's strengths to the defender's weaknesses. He cannot do so without a net assessment of contending military forces and strategies if he is to have a fair chance to estimate the possibility and form of a strategic surprise launched by the opponent. In this area as well, uncertainties will loom, inasmuch as only battle furnishes a true net assessment of contending forces under the precise circumstances of military encounters, and his analysis should encompass all hypothetical possibilities that are compatible with the available information. Even given these ideal conditions, the experience of surprise cannot be ruled out because of deficiencies of information or failures of the imagination. But the chances of being victimized by strategic surprise would be substantially reduced compared with the chances suggested by the historical record.

The real worth of relevant statecraft differs from the ideal image in several major ways that depress expected performance. First, both on the side of intelligence, the intended producers of strategic warning, and on that of decision-makers, the consumers of warning, the instrument is a bureaucratic organization which, in turn, is variously subdivided. While these organizations offer the usual advantages, such as bringing to bear substantial labor inputs and a variety of skills, they also entail disadvantages, such as the separation of function (e.g., of intelligence collection and analysis, military and political analysis, country specializations), and imperfect communications up and down between bureaucratic layers. Organizations, moreover, do not normally constitute and comport themselves in a manner calculated to optimize coping with any particular task imposed upon them because they are ordinarily required to address a number of more or less conflicting tasks and because they prefer to do things in ways that are comfortable to them and their constituents. Moreover, while intelligence organizations are largely manned by professionals with expertise related to the warning function, top decision-makers are not, and have not been trained in the business of reacting to and acting upon warning. They have arrived at their positions on the basis of quite different skills, and their staffs have been selected on the basis of criteria that are for the most part indifferently or not closely related to the matter of responding to strategic warning.

Second, organizations on both sides must cope with a scarcity of resources: funds, numbers of members, talent, special skills and experience, and —very importantly—time. They must, therefore, allocate these scarce resources; and whatever the chosen pattern of allocation, things of lower priority will be covered less well than those commanding high priority. In intelligence, if collection and analytical resources are allocated so as to favor important targets, other targets will receive less attention, and the possibility of surprise in these areas will tend to rise in proportion to the relative neglect. Decision-makers who are intelligence consumers suffer from the same constraints on a much larger scale, especially at the top levels where the agenda of government is vast and complex.

This problem of resource scarcity and its consequences is greatly aggravated by the fact that the experience of strategic surprise—while it may engender very damaging or even fatal results—is generally a rare event in the history of states. There are, of course, considerable differences in the situation confronting particular countries. As the example of Israel shows, some states (or states in particular regions at certain periods of time) face a much greater possibility of war than do most countries most of the time. That France became the victim of strategic surprise in 1870, 1914, and 1941 is typical. It cannot be expected that, and indeed would not be rational for, relevant organizations to devote large resources continuously to the task of minimizing the experience of strategic surprise. This constraint holds true even of intelligence organizations and, though naturally to a diminished degree, for those of its parts concerned with military affairs. Not only are such bureaucracies charged with many problems not directly related to war, they will also be engrossed in the production of current intelligence, and therefore will spend relatively little effort on hypothetical questions regarding rare events. Again, the necessity of dealing with current problems of policy (to which intelligence responds) is even more insistent and more absorbing with government leaders. To be sure, some shift in priority will occur on both sides of the organizational spectrum once crises erupt, and especially crises assuming dangerous properties. But, aside from the fact that the danger inherent in a crisis may be misjudged, even then the current task of crisis management is apt to receive a prior claim on time and other resources. Of course, a further shift of attention and effort will take place when the chances of war are recognized to be high, and even more so once it has broken out. However, this recognition may come tardily and, as many of our cases suggest, even then the specific inquiry into the possibility of strategic surprise may not rank high among the tasks bearing down on governments, the military and intelligence.

The real-world factors addressed above account for or contributed to the strategic surprises we have studied. Some of the identified problems are, in principle, capable of manipulation. For example, more resources can be allotted to intelligence in order to mitigate the consequences of scarcity, or to improve communication within and between bureaucracies. But essentially, these impediments to good performance in warning of strategic surprise are more or less inevitable and hence must degrade performance to a level of expectations far below what our ideal actor can be counted on to achieve. They greatly add to the defender's vulnerability. And on top of these common realities of political and organizational life are the well-known pathologies, examined in the preceding chapter, that afflict threat perception on the part of intelligence officials and policymakers, and that interact cumulatively with the impediments already discussed.

Even when the intake of information is, despite inevitable uncertainties, good enough to raise the question of surprise, misperception can lead intelligence astray. One can perceive reality only on the basis of assumptions or preconceptions of how the outside world is constituted and behaves. These assumptions may be based on abundant experience with particular situations and particular actors—which is what makes them persuasive—and yet prove mistaken in the particular case because situations are seen as looking more alike than they really are or because actors are able to change their behavior, or are assumed to behave as we would in the same situation. Once formed by individuals or, even more so, by groups, these preconceptions or mindsets tend to prove resistent to revision even in the face of discrepant information, and—worse—they shackle imagination. Being part of the professional identity of individuals and groups, they possess exceeding inertia. Moreover, doubts about assumptions, analyses, and conclusions may be discouraged if they would lead to revised estimates known to be disagreeable to policymakers or because warning of a possible event that is regarded as improbable would appear to have been unduly alarming when the improbable does not happen (the cry-wolf phenomenon).

The perceptual deficiencies are exhibited also by policymakers and their staffs. Indeed their impact tends to be greater with them than within intelligence organizations except for the possible consideration that individuals coming new to problems of threat perceptions may be less handicapped by preconceptions that have evolved and hardened in intelligence bureaucracies. But it is more likely that the preconceptions governing policymakers are cruder and more infused with prejudice than those prevalant among intelligence officials, and that they are more stubborn because, as pointed out in the preceding chapter, those in the seat of government have little time and inclination to learn. Since formulating collective threat perceptions and assessments is a time-consuming process, and time often is of the essence in warning, the time factor greatly contributes to the defender's vulnerability. On top of this, leaders show a strong predispostion to reduce complex and uncertain realities to simplified and hence more manageable images, and to resist perceptions that conflict with policy preferences. People tend to see what they would like to see.

Two views can be taken on whether these pathologies of threat perception—which are surely endemic—are likewise inevitable and therefore wholly to be put up with. It can be said that in perceiving reality we can operate only with assumptions that may prove erroneous; a high degree of misperception is unavoidable, and whether our estimates will be proven right or wrong is a matter of sheer chance. In many cases we have studied, some individuals or small groups, whose forecasts were rejected, made correct estimates; this does not necessarily challenge this thesis. These people may have been simply lucky. And it is a well-known observation that correct forecasts have sometimes been based on crude bias and remarkable ignorance. We are, however, reluctant to accept this view. The historical evidence we have seen is not conclusive on this question. Nor are we ready to accept the thesis on a priori grounds. Even if these pathologies have so often proved fatal, once fully understood they should not be wholly immune to remedy. Full awareness of the pitfalls should put us on guard and encourage the formulation and consideration of alternative assumptions. We subscribe to the second view but admit that the pathologies besetting threat perception are formidable and that they add much to the defender's vulnerability to strategic surprise. Whether one accepts the one view or the other is nevertheless crucial from the viewpoint of statecraft. On the first view, nothing can be done than to bow to the inevitable and go on from there. Any reform will be no more than palliative. The second view justifies efforts at ameliorating impediments as much as possible even if eradictating them is hardly feasible.

Nevertheless, our analysis of the obstacles to the range of threat perceptions that would greatly reduce the chances of becoming the victim of strategic surprise are so profound and pervasive that, taken together, they explain why, historically speaking, attempts at surprise have usually succeeded in inflicting it, even if the longer-run consequences of the achievement have often failed to present the attacker with a favorable outcome of conflict. Analysis, in short, supports the empirical finding.

REMEDIES

Extracting remedies for statecraft from the lessons encounters considerable difficulties. For one thing, many constituents of vulnerability are conditions that are unavoidable (e.g., the imperfections of information), or are necessary conditions of statecraft (e.g., coordinating the productivity and output of large bureaucracies, the preoccupation of governments with current problems of policy, or the difficulty of insuring proper attention by leaders to intelligence issues and estimates). However, none of these conditions is wholly incapable of manipulation. The degrading degree of their impact is not fixed. There are lots of little things worth worrying about that cumulatively are of appreciable consequence. We will not present a full list of these little issues because it can be readily derived from our analyses.

In searching for corrections on the bigger issues, on the other hand, it is hard, if not impossible, to avoid pieties, platitudes, and gimmickry. We will not, however, be daunted by this prospect because a bit a truth and utility is often contained in pieties, because platitudes are often ignored in the practice of statecraft, and because gimmicks occasionally work, despite *their* draw-backs, or at least force the bureaucratic mind to pay attention to a real problem.

To begin with the crucial platitude aimed at the intelligence side of state-craft, it seems to us imperative that statecraft not only become thoroughly familiar with the historical record on strategic surprise and the analysis of this record, but that it also internalize the lessons these analyses contain. The history of statecraft on this subject of surprise does not suggest that this has been universally accomplished. The lessons derived from historical experience should therefore form an integral part of professional indoctrination to be imparted in the course of professional training and in the ongoing process of intelligence work on matters of threat perception. The purpose of doing so would be to generate an ever present sensitivity to the pitfalls in collecting and analyzing relevant information.

It is more important, however, that the lessons of experience be transformed into institutional practices so that their consideration is not simply left to the discretion of bureaucracies and their individual members. In view of the key role played by assumptions in estimative analysis, it seems indispensable that potent preconceptions are subjected to challenge and that, on questions of possible surprise, such analysis operate with multiple sets of assumptions, including possible worst cases, as a matter of course, and that all hypotheses, which fit the information, be presented to policymakers along with an order of attributed probabilities, as well as the degree of confidence with which this attribution has been made. We are aware of the likelihood that, if this is done as a matter of course, it will tend to degenerate into uninspired and uninspiring practice. Nor do we ignore the fact that to engage in useful worst-case analysis calls for a high order of imagination, for our blindspots are naturally not obvious, and that this remedy will often fail to identify true vulnerabilities to strategic surprise. But if management insists unrelentingly on more than a mechanical search for alternatives to be considered, some estimative mistakes can be diminished if not altogether avoided.

Also needed in the province of intelligence is a unit continuously carrying on net assessments with the focus on the risk of strategic surprise, and amenable to augmentation when the danger of war rises to a seriously acute level. Since the defender's vulnerability to surprise is rooted in his disposition and weaknesses as well as in the attacker's resources and resourcefulness, it is ironic that intelligence efforts are directed only at the potential adversary and not also at the defender himself. Threat perception aiming at net assessment must look both ways. Important in such scrutiny of the outside world and in self-scrutiny is the matter of deception. Its purpose is to make the defender misinterpret his information, and it usually works best when it capitalizes on flaws in the defender's conceptions of the danger he faces, that is, when it stimulates and reinforces self-deception. Regarding analytical procedure, the group tasked with net assessment should not be satisfied with practising only the method of induction, that is, with a process of inference from observed indicators—which is standard for intelligence organizations. It must resort to deductive reasoning as well by asking: what would we consider doing if we were in the attacker's shoes? Novel considerations yielded by this effort would then drive new missions in the collection and analysis of information. Finally, the unit should be constituted with the capacity of reacting quickly to changes in the pattern of information and to changes in the behavior of the attacker.

The precise focus of such an organization would not be concerned so much with the surprising initiation of hostilities, which concerns the regular intelligence service or services, but with surprising military modes of attack. It can be taken for granted that military staffs do conduct net assessments regarding major potential opponents, but they do so for the most part with reference to the *defender's* strategic plans, not the *attacker's*. What needs to be added is a sharp focus on the possible intentions and plans for surprise of a potential attacker, on his military and associated political and administrative capabilities, and on the defender's vulnerabilities. To pursue such assessments is patently a challenge to the best and most experienced minds, and is up against the pitfalls in threat perception we have examined. Again and again, we have noticed that defenders overestimated their military capabilities relative to those of possible attackers, and that they failed to undertake assessments within the framework of strategic surprise planned by them.

This is crucial. North Korean military leaders had little cause to worry about their country's military strength in 1956 as long as they focused on the opposing forces hemmed in around Pusan, but they were vulnerable to the surprise landing at Inchon. In 1941, the British were confident that their vast naval superiority over the Germans precluded a German occupation of Norway in the teeth of this superiority. But they did not conjecture about circumstances under which this strength at sea could be largely evaded by German strategists. At the time of the Tet Offensive, American military leaders felt comfortable about the overall military picture in Vietnam, but failed to estimate carefully new means of waging war that might be available to the enemy.

It is also clear that such an intelligence unit must be composed of civilian experts as well as military personnel for two weighty reasons. First, the problem of surprise is not a purely military one. In searching for anomalies in the attacker's behavior, political and economic indicators should not be neglected. Second, except when they wish to justify demands for more resources, the military are often especially prone to overestimate their relative strength vis-á-vis opponents. It is easier to discover weaknesses in the opponent, whether realistically or not, than to admit one's own. Such a unit would benefit if it were staffed by experts both on long-term and shorter-term assignment. Long-term tenure is needed to insure institutional memory and the gradual improvement of intelligence methods. Shorter-term people could, upon entry, bring fresh thinking to bear and, upon leaving, spread sensitivity to the problems of minimizing surprise in the services to which they return. Finally, such a staff should be given authority to insert tasks for the collection of information into the allocation of collection resources.

Even if the preference of intelligence regarding strategic surprise were more or less improved, the improvement would touch only half of the problem. A *government* may be warned by its intelligence organization, but whether or not the defending *state* is warned depends on how decision-makers receive intelligence and react to it. Intelligence can mislead leaders by supplying faulty estimates or ignoring lurking dangers. But supposing it deals with various contingencies and uncertainties in cautious probabilistic terms that are fairly realistic, governments can ignore this input, pay insufficient or tardy heed, or draw inappropriate policy responses.

Our studies have shown that this part of the problem is far less remediable, if remediable at all, than is the production of intelligence, because this deficiency is anchored in the very nature of government and the normal process by which government leaders are chosen. To be sure, the problems presented by the consumption of warning are not invariably hopeless. Occasionally, states are headed by leaders who are, by motivating personal interest or by previous training and experience, close to matters of war, military strategy, and surprise (e.g., Churchill and Hitler). States that are continuously confronting severe and acute problems of military security, and have been engaged in frequent wars and war scares (e.g., Israel, Egypt), are likely to have leaders more alert to and more experienced in strategy and considerations of strategic surprise than do other states, and so may states that have themselves resorted to strategic surprise in the recent past. Their leaders, however, are still subject to most of the standard problems of threat perception we have discussed. The difficulties are greater for most states most of the time. For them, every conceivable repair of this weakness looks impracticable. Thus, one could recommend that officials with the requisite skills be made part of the immediate staff of innocent statesmen in order to insure that the consumption of relevant intelligence is sophisticated rather than uneducated. Yet unless top leaders are already keen on this range of their responsibility, such officials will not be appointed or, if appointed, will receive no more attention than the heads of intelligence, if they are not ignored altogether. As our historical cases indicate, only chance will cover, wholly or in part, this key component of the defender's vulnerability. This sour conclusion seems to us incontrovertible.

It is our overall conclusion that the business of minimizing strategic surprise faces odds that, though not exactly insuperable, are very formidable indeed. Improvements in statecraft can reduce the chances of being victimized by enough to render true improvements of statecraft worth making, even if they are demanding in ingenuity and other resources. But the costs of error are high and a basic vulnerability will remain as long as the threat of war is not eliminated from the system of international relations. Defending states can either accept this inherent risk in full, or reduce it by taking out insurance at a time when no concrete threats to national security are perceived, as individuals pay for the protection of life insurance although they do not expect to die for a long time.

For defenders, this insurance takes three forms, two of which have the purpose of discouraging attack. The first is to provide for adequate military deterrance and defense; the second, to pursue foreign policies that do not unnecessarily incite the aggressiveness and despair of other states and are thus calculated to minimize the population of potential attackers in the outside world. Such insurance, like all insurance, is costly in various ways. The instruments for adequate deterrence and defense are voracious of resources and, unless carefully suited to a defending posture can look threatening to others and end up by raising the danger of military aggression. Part of such a posture is a readiness to go on military alert whenever signs of serious danger, however ambiguous, have given warning, and careful advance planning for such action. In many of our cases, the defender was not on alert. Alerts, of course, are costly in resources and in looking provocative. But levels and configurations of military alerts differ in this respect, and designing, practising, and invoking alerts that are relatively of a low degree of costs and risks, and yet constitute worthwhile insurance, should be tasks high on the priority list of civilian and military leaders.

The third form of insurance accepts the possibility of being taken by strategic surprise and is intended to reduce its impact. The capacity to limit damage requires the doctrinal assumption by political and military leaders that an unforeseen attack by surprise cannot be ruled out. Based on this prior assumption, two measures would help to contain damage: an arrangement for command and control that possesses redundant resources and, in an emergency, allows for military decisions at lower levels in the chain of command, and the deployment of ready and highly mobile forces capable of rushing speedily to any breach.

Foreign policies designed to help remove or solve international conflicts of vital interest that might provoke attack are likewise not devoid of serious costs and risks. They may require concessions that are costly and, unless carefully suited to the purpose, they can be interpreted as weakness and thus encourage aggression. In these, as in all tasks of statecraft, governments and nations patently face trade-offs regarding how much risk and what sort of assortment of risks to accept compared with the opportunity costs of dimishing them further. And the evaluation of each of these options is beset by the same kinds of uncertainties and difficulties of perception that were uncovered in the study of strategic surprise.

Notes

1. While this chapter is based primarily on the preceding case studies and analytical chapters, its writing has also profited greatly from the forthcoming book by Richard K. Betts, *Surprise and Defense* (Washington, D.C., Brookings Institution). Of special interest is also Yu. V. Chuyev and Yu. B. Mikahylov, *Forecasting in Military Affairs, A Soviet View (1975)* (published under the auspices of the U.S. Air Force, Washington, D.C., Superintendent of Documents).
2. Erik Klippenberg, "New Weapons Technology and the Offense/Defense Balance, *Adelphi Papers*, No. 145 (London, International Institute for Strategic Studies, 1977), pp. 26–32; James Digby, "New Technology and Super-Power Actions in Remote Contingencies." *Survival*, XXI (March/April, 1979), pp. 61–67.
3. Martin Van Creveld, *Military Lessons of the Yom Kippur War: Historical Perspectives* [The Washington Papers] (Beverly Hills, Sage Publications, 1975), pp. 45–46.
4. Harvey Brooks, "Notes on Some Issues on Technology and National Defense," *Daedalus*, vol. 110 (Winter 1981), p. 134.
5. Ibid.
6. William H. Kincade, "Over the Technological Horizon," *Daedalus*, vol. 110 (Winter 1981), p. 116.
7. Ibid., p. 135.